Insurance Law in Argentina

Insurance Law in Argentina

Second Edition

Emilio H. Bulló†

Carlos Alberto Estebenet

This book was originally published as a monograph in the International Encyclopaedia of Laws/Insurance Law.

Founding Editor: Roger Blanpain
General Editor: Frank Hendrickx
Volume Editor: Herman Cousy

Wolters Kluwer

Published by:
Kluwer Law International B.V.
PO Box 316
2400 AH Alphen aan den Rijn
The Netherlands
E-mail: lrs-sales@wolterskluwer.com
Website: www.wolterskluwer.com/en/solutions/kluwerlawinternational

Sold and distributed by:
Wolters Kluwer Legal & Regulatory U.S.
920 Links Avenue
Landisville, PA 17538
United States of America
E-mail: customer.service@wolterskluwer.com

Printed on acid-free paper

ISBN 978-94-035-3557-9

e-Book: ISBN 978-94-035-3567-8
web-PDF: ISBN 978-94-035-3577-7

The Authors

Emilio H. Bulló was born in Buenos Aires, Argentina, on 23 October 1932.

He completed his JD from the School of Law of Universidad Nacional de Buenos Aires, República Argentina (1960). Emilio Bulló was Commercial Law Professor at the School of Law of Universidad Católica, Argentina; Universidad Austral, Argentina; and Universidad de Belgrano, Argentina.

He was active in several professional organizations, as Member, Vice President and President of the Argentine Branch of the Association Internationale du Droit des Assurances (AIDA); as Founder, Secretary and Vice President of Club de Abogados de Seguros de Buenos Aires; as Member of the Comité de Abogados de Bancos de la República Argentina; as Member of the Presidency Counsel of la Association Internationale de Droit des Assurances; since 1994, as Vice President of la Association Internationale de Droit des Assurances; and since 1995, as Member and Representative in Argentina from Instituto Europeo de España, and as Director of Insurance Law Area of Centro de Estudios sobre la Regulación Económica de la Universidad Austral.

He was also the former partner of Bulló-Tassi-Estebenet-Lipera-Torassa Abogados.

He acted as a legal adviser to various industrial, commercial, and insurance companies, banks, entities, and educational institutions.

He is the author of the book: *El derecho de seguros y de otros negocios vinculados*, volumes I, II, III.

He passed away on 13 November 2012.

The Authors

Carlos Alberto Estebenet was born in Buenos Aires, Argentina, on 23 October 1957.

He holds a JD from the School of Law of Pontificia Universidad Católica Argentina Santa María de los Buenos Aires (1983).

On the academic level, Carlos Alberto Estebenet is Insurance Law Professor at the School of Law of Universidad Católica, Argentina; Director of the Insurance Law postgraduate course at the School of Law of Universidad Católica, Argentina; and Business Law Professor at the Universidad Católica Argentina (1992). He was a representative of Universidad Austral to the European Community programme 'Red Alfa-Securus'.

He is active in several professional organizations, *inter alia*, Asociación Argentina de Derecho de Seguros; Argentine Branch of the Association Internacionale du Droit des Assurances (AIDA); Club de Abogados del Seguro; Colegio de Abogados de la Ciudad de Buenos Aires; International Bar Association; and Asociación Cristiana de Dirigentes de Empresa.

He is Senior Partner of BULLÓ Abogados.

In legal practice, he offers advisory services to financial institutions, the insurance and reinsurance industry, and business associations.

He can be contacted via e-mail at carlosestebenet@ebullo.com.ar.

Table of Contents

Table of Contents

List of Abbreviations

AACS	Asociación Argentina de Compañías de Seguro
ADEA	Aseguradores de Argentina
ADIRA	Aseguradores del interior de la República Argentina
AIDA	Asociación Internacional de Derecho de Seguros
ARS	Argentine Peso
ART	*Aseguradoras de Riesgos del Trabajo*
AVIRA	Asociación de Vida y Retiro
CAA	Comité Asegurador Argentino
INDER	Instituto Nacional de Reaseguros
IT	Information Technology
NGO	Non-governmental Organization
NRI	National Reinsurance Institute
SIN	Superintendence of Insurance of the Nation
UART	Unión de Aseguradoras de Riesgo de Trabajo
UBA	Universidad de Buenos Aires
UCES	Universidad de Ciencias Empresariales y Sociales
USD	United States Dollar
VAT	Value Added Tax

List of Abbreviations

General Introduction

Chapter 1. General Background Information

1. Geographical Locations and Other Main Data. In the first drawing up of section 35 of the National Constitution, the country is designated with the name of Argentine Republic, depicting the tradition that had been created around it. Geographically, the Argentine Republic is located in the southern extreme of the American Continent; this is towards the end of the South American shaping. It covers a surface of 3,761,264 km^2, including the portion located in Antarctica. Its continental part is one of a complete irregular polygonal figure that becomes thinner towards its southern extreme. Its greatest length of more than 5,000 km corresponds to the north-south axis.

It borders almost 10,000 km of the countries of Bolivia, Paraguay, Brazil and Chile. It also borders the Atlantic Ocean, with a coast of more than 6,000 km.

Argentina has been claiming for many years its sovereignty over the Islands Malvinas and Orcadas del Sur, both inserted in the South Atlantic Ocean, under the disputed domain of the United Kingdom.

Argentina's population, according to the last census in 2022, was nearly 46.04 million inhabitants.

The official language is Spanish. In many parts of the country, there are indigenous inhabitants from different origins, composed of few people that usually communicate in their vernacular tongues.

Due to the habitual education given in schools or institutes, in the last fifty years, the knowledge of English has truly spread. French and Italian have also spread as second languages.

The Gross National Product of Argentina for 2020 was close to USD 602.93 billion, according to official data from the government. The extension of the country determines a variety of regions giving shape to magnificent and diverse landscapes of generous dimensions and beauty.

Tourism is possible in almost any season of the year, either outside the vast southern territory or in the mountainous north. Having said that, it must not be forgotten the many existent points along the Andean mountain range on the west side or throughout the fertile Pampean prairie, the suitability of which for the production of substantial agricultural harvest or livestock of all kinds is very well known.

Although great respect is paid to freedom of religion, and it is supported by the Constitution, the main part of Argentina's inhabitants is Catholic (85%). Nevertheless and with a much lower presence, Protestant and Jewish religions can be named.

The official currency of the country is the Argentine peso (ARS); there are banknotes and metallic coins amounting to one unit.

§1. Political System

2. Government Form. The Argentine Republic is a Representative and Federal Republic, as established in 1853 in its National Constitution.

Thus, it is clearly stated that the power belongs to the people, but it is exercised by representatives that are democratically elected.

This federal characteristic has less intensity than in countries like the Swiss Federation or the United States of America because, in Argentina, the connection between the Central State and the Local States (the Provinces) has the following characteristics: (a) the subordination of the juridical order of these Local States to the Nation as these have granted supremacy to it; (b) the possibility of these Provinces to participate in decision-making processes cooperating with the Central State as reserved powers, that is, powers not delegated to the Nation; and (c) the coordination of their corresponding powers.

The Powers of State are specifically and organically distributed in three branches, which are oriented to a final coordination. In this way, a system has been established for the exercise of authority by a Legislative, Executive, and Judicial power. The Harmony of Powers that grants and requires the National Constitution has allowed for the equilibrium of functions.

3. The Legislative Power. This Power of State is bicameral and is composed of: (a) a Senate, whose members are directly elected by the people, in a number of three per Province and three for the Capital City. Their mandates last six years, and there are no term limits on re-election; and (b) a House of Representatives that is composed of representatives directly elected by the people, in proportion to the inhabitants of each electoral district. The duration of the offices of the members of the House of Representatives is of four years, and they can also be re-elected without term limits.

The Legislative Power or Congress of the Nation has as its fundamental mission the passing of laws at a national level. In this line, it is important to take into account that, different from what happens in other federative countries, the passing of substantial law, as Public Acts included formally or materially in the Civil, Commercial, Criminal, and Mining Codes, constitutes their exclusive power (this is not a power shared with the provincial legislative bodies).

4. The Executive Power. The power of the Executive Branch is exercised by a person called President of the Argentine Nation. In a word, it can be pointed out that this office is of a unipersonal nature and, as the Vice President, it is required, among other conditions, that the candidate to be elected has been born in the Argentine territory. If a foreigner, he must be the son or daughter of a native Argentine citizen.

The election for both offices is direct, and it is performed by the people of the Argentine Nation, the whole territory of the country constituting one sole electoral district. If certain minimum conditions – established by the Constitution – were not achieved, the election would be determined in a second round and by a majority between the two main opposing candidates that were elected in the first round. The term of the mandate is of four years. An individual could be re-elected for the immediately subsequent term on only one occasion. Any candidate can be elected after not having held said office for one presidential term.

5. *Additional Powers of the Executive.* In addition to roles as supreme chief of the Nation, chief of government, and politically responsible for the general administration of Argentina, the person in charge of the Executive Power also has several powers that are linked to other Powers of State, with a lower degree of influence than that specifically belonging to each of these powers. Thus, for instance, the President of the Nation has co-legislative powers with veto prerogative, according to the limiting provisions established in the Constitution, and with the enactment of bills passed by the National Congress; the President also has powers to issue regulations on the Public Acts that have been passed and enacted and even, under exceptional circumstances, he has powers to issue certain provisions of a legislative nature that will be considered by both Houses.

Regarding judicial powers, apart from the right to appoint judges, the President of the Nation may exercise the right to pardon and commute sentences. This power – although not truly one of the jurisdictional kinds carried out by judges – constitutes a true pardon, and thus it can be linked to a power very close to the judicial function.

Finally, as a significant aspect derived from the Constitution of 1994, it can be pointed out the novelty for the juridical tradition of Argentina, of a Chief of Cabinet of Ministries of the Executive Power.

This novelty was a political creation that could have had the intention of lightening the presidential powers, but that has hardly had those effects, as it has not truly modified the powers of the system originated in the Magna Carta.

The Chief of Cabinet of Ministries is invested with a clear preponderance or supremacy in relation to the Ministries or Secretaries of State, as it can be inferred from the powers that section 100 of the Constitution grants to it.

These last ones are in charge of tasks related to their corresponding fields of work, collaborating with their corresponding responsibilities as public officers with the President of the Nation and the Chief of Cabinet.

The President and the Vice President of the Nation and the Chief of the Cabinet of Ministries – as the Ministries themselves – are liable for impeachment before the Senate of the Nation, by exclusive accusation of the House of Representatives of the Nation, on grounds of bad performance or criminal offences in the exercise of their offices or common crimes.

6. *The Judicial Power.* With absolute independence from the other powers of state that have been previously analysed, the third power, the Judicial Power, is exercised by the Supreme Court of Justice of the Nation and by the Lower Courts that the National Congress establishes by means of their laws.

The nine Judges that, by means of special Act No. 23.774 from the legislative power of the year 1990, must compose the Supreme Court of Justice have been recently reduced to the ones currently in office but when these Judges leave their offices in the future, the number shall be reduced to five. The election of these judges corresponds to the Executive Power, with the previous agreement of the Senate, as long as they comply with the requirements established by the National Constitution, among which there is the condition of being a lawyer. They are irremovable, and they can only be removed by the same circumstances explained for the President of the Nation and with identical procedures.

Given the federal system in the country, the Federal Courts coexist with the local Courts of each Province, but the Supreme Court has its powers of jurisdiction in all cases, federal or not, by means of ordinary or extraordinary appeals, and in other assumptions through general, originary powers, such as those in which ambassadors, foreign ministries, and representatives take part.

The Judges of the Lower Courts of the Nation are irremovable from their offices as long as their good conduct lasts, and their removal corresponds to an impeachment jury composed of members of different scopes, including a wide range of areas.

7. Governments of the Provinces. In the federal system of government that was adopted by the Argentine Republic, as it has been established *supra*, the Provincial States or Provinces correspond to an organization that comes from the times of the viceroyalty, deeply rooted in the Argentine people.

It is a federative special type with a reserve of important rights to be exercised locally and the representation of the population to be carried out concretely by means of a system similar to the national one, except for some provinces where it has been decided to have a legislative power composed of only one House of Representatives.

Both maintaining a Provincial Justice to enforce substantial law, or the Province's own legislation, and the administration of education are conditions required to these states that, following the tradition, have their territory divided into departments or municipalities, divisions that, in turn, have a federal basement.

The Governors and Legislators of the Province, as well as the ones corresponding to the Capital City (Autonomous City of Buenos Aires), are elected by direct and universal vote from each district.

8. Political Parties. In the Argentine Republic, the Reforming Convention of 1994 included, among the incorporated novelties, the compulsory existence of political parties as necessary for running for elective public offices. Without prejudice of the right of association for useful purposes, the aforementioned demand implies an imposition that, to the judgment of many and in our opinion, turns out to be precisely inconvenient as it attacks the freedom of association or the contrary assumption, the freedom of not associating.

These political parties already have existed in the country for many years at both the National and Provincial levels, without the need for a regulation of a constitutional stand in order to guarantee their constitution and the freedom to participate in them, existing, in fact, laws of both jurisdictions regulating some aspects of their creation, their purpose, principles, and inner government. As it has been stated, to have incorporated the principle of presence of political parties with a direct influence in the participation turns out to be contradictory with the freedom to associate that protects its contrary, the freedom not to associate.

As a general rule, it can be said that, one way or other, in principle, even when two or three political parties can be granted in the national order, the first majorities and the most important minorities, none of them has per se the possibility of constituting the majority to win central government in relation to the two political powers: the Legislative and the Executive.

§2. Commerce and Industry

9. Agricultural–Livestock Production. Argentina has always had, as basis of its income, the exportation of agriculture and livestock, due to the predominance in its extensive territory of the fertile soils and the excellence of the variety of climates prevailing in its multiple regions.

Agricultural production has been, sometimes, intentionally disqualified for reasons of commercial competition. The assumption used by this negative position has been the indocile epizootic foot and mouth disease suffered by the livestock of different parts of the country and which consists of a feverish state accompanied by watery blisters that are formed in the mouth and between the hoofs of the animals.

This disease is certainly controlled now with the exception of sporadic and isolated cases that took place in small zones, as a consequence of the bad care of the animals, by failing to vaccinate them on time.

Towards the last two months of the year 2001, some outbreaks were detected, but these episodes were overcome once again, and the importations of meat coming from Argentina – which had been wrongly suspended – generated voices in their favour, above all, because the foot and mouth disease is a disease that does not transmit to man and because of the excellent quality of the meats produced in Argentina, coming specially from cattle raised in the open field with first quality grass.

The stockbreeding production of this unbeatable 'raw material' has allowed for industrialization of a transcendental sector, capable of generating products of a recognized class worldwide that are mainly exported as bovine meat for consumption and tinned meats.

Meat production from other species – such as ovine and porcine meats – also reaches a high level of quality, and thus, they are also export material. Although on a minor scale, dairy production and its derivatives constitute a similar business.

The industry related to agriculture, as well as the fine and coarse grain and crop exportation, has also good and traditional markets. Viniculture was consolidated a long time ago, and it comes from all areas of the country. Especially the Cuyean area – bordering the Andean range – continues to elaborate outstanding fine white and red wines, many of them deriving from stocks that have greatly adapted to the special lands of cultivation of the grapevines.

10. Other Industries. No less important for the economy of Argentina are other industries coming from the farming world, such as edible oil, by means of the production of olives, sunflowers, grapes, etc., as well as the oil industry, sugar, cotton, rice, and several other industries.

The exploitation and manufacturing of wood are also activities of importance, even when they require better plans of protection from the bad methods of production.

In another line, the mining industry is also important, with vast regions from which iron, coal, aluminium, as well as other minerals of permanent use are extracted.

Regarding petroleum, Argentina produces it in several regions, from north to south and, apart from its self-supply, it exports it together with some sub-products, among which, until not long ago, there was natural gas.

Thanks to several hydroelectric dams, electricity is also produced and exported to neighbouring countries.

Nevertheless, subsequent mistakes from different governments have given rise to different problems of an economic nature taking the country to a severe crisis of a very complex nature that has affected not only all the political and social structure but also the economic structure.

The unproductive expenditure generated – and still being generated – by national and provincial governments and the unscrupulous abuse of foreign credit have caused damage that has prevented the significant growth of the country.

§3. Financial Institutions

11. Banks. In Argentina, thanks to the favourable conditions that took place in the ten last years of the twentieth century, the performance of local and foreign banks turned out to be highly benefited, to the point that many diverse qualities of investments took place, bringing about acquisitions by predominant business groups of important commercial and investment banks.

The Central Bank of the Argentine Republic has existed for many years. Its Organic Letter is included in the legislation of Act 24.144. Its last modification was by Act 25.562 on 8 February 2002.

The main and fundamental mission assigned to the Central Bank is to preserve the value of currency, to which effect, among its powers, is the regulation of the amount of money and credit in the economy and the drawing up of rules at monetary, financial, and foreign exchange levels, all according to the legislation in full force at the moment.

The government of the Bank is carried out by means of a board composed of a president, a vice president, and eight directors whose eligibility in monetary, bank, or legal matters must be evident in not only professional competence in their financial area but also moral trustworthiness.

The appointment of all the members of the board is through the National Executive Power with agreement of the Senate of the Nation and for a period of six years, having the possibility of being reappointed.

By means of Act 21.526 and its modifications, the necessary conditions so that certain public or private entities carry out the intermediation between the offer and demand of financial resources have been established.

In this manner, financial institutions are regulated and classified as: commercial banks, investment banks, mortgage banks, financial companies, home or other property saving and loan companies, and credit funds.

Financial institutions, except for some very limited exceptions established by law, must have the company type of a corporation. The branches of foreign companies must have a representative office in the country with sufficient powers, pursuant to Argentine law.

The bank sector has undergone, in the past years, serious and severe problems, and although not many appropriate decisions are registered either from the governments or from the banks themselves, the reality is that they have fought the crisis oppressing the economy in general. At present, despite the lack of sufficient foreign or local investment, it is possible to say that the economic emergency (which had established special government powers) has come to an end. Nevertheless, as it has been stated before, there are difficulties of several natures, mainly in the political order, due to certain intolerance from those in power at present.

§4. Currency Legislation and Monetary Regulation

12. Public Finances. The administration of the public finances is established in the National Constitution as part of the powers of the National Executive Power, corresponding, only to some extent, to the Central Bank of the Argentine Republic.

The National Congress, by means of its two Legislative Houses, is in charge of passing the necessary laws, among which there is the annual budget that should indicate with certainty both the income sources and the allocations of expenses and investments.

The emphasis on this subject is placed on the fact that the House of Representatives has the exclusive right to initiate any bill intending to establish contributions.

As a consequence of passing the annual budget, it is their right to approve or discard the investment account.

Finally, it is worth mentioning that the national currency is the Argentine peso and that its value in relation to foreign currencies has altered, since the ending of what was called the convertibility plan in the beginning of the 1990s, to constitute a severe problem due to the existence of different markets apart from the official market encouraged by the Central Bank.

§5. Insurance: Organization and Distinctive Characteristics

13. Insurance Entities. The federal state is in charge of regulating the activity of insurance companies, whether it is about private or public companies, regardless of their legal form.

Such control is exercised exclusively by means of a unipersonal body called Superintendence of Insurance of the Nation (SIN) that is administratively under the National Executive Power as an office with functional and financial autarchy, as part of the Ministry of Economy of the Nation.

The investigative powers of the State are wide, and they comprise all the moments of the insurers, from the formalities pertaining to their creation to their possible forced or voluntary termination.

Apart from this investigative and controlling function, the SIN has the responsibility of drawing up the necessary regulations for the sector, regulations that must respect the principle of constitutional subordination.

This exceptional requirement of being the exclusive comptroller of the insurance activity provided for expressly in section 8 of Act 20.091 draws us to the conclusion that this is the only body of the State empowered for such a task and eliminates outright any other that exists or may be created without a modification of the aforementioned rule. Thus, the application of regulations provided for by the Consumer's Act and similar ones alien to the SIN does not correspond. This does not mean that laws coming from these sectors should not be applied. It is strongly emphasized that the application of laws regarding insurance corresponds exclusively to the SIN.

As a consequence of laws passed during the 1990s, the insurance activity has been released from the restrictions imposed on foreign capital companies, granting them nationality which is subject to certain percentages of ownership of capital and voting rights by foreign people.

In Argentine law, the Argentine nationality of a legal entity is defined by its creation in the country and the registration of its domicile therein, regardless of the origin of its capital stock.

There are different trade union insurance associations, among which it is worth pointing out the Argentine Association of Insurance Companies (Asociación Argentina de Compañías de Seguro (AACS)), which gathers companies of local origin and companies that are branches of international operators, adding up to approximately 60% of the market of property insurance.

It is worth mentioning other associations aimed at specialized risks: Insurance Union of Work Risks (Unión de Aseguradoras de Riesgo de Trabajo (UART)); Insurance of the Interior of the Argentine Republic (Aseguradores del interior de la República Argentina (ADIRA)), the Association of Life and Retirement (Asociación de Vida y Retiro (AVIRA) and Argentine Insurers (Aseguradores de Argentina (ADEA)).

Together with the first company mentioned *supra*, they have formed the Argentine Insurance Commission (Comité Asegurador Argentino (CAA)), comprising the 80% of the total market, where matters related to insurance in the Argentine Republic are discussed and resolved.

In the sphere of academic studies of the disciplines related to insurance activity, it is worth mentioning the International Association of Insurance Law (Asociación Internacional de Derecho de Seguros (AIDA)), operating locally by means of its local offices, as well as their university postgraduate courses in insurance that, for instance, are given in the Argentine Catholic University of the City of Buenos Aires (UCA).

The aforementioned course is, in our opinion, the most complete in the City of Buenos Aires and, year after year, has deserved an ever greater attendance of students, as well as the interest awoken, which attracts people from all over the country to carry out this study of a very well structured syllabus designed by the director of the seminar, Mr Carlos A. Estebenet, Esq., who has provided his invaluable help in the drawing up of this monograph.

Furthermore, many universities follow the way of UCA, for instance, Buenos Aires University (Universidad de Buenos Aires (UBA)); Catholic University of Paraná (Universidad Católica de Paraná, provincia de Entre Rios); Business and Social Sciences University (Universidad de Ciencias Empresariales y Sociales (UCES)).

Chapter 2. Historical Background of Insurance and Insurance Legislation

14. First Public Acts on Insurance. Once constituted as a nation, after the National Constitution of 1853 was drawn up (*see* paragraph 2), the Congress of the Nation undertook the task of legislating substantial law applicable to the whole country. Among the most outstanding legislative codes it can be mentioned: the Commercial Code written by the Congress of the Nation and Mr Dalmacio Vélez Sarsfield, and the Civil Code drawn up by this last one on his own.

Since October 1859, the Commercial Code started to regulate the State of Buenos Aires, which was not yet part of the Argentine Republic, and in September 1862 by Act No. 15 of the Congress of the Nation, it was declared a National Code.

One of the many modifications updating it was Act 17.418, which in 1967 completely substituted Title VI (of which sections 492–557 inclusive, from the originary code, were on insurance).

They constitute the regulations related to insurance, together with Act 20.091 on insurance entities and their controlling acts, Act 20.094 of 1973 on navigation (sections 408–470) and Act 22.400 of 1981 on insurance brokers' advisers.

Since August 2015, the Argentine Civil and Commercial Code is in effect, which has replaced the Argentine Commercial Code and the Civil Code.

15. Brief Historical Reference. Previous to this and as the territory that constitutes at present the Argentine Nation belonged to the Spanish Crown, the Spanish law was applied. These rules that, regarding insurance, have been guidelines, even for this part of the discovered world, as it is noticed in the Compilation of the Laws of the Indies of 1556, contained wise provisions on vessels, maritime insurance, and goods insurance.

The first insurance company of Buenos Aires comes from the end of the seventeenth century and belongs to the Royal Company of Land and Maritime Insurance of Madrid and, towards 1796, Manuel Belgrano (creator of the national flag), in his capacity as Secretary of the Royal Consulate of Buenos Aires, pointed out the pressing need of creating an insurance company, which appeared not long after, answering to the name of 'La Confianza'.

In a word, it is worth briefly stating that, after the saturation crisis of the English market that gave rise to the Bubble Act, there appeared in the market of the Río de la Plata (River Plate), many agencies of foreign companies that directly took out insurance. This was until 1860 when they started to establish their own offices in the Argentine territory, technically cooperating with the advancement of commerce in the now nationally organized Argentine Republic.

To finish with these precedents, it is worth mentioning that, in 1865, the first insurance company was constituted in the country when the Commercial Code had already been written.

16. Regulations of the Activity. The SIN has been taking care of the insurance operation by means of the drawing up of general and specific resolutions.

The former are rules of compulsory application for all the activity that, many times, has wrongly surpassed the limit of the purpose of creation of this body.

Unfortunately, in Argentina, the importance of insurance, commercially speaking, has not been seriously taken into account by many governments. Such governments, in many opportunities, have not considered the need of counting on a private industry of private first-line insurance (given the importance that such activity generates business in general).

The regulations referred to were often so divided into specific regulations that the possibility of respecting and applying them with a clear order turned out to be, many times, impossible or contradictory.

That is why, on 2 January 1992, the Superintendent of Insurance passed General Resolution 21.523 that made a complete revision on the existing regulations at the moment, with the aim of adapting them to important subjects, thus establishing provisions for fundamental issues as those pertaining to capital, reserves, previsions, etc., to allow for an appropriate surveillance of the patrimony, losses, obligations, and future of each one of the insurers, demanding balance sheets every three months.

This Resolution was amended by Resolution 38.708, dated November 2014.

Chapter 3. Sources of Insurance Law

§1. Legislation

17. The Insurance Contract Act. Adding information to what has been explained in paragraph 14, the current Act related to private insurance is No. 17.418, which, from its effective date in 1967, has not been modified.

The modification of its contents to reflect the changes that have taken place in the business since the first half of the last century is, undoubtedly, of a relatively urgent nature.

Nevertheless, such a modification should be comprehensively made, in relation to all the Acts influencing the insurance scope. It would not be convenient to only modify some of them or parts of them as the economy of the regulations would be altered and regulations must keep a conceptual and functional harmony.

Although Act 17.418 seems to have introduced original concepts related to the category of its provisions, Argentine law (by means of the Civil Code) already counted on regulations in such sense. The books of authority divided them into: (a) imperative precepts, that is, those which cannot be repealed; (b) dispositive precepts, that is, those applied to the extent that specific provisions have not provided otherwise; and (c) construction precepts, that is, those explaining others.

The Argentine Civil Code (section 1197), in the first place, contemplates the specific terms and conditions of contracts, granting them the protection of being rules that must be complied with by the parties, as if they were laws.

It is important to take into account that, after that, in section 1198, it is established that the contracts are agreed, construed and performed in good faith and according to what is plausible that the parties would have understood or could have understood, acting with care and caution.

In the second place, it is reminded that the same body of laws, by means of other rules, especially section 21, establish that the specific terms and conditions cannot render ineffective acts the observance of which are of public order and good customs.

The provisions of the aforementioned code, valid as general principle for the entire Argentine legal system, establish that the legal acts must be carried out with subject matters that are not contrary to those good customs.

What is attempted to explain here is that, from the beginning of the legislation, the laws and the judges enforcing and construing them have determined a path respecting the equality of the parties, not only in the legal aspect but also in any other aspect that may alter this perspective.

The new Argentine Civil and Commercial Code has confirmed the above-mentioned principles and has consolidated them into one legal instrument.

It keeps in effect specific laws on insurance and establishes an order of priority, namely: rules of the special law and the code that cannot be abrogated, specific rules of the contract, supplementary rules of the special law and supplementary rules of the code.

It further includes general rules on interpretation and, as a novelty, it regulates the contracts of adhesion to preestablished conditions and the consumption contracts, which clearly have an impact on insurance contracts.

It is indispensable to take into account that insurance law is absolutely alien to the existing supporting laws for social situations. These laws can be referred to social security insurance coverage, safeguarding accidents related to labour benefits or the activity they are annexed to, or motor vehicle accidents or other specific ones, which the laws have timely granted protection, due to the material and personal risks arising out of them.

In this sense, the validity and adequacy of the insurance coverage are not a matter of unworthiness or confrontation. It is only that insurance coverage deals with the application of very similar techniques with very different allocations, resources, and purposes.

That is why, in this monograph, reference will always be made, unless otherwise stated, to the insurance contract and the laws governing insurance in relation to its contractual form or the laws controlling it.

18. Authorization for Insurers. In Argentina, as it was previously mentioned in paragraph 13, the insurers are subject to very strict control by the regulations of Act 20.091, which includes, among the powers of the SIN, the specific power of authorizing their existence.

In this sense, section 2 demands that, apart from the valid creation of the entities in compliance with the type specifically required, the aforementioned Superintendence enables them to operate in the insurance field.

When this authorization is denied on the basis of market convenience or status of the market, it could be subject matter of a possible action filed before the National Executive Power (President of the Nation), lacking the possibility of a subsequent revision by the Judicial Power.

Such provision is established by Act 20.091 of Control of Insurers, but its unconstitutionality is evident, as it is contrary to the whole Argentine judicial system.

The authorization does not constitute a licence concession from the State because the insurance commerce is an activity of the individuals and not of the State proper. The State should only be in charge of the control of the activity, and in no way should it constitute an excluding subject that may grant or not the operation of business.

§2. Specific Binding Regulations

19. Insurance Commercialization. Without prejudice of what has been stated in the previous paragraph and of the fact that in Argentina for many years now there have been commercial entities integrated by the National or Provincial States, thanks to the long period where it was encouraged from many sectors of the country, the presence of the State in commercial and industrial activities. It is worth mentioning that, in our opinion, the insurance business is, by nature, of a private nature and that State capital should only appear in order to solve the absence of private investment and to the extent that it really meets an uncovered need.

Unfortunately, in Argentina, the State influence has been excessive and taken advantage of by the usual dishonest individuals that take profit for their own pockets or for the purposes of increasing their political 'clientele' by deceptive promises. The officers in charge of the SIN for many years, and because of an incredible passive attitude from the insurers, backed a wrong legal concept according to the principles that have always existed in Argentine law.

By applying a wrong criterion of Statism – that administratively existed in the country – the private activity was paralysed, and only the companies with capital and decisive votes of native origin of more than 51% could operate as local insurers.

This continued until the 1990s when, as a consequence of an action filed before said controlling authority by a foreign company, a favourable decision was obtained.

The natural consideration was the inadequacy of conceiving the nationality of a company by the origin of its capital, when a company must be considered a foreign company only if it has not been constituted in the country or its domicile is not registered in it.[1]

From that moment on, when the foreign insurers of international magnitude arrived in Argentina without the subterfuge of hiding all participation superior to 50%, the insurance market experienced changes of importance. Methods and systems were incorporated that the SIN and the monopoly from the State in reinsurance by means of the National Re-insurance Institute (NRI; Instituto Nacional de Reaseguros (INDER)) have not permitted for many years keeping the market away from the novelties that were taking place in the insurance world for a long time.

§3. Other Ruling Origins

20. Certain Restrictions. The limitations commented on *supra* are essentially similar to those established for other activities also regulated by virtue of their subject matter by means of specific rules of construction, restrictive to each operational sphere. These limitations are of different nuances than those exceptions that other regulations contemplating rights of another nature may impose.

The comment has its motivation in laws as the Defence of Competition Act (No. 25.156), which prohibits certain conduct related to the production or exchange of goods or services that has the purpose or effect of limiting, restricting, falsifying, or distorting competition or access to the market, or which may become an abuse of a dominant position in a market resulting in the prejudice of the general economic interest.

1. This brave and determined business position was taken by Mapfre from Spain who had invested capital with a majority of more than 50% in Aconcagua S.A. The latter's capital and votes have been to that date of Argentine origin. When obtaining a favourable and original resolution from the Superintendence of Insurance, many foreign insurance companies (which had concealed their majority investments in local insurance companies) followed and levelled their situation. In other words, this business position determined a profound change in relation to the wrong conceptualization of capital stock nationality.

Such Defence of Competition Act has created, to the effects of being applied, a specific Administrative Court with the remedy of appeal before a Judicial Court, only for some limited assumptions.

It is important to point out that the exclusive and excluding competition established by Act 20.091 in favour of the authority of the SIN has not been repealed by this Defence of Competition Act. Thus, should any insurer incur possible non-compliance with it, the Authority of Application shall continue to be the SIN, with the aforementioned characteristics of exceptionality and exclusivity.

§4. Private International Law

21. International System. Insurance, regarding its economic and technical aspect, mainly since its use has taken it to develop its benefits socially, has been a subject matter of constant and vast legislation in the laws of countries.

By analysing the regulations of different parts of the world, it is noticed a great similarity that generally orient them to similar or equal directions.

Regarding the insurance contract, beyond the institutions (which are also similar), the regulations focus on guidelines from each sovereign territory, which have formed as any other branch of positive law, that is, with ruling independence, although as time goes by, the younger laws have comprised similar and related sources.

That is why, since the last third of the twentieth century, it can be noticed the important tendency towards the unification of the different rulings based on the need of unifying similar systems that are separated or differentiated only on the grounds of belonging to different national states.

Thus, the favourable reception of the European Union which, since the beginning of the common feeling experienced by the European Community, has shown a noticeable advancement that is of public knowledge.

In insurance law and in the insurance contract law, something similar has taken place (which also happened in the exchange market): a line prone to a legislation of rules common to several states or countries. This has taken place in the European nations by means of the Insurance Directives.

Notwithstanding this, it is important to remember that in American law, there are precedents of importance as the Montevideo Treaties of 1889 and 1940, signed by Argentina, Bolivia, Paraguay, Peru, and Uruguay.

Additionally, as a subject of recent interest, there is the Merco insurance (Mercoseguros), that is, a common regulation in some aspects carried out in the South American Common Market (Mercosur) attempting, despite many difficulties, the association of Argentina, Brazil, Paraguay, and Uruguay (although there are certain domineering tendencies from some governments due to not only different but also opposing orientations).

Finally, it should be noted that the Argentine Civil and Commercial Code, in its chapter 'Provisions on Private International Law', establishes rules on international private law, including, without limitation, the free election of jurisdiction and of law on contractual matters.

The foregoing applies unless otherwise set forth in a legal provision.

§5. Legal Precedents

22. Judicial Decisions. The last source that appears as a possible precedent of the genesis of insurance regulations and the insurance contract is the construction that comes from the decisions made by judges when deciding in conflicts between parties or related to measures or provisions from the controlling authority.

These precedents in the analysis and explanation of the appropriate scope of laws are valuable in order to construe future conflicts.

The value thereof in their universally recognized nature as 'living law' and in constant change, in relation to the insurance law and the insurance contract, can be considered of an outstanding influence.

Chapter 4. Litigations and Arbitration

23. Judicial Authorities. As it usually occurs in the rest of the legal matters in Argentina and as it has been expressed in paragraph 5, in the country there coexist two different kinds of judicial authorities.

One judicial power is the federal or national power and is in charge of a Supreme Court of Justice of the Nation and Lower Courts, consisting of the Honourable Chamber of Appeals and Federal Courts of the Nation.

The other judicial authority is the one composed of the Judicial Powers of each one of the Provinces or States composing the Argentine Republic, according to its federal system of government.

It is important to explain that as the jurisdictions of the federal judges and of the judges and Court of Appeals of each province are different and independent from each other, the same occurs with the provincial jurisdictions and with the procedures followed in such jurisdictions.

As the last point of this subject, it must be considered that, thanks to the national and provincial laws that have been passed in line with the constitutional mandate and the construction jurisprudence of the case, there is no problem of difficult resolution at the moment in matters related to jurisdiction.

It could simply be established that the powers to judge habitually correspond to the provincial judges, be it in cases corresponding to Civil and Commercial Acts or Criminal Acts. The judicial instances in all jurisdictions are double: Judges of First Instance and Courts of Appeals, of more than one member, that take part in the appeal of sentences or decisions of the former.

Exceptionally, the Supreme Courts of each province take part as a Court of Appeals, a situation that is even more peculiar in the case of the Supreme Court of Justice of the Nation, as it carries out a specific role in maintaining the constitutional order regarding rule hierarchy (which starts with the National Constitution).

Matters related to control by the SIN are proceedings of investigation and possible penalties carried out and imposed by said institution.

The aforementioned Act 20.091 determines a manner of procedure that protects the freedom of defence, and the administrative decisions are subject to a remedy of judicial appeal by the insurer in question, pursuant to the resolutions of the Superintendence of Insurance.

There is no specific court on insurance matters in Argentina.

With reference to arbitration for the settlement of disputes in matters related to the insurance contract, the parties can agree on it after the insurance agreement has been entered into. Act 17.418 prohibits arbitration clauses from being included in the policies (section 57).

That is to say that the commitment of the parties to initiate the relationship of the insurance contract – even when it can refer in property insurance to the assessment value arising from a loss – cannot involve the substantial construction of the contract.

This arbitration proper may be agreed upon after the delivery of the policy to the insured so, in no way, can it be assumed that it was an imposition from the insurer.

If this was legitimately to become an arbitration, the conflict shall be resolved by such arbitration and pursuant to what has been set forth in the agreement. Remedies can be waived in the commitment.

Chapter 5. Consumer Rights

24. Legal Protection. Since 1993, there is in Argentina Act 24.240 called Consumer Defence Act, which has been modified by means of Acts 24.568, 24.787 and 24.999 and recently by Act 26.361.

This Act, in terms of supervision, in our opinion, does not turn out to be applicable to the insurance activity, as it establishes plural and different application authorities than the Superintendence of Insurance of the Nation, in no way repealing Act 20.091, which also turns out to be specifically established for the insurance activity.

However, in the Consumer Defence Act, the Court of Appeals (indispensable to safeguard such defence) is also different from the authority established by Act 20.091, which causes a profound uncertainty towards the Judicial Court with jurisdiction preventing a clear and true judgment of the Act.

As the Consumer Defence Act is a regulation of a punishing or penalty-imposing nature that establishes, apart from the application authority, the Judicial Court of Appeals, it is required that it is not contradicted by any other Act in force, as it would otherwise be inapplicable due to its unconstitutionality.

Notwithstanding this, it is necessary to take into account that, in Argentine law, there are sufficient rules that determine precise guidelines so that contracts comply with the general system. The subject is submitted to further consideration later on when the specific characteristics of the insurance contract are dealt with.

But it should be noted that the Argentine Civil and Commercial Code includes a specific chapter on consumption contracts wherefore, as long as the insurance contract is executed in the context of a consumption relationship, it will be subject to such protection rules, in the priority order mentioned herein above.

Beyond any criticism to the legislation passed on Consumer Rights and their objective application to 'consumers' or 'users' of insurance for judging possible infractions, it is worth stating that there are other observations made by different reasons and circumstances, natural to the Argentine idiosyncrasy and, therefore, to Argentina, subjects that are not analysed here as they exceed the matter of this monograph.

Chapter 6. Compulsory Insurance

25. Purpose. Among the multiple activities carried out in Argentina, as it is obvious, there are some tasks or occupations that, due to circumstances inherent to them or due to their external effects, are the subject matter of certain protections aimed at those carrying them out or those that may turn out to be harmed by neither sought nor wished effects.

As in other places, there exists the need to allow for the dynamics of the activity, in a manner that turns out to be useful to the community and, at the same time, helps the activity to achieve the indispensable safeguarding of such community, on account of the inevitable harmful consequences of the subject matter it deals with.

In other occasions, countries adopt the same type of protection in relation to occupations that, for different conceptions of justice, equity or merely political or power reasons, make such protection appealing to their leaders or to the electing majorities.

26. Examples. Examples of such activities are diverse tasks of daily life.

In day-to-day life, we take advantage of motor vehicles, which have an undoubted benefit for their owners or users but which, undisputedly, also bring about benefits to an infinite set of unknown individuals who take advantage of such means of communication.

Likewise, these third parties may suffer prejudices caused by the accidents taking place as a consequence of motor vehicle transit. The remedy of such deserves to be contemplated at a general level by the states, either by legislation of their own or by means of a compulsory obligation for all parties responsible for motor vehicle circulation.

Other examples of insurance with long history would be labour performance-related insurance (for in-house positions), or the safeguarding of those assisted by professionals in services of first need (as the ones coming from the art of healing or the art of advocating). The concrete examples are the following: civil liability for educational establishments and environmental insurance.

27. Legislation. Modern legislation has used the insurance technique as a means of protection. Legally, it is not possible to make it equal to the insurance contract, as their geneses are completely different and even opposed. One is originated from the free agreement of wills (to use the technique of insurance under certain conditions mutually agreed upon). The other is originated from the will of the law and the sovereign power of the people's will, being imposed for the benefit of those included in the regulation.

As it has been mentioned *supra*, some forms of compulsory insurance have a long history. Others are recent. In all cases, it seems indispensable to carry out a new study. This study should analyse in depth the subject in order to furnish the protection that has been legislatively ordered, with more effectiveness and a comprehensive sense of protection, the same as the modification of the 1990s in the matter of work accidents did, when insurance companies of the labour branch and their pertaining legislation were constituted.

Part I. The Insurance Company

Chapter 1. Its Form

§1. Mutual Insurance, Premium Insurance, and Others

28. Forms Plausible of Authorization. Under the provisions of section 2 of Act 20.091 (of Insurers and their control) published in the Official Bulletin dated 7 February 1973, only the following are authorized to operate insurance: (a) companies adopting one of the types of association compulsorily provided in such Act, which are corporations, cooperative insurance, and mutual insurance companies or mutuals; (b) branches or agencies of foreign companies (those constituted and registered abroad) of the types mentioned *supra*; and (c) bodies and official entities or mixed, national, provincial, or municipal entities.

29. Corporations. Under the form of a corporation, it is constituted what is called 'Insurance Company', fundamentally based on the collection of premiums in order to provide coverage for events established in the contract, plus coverage of administrative expenses and profitability as any commercial management.

Not only they must comply with regulations provided for in the Insurers Control Act but also they are subject to the regulations of the Commercial Companies Act (No. 19.550) concerning formalities regulating their constitution.

30. Cooperative Insurance. Under the provisions of section 1 of Act 20.337, cooperatives are entities founded on their own effort and mutual help in order to organize and render services according to the provisions established by law.

Among these characteristics, the following must be pointed out: variable capital stock and perpetual existence; no articles of association limit as regards the number of members or capital stock; only one vote granted to each associate no matter the number of their quota shares; acknowledgement of a limited interest of quota shares; minimum of ten associates except for the exceptions expressly provided; distribution of profits in proportion to the use of the company services; rendering of services to their associates and non-associates; and limitation of liability of their associates to the amount of quota shares undertaken. In case of liquidation proceedings, it is established the non-profitable destination of the property.

In the same way as corporations, they must comply with the formalities related to their constitution, pursuant to the provisions the law establishes in this respect. Notwithstanding that, they are also subject to the exclusive and excluding provisions of Act 20.091, which, in general, treat them in the same way as corporations.

The cooperative associations are favoured with some tax exemptions answering to the type of organization they are, and it must be pointed out the provision related to income tax (even when they pay a specific burden, as will be observed in Chapter 6 of this first part of the monograph).

In order to conclude this point, it can be stated that this associative form has been used in our country and that, at present, there are cooperatives performing in the insurance market with a production that, added to the mutual insurance companies, brings about the 8.2% of the total of the premiums received by the system.

31. Mutual Insurance Companies. Mutual insurance companies as they are defined by Act 20.321 are those freely constituted non-profit organizations by individuals inspired in solidarity with the objective of rendering mutual help before possible risks or assist their material or spiritual welfare by means of a periodic contribution.

Within the mutual services that section 4 of Act 20.321 lists and where reference is made to those companies which, by means of a contribution or savings from their associates or any other legal resource, have as objective to meet the needs of the associates by means of attaining different aims, insurance is specifically mentioned.

It is pointed out – as an important aspect – that the listing is not of a restrictive nature but it only exemplifies (as the aforementioned rule clearly states) that there may be other kinds of objectives, as long as they provide the associates with material and spiritual welfare.

The constitution of the mutual insurance companies is regulated by the specific Act mentioned in this item. Notwithstanding that, as their operation deals with insurance, the rules of Act 20.091 apply as from the moment of requiring authorization to carry out such activity.

Like cooperative associations, mutual insurance companies are exempted from certain taxes such as income taxes. This concept will be further analysed in Chapter 6.

§2. Public or Private Nature

32. Public Nature of Private Activity. Even when it is a clearly private activity performed in the commercial sphere, due to the kind of businesses it carries out, it has been considered an activity the performance of which should be carried out in full public view, as the main obligation payment of the insurer is related to the occurrence of a random and uncertain event.

In the protection of the insured, pursuant to what is established in section 1 of Act 20.091, the exercise of the insurance and reinsurance activity in any part of the territory is subject to the legal system of such Act and the control of the authority created by it, the SIN.

What has just been explained implies that, for our law system, we are dealing with an entity with a controlled corporate purpose, remaining thus subject to rules that establish the need to comply with certain requirements regarding strict control and publicity, with general informative purposes.

In this line, the controlling Act establishes that the insurers must register their operations in books and registers as established by the SIN (section 37) and submit to the holding of the annual general meeting, its annual report, general balance sheets, profit and loss statement, and statutory auditor's report or supervisory council as may be the case, accompanied by an auditing report drawn by authorized professionals external to the company (section 38).

Pursuant to section 40 of the aforementioned Act, the SIN, by means of its General Resolution 20.571 and circular 2591, has established that, in all cases, balance sheets from insurers must be submitted every three months.

Moreover, it turns out to be compulsory to submit the annual balance sheet for its approval, which publication is compulsory for all insurers.

§3. Factual Data

33. SIN Data from Analysis of Balance Sheets. According to the last information furnished by the SIN, issued with the annual report for the fiscal year closed on 30 June 2022, balance sheets of 192 companies were submitted.

From those, 121 corresponded to companies of general insurance, 5 to public transport insurance companies, 12 operated exclusively with work risk insurance, 36 worked exclusively with life and related insurance, and 18 with retirement income insurance.

For the purposes of showing the numbers that are dealt with in the Argentine market for the closed fiscal year, the total asset value of the market amounted to ARS 2,881,126,776,984 that, to the mentioned date (30 June 2022), brought about the approx. amount of USD 22.16 billion.

The total net worth represented 30.10% of the total of the assets.

The profit and loss statements amounted to the negative sum of ARS –92,360,722,174 (USD 710.46 million) after taxes, outcome of a global technical positive result of ARS 131,865,980,725 (USD 1,014.35 million) and a negative financial result of ARS –231,536,969,677 (USD 1,781.05 million).

The statements are corrected by inflation adjustment; otherwise, the result would increase in ARS –967,579,439,485 (USD 7,442 billion).

The gross production reached for the annual period under analysis was in the amount of ARS 1,714,609,227,005 (USD 13.19 billion) with a growth of 65% compared to the previous fiscal year.

The insurance signed as personal insurance represented 15.217% of the aforementioned production.

However, the total premiums for the area of property damage reached 84.78% of the total gross production.

From the total premiums earned by the general insurance, the branch of car insurance produced 46.49%.

If the approach of the analysis is directed towards the importance of the production depending on the type of insurance company, given that there are some companies operating with only one type (compared with some others that comprise several risks in their portfolio), some small differences in the percentages are produced that are indicated *supra*.

The general levels of retention of the market reached 90%. The total expenses of production and management of premiums plus the loadings reached 37.28%.

The total of the information included in this item comes from Communications issued on 29 September 2022 by the SIN.

Chapter 2. Access to Business: Authorization—Requirements and Procedures

34. Statutory Provisions. Only those entities listed in section 2 of Act 20.091 shall be authorized to operate insurance (*see* paragraph 28).

In section 7 of the Act, the requirements authorizing entities to operate in insurance are listed: those entities must be constituted pursuant to general Acts (subsection a); they shall have as exclusive purpose to carry out insurance operations (subsection b); they shall demonstrate a minimum paid-in capital (subsection c); in case of foreign companies, the five last balance sheets from headquarters must be attached (subsection d); they shall have a minimum duration as required by the nature of the type or types of insurance to be operated (subsection e); they shall adjust their insurance plans to what is established by section 24 of the Act (subsection f); they shall make their performance convenient in the insurance market (subsection g).

All this implies that authorization is necessary by the controlling body, which is in charge of observing that the total of the requirements named *supra* have been complied with.

35. Convenience of the Market Requirement. The last requirement mentioned in the preceding list (convenience of the market) is a circumstance that is linked to a political economic matter at a certain moment of history, and it is a matter not plausible of legal verification.

Resolution from SIN No. 13.828/77 was in force since 1977, by virtue of which it was not permitted to constitute new entities, so the only way of accessing the business was by becoming a shareholder of an already constituted insurer.

However, many years later, on 24 March 1987, Resolution 19.106 set forth the possibility to constitute retirement insurers and then life insurance companies. The latter Resolution were considered a landmark towards the opening of the market.

The constitution of Work Risk Insurance Companies was authorized as from the passing of Act 24.557 (section 26) and by means of resolutions of the SIN No. 23.334/96 and of the Superintendence of Work Risks No. 2/96 and 66/96.

Finally, by means of the drawing up of Resolution 25.804/98 (pursuant to Decree 2284/91), the prohibition of constituting general insurance entities or of any other type (Resolution 13.828/77) was repealed. Thus, at present, it is possible to access business by creating an insurance company from its beginning, no matter the type of insurance that wishes to be operated. This does not imply the repeal of section 7 subsection g, and it seems appropriate to sustain the unconstitutionality of such restriction.

The amendment answered to a deregulation policy initiated in the 1990s in different matters that specially reached the insurance activity.

The possibility of constituting new entities took place together with a modification and improvement of the capital requirements, both the original capital and those that fluctuate in relation to different parameters determined by regulations, as it shall be analysed in the corresponding chapter (Resolution 25.804/98).

36. Authorization to Commence Operation. According to what is set forth in section 8 of the controlling Act (20.091), the entities plausible of authorization shall only be able to operate insurance as from their registration before the Public Commercial Register in the jurisdiction corresponding to their domicile.

Such registration shall proceed 'when … the articles of incorporation [having been] approved by the corresponding controlling authority according to the type of company or association form undertaken, the SIN has granted the corresponding authorization to operate'.

There are no differences whatsoever in the treatment of entities in relation to the origin of the capital stock as, according to the law and regulations, the treatment shall be equal, having in each case to comply with the requirement established in the regulations of informative nature (section 5 of Resolution 25.804 of 24 April 1998) applicable to all potential shareholders.

It is necessary to clarify again that the control of performance as from its registration to operate, for all the insurance entities, is carried out by the controlling authority and no other, which holds this exclusive and excluding capacity.

Notwithstanding this, the SIN may request opinions regarding company matters to the corresponding bodies whenever such body deems it convenient (section 8 at the end of Act 20.091).

37. Additional Provisions. The Act also provides restrictions on qualifications to be a broker, founder, director, adviser, statutory auditor, member of the supervisory council, adjuster, manager, administrator, or representative of insurers, which restrictions, apart from including the provisions established in Act 19.550 of Commercial Companies applicable to any type of entity, establish other specific regulations regarding the criminal background of those intending to hold those positions (section 9 Act 20.091).

38. Reinsurance. In reinsurance, access to business is regulated by General Resolution 38.708 of 6 November 2014. This resolution takes into consideration the reinsurance system established since February 2011, whereby certain market reserve is created for reinsurers domiciled in Argentina.

Along these lines, it may be said that there are two types of reinsurers operating: the full reinsurers, which are known as local reinsurers. These are the ones organized under Argentine law and the branches of foreign entities.

In both cases, capital should be contributed to the entities, and its business scope has no limitation other than their capacities.

Second, we should consider limited reinsures, which regulations call 'Admitted Reinsurers'. They operate directly from their place of origin, and they are only required to be registered and to evidence their valid existence and net worth.

They may only act in individual risks higher than USD 35 million, in the retrocession market and by exception upon prior express approval by the supervisor for all other risks.

In a recent resolution, the supervisor established a schedule to gradually release the market up to 80% of the premiums during an eight-year term.

It is to be expected that such schedule accelerates based on the capacity required by the market and the reduction of costs, in order to avoid the participation of a local reinsurer without the appropriate capacity.

Nowadays, the legal framework issued by the supervisor allows admitted reinsurers to operate by certain restrictions:

They have a cap per contract of 75% of the premiums except in the following cases in which admitted reinsurers may operate by 100%: (i) facultative reinsurance: when the liability of the reinsurer/s is equal or exceed USD 35 million; (ii) in the case of Treaty (automatic contract), when the coverage is Catastrophic 'or by' Event and Catastrophe, non-proportional and the liability is equal or exceeds USD 35 million.

Chapter 3. Supervision

39. Role of SIN. As stated before, the control of entities operating with insurance and reinsurance is in charge of the SIN, which is the comptroller established by Act 20.091.

Such law establishes that the rules should be issued by the same controlling body by means of the issuance of general resolutions, apart from those particularly applicable to the activity of the controlling body in matters of jurisdiction and finally the issuance of circulars regarding construction or merely procedural and administrative circulars.

There is a compilation of ruling resolutions of the Act, General Resolution 38.708, part of which includes the total of general resolutions issued and not repealed or modified by such general resolution or by any other subsequent specific resolution.

The aforementioned controlling body comprises different aspects of creation, duration, and termination of the company as they are, as we have already expressed, entities with controlled corporate purpose.

§1. Solvency Control

40. Minimum Capital (a). Section 30 of controlling Act 20.091 delegates in the controlling authority the power to order, with certain uniform and general criteria, the amount and regulations on minimum capitals during the whole duration of a company.

According to the regulations of the Act, the minimum capital an insurer must count on arises out of the combination of three parameters, taking as guideline the highest of the three (General Resolution 38.708 November 2014, item 30.1.1).

The first of the parameters establishes a fixed minimum capital by type of insurance operated, which, given its nature, shall coincide with the original capital stated in the conditions to start an operation (*see* Chapter 2).

The second is the one pointed out by virtue of the premiums and loadings, which permits the insurer's assessment when it is under operation.

Finally, the third rule refers to the determination of the capital amount in losses.

41. Minimum Capital (b). The original minimum capital, according to the type of insurance, is established in the regulations and helps as orientation in order to consider the demands that the controlling authority imposes. The minimum capital required to all entities that were created as from 1 August 2016 are:

(a) To operate in the motor vehicle line, excluding the risk of civil liability against third parties for vehicles for public transport, ARS 104.250 million.
(b) To operate jointly and without distinction in each one of the types of liability insurance, and property including the motor vehicle line; aircraft insurance; to operate damages, comprising the types of fire and combined theft, robbery, and

similar risks, glass, transport, livestock, hail, technical insurance, and miscellaneous risks; and to operate contingency and credit insurance, except for mortgage credit coverage, a minimum capital of ARS 130 million.

(c) To operate jointly and without distinction in personal insurance comprising the risks of personal accidents, health, burial, and life (except for pension life annuity), and the coverage defined in section 99 of Act 24.241, the amount of ARS 52 million and entities should be constituted with exclusive corporate purpose.

(d) To operate in retirement income insurance (excluding pension life annuity and work risk annuities), and to operate retirement life annuity and work risk annuities, a minimum capital of ARS 87 million.

(e) To operate in work risk coverage as contemplated by Act 24.557, a minimum of ARS 87 million.

(f) To operate in mortgage loan insurance, the minimum capital shall be ARS 3 million.

(g) To operate in civil liability insurance on motor vehicles for public transport, a minimum capital of ARS 87 million in addition to the capital required to operate in motor vehicle insurance.

(h) For mutual insurance companies, which operate exclusively civil liability insurance of motor vehicles for public transport, a minimum capital of ARS 104.250 million.

(i) To operate as a local reinsurer, ARS 300 million.

42. Minimum Capital (c). The payment of the necessary minimum capital, whenever this was intended by means of assets and not cash, according to item 30.2.1 of the General Regulations, is limited in order to improve the effectiveness and guarantee of the instruments supported.

The aforementioned limitations do not imply a prohibition, and they rather refer to the following aspects: differed charges, investments and available funds deposited abroad, rural or estate located in non-urbanized zones or imperfect titles, shares trading in the stock market, any other investment that does not correspond with what is expressly provided for in the act of reserves or is not authorized by the controlling body and finally, receivables accounts.

Investments with the limitations provided in the regulations determine what is known as countable assets to the effects of paying the minimum capital.

43. Minimum Capital (d). Section 31 of the controlling act establishes that, when the minimum capital turns out to be affected by any loss, the insurer shall be summoned to give explanations and take the necessary measures to maintain the integrity thereof.

To such effects, the insurer shall submit a plan on regularization and rehabilitation. If such plan is not accepted by the controlling body, the capital shall be reimbursed in thirty days.

In such a scenario, the investment unavailability shall be declared (section 86 of Act 20.091).

There is freedom for the purposes of establishing the retention tables; nevertheless, the controlling authority shall be able to draw observations taking into account the regulating rules (section 32 Act 20.091 and item 32.1 of General Resolution 21.523).

§2. Supervision of Tariffs and Insurance Conditions

44. Authorization Requirements. According to what is set forth in section 24 of the controlling Act, to operate a type of insurance the insurer must be expressly authorized.

The insurance plans, as well as their technical contractual elements, must be approved by the controlling authority before their application, as established at the end of section 23.

Plans shall necessarily contain the text of the insurance proposal and of the policy, the premiums, the technical grounds, and the calculation basis of the technical reserves whenever there are no applicable general rules (section 24 of the controlling Act).

In the same regulation, special rules for life insurance are established, according to which there shall be stated: the text of the questionnaires to be used, the principles and technical basis for the premium and pure reserves calculation, and the basis for the calculation of the salvage values of settled insurance and loans.

It is further necessary to attach an authorized actuarial opinion.

Notwithstanding what has been stated, the regulation in its item 23.1.1 establishes that the insurance entities shall be able to use plans, clauses, and other technical contractual elements – applicable to such lines of insurance – approved by general resolutions.

45. Premium Requirements. The controlling Act in its section 26 establishes that the premiums must be sufficient for compliance with the obligations of the insurer and its financial economic capacity.

According to the regulations, insurers shall freely establish premiums, which shall arise from the statistical analysis of the loss experience, expense level, and other elements, with technical reasons supporting them to the effects of being authorized by the controlling authority (item 26.1.1 of Resolution 38.708).

The controlling authority has the right of observing premiums that turn out to be insufficient, abusive, or arbitrarily discriminatory.

Minimum premiums shall be fixed whenever the stability of the market is affected (section 26 at the end).

46. Policy Requirements. Regarding the contractual terms and conditions of the policy, they shall adjust to the provisions of Act 17.418 (insurance contracts), and the controlling authority shall take care of the fact that all the conditions are fair (section 25 of controlling Act 20.091).

There are certain imperative regulations for which modification by agreement of the parties is not possible, and others that can only be modified in the insured's favour (section 158 of Act 17.418).

Upon the approval of the contractual conditions, the controlling authority shall take care of the fact that the conditions are compatible with such regulation as with any other guideline of our law, mentioned in this monograph.

All this implies that all contractual conditions to be used shall have to be previously approved by the SIN.

Chapter 4. Technical Reserves and Investments

47. Loss Reserve Requirements. Technical and pending loss reserves (that correspond to constitute) shall be determined in general by the controlling authority (section 33 Act 20.091).

Besides, they shall constitute amortization, prevision, and reserve funds as provided for in general, without prejudice of the funds that are, in particular, established by each entity (section 34 Act 20.091).

Thus, the SIN is empowered to issue regulations for the purposes of establishing the necessary reserves to comply with the obligations undertaken by the insurers in the contracts.

Therefore, ongoing risks reserves (item 39.3.1 of Resolution 38. 708) can be differentiated from those constituted for outstanding loss reserves (item 39.5 of the same resolution).

In the ongoing risk reserves, specific regulations are applied defining the manner of calculation, differentiating possible risks from the transportation of goods, public transport, and credit and contingency risks.

In the regulations related to reserves for outstanding losses, specific rules with alternative technical methods are issued (item 39.5.2), including those implying the calculation of the IBNR and the IBNER.

48. Motor Vehicle Insurance Requirements. For motor vehicles insurance, there are specific rules (item 39.6.0 of Resolution 38.708, pursuant to Resolution 24.874 of 1 November 1996).

Moreover, pursuant to what is set forth in item 39.5.10.3 of the regulations, it is provided for the 'correction in the calculation of the liabilities for outstanding losses for direct insurance', that is, no other thing but the liabilities added for insufficiency in the calculation of the outstanding losses at the closing of the previous fiscal year.

The reserve for deviation of losses established in item 39.4.1 of the regulating resolution pursuant to the text of Resolution 38.708 is also applicable in the motor vehicle risk, which, by virtue of a calculation in which the variable 'risk exposed vehicles' is applicable, demands a provision for additional liabilities.

All this is to the extent that the expected risk ratio suffices in comparison with the amount of losses in the last twelve months.

49. Loss Reserve Investment Requirements. Act 20.091 establishes in its section 35, in which instruments and property the amounts of the total of reserves and deposits in guarantee, retained to the reinsurers, the capital, the legal reserve, and the provision funds may be invested, '… preferring those that have greater liquidity and sufficient profitability and guarantee …'.

In a word, the investments that the regulations establish are the following:

(1) Bonds and other public national debt instruments or instruments guaranteed by the Nation, and bonds of provincial debt.
(2) Public bonds of foreign countries up to the amount of technical reserves for policies issued in currency of said country.
(3) Negotiable obligations of authorized public offer:

   (a) Loans secured by a mortgage or pledge on property located in the country.
   (b) Real estate located in the country.
(4) Corporate shares that trade in national or foreign stock exchanges:
   (a) Loans secured by bonds, debentures, and shares of the aforementioned entities.
   (b) Financial operations guaranteed in their total amount by banks or other financial institutions authorized to operate.

50. Allocation of Investments. It is a power of the controlling authority to establish the percentages of investment of the aforementioned property and challenge the investments that do not meet the required characteristics of liquidity, profitability, and guarantee.

In item 35 of the General Resolution on these matters, the related regulations are dealt with. According to Resolution 38.708, it was established a specific system of custody for the investments.

It is pointed out that, according to the law and the regulations, the insurer need not request authorization to carry out the aforementioned investments as the principle of freedom of investment operates.

Therefore, beyond the investment established by security reasons by law, the insurers are free to invest their property with the general prudence of the case. In the aforementioned sectors, investment must be done in the aforementioned property, as provided by law. If the insurer fails to do so, the effect shall be the impossibility of counting such investment for compliance with the solvency regulations.

Chapter 5. Accountancy

51. Accounting Records. According to what has been set forth by section 37 of Act 20.091, the operations must be registered in books and registers, as provided for by the controlling authority.

Moreover, they shall submit to the SIN an annual report, general balance sheet, loss and profit statement, and statutory auditor's reports or supervisory council, with an auditor's report from an external professional (section 38). This information must be submitted before this body at least thirty days before the shareholders' meeting, where the results at the closing of each fiscal year shall be considered. This will compulsorily be carried out, pursuant to Act 20.091, on 30 June of each year, except for the case of an agency or branch of a foreign company (which will do so at the moment its headquarters does).

In section 39 of Act 20.091 is established the power of the controlling authority to issue accounting rules and establish a uniform accounting plan for the whole market as well as uniform rules for asset assessment (section 41 of the controlling act).

Special authorization shall be previously required for exemptions from these regulations.

In item 39.1 of the regulations, guidelines are established for drawing up of financial statements, the general rules (39.1.1), the limit values (39.1.2), and the specific regulations (39.1.3).

There are differences in the balance sheets' structure depending on whether it is a financial statement that must be made public (item 39.6.1 of the regulations) or if it corresponds to intermediate periods (item 39.7.1 of the regulations).

At the same time, the payable obligations coverage statements and receivable paid losses must be submitted monthly (item 39.8 of the regulations), which are simply statements of financial situation, pursuant to the guidelines established by the same regulations.

52. Accounting Audits. In item 39.13 of the regulations, it is determined the reach and forms of accounting audits, all this pursuant to Resolution 38.708 (General Provisions on Accounting and Actuarial External Audits).

There, the modalities for the exercise of the auditing activity are established, a register is created where all those professionals carrying out auditing tasks in insurance companies must enrol, and the conditions and impediments for performing.

The minimum procedures for accounting audits are provided for in item 39.9.2 of the regulations. There, the tasks to be reviewed are established.

In item 39.9.3, there are rules of performance for actuaries, establishing the modalities for their activity, a special register, the conditions for their performance, the impediments, and the descriptions of minimum control procedures.

Finally, in item 39.9.4, all regulations regarding the form of the reports are gathered.

Chapter 6. Taxation of the Company

53. Forms of Taxation. As with other activities of the economy, insurance is included in the general rules in full force and effect on taxation, leaving the insurer under the effects of the current taxes. Nevertheless, it is worth describing each one of the existent and special effects that they produce in particular.

Income tax is applicable to insurance companies as a derivative from the general system for the operations of both insurance and reinsurance, which in both cases covers the risks in the territory of the country or refers to individuals that, at the time of entering of the contract, resided in it (Income Tax Act, as amended by Decree No. 649/97).

Insurers constituted as cooperative and mutuals are exempted from paying income tax (cf. section 20, subsections d) and g). Notwithstanding this, they pay the so-called Special Contribution on the Capital of Cooperatives (Act 23.427), which is calculated on the difference between Assets and Liabilities at the end of each fiscal year, according to the rules of assessment established by law and a rate of 2%, applicable on such tax base.

The tax on Minimum Assumed Profit is applicable on the basis of assets of the company, evaluated in the manner determined by the Act that has created it (Act 25.063).

Such tax is applicable even when the fiscal year was negative for the insurer.

In the particular case of insurers, 20% of taxable assets is taken as the tax base. Property corresponding to insurers constituted as cooperative entities or mutual insurance companies are exempted.

A rate of 1% is levied and, as payment in advance, income tax corresponding to the fiscal year on which such tax burden is charged is taken from this tax.

The tax on debits and credits in current accounts is provided for in Act 25.413 and applies to the debits and credits performed on accounts opened in institutions regulated by the Financial Institutions Act.

The fixed rate is 0.6% and is determined on the gross amount of debits and credits and taxable operations, without deductions or increments of any kind for commissions, expenses, or similar concepts.

It must be taken into account that, as from the passing of Act 25.345 and with the purpose of preventing tax evasion, it was established that payments carried out as from a certain amount – at present fixed on ARS 1,000 – must be necessarily done by check, credit card, credit invoice, deposit in financial institutions, drafts, or bank transfers, with which it is evidenced that tax is levied over most of the transactions.

Until the beginning of 2009, 58% of the amounts entered were taken as credits against income tax and Value Added Tax (VAT). With the enactment of Decree No. 315/2002, this possibility has been repealed with the aim of reaching a greater fiscal equilibrium.

The accounts for collection of funds and for the Administration of Labour Risk Benefits (ART (Administradoras de Riesgos del Trabajo)), life and retirement income insurance companies are exempted from this bank account tax.

Also exempted were those who were exempted from the income tax, but this benefit was suppressed by means of Act 25.453.

Gross income tax is a direct tax on turnover, and its tax base in the case of the insurance activity is constituted by everything that implies an income from the rendering of services or a benefit to the entity. It is formed, therefore, by the premiums, plus the accrued loadings, net of reinsurance, and losses.

It is a local tax and, for instance, in the City of Buenos Aires – Fiscal Code, Act 541 – levies a charge on this activity with a higher rate than the one provided for most of the other activities also levied (4.9% in comparison with the general rate that turns out to be of 3%) according to the Tax Act in full force and effect for the year in course (Act 746).

Part II. The Insurance Contract: General

Chapter 1. Generalities

54. Concept. The insurance contract, as the name and our law indicates, is nothing but a contract. With this, a clear definition appears because the word 'contract' has a very well-defined meaning that cannot be used in another sense but the specific one, that is, a concrete legal phenomenon supported on the fact that, by an agreement of wills of two or more individuals, legal relationships are generated, modified, or terminated, between the parties.

In this manner – and with all simplicity – it turns out very clear that the insurance contract has not and may not have any other notion but that of belonging to the contract category.

This clarification is made because considering the insurance contract only under the conceptual insurance techniques is certainly a mistake that disrupts the fundamental bases of the law of our country.

One situation is that the insurance contract be analysed, construed, and applied under the legally corresponding guidelines, pursuant to the legislation in full force and effect. Another very different one is that it is intended to comply with it from perspectives totally alien to it, as those corresponding to institutions that the law creates or regulates for general interest or strictly social reasons. An example of this case would be the coverage granted for damages derived from work accidents, or damages coming from group life insurance, or damages coming from traffic accidents or collective life insurance. All these cover a balance that, once saved, will grant an economic base that will enable, after a set period of time, an amount of retirement or a pension for death of the policyholder.

In other words: if we are before an insurance contract, no matter its type or subtype, it must always be taken into account as something very well circumscribed to a defined set of laws. It cannot be treated as if something of another nature was being considered, as would be the case of those subjects deriving from a legal provision absolutely different to the agreement of wills and thus, with their own shape and circumstances – alien to them – and their species, which, in law, is called contract.

We understand that at present, in all countries and for some reason alien to contractual nature, one of the parties of the insurance contract necessarily has to be an insurer with characteristics defined by Public Acts. The State's control over the insurer is required in order to safeguard those that turn out to be any of the other parties, that is, the policyholders or co-takers, the insured, and the beneficiaries, as will be seen later.

This means that, in Argentina, in order to take out insurance, the party that assumes the risk has special requirements to comply with by means of Public Act No. 20.091. These regulations, which widely regulate the activity, refer to both the minimum capital in order to validly constitute as insurer and diverse legal conditions of company type and others as it has been seen *supra* in Part I of this monograph.

55. Specific Characteristics. The insurance contract, apart from maintaining the characteristics that all contracts have in the Argentine law, has some specific ones:

(1) It is a consensual contract because for its existence only the agreement of the wills of the parties is needed, and it does not require any other additional element. As, for instance, the delivery of the policy.
(2) It is an aleatory contract because it is subject to the random occurrence of a future and uncertain event, so that the advantages or disadvantages in favour of one or the other party may occur.
(3) It is a predetermined contract, a characteristic that comes from the specification of agreements in which terms and conditions are solely attributable to insurers.

Moreover, there are insurance relationships that do not participate in the conditions of a contract as, to our criterion, for instance, is the case of compulsory insurance for motor vehicles (and other coverage widely used by the insurable and massively commercialized by the insurers). It is also worth pointing out that, legally, these insurance relationships have no characteristics of a contract but, in reality, they are different features that correspond to legal or social obligations or duties and that, technically, they use methods and systems similar to those applied by the contractual insuring activity.

A characteristic must be also pointed out that has nowadays been attributed to contracts, although there are many individuals opposing it, among them ourselves. This last characteristic: the predetermined characteristic (also derogatively called by some books of authority by other less objective names as adhesion contracts). With all this, what is intended is to force the construction of the insurance contract in favour of the insurer's counterpart, either the policyholder or taker of the contract or the beneficiary of the compensation or of the agreed amount (depending on the type of insurance, property or life insurance). This assumption is totally controversial, and much more controversial are the consequences of this irrational and blind posture. The subject raises justified concern because, even in countries where the subject is openly discussed, where authors sustain that all insurance contracts are adhesion contracts, there are explanations restricting this characteristic to narrower limits than the ones seemingly portrayed. For instance, in this same collection of insurance law texts (the Denmark Insurance Contract volume that has helped as formal guide for the adaptation of this present monograph to the standards set by Kluwer International), several exceptions can be distinguished that shall be introduced under the title of the example (Part II, Chapter 1. Generalities, paragraph 54).

In order to conclude this item, from the summary of the position arising out of the chapter contracts in the Argentine law, it is clear that any interpretation of any of the specimens of this kind of legal institution must agree with the general guidelines incorporated in our law, particularly the concept of good faith covering the whole perspective with its always proportionally coordinating force.

Such good faith has been the engine – by means of the books of authority – of the idea that, in the case of doubt in the construction of an agreement, the decision must be for the benefit of the policyholder and insured, that is, against the insurer, the creator of the policy that documents the contract.

Without disregarding the significance of the books of authoritative commentary that have ruling presence in many countries – practically in the universal jurisprudence – it is essential to remember that the differential model support is the simple fact that our modern world considers legal freedom and equality necessary in order to be able to deal with contractual theory, which implies and demands the economic equality of the parties, a circumstance that is not present in several contracts due to the difference that operates between the parties, either by consequence of their different qualities or by the subject matter of the contract.

In this sense, from all the analyses that could be made, it seems convenient to rescue clear facts that appear when economically the contract being carried out implies an activity that may be grouped under minimum but yet important distinctions to be made as mass characteristics. Thus, the person who obliges himself to deliver goods or render the promised service is more interested in considering the general economic results produced from the benefits than those proceeds coming from each business in particular, whereas each of its co-takers, as it is obvious, is interested individually and distinctly in each one of these results.

In all this – as in the majority of the fights for rights that have been shaping law as ordering behaviour – the experience of a society cannot be coldly and indiscriminately transplanted to another society that does not share the same principles of the former, as the needs and factors of power are different.

If we take a look, for instance, at our country with a historical perspective, we shall see that we have always received with years difference in the principles, theories, and realities that have been developed and assumed by others of greater prestige in the world, especially in Europe, the continent from which our environment predominantly comes.

It is important to point out that, even when the books of authority, as previously said, have inspired on a world level the expression that when in doubt the principle of acting against the one stipulating the conditions of the insurance contract must be favoured or it must be a priority, there are sufficient qualified opinions that have raised interesting questions to such principle. In the first place, these theses of not applying to the extreme ideas as the ones just mentioned are widespread, as they may lead to unjust or unequal constructions and not to situations with seemingly different objectives that, deep down, they were camouflaging. In the second place, there are other cases to quote in which the aforementioned principle applies with certain very important modifications as, for instance, considering the authentic constructions given by our own Acts on insurance or own insurance contracts.

Something to add to such an important subject, which requires much more space and time in order to grant the true dimension that it requires at a worldwide legal level: in Argentina, even when there are judicial decisions of importance regarding matters of contractual predetermination and their derivations, it is worth mentioning that, from the writing of the Civil Code more than hundred years ago, there are rules that have permitted and caused constructions of contracts with a sense of equality.

Finally, as a thought to be elaborated deeply, we repeat it is necessary to distinguish between the insurance contract and the insurance that is placed or commercialized under other guidelines than those of the contract, as the latter answers to social or necessary impositions, safeguarded by laws that use, in the benefit of the objective pursued, the same technical system supporting insurance contracts.

56. Good Faith. Another characteristic of the insurance contract, pointed out specifically by much legislation, is that of being a contract of good faith.

In Argentine law, the condition of good faith is a natural attribution of all contracts and not exclusively of the one mentioned. The Civil Code itself establishes so in section 1198, in the chapter devoted to the effects of contracts in general.

This precisely brings out that the characteristic of good faith acquires in the insurance contract a very special meaning, which is exquisite and requires the qualifying adjective of bountiful.

It is unnecessary to mention that for technical reasons incorporated to the insurance contract, legally the contractual structure cannot be alien to those technical and human reasons that have determined its validity.

However, given that the hope of the beneficiary of receiving the promised consideration by the insurer – if the random event should happen – shall, as priority, depend on its future behaviour, it turns out to be true that, in this contract, the parties owe each other something else than in any of the other habitually commutative contracts.

The principle of good faith as it has been pointed out *supra* has been incorporated as rule of positive law in the general legislation of Argentina. It has not ceased to be the moral notion contained in the roman formula *honeste vivere, alterum non laedere, suum cuique tribuere*, which mentioned the good faith in the three periods of legal life: contracts, extra-contractual conduct, and property distribution.

The Supreme Court of Justice of the Nation in a sentence registered in their inner registers (Judgments, 17:362), many years ago, sustained that '[I]t is a general principle that contracts have to be performed and oblige to not only what is expressed in them but all the consequences that equality, the use or the law attribute to the obligation according to its nature.'

The construction of the insurance contract must be carried out in the same way as any other contract, with the annexed guidelines that correspond by law to others participating in features common to them.

In the same section 1198 of the Argentine Civil Code that has been mentioned at the beginning of this paragraph, when legislating in general for the whole contract gender regarding effects, it is established that it is legally based to consider what the parties understood or could have understood, acting with care and caution.

Apart from this, in all the other concepts composing the aforementioned rule under the diverse headings, different guidelines of an intense content are provided in order to achieve their most fair interpretation.

With what has been just stated, it is important to emphasize very specially that, in Argentine law, there have always been behaviour criteria to judge profoundly and adequately the effect of all the contracts which, according to sections 959 and 961 of the Civil and Commercial Code and in relation to the parties and their successors, have the same force or predominance as the Public Acts formally stated as long as the legal equality was not affected by factual circumstances.

In other words: the matter to be posed is whether legally the consent given by a party would be free consent where the party only chose to carry out a business because its performance was merely necessary, but that did not have the opportunity or chance to analyse or discuss several or all of its significant clauses.

It would be impossible in a limited space as the one provided herein to analyse further onto some specifics contained in our laws about the construction of contractual terms, but we deem convenient to point out as example sections 2 and 1061 of the Argentine Civil and Commercial Code of notorious importance and that respectively state:

> If a civil matter cannot be solved by the letter or spirit of the law, the principles of their analogous laws shall rule; and if even then the matter was doubtful, it shall be redeemed by the general principles of law, taking into account the circumstances of the case, the purpose of the contract and the common intention of the parties.
>
> [P]articular terms and conditions may not render ineffective the Public Acts which observance are of public order and according to good customs.
>
> The judge must resolve by a reasonable grounded decision (section 3 Civil and Commercial Code).

We cannot go on without mentioning that in the Insurance Contract Act, there is section 158, which refers to a certain order of preference in its regulations. Without prejudice of carrying out a specified distinction of this provision, it may be affirmed that it resembles the traditional legal scheme of imperative and dispositive rules, which has always been part of the system of law in our country and that has firmly prevented any kind of abuses.

In order to conclude this item, from the summary of the position arising out of the chapter on contracts in Argentine law, it is clear that any construction of any of the specimens of this kind of legal institution must agree with the general guidelines incorporated in our law, particularly the concept of good faith covering the whole perspective with its always proportionally coordinating force.

57. Special Elements of the Insurance Contract. The insurance contract, apart from the elements of every contract (parties, subject matter, and relationship), has other elements that are very special to it and that are considered essential, that is, substantial.[2]

---

2. As necessary clarification it must be remembered that the essence of each being is that for which it truly is, regardless of its accidents or qualities which may subsist, change or cease to be, without altering the fundamental idea of its medullar identity.

In other words, the insurance contract has in its drawing up elements the absence of which would determine that what is being dealt with is not an insurance contract. It would be any other thing, maybe another gender of contract or terms and conditions, but in no way reference could be made to an insurance contract. Before analysing each one of these characteristics, it is necessary to spend some moments reviewing insurance types.

The Argentine Insurance Contract Act No. 17.418 has attempted to achieve a classification with a distinction criteria supported in the different nature of the insurer's service, that is by means of the different obligations that the insurer assumes as from the moment in which the contract is entered into. This purpose is evidenced by means of the definition that the insurance contract poses in section 1 of Act 17.418, which text is transcribed in the note *infra*.[3]

It must be noticed that the mentioned Act separates by the letter and sense it uses, in a very definite way, insurance contracts aimed at compensating damages from those that do not aim at such purpose; thus, they are not linked in any manner to the concept of insurable risk that, as it will be seen later, is a natural element of property insurance contracts or damage property insurance contracts, whatever the preferred denomination.

Incidentally, it is clarified that this last denomination turns out to be very narrow as it seems not to include all civil liability insurance or insurance that covers civil liability of the insured or the case of credit and contingency insurance.

The principle of compensation that characterizes this type of property contract, which is the main concern of Argentine Act 17.418 – since many sections have been incorporated into it – fundamentally establishes that the insurance brings about compensation for damage that effectively would have resulted in the insurable interest of the insured if the future and uncertain event occurred, which concrete consequences were sought to be avoided with the specific insurance.

As this type of insurance has been – in history – the first that became a matter of negotiations, mainly in the maritime sector as it is widely known, it seems undoubted that the term 'risk' in the insurance business was a strict derogative term at the beginning which referred to average or impairment and, in consequence, the ideas of need, risk, and damage have been very related.

Thus, the risky event has been confused in the jargon of insurance with the threat of being in danger of experiencing an economic need, or demand for sufficient means to remedy it.

It is interesting to remember the Latin expression *risi cari*, that for some authors derived from Italian, another of the romance tongues, to *risco*, and that due to its meaning of surrounding a headland at the sea, evidenced the difficulties navigation was experiencing in the fifteenth or sixteenth century, as the danger of unforeseen events from the long and hidden shape of things.

Also in Spanish, the language we are using in the original version of this monograph, the word 'risk' also has a meaning of great importance, which has legal basis and is applicable to the insurance sphere, that substantially differs from the one previously seen and that even reaches the common language. 'Risk', apart from

3. 'There is an insurance contract when the insurer obliges, by means of a premium or quotation, to compensate a damage or comply with the service agreed if the expected event occurs.'

expressing the possibility of damage or the danger of damage or a total or partial loss of property, represents also the concept of contingency. This is the possibility of the event occurring or not, regardless of the type of consequences arising thereof, that is, that the consequences are innocuous or harmful.

In this same sense, a third definition of risk is provided by the Spanish Royal Academy of Literature as 'each one of those contingencies that may be the object of an insurance contract'.

Summing up: for insurance and for insurance law, risk implies the contingency or possibility that an event may or not occur, regardless of the quality effect, even when the species of property insurance or damage, as it has been previously stated, requires, for the intended compensation to be covered, that the event occurred is harmful. This meaning of simple contingency that is the one to be granted excluding any other to the concept applicable to the term 'risk' is of paramount importance since, if risk was conceived in the originary sense of the term mentioned some paragraphs before, it would require the occurrence of a misfortune, a concrete damage, for insurance to be thought as a differential legal idea from another contract or related feature.

Risk as possible event to occur in the future is the distinctive element of the insurance contract, and that works for both the species of life insurance contract and related ones. It must be very clear the difference between risk as subject matter of an insurance contract and the idea of risk as contingency of the obligation, upon which the economic advantage or disadvantage of the contract regarding the parties involved shall depend.[4]

Coming back to the division or classification stated in Argentine Act 17.418, we noticed, on the one hand, the denomination of Property Damage Insurance, which in Chapter 2 is listed in paragraphs 60–127 and, on the other hand, the Insurance of the Person denomination, which, in reality, essentially refers to life insurance as it shall arise out of the reading of paragraphs 128–156, which appear in Chapter 3.

In order to avoid confusion for the reader, it is clarified that Act 17.418 called Insurance Contract Act still contains some sections, up to section 164, which refer to generic subjects or formalities that are of no interest to the item under analysis.

Briefly, to summarize what we have been mentioning *supra* regarding the substantial elements and species of insurance, it is essential to point out that such substantial elements – risk, premium, and the insurer's rendering of services – shall be analysed as generic guidelines to all types of insurance (life and non-life or life and property) and not as ingredients of one or the other species mentioned.

58. Risk. It has been stated in the last paragraph that risk constitutes for Argentine law an essential element of the insurance contract, regardless of its species. Apart from the fact that the term 'risk' is of a changeable nature and that has several meanings, if we hold onto the idea that, in insurance law, we are dealing with a future event of possible but uncertain occurrence – whether in its occurrence or in

4. In the following heading of this monograph when it is analysed the risk as element of the insurance contract in particular, we shall come back to the concepts stated in the text that are part of ideas exposed in the work *Insurance Law and Other Related Businesses* (*El derecho de seguros y otros negocios vinculados*), vol. I, 114 and 170 (Buenos Aires: Abaco Press, 1998).

the term of occurrence – and we admit so, regardless of the production of the damage in the obliged sense of danger, the idea that we are dealing with the legal subject matter of the insurance contract turns out to be completely correct, as established in section 2 and again in section 60 of the Argentine Insurance Contract Act No. 17.418.

In some life insurance, the fact originating the loss for the insurer to make the payment of the assured amount to the beneficiary cannot always be called damage objectively. In the possible and frequent variable of an alien third-party beneficiary, the event of the death of the insured, that is, the event causing the loss generating the payment, is not an event that causes damage to the aforementioned beneficiary. The same occurs in the case of endowment insurance or of survival insurance, in which survival of the insured-beneficiary shall always be considered a fortunate and not harmful event. Thus, it is important not to confuse the risk as subject matter of the insurance contract – and, therefore, essential element thereof – with the concept of risk as factual contingency of the aleatory obligation, on which the economic advantage or disadvantage of the contract regarding the parties involved shall depend.

When legislating about the life insurance contract, Act 17.418 does not require at all the existence of an insurable interest or a beneficiary third party or the taker of a coverage on behalf of a third party. It just demands, in the case of a third party as insured, its conformity in relation to the insurance that a different policyholder may take.

Following the item contained in the previous paragraph, it shall be remembered that in the insurance contract, the acquisition of the right is not subordinated to the verification or not of the risk established as covered. The occurrence of the risk of the loss grants the right to the beneficiary to collect, but it does not affect the existence of the right as this has been established as from the agreement of wills, that is, from the entering into of the contract. That is the reason why, in our law, the insurance contract, although aleatory, is not conditional, as in that assumption, the right would not be earned or lost by the creditor but at the moment when the condition occurs.

Since the risk is, legally, the subject matter of the insurance contract and, at the same time, it is the advantage of one of the parties and the disadvantage of the other in the contractual existing relationship, the rich and polysemous quality of the term is clear, as shown *supra*. The need for cautious behaviour when analysing these concepts also is noticeable since the difference between the meaning that may be agreed from the legal standpoint and from any other as, for instance, the economic or technical standpoints is notorious (without inclining towards a radical distinction of this institute, as if one or the other scope were alien to each other).

59. Description and Declaration of Status of the Specific Risk. As starting point of the problem about the importance of the declaration of the risk by the policyholder of the contract, it is necessary to remember and to take into account that we are not dealing with a generic risk of a specific kind of subject matter of a specific contract, but with the concrete, specific risk of each one of those contracts.

Considering one specific contract, we will always deal with the risk particularly described, and it could not be construed in excess or defect in relation to what is established in the agreement of wills. In this line, provisions of Act 17.418 shall always be dispositive as the parties have wide powers to agree to everything about it, due to the relation that necessarily must exist among the agreed risk, premium paid to the insurer, and service promised for it, in case of the loss being verified.

The risk determined by the agreement of the parties generally submerges in the risk nominated in a general way, for example, what occurs in the fire insurance of a defined real estate regarding the term 'fire insurance'.

What is desired to point out is that, even in simple situations as the one just mentioned, each individual contract covering the damage caused by a fire to real estate in concrete must indispensably be analysed by itself and not through the contents of the insurance law regarding fire, as neither should it be analysed by using the text of another fire insurance policy nor any other type of policy.

In this way, it is determined that the construction of the risk covered by a specific contract must be strict and cannot be the subject matter of construction of another insurance policy documenting another contract.

Another is the matter when interpreting an insurance contract taking into account problems different from those referred to the risk itself. In summary, the extensive construction of the risk is not possible.

It is clear that what has just been explained does not imply a restriction to the construction powers of the jurisdictional power whenever there are elements – which are not forced – that bring about confusion. Whenever the extension of an agreed risk is the matter in question, the restriction in the construction must be prudent because the relation of risk-premium-obligation assumed by the insurer requires to be maintained so as not to be technically broken.

The determination of the agreed risk must be carried out by following these instances: (a) the grounds instance; (b) the temporal instance; and (c) the space instance, in a way that the risk gets to be completely identified, through the harmonic game of these three guidelines. This shall provide us with the origin of the aleatory event, the time when it must occur, and finally, the place where the occurrence must take place, so that the event can be thought as a loss triggering the insuring obligation of paying the agreed amount, in case of life insurance, and of compensating within the insured amount in property insurance.

Argentine Act 17.418 of insurance contracts does not include provisions of any nature regarding the characteristics that the loss must have. Although some pertinent comments will be made later on, it suffices to mention the indispensable circumstances in order to hint the situation.

The occurred risk may be considered in Argentine law as the event that may give rise to the loss, that is, the obligation of the insurer to satisfy the agreed service, whether it is the amount or compensation provided for in case of life or property insurance.

To this respect, it is important to clarify that the term 'loss', despite its origins and meanings, can perfectly be attached to insurance law. It is true that in day-to-day language, loss means something terrible, unhappy, and tragic, with close reference to fortuitous damage or losses generated by an unfortunate event, in particular a crash, shipwreck, fire, or analogous event. Yet, it is also true that the Spanish Royal Academy of Literature as sole authority ruling the Spanish language has granted to this term in the case of the insurance activity the scope of occurrence of the covered risk in the insurance contract, which determines the commencement of the insurer's obligation.

Therefore, the term 'loss', since the beginning considered as something terrible due to those omens forecast by the flight of birds to the left (*siniestra* in Italian meant left and was a bad omen), would have seemed to invade our insurance scope. Nevertheless, by the use of such term in Argentine Act No. 17.418, the idea technically conveyed is the wider concept already mentioned. For instance, in several of its sections, the term 'loss' refers indistinctly to both damage property insurance and life insurance, and it has been already stated that, for that Act – as life insurance has no insurable interest – there cannot be property damage to be compensated, thus the expression contained in section 1 and transcribed in note 3 of this item.[5]

Something else supports this idea that has been pointed out about the loss, namely the fact that in section 1 of Act 17.418 precisely – moving away from the idea of loss as something terrible, damaging, and harmful, typical of property insurance – the expression 'unforeseen event' is used, protecting the fact that the loss, as occurrence of the agreed risk, remains alien to the exclusive and excluding characteristic of damage, danger, or sad event, at least in the legal consequences related to the insurance contract.

60. Duty of the Policyholder of the Contract. Misrepresentation of Facts. The declaration of the risk in Argentine insurance law is a burden that corresponds to the taker of the contract although, in certain occasions, it also corresponds to the insured. The different roles in the insurance contract legally correspond to different individuals who may take part in the relationship with the insurer. The person who carries out the insurance contract with the insurer is called policyholder, that is, the taker. This person, who can be the same as the insured, is legally different in his contractual position and, consequently, may have a concrete existence different from the insured that – as it will shortly be seen – has another role in the relationship.

The policyholder or taker is the person who covenants to pay the premium, although in certain assumptions contemplated by Act 17.418, the insured and even the beneficiary can see themselves engaged by special circumstances. Reference is made, for instance, to an insolvency assumption in the case of third-party insurance (section 27 of Act 17.418) or failure to pay insurance (section 27, subsection 2).

In Argentine law, in property and non-life insurance, as they have been recently denominated, the insured is the individual who owns the insurable interest, that is, the person who exercises a lawful economic relation with the property the insurance contract refers to. In life insurance, since there is no such thing as insurable interest, the insured is the person on whom is the insured risk. Finally, the insured is the beneficiary who, in both types of insurance (life and non-life insurance), is the natural holder entitled to the amount that the insurer shall pay if the loss takes place.

In this sense, the quality of insured and beneficiary is frequently combined in one person, usually in the property insurance species. In life insurance, this identity is

5. Thus, the difference in compensating a damage (property insurance) and complying with the agreed benefit (life insurance).

not present in the case of death insurance, as necessarily, the beneficiary has to be different from the insured, that, as mentioned before, is the person on which the risk falls. In this case, if the insured were also the beneficiary, obviously, the occurrence of the loss – the death of the insured – would imply the impossibility of the right to collect the insured amount on account of his passing away.

The title of this heading refers to the fact that the obligation to describe a risk is on the taker. This legal burden of precontractual nature is related, for Argentine law, to the adoption of a very special behaviour of extremely good faith, which translates into informing the insurer concerning everything that is known about the risk for which coverage is intended.

For Argentine Act 17.418, the declaration of the true risk status is a technical requirement, and not one that answers to one's will, but a technical requirement where the insurer is required to locate the risk subject matter of the contract, within the risks similar to it, according to its business, to complete the indispensable relation among risk, premium, and rendered service.

Thus, the wrong description of risk, even when acting in good faith, under certain circumstances, may render the contract void. This institute is called misrepresentation, as indicated in Article II of Chapter I of Title I of Act 17.418 of insurance contracts.

The regulation established in section 5, which is the one containing the aforementioned nullity principle, demonstrates that in Argentine law, misrepresentation is a legal institute related to a technical aspect and not caused by a legal circumstance.

This arises primarily from the provision establishing that, in order to judge the significance of the misrepresentation claims, the participation of experts before the judge in the proceedings must determine whether the misrepresentation would have prevented the insurance contract or modified its conditions.

This regulation deserves further study, as it is precisely a guideline of original nullity, arising out of a profoundly technical matter for the law regulating the insurance contract in Argentina. It changes deeply the judicial system ruling in the whole country concerning a topic of permanent discussion among judges (the constitutional rights and obligations coming from the fundamental principle of independence of the judicial power regarding the other powers both nationally and provincially).

A judge has wide powers to construe all evidence that would have been submitted – when sentencing in the proceedings under his jurisdiction – without any restrictions but the law and the coherence of his healthy logic. This broad definition includes the experts' opinion, but the free will of the judges imposes over the experts conclusions pursuant to the procedural law.

The nullities of legal acts for Argentine law are very restrictive constructions as they are alterations of elements of the voluntary act. The error, fraud or duress implied require very assertive guidelines with a profound knowledge of the law, which sometimes needs strictly the technique of a science in particular.

The same may be argued about the nullities of legal acts arising out of bodily injuries. That is why the respect to the extreme of the powers granted to judges has been maintained, despite the advance of technology in all branches of knowledge.

Nevertheless, insurance law, expressly supported by jurisprudence and precisely in the need arising out of insurance professionalism, has accepted with distinctive singularity the requirement of an expert criteria in the matter regarding the indispensable influence on the consequences that would have brought about the knowledge of the insurer of the true status of the risk declared by the taker or insured in the case under analysis.[6]

In other words, it is worth mentioning that:

(1) it must be understood that the institute known in insurance law as misrepresentation is related both to the wrong declaration of the status of the risk as it is an incomplete declaration and a false declaration of the risk, that is, a false, not genuine, declaration that does not correspond with reality;
(2) the indispensable judicial evidence of misrepresentation may be verified by any of the usual methods, including, of course, a confession from the responsible person. It is the intervening court's duty to take the declaration to have it as accepted;
(3) the significance, importance, reach or penetration of the misrepresentation taking place and accepted as a fact by the Court, on the contrary, is not a matter of the judge's appreciation but of the specialist experts in the matter (e.g., actuaries), that are the persons who can validly issue an opinion in this respect.

Consequently, the nullity of the insurance contract invoked by the insurer cannot be claimed without the experts' conformity in relation to the fact that the origin of the misrepresentation is the requirement established by law to prevent or modify the contract conditions if the insurer would have known the status of the risk.

The misrepresentation institute, alien to the nullity caused for vices of the will, coexists with this in the insurance contract, because the will may have been affected by these vices, and even the contract could have been influenced by simulation and dishonesty during its effectiveness due to the supervening bodily injuries.

It must be clear then that the occurrence of a misrepresentation permitting the declaration of nullity of the contract due to this precontractual cause affecting the technical aspects is no impediment for other causes of supervening or accompanying nullity at the moment of agreement of wills to be invoked with nullifying effects because they would affect the legal and not technical or technical rules circumstances.

The fact of incurring in a willing or unwilling misrepresentation, that is, even acting without bad faith on the part of the taker or, if it were the case, on the part of the insured, separates misrepresentation regulations from the conditions established, for instance, by English law when making the provisions of the institutes of deceitful or fraudulent information and of spreading and disclosure (where there must always be the intent, which at least must be able to constitute a significant assumption).

---

6. Section 5 of Argentine Act 17.418 under analysis states: 'All false declaration or misrepresentation of circumstances known by the insured, even acting in good faith that, to the experts' opinion would have prevented the contract or modified its conditions, if the insurer had known the true status of the risk, renders the contract void.'

The most outstanding and distinguished jurisprudence of the courts of Argentina has required for the misrepresentation to have effects that the deponent is aware of the error because, as it has been sustained, it cannot be said what is not known.

It is our opinion that, evidently, the lack of knowledge from the deponent of the matter silenced or deformed is a *sine qua non* but, at the same time, in order to accept the ignorance as excuse of an absolute type, it should be necessary that the subject of the obligation would not have been responsible for that ignorance, as his ignorance over something that normally and naturally he should have known could not be considered an excusable ignorance.

To see misrepresentation as a problem derived from a technical aspect and not a legal aspect with special influence in the agreement of wills does not mean that the declaration of the true status of the risk may be considered exclusive incumbency of the insured or taker of each contract. On the contrary, the taker has a clear space of action for which he is responsible. In fact, the insurer, of the two parties to the insurance contract, is the party holding the main and wider knowledge of the technical aspects and the one assessing, in each case submitted before him, the location of the risk as well as its frequency, in order to establish the guidelines for the premium and limit his obligation in each one of the events that may take place, that is, to cover the losses.

Consequently, it could never be alien to the taker of the insurance contract to declare the true status of the risk and, in this sense, as the taker will always, in relation to the insurer, be the less technical party, it turns out to be logical that said insurer provides its counterpart with sufficient help as to guide him towards those answers that shall be necessary in order to make a correct assessment of the risk. In other words, the insurer shall be responsible if he fails to mention to the taker during the declaration of the status of the risk those concepts considered essential.

In this sense, it is worth pointing out that, for instance, the insurer that omitted carrying out an adequate questionnaire for a correct and consistent declaration of the taker and that, as a consequence of that failure, omissions and mistakes would arise, could not claim the nullity of the contract *ab initio* on grounds of the taker's misrepresentation. Evidently, assumptions are of various analyses because there are at stake personal aspects of the takers and even situations in which bad faith could be assumed.

As extreme variants of the nullity that brings about misrepresentation or false precontractual declaration on the true status of the risk, it is necessary to point out that, with the agreement of the insured – and if it were the case – the taker, when the misrepresentation has not been fraudulent and it turned out to be timely claimed by the insurer, the insurance contract may be validated by readjusting the premium to the real status of the risk and in life insurance when the contractual nullity was prejudicial for the beneficiary, the readjustment may be imposed upon the insurer, as long as the contract permitted so, to the judgment of experts and pursuant to the commercial practices of the insurer.

61. The Premium. Continuing with the analysis of the elements of the insurance contract mentioned in paragraph 57, the premium is the second one established as essential.

The premium, that is, the consideration that the taker must pay when entering into the insurance contract, technically, is the price of the expected cost of the individual risk assumed.

Argentine legislation, as it happens with many similar legislations appearing in the first half of the twentieth century, contains apparently very rigid provisions stating that the premium must be paid at the beginning of the insurance contract and, in the case of life insurance with instalments, at the beginning of each one of those periods, specifically, the annual payments.

Nevertheless, such severity in section 30 of Act 17.418 which seems ratified in its subsequent section 31 is only apparent since – as in the other legal systems mentioned – restrictions to this rigid measure were introduced through other regulations (as the arrears in payment by the taker entails the cessation of the responsibility undertaken by the insurer).

In the first place, it must be taken into account that the system of premium payment in life insurance with mathematical reserves in Argentine legislation is different, the reason why, at the moment of dealing with this type of insurance, some corresponding comments shall be made.

In the second place, it must be noted that a subject that has been discussed for a long time – although now it does not look so appealing anymore – is whether the payment of a premium should be considered as an obligation of the taker that comes from the principle of divisibility or from the principle of indivisibility of the premium. To defend the indivisibility of the premium it permitted to the theory to state that, whenever the taker was in arrears, it should follow the cessation of the contract due to the non-compliance of the fundamental obligation derived from the contractual quality of the insurance contract as it cannot be thought the possibility of dividing the premium.

Later, the books of authority changed their orientation in order to adapt to the realities that the business imposed by means of its evolution in time and, from then onwards, the opposing stand started to be conceived, that is, the divisibility of the premium as basis of the insurer to retain the premium portions corresponding to the time during which the risk was covered, in those contracts that were suppressed due to legally established circumstances.

In the Acts, there are examples that determine the return of the already paid premium portions whenever there are reasons that favour such behaviour – as lack of the insurable interest by loss of the property on which it fell – in relation to the term in which neither technically nor legally it would be possible to keep the contract.

This change brought about the adoption of its consequence that was obviously the possibility of paying the premium by parts since the contractual condition of the contract was not prejudiced. The term did not bring about the reduction of its intrinsic value as there were added the corresponding interest or revaluation which reinstated the agreed price its equivalence and the possible profitability that the insurer would have obtained if he had collected the premium, at the beginning as consideration.

However, the application of penalties for arrears was logical, both partial and total, but these penalties could not get to the extreme of making the obligation of paying the total agreed amount subsistent when the obligation of the insurer of coverage did not subsist.

In the Argentine law, in which the protective Act of the insurance contract No. 17.418 comes from legislative bills generated by important scholars of insurance law including the conception of premium indivisibility – as that was the prevailing concept in those years of the decades 1950s and 1960s – the assumed immutability of the rule of inflexibility that seemed to be strongly present was not so. In other provisions of the same Article VIII of the Act, it is presumed the granting of an implied credit for the payment of the premium according to circumstances which may take place; credit that, undoubtedly, implied the adoption of the principle of divisibility.

And it is left with no thorough comment – so as not to introduce topics that the subtleties of the language may not recommend – the thoughtless act in that same section 30 of Act 17.418, with concepts that, in spite of being used differently, are legally equivalent. I am referring to those of 'the premium is owed' and 'but is not payable' that practically, one after the other, appear in the same paragraph.[7]

As the payment is of a nature substantially of the convenience or need of the parties, it is our opinion that the term of payment is exclusively their will's domain as no one better than them to solve this matter of prices as it occurs in all contracts.

It is clear that the taker in arrears could bring about the rescission of the contract and the payment of the premium proportional to the term of risk that, according to the contract, could have been covered by the insurer, plus the additional amount that – with justice – could have been determined as penalty. We stressed the point that, as in any other contract, the rescission of the agreement cannot have abusive penalties. (Penalties should always be equitably adjusted.)

Resuming the Argentine legislation in order to end this subject, it is necessary to state that, from the moment Act 17.418 became effective, by inadequate resolutions taken by the SIN successively issued, the term to pay the premium became a practically compulsory variable, thanks to impositions that were generalized in all types of contract, despite undergoing during many years the pernicious situation of abnormal inflation.

As a consequence of this, the cash payment of the premium does not usually occur and the policyholders – whatever their insurance line – opt for the variable of paying in instalments to the detriment many times of the timely entry of funds to the insurers or sometimes even totally in arrears.

We shall later on see other characteristics of the premium and its commercial elements.

62. The Rendering of Service of the Insurer. The third of the substantial elements listed regarding the insurance contract is the obligation or service rendered by the insurer.

As it has been previously emphasized, section 1 of the Argentine Act No. 17.418, in an attempt to settle the discussion of the books of authority that existed on the insurance contract (not today) in relation to its monist or dualist conception, released a definition that tried directly to contemplate the two possible types: property insurance and life insurance. For these purposes, it was assigned to one and

7. The first part states 'The premium is owed from the entering into of the contract but it is not payable but against the delivery of the policy.'

other species the concepts of compensation of a damage and compliance with the agreed rendering of services, referring to the consideration of the insurer caused by the obligation of the policyholder to pay the premium.[8]

As it was sustained in Volume I of the book about insurance law and other related businesses mentioned *supra*, the insurer's rendering of services is not circumscribed to the obligation of payment of the loss when the risk takes place, as such obligation would not exist when the loss did not take place and, notwithstanding that, the contract would validly continue to be carried out.

The insurer's rendering of services considered as a substantial or essential element of the insurance contract is the 'assumption of the risk' by the insurer. In this way, it must always be clear that the reason why the taker of the insurance contract is contractually obliged to the payment of the premium is, following the relevant remark of the Spanish professor Joaquín Garrigues, the genetic obligation of the insurer of complying with its commitment of coverage if the loss took place.

One substantial part of the obligation of the insurer is the compliance with the payment of the corresponding amount, whether it is a compensation or an agreed amount, whether it is a property or a life insurance contract.

In the Argentine insurance law, there are no conflicts regarding the obligation of the insurer to pay the loss within the terms established by Act 17.418, in order to protect the insurance beneficiary.

The duration of this term has been established in a different way depending on whether it refers to property, life, or similar insurance.

In the first case, as the insurance contract on damages or property is a compensation contract, to the extent that the insurable interest means the application of the proportional rule, it shall be precise to previously establish the amount of the loss occurred.

In order to comply with this purpose that, in turn, allows for the insurer's lawful enquiries corresponding to his right, some proceedings are established within an adequate term, in order to cover the duties imposed on the insurer: the compliance with the burden of informing the insured, and those related to the event occurred or the amount of the loss.

An – almost always – appropriate jurisprudence of the Courts has also correctly applied the legal terms, above all, the thirty-day term, strictly established to pay the beneficiary the compensation amount.

In the case of life insurance Act 17.418 has provided for an inferior term as, except for the need to evidence details of the loss by the beneficiary or of its own right, the payment of the assured amount is of less duration to the one established for the non-life insurance.

8. *See* the text of s. 1 in the preceding n. 3.

Chapter 2. Insurable Risk

63. The Insurable Interest. In previous paragraphs, reference has been made to the fact that in the insurance contract there are three essential elements, that is, those that must be present for a contract to be an insurance contract and not something different.

These three mentioned and described elements are the risk, the premium, and the obligation or rendering of services of the insurer.

When expressing these concepts again, the aim is emphasizing that, although there is a clear difference between the property and life insurance contract and although both belong to the gender of the insurance contract in which these three elements must compulsorily appear, there is no doubt that each one of these species might have other elements without which each family or variety could not be considered.

In the Argentine Insurance Contract Act No. 17.418 as it has just been stated, there is an essential and exclusive requirement for property insurance.

Section 60 and subsequent sections of said Act provide for the insurable interest as a compulsory requirement so that the risk intended to cover turns out to be a legally insurable risk, in the same way that the lawfulness of the subject matter of a contract is required.

This legal requirement for this species of insurance contract is not sustained in life insurance cases for, as it will be seen, there is no obstacle for this kind when the life of a third party is insured.

In life insurance paid upon death of the insured, it shall be required the written consent of the insured third party or his legal representative when it is about a legally disqualified person.

When referring to the insurable interest, it is important to establish with the greatest accuracy what the Argentine legislation understands by it. The aforementioned section establishes that any risk may be the subject matter of an insurance contract whenever there is a lawful economic interest in that the loss does not take place. This legal provision is in the chapter of property insurance, and that fact speaks for itself about the limitation of this last insurance type and about the need of concurrence of the insurable interest. We are also left in the same differential sector as the idea of loss of the species of property insurance, which is related to something harmful and not simply to an event depending on a random variable – as it has been previously established – a unifying generic factor of the subject matter of different kinds of insurance contracts.

The origin of the legislative introduction of this element as significant for damage and property insurance law took place in the French Act of 1930, and the books of authority of several German authors analysed it more deeply.[9]

The lawful economic relation over property or things or over a universality of one or the others of the loss not occurring may appear in many ways (and not only under the sole aspect of the relationship of ownership).

9. Ascarelli Tulio, *Studi in tema di contratti,* 358 (Milan: Giuffré Press, 1952).

In Argentine insurance law, the insurable interest as a substantial element in the many types of property insurance contracts must exist at the moment of material commencement of the coverage, but indispensably, it must appear at the moment in which the loss occurs or the event from which the insured responsibility derives.

The lack of insurable interest at the moment of occurrence of the expected risk in an insurance contract determines the release of the insurer from his obligation to comply with the main rendering of service, that is, to compensate the insured, given that the latter does not truly exist due to the lack of such an essential element. Interest cannot be spoken about in abstract, but it responds to the idea of ownership and, therefore, of an insured.

The property insurance contract has a clearly compensatory function that fundamentally is not and cannot be source of benefits or of gambling. Thus, in such type of contract, the obligation of the insurer has as purpose just the redress of a damage truly experienced by the holder of the protected insurable interest. The function is compensatory and cannot imply the enrichment of the insured-beneficiary.

In this line, it is convenient to confirm that, in Argentine law, in the species of property insurance, ultimately, the real value of the insurable interest at the moment of occurrence of the loss constitutes the highest limit of the payment obligation but always, within the insured amount.

64. The Proportional Rule. It is finally pointed out another consequence of the compensation principle that derives from the element of insurable interest under analysis. Reference is made to another aspect of compensation related to the aspects of overinsurance and underinsurance, and that is known as proportional rule.

From the compensation principle that we have been analysing, it is pointed out that, only at the moment of occurrence of the loss, the real value of the insurable interest will be known. Its determination in the policy by means of an amount of money (insured value), only in certain respect, has a sense of maximum limit, as the premium has been calculated and established in response to that amount. However, it has an approximate value sense estimated by the policyholder regarding the interest to be covered. (The policyholder is the person who, at the moment of taking out the insurance, knows or must know, at least, its magnitude.)

When at the moment of occurrence of the loss, the insurable value is superior to the insured value, whether this was due to a real increase of the mentioned property or due to the decrease of the insurable value because of a devaluation of the currency in which it was expressed, such infrainsurance shall require the application of the proportional rule provided for in the second subsection of the transcribed section 65, from where it can be noted the function of the insured amount of reflecting the proportion of the loss suffered.

65. Insurable Interest and Types of Insurance Contract. Previously, in some parts of this monograph, it has been briefly mentioned the existence of different types of insurance contracts in Argentina, as it occurs in other countries.

The fundamental difference is on the need or not of the element that has just been mentioned, the insurable interest. Even when in property or damages insurance contracts it is required, that is not the case in life insurance contracts.

What is more, as it has been stated, life insurance – upon the death of a third party and, therefore, alien to the beneficiary and the policyholder – only demands the consent of the insured person. The same would operate in the assumption that the risk covered was any of the ones affecting the health of the insured.

In this sense, Argentine insurance law has very distinct origins to British insurance law, for instance, where life insurance was suppressed, the fact that motivated later on – as a way of avoiding certain abuses – the need to arbitrate the existence of a specific insurable interest derived from family or marriage bonds or by the real existence of the benefit.

Chapter 3. Formation of the Insurable Contract: Its Conclusion

66. Nature of Contract Formation and Conclusion. In Spanish, the language in which all Argentine regulations are written, the terms 'formation' and 'conclusion', although with similar meanings, cannot be considered synonyms. In fact, the term 'formation' conveys an idea of movement and of time during which something is going towards its termination and consequently, it contemplates situations that take place during that term. On the contrary, the term 'conclusion' is a more static concept, that is, that the time dedicated to produce, to do something, has elapsed and we are facing the completed thing.

That is why we have used in the title of this chapter both terms ('formation' and 'conclusion') as we are going to refer to two different moments in the creation of the insurance contracts.

It is our opinion that, when we make reference to the insurance contract in all the modern legal systems, certain difficulty is present (which arises out of the fact that, generally, there is a multiple and intertwined mechanism or procedure that enables its formation as such).

When we penetrate the insurance contract institution and we accommodate to its principles, rules, and effects, we can visualize that, at least, we can separate much clearer, two moments.

The first, with a clear objective aiming at finding the kind of contract needed and intended and, the second, which brings about the coverage of the risk by the insurer and the development of the contractual time during which the effect will take place.

The first moment – and given that the insurance contract is a contract of consensual nature (*see* paragraph 55 and its characteristics) – takes place during the time in which the parties initiate the necessary formalities to agree to the concrete risk that shall be covered.

For those purposes, said parties require the pertaining information, whether directly or by intervention of a commercial intermediation between their representatives, independent brokers or third parties involved, not only regarding the risk itself but also in relation to the coverage conditions, contract duration as well as the price and requirements to comply with during the term and after the occurrence of a loss.

Even when there exist in this instance certain similarities with the *pour parler* (preliminary negotiations) existent in the introduction of the contract, the difference between them and the central idea of this paragraph is clear, as the *pour parler* may or may not extend greatly because its nature is simply clarifying and illustrative of details.

However, in the insurance contract, the data that must be provided by the parties is significant, as it refers to technical and legal aspects, indispensable to be known or made available for the counterpart so as not to induce it to a misinterpretation of the risks and clearly establish the guarantee that the insurer would render if the contract took place.

This information, in certain legal systems as the French, as from the Act of December 1989 and Decree 90-827 of September 1990, has been expressly placed over the head of one or another, pursuant to the nature of the ends pursued.

In Argentine law, the duty to precontractually inform – as it has been already explained – is expressly contained in the insurance law contract in relation to the policyholder, and it refers to the status of the risk that is intended to cover. Yet – as we have already explained towards the end of item 52 – the obligation to declare the risk may not be considered as something absolutely alien to the insurer.

On the contrary, it corresponds that he also takes active part in achieving this purpose by collaborating in good faith with the policyholder's compliance with such burden of informing about the true status of the risk that he wishes to insure. His obligation in this assistance is related to providing the policyholder with an insurance contract with the necessary bases and elements for him to declare the risk with the necessary adequate limits to technically convince the insurer.

As long as the insurer intending to commercialize the insurance is the expert part of the contract in both the art and science and marketing of the insurance, he must know what is of interest to assess the risk offered and his responsibility in the matter, and, therefore, he must draw up the questionnaire that shall be used by the policyholder in order to reach the objective we are dealing with.

If the insurer makes the incorrect questionnaire or this questionnaire induces mistakes in the taker's answers so as not to tell the insurer effectively the true status of the risk, the taker would not be liable of sanction by misrepresentation in any of two variants, except when his acts are fraudulent, that is, with the intention of benefiting from the insurer's prejudice.

In relation to other precontractual obligations of information corresponding to the insurer, in Argentina, there is no such political influence as extreme as it occurs in other countries.

It is expressly pointed out that we are referring to the influence on policies of consumer protection, as its relative weight is tightly related to the electoral influence that consumer associations have in other countries. In Argentina, they have not yet achieved enough potentiality as to become predominant, notwithstanding that they could become so in the near future, as long as the scheme of power is penetrated.

In Argentina, where the influence of independent insurance brokers is of great importance and also is traditionally established in the vast territory of the country, the custom of formulating insurance requests verbally by such agents takes place very often, most of all concerning simple risks (including massive taking out of insurance or general requirement insurance by quantity of potential insured, as is the case of motor vehicles or some group life insurance without mathematical reserves).

The lack of a written document for insurance of this kind has not caused great problems in our country, which, despite the terrible economic situations we have undergone, means that absolute good faith on the parties to the contract still exists.

In relation to the closest analysis on a possible misrepresentation, the lack of the application and consequently the inexistence of elements in order to consider such situation, ultimately all this cannot affect either the taker or the insured, as it is a contractual agreement of acceptance of the insurer to the proposal of the insured based on the habitual formula that states that the insurer usually has the support of the insurer's drawing up.

Coming back to the main matter, that is, the formation and later the conclusion of the insurance contract, it may be said that, in Argentina, freedom is wide as there are no limitations concerning the form of carrying out the drawing up of the contract or restrictions, as the Act does not provide for any details.

In this sense, it is worth pointing out that: (a) usually in all contracts there are intermediaries who specialize in the commercialization of insurance and that may offer the insured assistance regarding his insurables; (b) individually, the coverages turn out to be simple both in life insurance and in non-life insurance; (c) due to the Statism present in the country during many years, until not long ago the intervention of the SIN was an obstacle in the commercial freedom without rightly protecting the insured rights. Such interventionism consisted mainly of an unnecessary control over the texts of uniform policies for the whole business with which all differences that could have meant a benefit to the insured were erased. Everything was the same as any difference would not have been acknowledged. Also, the establishment of uniform premium fees took place, according to authorizations given by such body in close connection with the NRI, a State institution.

To conclude, the texts of the policies document the consensual contracts and – as we shall *see* later – they have an evidentiary function. They have been and they continue to be of a uniform or at least similar drawing up.

In the case of complex transactions due to the risks involved or their variety, the letter of the contract is previously analysed by the parties, usually on a model written by the insurer but with no absolutism.

The second moment in the formation of the insurance contract is when the contract finishes, that is when the agreement of wills takes place, in other words, when the consent of each of the parties is unequivocally expressed (the moment that contains the essence of the contract).

The declaration of the common will that brings about the termination of the moment of formation of the contract, at the same time, gives rise to the last phase of relation of the related parties, which normally will come to an end with the termination of the term of risk coverage without this having taken place or with the occurrence of the loss and the subsequent payment as agreed.

67. Consent, Insurance Policy and Proposal of the Contract. As it has been stated, when commenting the characteristics of the insurance contract in Argentina, the contract is consensual. According to section 1140 of the Argentine Civil Code, the contract is concluded in order to give rise to their own effects once the parties have reciprocally manifested their consent.

The documentation of the contract is carried out by the insurance policy, the same as in many civilized countries. This documentation and even the need of certain legislation of granting some meaning to its delivery to the insured or policyholder does not bring about any alteration to the consensual quality of the contract that Act 17.418 clearly states in its section 4.

Argentine law, in spite of being categorical when referring to the consensual characteristic of the insurance contract, in section 30, wrongly determines an unadvisable behaviour, as the granting of credit must be a matter restricted to the agreement of wills.

This consensual characteristic determines that the insurance proposal does not oblige the taker or the insurer. This logical circumstance is, nevertheless, established by section 4 of Act 17.418. In our opinion, the regulation mentioned the importance of one of the elemental principles of the contract before some books of authority that had spread during the years of the drawing up of the Act. Notwithstanding what has been said, it must be pointed out the special difference that regarding consensuality establishes Act 17.418 in the renewal of insurance contracts.

There is no such thing, except for some exceptions, in our law as the implied or automatic renewal of contracts. Thus, after their term of duration, the contracts expire. In order to continue with the rights entitled to each party during the contract, they should decide to continue with their relationship by means of another agreement of wills called extension of the contract.

This extension can be made before the expiration of the term established in the contract or after it and pursuant to what the interested parties may determine regarding the time that could have elapsed until the renewal of the term.

In the insurance contract, the situation is identical and the insurer must comply with its part in the agreement until the agreed term. The parties can extend their obligations and burdens belonging to each of them, establishing the extension that they deem appropriate, as it has been mentioned.

This – that customarily is called extension – is in plain words a new contract. In many cases, it occurs almost mechanically, due to its convenience for the business of both parties. It is a simple development in order to achieve the continuity of the insurance that already took place once. It avoids the solution of continuity of the coverage of the risk, which, in relation to the insurer, translates into the possible loss of the client and, in relation to the insured, the lack of coverage.

In some massive contracts – as the ones related to motor vehicles – there are developments of such technical certainty that the insurer can fix parameters to establish the income premium. It refers to trademark, model, motor characteristics, colour, location of damage if any, and deductibles.

The insurance policy that also in our law contains general clauses for all types of contracts of the same type or at least of the same species and special clauses for that contract, and also for that same species of contract (property insurance and non-life or life insurance), has the characteristic of being a sole copy[10] signed only by the insurer and issued by the insurer. This, that customarily happens, is a contract among absents, a form that is different from the more habitual contract which is between presents in which the parties are one in front of the other.

The influence of this practice is induced by section 4 of Act 17.418, which in its third subsection referring to the proposal of an extension of the insurance contract, considers it accepted if the insurer does not reject it within the term of fifteen days from received, except in Insurance of the Person.

It is clear that if the parties decide to document the insurance contract by means of a formal agreement between presents, there would not be any objection since the form by means of a proposal and acceptance, fact that takes place when the offer is initiated by the policyholder, is just a non-compulsory proceeding.

10. The Argentine Civil Code establishes that bilateral contracts must be drawn up in as many copies as there are parties to them.

In this same sense, it is worth pointing out that the proposal may come from the insurer, being unimportant who draws it up, except for those items where the own activity of one or the other is indispensable.

68. Insurance Policy. Form and Evidence of the Contract. The insurance contract may contemplate three different durations:

(1) In the first place, there is the formal duration, that is, the one that commences at the moment in which the agreement of wills starts. From that moment on the parties are bound to the obligations of the contract although they can postpone its effects if this was so decided. This would be the case of a guarantee to the insurer's charge that will not have effects but as from certain term (twelve hours of an established day or as from the commencement of a given trip).
(2) In the second place, the material duration, that is, that related to the moment in which the guarantee effectively commences by the insurer. In this sense, the differences between the duration of one and the other can be clearly appreciated.
(3) In the third place, although legally less important, we have the technical duration, that is that related to the period taken into account to calculate the premium which coincides with the material duration, starting at the moment in which this, in turn, commences.

On the matter of the evidence of the insurance contract, as essential starting point in Argentine law, it is worth repeating the principle of consensual contract. Regarding the required contractual form, it is important to clarify that there is no established form as the prevailing principle is its inexistence for the insurance contract.

Form and evidence are two different matters that have items in common but it is important to establish their difference and thus their different effects. The form of a legal act or of a contract are elements that may be vital depending on what the law establishes, to the ends of such contract or legal act validity (for instance, the public deed for the constitution of a mutuum secured by a mortgage or the writing form for a last will).

As a way of confirming what has been said, it is worth synthetically pointing out that, in Argentine law, neither Act 17.418 of insurance contracts nor Act 20.091 of Control of Insurers provides for any form. Only to the ends of a better evidence of the insurance contract, it is determined the written document (policy) regarding which it is pointed out its characteristics intending the protection of the insured by means of the State control over its texts, point that we have timely criticized.

Despite certain imperative tone that Act 17.418 adopts in its section 11 related to the policy and its existence in order to evidence the contract as sole means, the concept is immediately rectified creating a contradiction. This conflict of opinions and, beyond the unequivocal words used, the construction of the law must be carried out as it has been sustained, in the sense that there cannot be made reference to only one means of evidence. This position would go against the principle of freedom of contractual consensus. The policy is a probatory means, the most important and categorical, but it is not of an exclusive nature. Thus, before its absence or non-existence, another appropriate means of evidence may be presented if the principle of written evidence – as it occurs in any other contract – was respected.

The fact that the policy issued by the insurer effectively evidences the insurance contract it documents does not mean in the matter of property insurance that such effectiveness refers to certain characteristics of the insurable risk or its value, which depends exclusively on the will of the taker of the contract (individual that legally can coincide with the insured as it has been pointed out). In this sense, the policy does not evidence at all, although it has been written and signed by the insurer, the ownership of the insurable interest or the value of the property of such insurable interest.

Argentine Law 17.418, in the case of a loss, does not refer to the need to demonstrate the preexistence of the insurable interest and its value as burden or obligation of the insured but, from the context of its terms, it arises that it is his duty – whenever there had not been an acknowledgement from the insurer – to evidence them after the loss has taken place, as means of preserving in this type of property insurance the unavoidable principle of compensation. However, this duty is imposed by the terms and conditions of the policies in the market. As correction to excesses in the application to the extreme of this modality and principles, jurisprudence has moderated certain unjust situations that the practice presented when, before the occurrence of losses, the probatory documentation of one or the other is lost and not always can it be verified by other assertive evidence means. In this kind of situation, judges in general have resolved that the indications contained in the policies serve as assumptions.

69. Challenge to the Insurance Policy. The content of an insurance policy may be partially or totally challenged by the taker of the contract.

It could happen that the person referred to as taker and that, as we have seen, is the one obliged to pay the premium, does not acknowledge his intervention, or that the contents of the policy regarding the contractual terms differed from the proposal that he would have made to the insurer. That is to say that the insurer has issued a policy that is not documenting a valid contract because the person the insurer attributes the proposal expresses its inaccuracy or because such person (the taker) sustains that the proposal of contract has differences with what is written in the policy issued by the insurer.

The first scenario, though uncommon, may occur in general due to information or interpretation errors or, in isolated cases, due to a bad performance from those that one way or other may profit from the existence of contracts.

Act 17.418 has rightly made only reference to the second scenario. The part of the insurance contract in which the content of the policy differs from the taker's proposal may be challenged by the person who is also entitled to terminate the contract.

The subsistence of the contract – in the part that does not differ – permits the part differing not to be implicitly validated if the taker of the contract has duly notified his right and the existent difference by a claim, within a month of having received the policy pursuant to section 12 of Act 17.418.

The term of a month mentioned before starts when the taker receives the policy where the difference is noticed.

In any case, as guideline to construe such legal regulation, it must be taken into account that any doubtful situation arising from the facts to be considered could not be considered contrary to the rights of the taker as the writer of the policy is the insurer.

70. Contents of the Insurance Policy. Annexed Documents. Argentine insurance contract law, following one of its precedents, the French Act of 1930, has regulated in detail in section 11 the content of the policies, regardless of the type of contract they document.

The requirements regulated by the rule, in reality, respond to the need that the contract instrumented by the policy documents all its essential elements; the ones related to: identification of the parties, subject matter of the contract, that is, the risk that it covers, the insurable risk (for property insurance contracts) or the insured (in life insurance), premium or quotation to pay by taker as well as the assured amount, and the general conditions and, possibly, the specific conditions for each contract.

It has been mentioned that, during the years in which the State became the rector of any activity under the influence of civil and military governments that for many years acted with extraordinary powers, the SIN excessively regulated the market without any rational sense as, instead of issuing truly protective rules on those matters that required so, absurd interventionist rules were issued that did not bring about any benefits. According to direct experience, policies projected by insurers were turned down. The Superintendence of Insurance had enforced and made compulsory plans for the reduction of text in which the most significant rights of the insurers and the takers were stated and where the 'small letter' was erased (when it turned out to be necessary as they were transcriptions of the laws). The intention of these insurers of international traditional prestige was simply to achieve more certainty and comprehension for those requiring policies that were clear and easy to read, which may be, as sole important requirement, contained in the mentioned section 11.

When the parties agree to modify the insurance contract, the insurer documents the changes in the policy issued, by means of supplementary documents that, in insurance law, are called endorsements, a term that differs from the term used in banking law for the lawful transmission of ownership.

As it derives from the previous paragraph, even when the endorsement is a unilateral manifestation of the insurer, the modification to the contract it documents has to be agreed upon beforehand between the parties involved.

In the insurance contract, there is another document that typically appears and it is called *Certificate of Provisional Coverage* (*Provisorio De Cobertura*), which is mentioned in section 30, Act 17.418. This document, also called coverage note or guarantee note or simply coverage or guarantee letter, is a very brief and concise document that substantially contains the existence of the contract of insurance with special mention of the risk, coverage, or contract commencement, but that does not refer to the points that are usually contained in policies. They are issued by the insurer, very informally, on account of time constraints, to give security to takers and insured parties. They are also usually issued by insurer's representatives as a need of satisfying such counterparts and covering only the essential elements of the contract they are undertaking.

Chapter 4. Obligations of the Insured

§1. Description of the Risk

71. In General. In paragraph 60 and subsequent paragraphs corresponding to Chapter 1 of this second part, some duties of the insured (taker) have been pointed out, both regarding the contractual time and the precontractual time. These subjects were developed in relation to the premium of the contract and the declaration of the risk and now they will be seen in a more systematic order.

The title has referred to something wider than the obligations of the insured. In fact, both the taker and the insured of the contract (according to the explanation given on the names that in Argentine law differentiate the parties to the contract regarding their legal positions – *see* paragraph 60) must comply with burdens or obligations.[11]

Even though it is not necessary to comment on the differences between burden and obligation, to the sole effect of measuring their consequences, we are going to make a brief consideration on their differential practical effects.

Where an obligation invariably grants to the part suffering the non-compliance of the other the right to require the termination of the contract or the power to demand compliance, the burden only provides the person who suffered the consequences of the non-compliance the right to be released from its own duties and claim a compensation for the damage the non-compliance could have caused, without granting the power of demanding the party in breach the compliance with the burden in question.

In this line and to continue portraying our legal system, before going through each obligation of the insurer, a list of duties will be provided.

In principle, without being established by Act 17.418 as an enunciative or treatment method, it is possible to classify burdens and obligations of the taker and the insurer as before or after the possible occurrence of the loss. With the same time parameter, it has been pointed out the contractual and precontractual burden.

However, the situation mentioned in paragraph 67 *supra* about the possible distinction between insured and taker or policyholder is no impediment if it is taken into account the habitual circumstance of identification in practice of the two features; thus, the taker and insured legal characteristics (especially in property insurance) shall be dealt with in this chapter *mutatis mutandis* (the necessary changes having been made).

72. Duties to Comply with Before the Occurrence of the Loss. Here there appear all those duties (obligations and burdens) that the taker or insured must carry out from the precontractual time until the moment immediately prior to the occurrence of the loss.

As first duty (and section 60 of the paragraph is repeated), it must be mentioned the precontractual burden to declare the correct status of the risk. Such burden of the taker that also falls on the insurer in property insurance on behalf of a third party,

11. The term 'duty' is used to make reference individually or together to obligations and burdens, considering it as gender of these two species.

pursuant to section 10 of Act 17.418, is established by the mentioned Act as a burden that is not directly related to any vices of the will but with the technical aspect of the correct location of the risk in order to achieve its homogenization.

It is so much a burden and not a duty that the insurer could not attempt any action whatsoever to force the taker to comply with the correct declaration of the status of the risk subject matter of the insurance.

The insurer can only claim the nullity of the contract if the taker has incurred misrepresentation or false declaration of the risk or inaccuracy of the declaration thereof. This nullity shall be declared within three months from the occurrence of the misrepresentation of the policyholder. It implies to render ineffective *ab initio* the contract, other consequences being applied if the taker of the contract would have acted in bad faith. This three-month period can be shortened if the knowledge of the misrepresentation appeared as a consequence of a loss. This fact should reduce the term that the insurer, pursuant to law, has to issue a decision about the right of the insured-beneficiary to receive the amount of compensation or the assured amount according to the cases of property and life insurance. Also, there are specific situations: (a) when the misrepresentation is not fraudulent, if the taker agrees, the insurer can readjust the premium to the true status of the risk; and (b) in the same case of non-fraudulent misrepresentation, the readjustment may be imposed on the insurer in life insurance as long as the nullity was prejudicial to the insured and the contract, in the experts' opinion was readjustable according to the commercial practice of the insurer (i.e., he had entered into similar contracts before).

These rules are provided for in section 6 of Act 17.418. They are imperative in the insurer's benefit because they can be repealed by establishing a provision in their favour.

§2. Payment of Premium

73. Continuation of Item. As second duty of the taker of the insurance contract can be indicated the payment of the agreed premium.

This duty is an obligation of the taker and not a burden, as its compliance shall not bring about the right for the insurer to claim the payment without prejudice of the application of penalties that, one way or other, could be established.

The insurance premium – as it has been considered *supra* in paragraph 61 – is the price of the insurance contract that pays the taker. As it is a bilateral contract form, the premium is the cause of the genetic obligation of the insurer, as established in section 1 of Argentine Insurance Act No. 17.418.

The Act recognizes the different accepted denominations. Reference is made to a quotation that is used in mutual insurance companies or cooperatives in which, respectively, to become an insured it is required the quality of member or in which an insured for being so, automatically becomes an associate and premium which, besides being used for the rest of insurance companies, it is also used to generically denominate the price, as it has been just commented.

The premium is constituted by different elements of which the most significant one is the one that purely represents the theoretical value of risk because it expresses a monetary value. This premium is known in insurance and in insurance law as a pure premium, technical premium, or risk premium, and, essentially, it depends on the risk or, in other words, on the probability and intensity of the risk subject matter of the contract.

That is how the pure premium is established by multiplying two conceptually invariable data in property insurance: the premium rate and the amount of the insurance price (capital assured) that, however, should correspond to the real value of the insurable interest. The rate of the premium is reached by means of the product of the factors of frequency and intensity of the risk coming from the findings of statistics in both one case and the other (vulgarly known as probability and average cost of the risk). Once having clarified the conception that the technical premium only means the coverage of pure or technical risk, it is important to take into account that the monetary amount product, following the equations that could be made in each case, could not compensate the expenses that, at a company level, must be made to both commercialize the insurance and administer the business.

We habitually know those expenses as charges of the premium and they include those from both a commercial and a fiscal origin.

The former gather the expenses or costs of acquisition of the insurance contracts and those coming from the commercial performance of the insurer. The technical or pure premium plus the commercial cost is called commercial premium or net premium. The costs of acquisition are those that give a return to the production of insurance contracts either by commissions, wages to intermediaries, or those carried out unproductively to maintain the necessary sales structure. The costs derived from the commercial performance of the insurer can be defined as those coming from the regular administration, which include a stable personnel payroll, hired professionals, regular expenses of a company, and general taxes that companies must pay.

The tax charges are the burdens that fall on the production of insurance in charge of insurers (tax rates or contributions established on specific types of insurance).

To conclude this subject, the commercial premium is constituted by the pure premium plus the commercial costs, added to the tax costs, and is known as total premium in many markets and in Argentina as *gross premium*.

In relation to the payment of the premium in Argentina, pursuant to the customs and especially to the regulations established by the SIN, in our opinion, without any legitimacy, the cash provided for by Act 17.418 when taking out insurance has turned into the obliged granting of credit that has been established partly in cash and its balance in instalments, the total maximum duration of which cannot exceed the expiration term of the insurance contract, which varies pursuant to the conditions of the market.

In life insurance, the payment of each instalment is in keeping with what is established for each type of contract. As mathematical reserves are constituted and there are salvage rights, part of the commercial operation is financial.

In any case, the fact that to pay the gross premium there is the possibility of credit granted by the insurer does not prevent consideration of the obligation as of prior compliance to the occurrence of the loss – as we have classified it – since the credit of the insurer is equal to the payment in relation to the grounds of his genetic obligation of coverage. However, in the voluntary or compulsory granting of credit on the insurer's part for the taker to pay the gross premium, some penalty guidelines can be established in the case of arrears in one or more of the agreed instalments.

These penalties, habitual in all contracts, may decide the suspension of the instalments and coverage and even the termination of the insurance contract on account of the taker's fault.

§3. Obligations in Case of the Insurance Event

74. End of Item. Apart from the two duties mentioned before, there are some other duties on the insurer's part that are generally established by agreement of the parties and whose listing could be impossible since it would depend on the type of insurance, the type of agreement carried out, and the purposes specifically pursued. These duties tend to order a type of behaviour from the insurer in relation to the risk/subject matter of the contract specifically or in relation to the insurable interest of the insured.

In this sense, and as mere example, we could quote some agreed-upon charges in a fire insurance contract, those related to the possibility of changing the destination or use of the real estate subject matter of the insurable interest or where things (goods) assured are located.

In an insurance contract of theft or robbery located at a specific real estate, it would be an example of agreed-upon duties, the installation of preventive measures by the insured, such as protective metallic curtains, or alarms, or, in transport insurance, the altering of the projected trajectory.

In some occasions, there could be obstacles in order to differentiate whether an existing condition is, in an insurance contract, a burden or a coverage exclusion.

This matter brings about some significant problems as, pursuant to Act 17.418 and to both Argentine and foreign authoritative treatises, to clarify which institute it belongs to is fundamental for both parties to the contract. If we were dealing with coverage exclusion, this would suffice for the insurer to be released by the simple reason of non-existence of a risk covered, but if it was about non-compliance with a contractual burden, it would cease to be simple as there is a whole sequence established by section 36 of Act 17.418.

In relation to all this, it is worth remembering the demand to be strict in all matters related to the description of risk.

§4. Special Obligations in Case of the Insurance Event

75. Duties to Comply with after the Occurrence of the Loss. This item comprises – for explanatory purposes – all the duties that the insurer must comply with, after and at the moment of the occurrence of the loss.

In our law, similar to what happens in other systems, the main duty after the occurrence of a loss is to inform the insurer of the event (or of what, at least, seems to be the precedents necessary for the insurer's promised obligation to proceed).

It is clear that, in complying with this duty, the difficult task of establishing if a given event represents the occurrence of the loss cannot be left to the insured's luck, and so to notify it to his counterpart. This task belongs to the specialist in the matter, the insurer, who will be able at his own expense to carry out the corresponding investigations to establish – if it corresponds – the inaccuracy of the occurrence of the loss when there has been an excusable error from the insured.

It must be taken into account that it could happen – as it usually does – that before a fact that produces an effect equal to the one that could be caused by the loss (e.g., a fire, a death), the cause of such event is not included within the risk covered. Sometimes this occurs due to an exclusion or, explained in a more technical way, the event taking place, although of the same physical nature that could cause the loss, was not included in the causes of risk determination or occurred outside the time or the place or the sphere established in the contract (temporal and special risk limitations).

That is why, regarding the insured, it would be convenient to notify the insurer of all the events that may be of a similar nature to the occurrence of the assured risk (covered risk).

Act 17.418 has established a term counted as from the day of occurrence of the loss so that the insured notifies it to the insurer. This should not be taken as if the insured was not the only part of the contract obliged to inform. (This is established in Act 17.418 and it is also our opinion.)

To have expressed that this informing duty is one of the insured duties as owner of the insurable interest in property insurance has been a licence that we have decided to use in order to preventively contradict any mistake that could arise from the possible error that section 46 first part of Act 17.418 may lead to induce if it was interpreted literally in the words used of the taker and rightful owner.

In reality, although the interest of the insured verifying the event that could legally bring about the occurrence of the loss is of both parties, Argentine law has put an emphasis in that the person of the insurer be timely informed in order to carry out his investigations.

Therefore, though wrongfully, for Act 17.418, the important thing is the knowledge by the insurer, regardless of the person who informs or that has the duty to inform, which seems to us to be an error to the extent that the insured-beneficiary in the terms of property insurance must be very much concerned about complying not only with the term of notice but also with the manner of portraying such information.

In Argentine law, as duty of significance to be complied with by the insured – after having notified the event appreciated as loss – there appears the burden of notifying the insurer and, to his request, of providing all the information necessary for the verification of the occurrence of a loss and the determination of the extent of the rendering of services he must comply with.

This obligation that is a necessary complement of the notification – which had been seen in the first item of paragraph 73 – contemplates as significant the requirement of collaborating in the determination of the importance or intensity of the loss.

The penalty for the failure to comply with this duty does not always produce irreparable consequences for the insured. Distinctively, Act 17.418 uses minor consequences than the ones provided for in the case of the omission to notify the event and the probable cause of the loss.

Section 48 establishes the same penalty of loss of right to be compensated in the case of malice in the non-compliance, with fraudulent exaggeration of the damages caused by the event or with the employment of false evidence to justify damages.

This means that the assumption of omission of notification of the event originating the loss in the legal sense suffices (without the need to consider the behaviour of the insured).

Exceptions to such a situation – that, as it has been mentioned, come from section 47 of Act 17.418 – refer to situations of a general order that are contemplated in Argentine law as defences in all cases of non-compliance (fortuitous case or act of God referring to those assumptions where events have not been foreseen or if foreseen could not have been avoided – sovereign acts or acts of nature) or when it is evidenced that the non-compliance was derived from an impossibility caused by an irresistible event.

In the line we are explaining, the lightest possible sanction seems advisable for the cases in which the insurer was not provided with the necessary information (so that he could verify the extension of the loss). If the insurer knows the event of the loss, he may establish by different means the situations occurred, on account of his permanent professional experience, that is, the extension of the loss for appropriated assessment fundamentally for cases of non-life insurance.

As guideline for a correct interpretation of the effect that produces the burden of reporting the occurrence of the loss, it shall always be illustrative to link the legal and contractual regulations related to the duties to comply with by the insured before and after the loss, with the corresponding behaviour of the insurer and the fulfilment of its main obligation that is to comply with the rendering of services agreed in the case of the loss.

This last precept referred to the behaviour of the insurer is regulated by the same Insurance Contract Act in its sections 49, 51 and 56 that, later on, shall be considered when dealing with the obligation of this party to the insurance contract.

It must be taken into account that, as from the moment of the loss, in most of the insurance contracts (it occurs with all the contracts of property insurance and great part of life insurance contracts), the situation of the insured is of anxious expectation to receive what the insurer must pay him.

Obviously, the economic capacity of the beneficiary of the service turns out to be of a lesser importance; this expectation easily evolves into anguish, and thus, the time after the event has been informed is the time in which the insurer must respond with celerity and with maximum good faith in compliance with all his obligations.

Within the duties previously mentioned, there are duties that may be considered natural, regular, or undisputable, and which may or may not be specified by law. Among the specifically contemplated, it is important to note that sometimes they are conceived as derived from other institutions. These must be pointed out as not causing the loss or avoiding and informing the risk aggravation, coming from essential specifications of the insurance contract linked to the need of the risk to be alien to the will of the insured and that, since it would technically affect the contract, the risk continues to be the same during the whole effectiveness for the contract.

76. Contrasting Pre- and Post-loss Duties. As a help to remember systematically, it could be agreed that these duties that we have mentioned imposed the insured certain activity to prevent the occurrence of the risk and, in the case of property insurance, the activity demanded to the insured is also to carry out acts of rescue, to diminish both the damaging effects of the loss and the extension thereof.[12]

In this sense, we can consider the duties to be complied with by the insurer before the occurrence of the loss as measures of prevention and the duties to be complied with after the loss as rescue measures.

In the conventional system that Argentine law establishes in its section 36 and that is the imperative regulation, only changeable in the insured's benefit, it is determined that if the loss has not occurred and the insurer learns that a burden is not being complied with, he must bring forward the expiration of rights on the insured, coming from the contract within the term of a month from the moment of having become aware of that fact.

If within this pending month the loss occurs, the case shall be treated as if the insurer would not have known of the non-compliance, and the services shall be paid, as long as the non-compliance of the insured would not have influenced in the occurrence of the loss or in the extension of the obligation of the insurer.

This assumption – which we will exemplify in order to improve understanding of the law that favours the insured – must be solely referred to the case of burdens and obligations imposed on the insured to comply with before the loss occurs, that is, as it has been previously commented, in the assumptions of the preventive measures to collaborate in the avoidance of the loss.

This would be the case of having agreed – at the insured's expense – to arbitration of security measures in order to make the theft of assured goods difficult by means of the installation in the premises of an alarm system working twenty-four hours as from a specified date.

If the insurer notices that, after the established moment, the alarm has not been placed and, therefore, the burden has not been complied with, he would have only one month to claim the sanction that has been previously commented.

In case a theft was committed within that month, the insurer shall not respond, solely if it was verified that the theft could have been committed because of the lack of alarm. Otherwise, the rendering of services should be fulfilled.

Apart from this, there are certain precepts that expressly or implicitly transmit orders of action or principles that clearly establish certain behaviours that must be assumed by the insured in property insurance or the beneficiary in life insurance. They are provisions that have the same nature as the insurance contract and, as it is logical, the essence of the contractual theory. These behaviours oblige the persons they are intended for to act in keeping with them, without transgressing or violating them, throughout the whole insurance contract (as it would be the avoidance of the production of the loss or the event that could cause it).

12. It must be taken into account that certain insurance contracts that Argentine Act 17.418 considers as 'insurance of the person' could not, to our criteria, be interpreted as life insurance since, in reality, they are not 'fixed price contracts', but compensatory. We are mentioning contracts that cover labour accidents or life insurance without reserves and that, in case of legal disqualifications, grant a supplementary right to collect amounts of money, pursuant to the percentage of the disability that the contract would have provided for.

Act 17.418 in section 70 releases the insurer when the insured or the beneficiary of the insurance contract or the taker would have caused the loss, fraudulently or with gross negligence.

It is necessary to clarify the behaviour punished, called by law 'causing of the loss'. As we have mentioned before, loss only can be considered as the event that, pursuant to the contract, implies the occurrence of the risk. In reality, the expression contained in Act 17.418 and that we have previously mentioned in quotation marks contemplates in a wide sense the word 'loss' as, evidently, what is punishable is the action of causing, producing, and inciting the incident that has the potentiality of constituting legally the loss in the corresponding insurance contract. The loss – referring to this legal phenomenon – typical of the insurance law is a complex concept that is formed ideally by the intellectual elaboration that combines a series of previous ideas.

It should be noted that the legal principle of section 70 mentioned two paragraphs *supra* never could have been referred only to a conduct causing the loss as a technical-legal purity conception since this precept would only refer to a very complex behaviour on the insured's part almost impossible to prove. It is important to notice that the concrete risk that constitutes the subject matter of an insurance contract must be future, certain and alien to the insured, beneficiary, or taker. In other words, the will of any of the three persons mentioned, except for their specifications in life and non-life insurance contracts, must not be a priority in the possible occurrence of the expected event and, on the contrary, the parties must be always alien to the production of the event.

Even in the case of a risk linked to the insured behaviour in property insurance as, for instance, civil liability insurance, the distinction is clear as it refers to misconduct liability.

In order to conclude this item, it is worth mentioning that the causing of loss punished by section 70 of the Act is not counted as such if the behaviour that could surround the idea of the loss was caused in order to prevent the event or lessen its consequences or for a humanitarian duty generally accepted. In this matter, the jurisprudence has been and will be of significance due to the indispensable categorization that in many adversarial proceedings must be only assumed via construction of concepts so special in law as malice, fraud, negligence, recklessness, and even those of malicious intent, gross negligence, humanity duty.

(a) Behaviour Tending Not to Infringe the Duty to Avoid or Diminish the Damage.

This demand is completely legal as it is provided in section 72 of Act 17.418. Moreover, for this Act, the subject is related only to property insurance as the aforementioned rule solely refers to the damage derived from the occurrence composing the risk. This concept is repeated in the second item when, referring to the punishment for the violation of this established behaviour, it is expressly indicated the obligation to compensate, a verb that prevents us from considering life insurance, pursuant to the provisions established in sections 1, 2 and 60 of Act 17.418.

The behaviour that is now under analysis is completely of prevention; human behaviour in this case is imperative but underlying to the whole subject of insurance as it benefits the institution. It is worth remembering that, in the Association Internationale de Droit des Assurances (AIDA), we have developed for many years a work group of the Council of the Presidency. The duty to avoid or lessen the damage that an event may bring about regarding property, subject matter of the assured interest in Argentine law, is contained in Article IV under the title Salvage and Verification of Damages, thus confusing two institutions of different nature, as verifying the damages occurred implies verifying those that eventually would have caused the loss event.

There are certain situations coming from events that have the potential of legally bringing about the loss in life insurance due to the death of the insured. Act 17.418 provides some cases that prevent as consequence of certain types of death of the insured a specific coverage exclusion or release of the insurer and that are coincidentally assumptions established by other legislations.

The first of these assumptions – in which the risk is excluded and the law establishes it as the release of the insurer from having to pay the amount assured to the beneficiary – is the case of suicide of the insured, an act that is materially bringing one's own life to an end which is linked with a voluntary act of the suicidal subject.

The qualification of voluntary act that section 135 of Act 17.418 requires has nothing to do with the external behaviour of the insured as, given we are dealing with suicide, the action of suicide always implies to kill oneself (Latin pronoun *sui*). It is related to the interior attitude since if the insured was not in a state of mental disruption or mental illness, it could not be considered as a knowledgeable voluntary act with intention and freedom. Neither is it the case of a person who takes out a life insurance on his own life or on a third party's life, having as guideline the possible death of the insured due to a more than likely suicide. This assumption would imply the nullity of the contract by fraudulent misrepresentation of the taker or of the insured and rejects the coverage exclusion.

The second of the cases that have been pointed out in the first paragraph of this item is the deliberate production of the covered event, that is, the deliberate death of the insured by an illicit act by the taker of the insurance contract, pursuant to what is established in the first paragraph of section 136. The strictly technical grounds for this assumption are identical to the one analysed before, suicide, that is, behaviours that bring about death not from a random event but from the will of the parties.

Lastly, the third case is the death of the insured during the course of criminal acts and due to the lawful application of the death penalty.

In other words, section 137 releases the insurer from obligation if the insured passes away as consequence of criminal conduct, the jurisprudence determining that these acts must be with defined purposes, previously arranged or combined behaviours intended to accomplish a crime.

There are no precedents of the second aspect mentioned, the release by death penalty, after the effectiveness of Act 17.418 because it has been erased from Argentine law.

Another behaviour that is specifically pointed out and that has not been included in what we have seen before – as Act 17.418 considers it a punishable behaviour of the beneficiary and not a releasing behaviour for the insurer – is established by section 136 in its second item. It is the deliberate causing, that is, irreflexive and intended causing of the insured's death by means of an illicit act from the beneficiary.

Here, the direct penalty on the beneficiary does not have technical support, but it is sustained by exclusively moral principles. This is clearly shown if we think that the insurer is not released at all and continues to be contractually bound to the assured amount regarding someone that is different from the beneficiary. In this line, the direct punishment of such behaviour is logical and must be agreed with, as the legal regulation must respect morality and public order. Nevertheless, the legal solution of section 136, paragraph 2 of Act 17.418 is incomplete and even contradictory regarding the event triggering the loss because, if this intentional offence ceases to be at random, a characteristic of insurance, that is enough reason to receive the same treatment since his author is the person that could be directly interested in the occurrence of the event, by means of the death of the insured.

Therefore, it is not compatible the legal solution of the problem[13] as the legislative policies for the protection of the assignees of the specific insurance taker oblige the insurer to pay the agreed service, as it is widely established by the last paragraph of section 145 of the Argentine Act.

Here it has not been taken into account that a better solution would have been to provide for the release of the insurer (as another assumption of random breakage of the contract) respecting the taker or his heirs the right related to the mathematical reserves, granting them rights to the subsequent salvage of value.

The quality of the illicit act established as necessary characteristic of the two recently analysed paragraphs of section 136 of Act 17.418 is established by Title VIII of Book II, Article II of the Civil Code by means of sections 1066 and 1072.[14]

As general rule, for a voluntary act to have an illicit characteristic, it requires fundamentally and indispensably that it is expressly prohibited by law and to be deliberate, it requires intention, that is, acting with malice, including malicious intent which is constituted when thinking in the obvious possibility of the result of an act. This would allow in our law the application of provisions that we have been considering for the acts caused with gross negligence, which, although not linked to intention of any kind, practically do not separate from malice.

Certain conduct is so extreme that it is impossible not to represent the possible consequences of an almost certain effect, as, for instance, would be the assumption of manslaughter by driving at high speed. Although the doer of the action did not have the intention of killing any person, the danger that could be caused by high speeding was evident.

In this line, it is worth pointing out that in Argentine law there is no such thing as justice establishing different degrees of guilt pursuant to different objective parameters. Thus, when the law establishes a conduct that deliberately is aimed at

13. Nevertheless, among the last legal modifications in insurance matters of the twentieth century, in France in January 1981, it was established in s. L 132-24 of the Insurance Code, a regulation similar to the Argentine Act under criticism.
14. It is impossible to bring to this monograph a complete but synthetic analysis of the problems of an illicit action or omission. However, we deem such a thing unnecessary, as illegality is a concept of law universally valued.

'causing' the death of the insured, it is not possible to interpret extensively the concept of gross negligence or severe gross negligence.

In Argentine law, the construction is not carried out on the gradation of the fault, some isolated decisions have been made in assumptions as the one mentioned two paragraphs before, and thus the doers of such accidents have been judged for negligent (manslaughter) and not malicious homicide.

77. Contractual Burden Versus Coverage Exclusion. When two paragraphs before, the subject of obligations and burdens was commented on, a prudent division was made into those that must be complied with prior to the loss and those that must be complied with after the loss. The existence of legal rights was also commented on, that is, rights imposed by law and the existence of contractual rights that in insurance law are known as contractual burdens. The contractual burdens, as long as they do not affect any other imperative regulations – as these are unchangeable – are valid in our law, with the application of general exceptions that, at the same time, are habitual in the whole Argentine law as when agreements are abusive, contrary to morality, good customs, and public order.

These contractual duties must not be confused with coverage exclusion guidelines. Although this item has been mentioned, it seems significant to refer again to it, as the effects of one or another assumption are totally different. There are no systematized methods in order to generalize in such an important matter since, according to Argentine law and the legal treatises locally and internationally, the determination of the legal institute is fundamental for the parties of an insurance contract. If this was a coverage exclusion, it would suffice with the release of the obligation of the insurer for the simple reason that it is not a risk that has been subject matter of a contract; that is, it did not form part of the guaranteed coverage by the insurer.

However, if this was about non-compliance with a contractual burden, the process of unravelling the matter would be completely different. Concretely, as it has been said, whenever we are dealing with the description of risk, the contract must be very strictly interpreted as the risk must be equal to the amount of the rate of the premium and to the insurer's obligation.

Please note that section 36 of Act 17.418 provides that in property, in order to apply the expiration of rights that could contractually be agreed whenever a burden or obligation is not complied with by the insured, the non-compliance with a duty after having occurred, the loss shall only bring about the release of the insurer when said non-compliance influences the extension of the insurer's obligation.

78. Risk Modification and Aggravation. The following matter is provided for in Act 17.418, Chapter 1, Article X, sections 37–44 inclusive. Even though nothing has been expressly stated, the fact that they appear within such Act permits us to consider them as generic for both types of insurance, that is, life and property insurance.

In fact the matter to be dealt with here could have been dealt with in paragraphs 57, 58, and subsequent sections when reference was being made to risk as one of the elements of the insurance contract.

Nevertheless, we have preferred the following model advised by the publisher (following the example provided by the monograph on Danish law) for the benefit of readers. The concrete risk – that has been analysed and established as subject matter of the insurance contract and that also works as a technical element in harmony with the agreed premium and with the obligation assumed by the insurer in case of its occurrence – justifies the institute of risk aggravation, which always produces an increase in the probability or intensity of the occurrence of the loss:

(a) *Modification of the Risk That Does Not Imply Its Aggravation.* In first place it is worth pointing out that not every modification of the concrete risk of a contract brings about its aggravation. Towards the end of this paragraph and once the matter of aggravation has been done with, reference shall be made to other modifications of the risk that although they may be linked to aggravation, could not participate in this concept.

(b) *Aggravation as Modification of the Original Risk That Increases the Probability or Intensity. By contractual risk aggravation, it is understood, in general, a modification of the risk originally assumed by the insurer that may influence the probability or intensity of its occurrence by increasing it. In other words, the aggravation when compared with the initial risk shall bring about an unexpected imbalance in the equilibrium that should be kept among risk, premium, and rendering of services of the insurer, technically affecting the business and, at the same time, the contract that supports its global business, on technical guidelines preserving the insured reciprocity and the premium funds. From this, it is deduced that the legal aspect is harmed, as this is the support of the technical aspect and vice versa.*

It is important to distinguish with accuracy the net difference between risk aggravation and risk exclusion. The exclusion of the risk informs of certain will of the insurer of not covering that determined risk. In laws where, as it has been stated, the determination of the grounds for exclusion risk is required by modality circumstances – as occurs in certain cases of compulsory insurance or in some countries such as France – the problem is less important.

Since in Argentina there is no regulation, although the policies usually indicate the coverage exclusions in a clarifying or confirmatory way, the description of risk, in general, is made in an affirmative form in contracts, mentioning the risks that are effectively covered. In this way, if an assumed aggravation was an exclusion of the risk, the subject would be different and the institute of aggravation would not apply. Moreover, it must be taken into account that the increase in the value of assured interest (in property or damage insurance) does not constitute risk aggravation, except for exceptional reasons of the same risk since the basis of the premium does not change, and there are remedies that depend on the assured amount, the proportional rule, and the underinsurance.

An exception to this case would be security theft insurance, in which the increase of the insurable interest security at risk (e.g., the transfer of a greater amount than the originally agreed upon) could be the cause of the occurrence of the loss. The same example applies to misrepresentation.

Finally, the case of accrual of assets in fire industrial risk insurance can be mentioned that is quoted by the books of authority. In this item (b), within the concept of aggravation, it was implicitly included in the increase of the probability or intensity, the modification in the same sense of certain personal conditions of the insured that, as the others, were or could have been taken into account by the insurer in order to locate the risk of the proposal and, in consequence, following such guidelines, carry out the contract.

Some of these particular conditions of the insured have a special system as, for instance, the change of profession in life insurance (*see* section 133 of the Act), others, in relation to their nature and the general system (those are the ones related to moral and random risk).

(c) *Duty to Maintain the Status of the Risk.* The duty to maintain the status of the risk – which is closely tied to declaring it to the insurer – must be connected with the possibility during the term of an insurance contract that things could modify their original status, not only due to the insurer's behaviour but also due to third parties, alien to the relationship insured-insurer. This is reflected by the institute we are analysing and, even when it has practically the same grounds as misrepresentation, it substantially differs from it regarding its effects by not falling with severity on any of the parties.

The duty to maintain the status of the risk ultimately translates into not aggravating the status of the risk that, as it has been mentioned, is established in the qualitative aspect of the risk as the aggravation; in order to be so, it must influence the risk in connection to its probability (frequency) or intensity or both at the same time. In comparison with the risk declared – that was taken into consideration for the contract in the opinion of experts – if it had existed at the time it was agreed upon, it would have prevented the contract from being or modified its conditions.

(d) *Aggravations Derived from Events Related or Unrelated to the Insured.* The possibility of risk aggravation coming from events related to the insured or alien to him has been stated, and it is essential to establish the first important difference in our system, in comparison with the ones used to legislate on misrepresentation or false declaration of the risk (dealt with in paragraph 60).

Not only are there opportunities during the duration of the contract when an aggravation of the originary risk must be accepted by the reality of the facts carried out by third parties, but also, in some occasions, it could be unfair to apply a penalty of nullity over the aggravation of a risk caused by one's own acts.

In principle, Argentine law establishes different proceedings in one case or another, and it clearly determines, in section 38, the behaviour of the taker before one or another situation. If the event or events causing risk aggravation are of one's own, the person must notify such aggravation before it takes place, which is either before carrying out the action that would aggravate the risk or at the moment of its appearance. The aggravations caused by an event alien to the insured must be equally notified to the insurer at the time of awareness.

Act 17.418 has not made any clarifications regarding what is the meaning of the terms 'event of one's own' and 'event alien to one'. According to their interpretation shall be the answer. The words in question have a unique possible meaning when we are not referring to exclusive rights of individuals. Both 'event of one's own' and 'event alien to one' must be interpreted by extensively applying them to the assumptions as described by our laws and in no way to exclusively one individual.

(e) *Time of Occurrence of Risk Aggravation.* The institute of aggravation of the risk applied to aggravations produced after having agreed to the contract, as it is established in section 37 of Act 17.418 by provisions of section 44 of the same Act, is also applied to those aggravations that may have taken place between the insurance proposal and its acceptance, that is, at the moment of agreement of the contract.

Misrepresentation or false declaration of the status of the risk, as it has been seen, only includes the precontractual period as the events and actions of one party or the other are carried out at a moment when the agreement of wills has not yet taken place. That is the reason why we are dealing with an institute whose effects – as well as purposes – are precontractual.

Precisely as precontractual duty of the insured (taker) of declaring the status of the risk,[15] the influence of its non-compliance brings about regarding the contract, pursuant to section 5, the nullity of the insurance contract, as long as certain conditions established in said regulation are present. Yet the main assumption is the silence or the falsehood of the insured at the moment of enforcing its declaration of the risk, circumstances that bring about the possibility of a wrong technical analysis by the insurer.

In the case of risk aggravation produced after the declaration and at the moment of acceptance by the insurer – also in a precontractual period, pursuant to the characteristics provided for in section 37 of Act 17.418 – this does not grant the right to invoke the nullity of the contract but the termination thereof. There are no explanatory grounds either in the preliminary drafts of the bill or in the same Act explaining the reasons for such a regulation. We think that the lesser legislative severity answers to the principles stated in item (b) *supra*.

(f) *Consequences of Risk Aggravation.* The following can be pointed out:

(1) The fact that there are some substantial differences in the case of property and insurance of the person (in the terminology of our law) regarding the application of the institute of risk aggravation (*see* item (b)) does not prevent us from extracting the more general concept; according to Regulation 17.418, risk aggravation in insurance of the person is not applicable regarding the contract termination, except for the expressly provided assumptions: those of section 131, where the age of the insured exceeds the limits of commercial practice of the specific insurer (non-insurable risk for that insurer, pursuant to his experience and habit in the matter, as he could not form a

15. About risk, all that is known and how it is known is a duty discovered by the distinguished author Mr Vivante. This guideline is rescued and broadened by the judgment on the succession lawsuit *Risso Patrón v. Círculo Cerrado* and 'Plus Ultra of the Court of Appeals in Commercial Matters of the Federal Capital City', *Legal Journal for Insurance, Responsibility and Companies* (*Revista Jurídica Argentina del Seguro, la Responsabilidad y la Empresa*) 17/20, 151 et seq (Buenos Aires: Impresit Press).

premium fund of homogenous risks); those of section 132 where the contract would have provided for the specific grounds for aggravation; and those of section 133.

(2) We have previously advanced two possible sources or possibilities of occurrence of an aggravation: the one consequence of one's own behaviour and the other owed to the behaviour of third parties. It seems a fair and clear regulation of section 39 Act 17.418 that establishes a different criterion to section 40 when establishing a first consequence, different for the two possibilities of occurrence of risk aggravation. In both cases, the assumption is that the risk covered has not yet taken place; that is, the occurrence of the loss has not been verified. In the first case, as the duty of the insured is to notify the insurer of the aggravations or events that would bring it about before its occurrence (section 38), the Act in such section 39 decides that immediately after their occurrence, the coverage is suspended and, further, that the insurer shall have a term of seven days from having this knowledge in order to notify the insured his will of terminating the contract. In the second case, as the duty of the taker (insured) is to notify the insurer of the aggravations caused by an event alien to him, immediately after knowing it, the legal decision (section 40) in order to be fair with the possibility of not knowing it – and even with the possibility that the taker would have permitted or caused the event alien to his will – does not establish the suspension of the coverage, but only provides the insurer with the power of notifying his decision of termination of the contract within the term of a month and with seven days prior notice, as from having knowledge of the aggravation. This solution comes with a logical exception: the total application of section 39 (suspension of coverage and notification or termination in seven days as from knowing).

(3) In the assumption that pending the notification – as long as this was not due to the negligent lack of notification from the insured or taker – or despite not having been notified, the insurer would have known the aggravation at the moment the notification should have been made (section 40, second part) and the loss had taken place while the subsistence of the aggravation, the insurer shall not be obliged to comply with the rendering of services. This penalty is logical, taking into account that, due to the circumstances (production and occurrence of the risk), the contract has finished and there is no possibility of termination or readjustment of any kind. The insured has not complied with a burden or obligation and the penalty that the contract imposed on him. It is worth mentioning that, by including the regulation under analysis in the second part of section 40, which title makes reference to the aggravation caused by an alien event and having been regulated the case in reference to acts of one's own in section 38, it is obvious that this second part only will be applicable before the occurrence of the loss in the case of lack of notification of the aggravation, due to an event alien to the insured. It is important to take into account the governing regulation behind all these regulations, which states the duty to inform the insurer, immediately after knowing the aggravation by events caused by third parties and, in consequence, the delay in acting or the knowledge that the insurer may

have had of this aggravation, pursuant to law, shall be matters of construction; therefore, a detailed case study is not plausible.

(4) It has been already indicated that the effect of risk aggravation is to support the insurance right to terminate a contract. As it happens in the case of misrepresentation, there is a formal matter that is unavoidable, apart from the conditions established by the substantive law. It is the notification within the aforementioned terms of the use of such right to the taker. Here, the same considerations apply as stated in relation to any other part of the insurance contract in concrete, as certainty regarding the future actions. However, the power to terminate is provided by law and, therefore, it does not require any judicial decision; in the assumption that the insurer enforces it, by means of a private (not judicial) notification, it does not need, later on, to file any judicial action. If any of the parties to the insurance contract in question challenged the right of the insurer to enforce the special clause of termination, the insurer, within the expiration term, must file a judicial action to the end of bringing about proceedings for the expert's opinion. Nevertheless, it is our opinion that the judicial action is not excluding, as the parties may submit the issue by alternative means, in which assumption we would favour the consideration of the expert's opinion as it is legal evidence with the same connotations and modalities considered when dealing with misrepresentation.

(g) *Modifications of Risk.* Previously, in item (a), we mentioned that we would comment on the modifications of the risk that, in connection with the institute of aggravation, may or may not take part in their concept. It is not that the matter of aggravation of risk has finished with the previous pages, but, in our opinion, the extension of the many variables to be introduced would be simply undreamed of. Such matter should be subject of a specific monograph as the Association Internationale de Droit des Assurances did in 1986, when in full session the Argentine Professor Morandi addressed the Congress of Budapest.

It has been already mentioned the exclusion of the risk when the insurable risk increases. Now, other brief references regarding abnormal risk, transitory aggravation, aggravation of the aggravation, and decrease of risk shall be made:

(1) Abnormal risk: this is a concept that has been developed by some books of authority in the last years, but that does not differ much from the constructions regarding aggravated risk and excluded risk that do not add up to make a particular species of this gender. The Italian report to Budapest in 1986 attempts – as well as the Mexican – to grant it a specific category but, up to now, it has not had an adequate convincing stand.

(2) Transitory aggravation. Some books of authority sustain that transitory aggravation (as a transitory state of intoxication causing a loss of civil liability insurance) is not important. In our law, the state of intoxication in the drawing up of the conditions of the policies of motor vehicle civil liability does not constitute aggravation, but exclusion of the risk and any loss under its influence would not be covered. Another would be the case if we referred to transitory aggravation as the aggravation that due to its short duration

does not permit its notification or even a real influence on the service of the insurer, either because its essence or nature would not have such influence or because, during such a brief term, it did not have negative permanent consequences on the status of the risk.

(3) Aggravation of an aggravation of a risk. The item obviously refers to the aggravation of the risk of a prior aggravation accepted by the insurer. This new aggravation must be assessed in relation to the status of the risk, after having been accepted the first aggravation.

(h) *Relationship of Cause.* To conclude the study on the aggravation of the risk, it is convenient to make reference to the need of existence of a relation of cause.

Up to now, the analysis carried out and the legal regulations in the cases contemplated as special grounds for the termination of a contract have made reference, although not expressly stated, to the existence of a relation of cause either between the aggravation proper and the fact or facts triggering the loss or between the event determining the aggravation of the risk and those triggers of the loss as, ultimately, there is no other concept arising out of the institute, pursuant to section 37 of the Act.

In some occasions, it occurs that the aggravation of the existent risk did not influence the occurrence of a loss. This may happen in contracts for which the subject matter involves different risks or the same risk as consequence of different events and, in the loss affecting the contract, the aggravated risk or cause of production would not have had any influence.

It is our opinion that when the aggravation is insignificant regarding the occurrence of the loss, the right of the insurer to terminate the contract does not proceed. It is clarified that the term 'aggravation' being used in the regular usage as 'aggravation of the risk' in insurance is no other than the one established in section 37 of the Act since there would not be aggravation with the special effects established by regulations if the risk that increased its frequency or intensity would not have prevented the contract or modified its conditions to the experts' opinion.[16]

16. It is worth noticing once more that the law demands 'expert opinion' with the same intensity that it has demanded in the case of misrepresentation. What has been said in relation to such legal evidence is equally applicable to the aggravation of the risk. In this manner, the termination of the contract, in case of being contested, requires that, in the process of knowledge pending before the claim of the insurer, the experts' opinion is inexcusably carried out.

Chapter 5. Obligations of the Insurer

§1. Complying with the Assumed Rendering of Services

79. Generalities. It has been previously stated that the taker or insured's obligation of notifying the loss and complying with all the other legal and contractual burdens, pursuant to section 46 of Act 17.418 or the specific insurance contract, must be connected very closely with the insurer's obligation of complying with the rendering of services. This obligation to comply with the rendering of services or the payment of the compensation if the loss occurs in life insurance and in property insurance, respectively, appears as a precise consequence of the notification of the loss. Thus, it is logical to understand that the insurer, before the event of being informed of the occurrence of a situation that may bring about legally the loss in insurance law, in the first place is entitled to investigate whether the content of the received notice may or may not give rise to a loss, that is, and we repeat ourselves, whether the occurrence of the risk/subject matter of the contract is a loss or not, as the taker or insured, not being a specialist in the subject, may incur an excusable mistake of taking for loss something that is not.

The simplest example is to confuse the risk of theft with other related crime features, which may imply the dispossession of the thing that has been the matter of the insurable interest (petty theft, infringement), making reference only to property or damage insurance.

The insurer is entitled to investigate the notification, the details of the event, either by means of acceptable requirements seen as insured (taker) burdens or by means of own tasks carried out by himself or by third parties, intended to establish with the highest accuracy both the existence of the loss and its extension.

Act 17.418 is sufficiently clear for the purposes of analysing each and every one of the regulations devoted to this matter in general. Yet, it is only important to bring to the consideration of the reader those items in which there might be some problems needing further study.

The insured has, as prerogative, the unavoidable obligation from its insurer of issuing a decision, in the shortest and most prudent time, about what its behaviour would be regarding the notification submitted. It is at this opportunity when the insured finds himself in an uncertain situation that things must be solved with the utmost good faith by his counterpart. That is why the law has established a strict period for the insurer to notify his insured or beneficiary of his decision regarding the right invoked, pursuant to sections 49 and 56 of Act 17.418. This term is of thirty days for property insurance (section 56).

For insurance of the person contracts, as they are called by Act 17.418, as there is a specific provision in section 49 regarding the commencement of the term for the payment that the law grants in relation to the term granted for property or damage insurance, its strict application would be challengeable, since it would not grant the insurer a specific term to deliberate. Thus, both terms 'deliberation' and 'offering of payment' shall expire after fifteen days counted as from the notification of the event or from the reception of the supplementary information requested by the insurer. This conclusion is more beneficial for the insured and for the beneficiary and, at the same time, more fair for the insurer for the purposes of issuing the correct decision.

The terms of thirty and fifteen days – as it has just been appreciated – have been established by law, so that the insurer answers the insured or beneficiary regarding his acceptance or not of the insured's right to claim a loss – legally speaking – and if it corresponds for him to receive the compensation or rendering of services, consequence of the insurance contract. These terms are peremptory, which means that, once expired, the immediate arrears of the non-compliant operate.

Nevertheless, as the insurer has the possibility of requesting information or supplementary instrumental evidence of the claim (section 46 of Act 17.418), during the delay in the provision of such requirements, the interruption of the term is contemplated not only by section 56 of Act 17.418 but also by the pacifist construction that the Argentine jurisprudence has granted section 49 – which sets out a custom in this sense.

The commencement of these terms so that the insurer issues a decision, pursuant to the insured right, takes place the following day as from the reception of the notification of the 'loss' notice that, at the same time, as we have seen *supra* must be forwarded to the insurer, complying with strict terms. The term is so interrupted that, from the letter and spirit of the mentioned section 56, it clearly arises that the term of thirty days starts from the reception of the supplementary information stipulated in section 46.

The right of the insurer to request supplementary information from the insured or, even to other individuals or institutions, with the collaboration of the insured – as it has been seen – must be reasonable (as indicated by legal terminology), that is, sensible.

Within the necessary moderation, we must include the possibility derived from the opportunity of its claim as, to the extent that the term is interrupted, erasing the effects that would naturally cause a prior reclamation; it is clear that the insurer must use this right timely and when it is convenient, proposing the claiming of all the supplementary information he will need as soon as possible and all together.

This will happen except when the supplementary information appears indispensable through an answer or an element of an answer made known by the insured (taker) or arising with the same characteristics from information obtained from other sources or from the instrumental information provided by the interested party or by alien causes not performed by the insurer to his benefit.

This is very important as it falls within the scope of possible effectiveness of the insurer's rights to file demurrers, pursuant to law by means of sections 36 (extinguishment) and 47 (his right of being released due to the loss of being compensated of the insured).

In fact, the books of authority coming from our organizational regulation system and the general and specific regulation arising out of section 75 of the Insurance Act establish, together with the books of authority of own actions, that one party cannot take advantage of situations generated by the counterpart which in some way required some sort of validation on his part. In the case under analysis, if an insurer, after knowing the existence of one or several events caused by its counterpart, determining the substantial non-compliance with some burden, without invoking such non-compliance, carried out acts which inexcusably meant to preclude a state previous to those acts, the unavoidable construction would be his intention of not seeking protection from the right that originally could have protected him or the laws determining the not-timely invoked non-compliance. For that circumstance, he cannot accept to do it later.

In this sense, it is clear the importance that bears the correct and prudent construction of the situation presented with its specific details. Thus, for instance, if from the nature of the event occurred and of the risk/subject matter of the contract, it arises or may arise with seriousness and certainty, from the first moment of being the notification received from the insured, that we could be dealing with a loss in the sense legally defined by insurance law, an attitude as the one pointed out would be evidenced in the fact of not immediately filing the demurrer for the unmistakably tardy notification (and in its place, starting an absolutely unnecessary investigation because of the evidence that the facts concisely exposed provide).

It does not matter who carries such investigation as long as it is the insurer or third parties commissioned by it. Yet, it should be taken into account that there are complex situations that require more precise information in order to decide correctly. Even when the insurer may and must know – due to his professional characteristics – the concrete subject more than the insured (and not only the circumstances causing complexities), the insured is the party on which the burden lies. As such, he must evidence the occurrence of the loss, starting by the event that initiates the development and concretion thereof.

What must be substantially present is to see whether the labour carried out by the insurer is the one corresponding to a professional whose interest must be to find the truth rapidly, seriously, and well adjustedly, or if, on the contrary, it is noticed that on his part he engages in manoeuvres intended to unnecessarily delay the terms. As it has been previously pointed out, when dealing with good faith actions, we consider that these are the moments when the insurer's attitudes must be judged under these perspectives.

It must be taken into account – as has just been expressed – the complexity or the simplicity of the particular case and, at the same time, the conduct of collaboration of the insured in response to the reasonable informative requirements from the insurer since his doubtful behaviour in providing them would not be precisely adequate for the person whose immediate objective will be to try to lighten as much as possible any difficulty in order to receive the promised services from the insurer, despite the general shock caused by an experience like a loss.

The law declares the arrears of the insurer as debtor of the obligation of payment from the mere expiration of terms (section 51 at the end).

This provision in reality coincides with section 509 of the Civil Code, but is not redundant at all because it must be remembered that Act 17.418 was drawn up prior to the reform of the Civil Code.

§2. Term for the Payment of the Owed Rendering of Services

80. Term for the Payment or Compliance with the Rendering of Services by the Insurer. It has been previously dealt with as central subject the obligation of the insurer to issue his decision in a defined term (on the right that he understands, assists the insured to claim the collection of his compensation).

As has been previously mentioned in paragraph 79, the payment of the compensation or the obligation assumed by the insurer in case of occurrence of the loss must be complied with within a compulsory term that cannot be a matter of different terms and conditions but those in favour of the insured or the beneficiary. This term has been established by section 49 of the Act in different terms for property insurance contracts and insurance of the person contracts.

In fact, although in both situations the number of days is the same as it has been fixed to fifteen, the calculation differs because, in the first case, the time commences to elapse once the term in section 56 has expired, the amount of the compensation is fixed, or such amount is accepted. If it were the case of insurance of the person, the commencement of the term would be with the notification of the loss or reception by the insurer of the supplementary information, if corresponded.

The provision of the Act is not very clear, and only the insurer's good practice in business has prevented an insensible spreading of conflicts. In fact, although the law established a term to deliberate and the faculty of the insurer to interrupt it (sections 56 and 46), there is no provision that authorizes the insurer to extend the time once the term of section 56 has elapsed. For instance, so as to count on an additional term in property insurance to estimate the compensation to be paid and carry out the proposal to the insured (as it would suggest the wrong text of the first part of section 49).

In day-to-day business, the insurers, after the thirty days that the law provides for, in order to decide about the right of the insured, and if the determination of the amount to pay did not offer major problems, in general, establish it by agreement with the insured and, in case of disagreement, an amount accepted by both as minimum is determined and the lines discussed or their amounts are left for a later solution. If they do not agree, it is offered to pay and it is paid what has not been discussed, within the term of fifteen days.

On the contrary, if it is a loss which determination of damages, both on account of their dimension and of their valuation, once accepted the right of the insured or, more specifically, once the insurer has deliberated and accepted the loss (within the original thirty days), the liquidation of these two matters (the dimensions of the damages and the economic extension and thus the determination of the amount to pay) is of a variable lapse, according to the special circumstances of each case.

In order to arrive at a solution, it must be considered the complexity of the situation, the diligent conduct of the insurer – measured even by means of the tasks advised by him or by the liquidators that the insurer may have hired – the conduct of collaboration of the insured and very especially, the good or bad faith.

It should be noted that the difficulties will not be at all the same and, in consequence, it could not be estimated in the same lapse the situation arising out of the damage to the mudguard of a motor vehicle of a recent model of national manufacture than the one presented by a corrosive substance factory on account of a fire or any other industry, in which it should be contemplated the raw materials rescued and still usable, from those rescued but unusable.

That would be the classic example of wines that, even recovered in their bottles, the heat could have affected severely and, regardless of the external impression, turn out unfit for their consumption.

It must be pointed out that the habitual experience tells us in cases of difficulty that the regular situation is that both the insured and the insurer work in the liquidation of the damages of the loss in harmony, trying to arrive at the correct conclusion as soon as possible, finding technical solutions and even special agreements in all those assumptions of impossible application of known guidelines.

In any case, from the thousand problems that can appear, according to the different cases, it is important both that the insurer does not remain without receiving for an extensive period of time the rendering of services that has been acknowledged as owed once the loss was recognized and that the amount to be discovered or determined is not left uncertain as an illiquid sum and, therefore, non-payable.

In order to cover the imbalance that could be produced on the insured (thinking of some assumptions of halt of the insured's industry and the existence of a right already recognized for the rendering of services for a coverage of 'loss of benefit'), laws have fixed a provisional right of the insured to perceive a percentage of the maximum amount to which they can aspire, the assured amount, which was originated in a very old practice and that our law shows in section 51, through the establishment of a minimum limit of half of the rendering of services acknowledged or recognized by the insurer (as it is presumed that he has already estimated the damage and recognized the right).

Besides, our law provides for another assumption: the course of a term from the moment the insurer assessed the damage. This assumption in our opinion, if literally admitted, would be unfit for our legal system, as it has been noted in the similar case of section 49 (cf. *supra* in this same paragraph).

The insurer, once the right has been acknowledged, counts on fifteen days for the payment or for the offering to pay to cause the necessary arrears of the insured (taker or rightful successor) and be then able to attempt the payment by consignment. In this lapse of fifteen days, extensible by agreement of the parties or by own requirements intending to determine with precision the dimension and the economic extension of the loss (not in life insurance but yes in property insurance and insurance of the person as the legal terminology calls them).

This term, once the conventional or necessary extensions mentioned have elapsed, does not allow for a new extension of a month as it appeared to point out in section 51 of Act 17.418, but such month starts as from the moment when it was expressly or implicitly acknowledged the right of the insured. This lapse is sufficient in most of the cases to have a close idea of the dimension and, at least, possible economic extent of the rendering of services of the insurer.

It is our opinion, then, as generic construction of section 51 in this part, that the insurer, one month after having the right of the insured recognized, before his specific request, must carry out a determination, obviously estimative, logical, and essentially provisional of what its rendering of services would be, and it shall be obliged before the insured's request to carry out a payment of similar characteristics, but without exceeding 50% of the provisional amount estimated, as long as this term of fifteen days of section 49 could not be complied with, by the specific difficulties of payment of the specific case.

In this line, the law in a first perspective would seem to modify the criterion of the Civil Code regarding the obligation of partial payments but, if its meaning is understood rightly, we can coincide in that we are not dealing with a partial payment but an advance payment of a service that is not yet liquid since, although the essence of what is owed is known, there is no information as to how much is owed, a dimension that could not be known, either, at this stage so as to generate a concrete commitment.

81. Assessment of Damages by Expert Opinions or Expert Judgments. There is another possibility that has not been much used in our sphere, except for the cases of large insured companies that have an adequate organization for the assumptions of losses in property insurance contracts. We are referring to 'arbitration trials', as defined by section 57 of Act 17.418.

The method should have been another. Even sustaining the monist criterion as gathering agent of insurance – a starting point which today is criticized – and even having looked for a solution by means of section 1 of Act, the subject 'rendering of services of the insurer' should have been separated in life and non-life insurance. This is mentioned because, later, when the insurable interest is considered (an indispensable element in property insurance or damage property insurance, and non-existent in personal property), it shall be more clearly noticed the influence of the value of such interest in the amount of the rendering of services to pay to the insured.

This arbitration method is incorporated by section 57 as solely possible for the damage assessment and, as it is a dispositive regulation, the parties are free to use it or not, leaving the formulation of their stipulations to the free agreement of the parties (except for the respect of the imperative ruling that may exist in relation to the arbitration regulated by the applicable Procedural Code).

It is important to point out regarding section 57 of Act 17.418 some attempts of wrong construction which are easily evaded by the correct reading thereof – a fact with which the majority of Argentine jurisprudence agrees.

The regulation commented – and we insist on what we have just said – does not prevent the establishment of an arbitration for the assessment of the damages that a loss may bring about regarding the property that is the subject matter of the coverage in a property insurance contract, even when the item is part of the text of the policy. Section 57 only limits the right of the parties to establish within the contents of the policy a commitment to arbitration, regarding the substantive meaning of the matters that could arise between the parties, and thus subtracts the insurance contract in question from the natural judicial construction.

This limitation of the right is only temporal as the nullity penalty does not affect the agreements that the parties could freely achieve in other subsequent moments. The law punishes with annulment each arbitration agreement included when entering into an insurance contract, whether by general clause or by means of a specific express pact. It is precise to point out that neither does it pursue the arbitration for the assessment of damages nor does it pursue to combat the arbiters' judgments, perceptibly agreed outside the policy documenting the contract. In other words, the clear intention of Act 17.418 is to prevent the insured from being conditioned to clauses separating him from fundamental rights as the judicial jurisdiction.

If after the entering of the contract it was decided to waive such right and it was understood that other alternative means – such as arbitration – would transmit him an acceptable security, he is in total freedom to consider it and agree upon it.

In the same sense, it is worth remembering that the regulation of the first part of Act 17.418 that prohibits compromising the jurisdiction to arbitration as interpreted in the contract is a protective provision of the insurer that originally was introduced to the insurance law of Argentina to correct a doubtful practice of the insurers. This practice consisted of agreeing on an arbitration regarding all the contents of the contract. The law does not prohibit arbitration regarding the assessment of damages causing a loss as this is a technical matter, which most of the time must be elucidated by experts in the special subject in question and inclusively is related to the event or events of the occurrence of the loss.

What is more, it is customary that many general conditions establish, from the beginning of the contract, a reciprocal agreement to resource the expert's opinion in the assumption of criteria or price disagreement, in order to subtract from judicial proceedings, always longer and more expensive.

From the same approach, it would be convenient, as from the agreement after the moment of taking out insurance and after the policy has been issued, to submit to arbitration some types of conflicts between insurer and insured even from a preventive standpoint, not only in keeping with the most modern current policies around the world but also with those recently spread in Argentina of using alternative methods in order to settle insurance conflicts.

Despite the old age of the legal institute of arbitration, it has not been used a lot in our sphere for different reasons that do not correspond to analysis at this point. Today, there seems to have taken place a return to the past in this matter, and, regardless of the reasons that are not important to our study, the reality is that every time with more frequency these means of alternatively reaching decisions are being used. Arbitration is the example par excellence, although mediation is also prominent, whose outcome is not compulsory.

§3. The Damage Adjuster: Modality

82. Damages Assessment – The Adjuster. As from the compliance with the obligation of the insurer that is present since the moment when he expressly or implicitly accepted the right of the insured – although there is not yet a liquid sum to determine its enforceability – the independent work of the adjuster of the loss is, apart from habitual, convenient to reality.

The task of the adjuster essentially consists of carrying out the correct assessment of the extent and value of the damages, and for that he acts independently from the insurer, reaching conclusions that are not compulsory for any of the parties but that can be accepted by them, if they agree with the information of the adjuster and, in such case, enter an agreement.

This adjuster is not the expert we read about in section 57, but an expert appointed by the insurer, according to the custom in this business in our country but

– as it has been rightly pointed out before – for the sole determination of the extension of damages and their assessment. The appointment of the adjuster is not subject to any restriction and does not prevent or condition the insured from appointing another adjuster on his part, for the control of the case and to relate with the insurer and the adjuster that he has appointed.

83. Recapitulation in Procedures for Payment. Given the extension of these topics, due to the specification of the matters dealt with, it turns out to be convenient a brief summary on the scenario presented to the insurer when the loss is notified. In the first place, the obligation to solve everything that arises out of the notification of the taker as he had understood it corresponds exclusively to the insurer.

The first task to undertake by the insurer after the notification is the assessment thereof, with reference to a special term of thirty days to decide upon its rejection. Silence during that lapse equals acceptance of the event as loss from the legal standpoint, not enabling later on to revert the consequences of such acceptance, except for the assumptions of fraud or use of fraudulent evidence by the insured.

The second task and obligation of the insurer – as it has been previously analysed – is to pay the benefits and, for that, in many cases, is needed a profound analysis of the specific situation of the loss, the extent of its effects and the insurable interests involved, appropriately examining those circumstances and elements that can only be concretely established. It must be taken into account, for instance, that only to arrive at the conclusion of the preexistence of the property that has been subject to the insurable interest of a fire insurance with total apparent intensity, it is frequently necessary to use methods of inspection of ashes, volume of the premises containing them, in order to establish the amount to compensate. In many cases, studies have to be conducted, the combination of different subjects of insurable interests analysed, and the existence of privileged creditors verified.

For this analysis and study, the obligation of the insurer will be to carry out different tasks, subject to the control of the insured with expiration terms. These tasks vary a lot as they will multiply in correspondence with the growth of business, that is, depending on the number of operations. As a consequence, it is not only more favourable to his interests to hire third parties for these activities (it avoids him cost repetition, dispersion of efforts, multiplicity of inner responsibilities, and other expenses that may arise from the company's administration). But also, it turns out to be more favourable for the insured as, when this aspect of liquidation, for instance, is delegated to a third party, as company or independent business, this company responds to its own interests and conducts itself according to an ethical behaviour alien to the convenience of the parties.

Also, professional adjusters are specialized in one or more types of cases, which allow them to acquire experience and certainty in their technical concepts as well as in regard to the values of the articles or goods that compose these aspects.

The simple fact of outsourcing this activity – as the fact that control is exerted over this activity by the SIN (sections 68 and 70 of Act 20.091 and corresponding regulations) – improves considerably the rendering of services as well as adding the benefit of the quality of work of this professional adjuster, namely, the independent criterion of the individual from his employer, who precisely hires him for that reason.

It is clear that this point depends fundamentally on the quality of business of both the insurer and the adjuster. In this sense, given the development of business, it is not common to suspect the permanent quality of some property and services that are offered by certain companies or professionals, even when it is important to maintain the State's control. The custom of appointing this type of adjuster by the insurer, appointment that takes place exactly as from the notification of loss or the event considered the loss, does not prevent at all that the insured does the same with identical characteristics. This principle that is contained in section 75, although it is included under the article dedicated to the salvage burden, must be interpreted as a general provision not applicable only to this case.

The commercial custom, as well as the brevity of the terms before certain circumstances, made the duty of the adjuster to advance provisionally on the grounds of investigations intended to determine the possible extension of the damage, which in certain occasions connected it to the same event that may have given rise to the assumed loss. The insurer, notwithstanding these advancements, within the period of thirty days that we have seen before, used to issue and issues – following his duty – a decision on the rejection of the event as loss or the loss as loss itself, disallowing, in consequence, any benefit of the taker (insured) regarding it.

The uses and customs of our business have considered prudent the appointment of the adjusters from the moment in which the loss has been notified by the insured. These adjusters, by practice, have assumed in many opportunities when it is required, a two-stage task: at the first stage, they are investigators trying to find the truth about the occurrence of the loss, its causes, the exact apparent dimension, and they attempt, together with the intervening public authorities, to protect the remaining property and the public security that could have been affected. Once the problem of the loss has been legally resolved, they carry out a second activity that is their own activity and that has been referred to before but that, in many opportunities, has even started provisionally to the effects of saving time in the benefit of the two parties and of its own work.

It must be understood that both aspects can and usually are absolutely mixed during the first moments of the occurrence of any kind of loss, especially in those of importance. (Note that the word 'loss' has been used now, not only in its sense of insurance but also with a wider meaning as we are referring fundamentally to property damage insurance and, in consequence, there are connotations of damages or prejudicial effects.)

84. The Insurable Interest: Its Importance in the Occurrence of the Loss—Its Influence on the Insurer's Payment. In order to continue dealing with the insurer's obligation of paying when the loss takes place, in the assumptions of property or things insurance contracts, it is important to analyse a fourth element that only exists in this type of insurance since, in life insurance, for Act 17.418, such requirement is not necessary. This element is the insurable risk.

When we were analysing the elements of insurance, we mentioned three essential elements that cannot be absent in an insurance contract for it to be considered an insurance contract and no other thing (risk, premium, and rendering of services of the insurer), all that, at least, at this stage of business, from its both technical and legal point of view.

When expressing this concept, to be absolutely clear, it is necessary to emphasize that, even when there is a difference between gender and species from insurance contract as main line and damage property insurance (damage, things, or liability) and life insurance both as family thereof, it is undoubted that these varieties can have, at the same time, some other element in their composition, without which its existence as contractual species within a common gender could not exist.

As it has just been stated and also previously dealt with, Act 17.418, section 60 and subsequent sections establish, as essential element, the insurable interest.

We partially agree with this subject following what was stated by the Spanish Professor Garrigues, in his work *Land Insurance Contract*, 2nd ed (Madrid), regarding the fact that in the property damage insurance contract, apart from the subject matter and the cause, there is another characteristic element that we do not find in other contracts: that element is the insurable interest.

It can be argued that the insurable interest is a property relationship that a person has over one thing or right to avoid the occurrence of a risk that would cause a decrease in its value, or, simply, property damage to the owner of such interest.

The French Act of 1930 introduced this element as significant for damage insurance when prescribing that any individual with the interest of conserving one's property can have it insured and that all direct or indirect interest upon the non-occurrence of a risk may be subject matter of an insurance contract.

This broad regulation of the repealed French Act of 1930 allowed for the free will of the parties to determine the risk to be insured, as long as such interest was of property content and not purely sentimental, in a way that the risk occurrence implied a loss.

From this principle, the opinion of many authors started to derive in the sense that, in damage property insurance, the subject matter of the insurance is the insurable interest (property or goods in the broad sense). Most authors after 1930 subscribe to this position.

We, however, do not share this position, and neither does the Argentine Act 17.418 that certainly establishes the idea of considering the risk as the subject matter of the insurance contract and the insurable interest as an additional element or an indispensable element attached to the contract, as expressed in sections 2 and 60.

In such a specific manner, the Argentine Act establishes the risk as subject matter of the insurance contract that, in the general provisions, that is, in those provisions that should be common to any type of contracts, section 3 refers to the non-existence of the risk as grounds for the nullity of the contract, omitting any reference to the insurable interest, a subject that is only defined in its special part (damage property insurance) legislated in section 81. The insurable interest may present in many ways and not only under the aspect of a relation of ownership of a thing. Only a lawful economic relation over property or things or over a universality of one or the others of the loss not occurring suffices, so that the circumstances are given.

Our Act 17.418 has regulated the effects of the non-existence of the insurable interest at the moment of commencement of the material effectiveness of the contract (section 81), with different reaches to the commonly legislated by the Civil

Code in the matter of nullities of legal acts. The additional regulation provided in the last part of the mentioned section 81 would establish a limit to the rights of the insurer.

85. Opportunity of the Existence of the Insurable Interest in Order To be Entitled to the Insurer's Rendering of Services. The insurable interest, the essential element of the damage property insurance contract in any of its subspecies, must exist not only at the moment of material commencement of the coverage but also fundamentally at the moment in which the loss of the fact from which derives the insured's liability occurs (liability insurance).

The second item of section 81, when referring to the behaviour of the parties in relation to the payment of the premium when the insurable interest disappears after the commencement of the coverage, textually refers to what is set forth in a similar subject by section 41 of the same Act 17.418 (which, in turn, refers to the behaviour in the case of termination of the contract due to aggravation of the risk).

This reference to the solution provided to the rights and obligations of the parties regarding the payment of the premium strengthens the criterion established in the aforementioned item, regarding the possible contraction in the scenario of the disappearance of the insurable interest as attached to the risk (sections 2 and 60). Although they are different institutes responding to different concepts, they permit certain analogies in relation to their effects, since – as we have seen – to our criterion, it plays an important role in both of them, the subjectivity with which the risk is contemplated in certain occasions.

Yet, beyond the effects on the premium, the non-existence of the insurable interest at the moment of the loss causes the release of the insurer from his obligation to comply with the main rendering of services, that is, to compensate the insured. This is because this interest truly does not exist, as an interest cannot be spoken about in abstract, but it responds to the idea of ownership and, therefore, of an insured.

Damage property insurance has a compensatory function that cannot be the source of benefits or of gambling. The contract's aleatory characteristic responds to that person that has an interest in the property or in its rights and not to a person alien to such interest.

86. The Principle of Compensation. The insurance contract is a compensation contract, which cannot arise out of a benefit in favour of the insured, but only out of compensation to the maximum limit of the loss or damage underwent. Thus, it cannot imply the enrichment of the insured.

Therefore, the insured's obligation has the purpose of redressing the damage suffered, and not of placing the insured in a situation better than that which he would have had, had the loss not occurred. Thus, it can be affirmed that, ultimately, the limit of the damage, framed by the real value of the insurable interest at the moment of the loss, shall determine also the maximum limit of the insurer's rendering of services. This is a longstanding concept and comes from the very first manifestations of maritime insurance, immediately extended to land damage insurance as soon as the mechanism developed in this line.

These guidelines are expressly contained in our law, starting by the governing regulation section 61, where it is stated the obligation to compensate the insurer, with the meaning of compensation. As it is well known, the traditional grounds of this compensatory principle are two fundamental conditions:

(1) The fear of the occurrence of intentional (voluntary) losses that could give rise to benefits that do not correspond to the insured if it was permitted for them to collect amounts superior to the value of their protected insurable interests. If there was no legal protection towards the principle under analysis, insurance for amounts very much superior to the real value of their assured interest would be encouraged, as well as the proliferation of losses caused in order to profit from the differences. It is not being judged the possibility of proving fraud of the insured, but it would be reckless not to point out the existent restrictions to prove such fraud as of bad faith. All this is without prejudice of mentioning and pointing out the inconveniency for any economy of the intentional destruction of property. It is also pointed out how frankly immoral would turn out to be the encouragement by a defect on legislation of an unjust and false enrichment.
(2) The danger of turning the activity into a gamble or bet given that if the compensation was not conditioned by the effectively occurred damage, in certain losses – which cause is only the act of nature as, for instance, it may happen with fires or hail insurance – without the limit imposed by the regulation in question, insurance could become a gamble or bet as, in areas of frequent occurrence of such risks, it would suffice to insure against those risks for values superior to those of the corresponding insurable interests, so that the chance determines an enrichment, by means of something that would really constitute a gamble or a bet and not a real protection.

87. Consequences of the Principle of Compensation. In our opinion, as it has been mentioned, the first part of section 61 of Act 17.418 points out not only the principles we are making reference to but also the consequences arising thereof. This regulation states that 'the insurer obliges himself to compensate, pursuant to the contract, the property damage caused by the loss'. The expression 'pursuant to the contract' has some readings or constructions. In the first place, the compensation owed shall be in accordance with what has been agreed by the parties since both the risk and the insurable interest are clearly contractual aspects, alien to any imperative provision of the law and determined by the agreement of wills. Both elements form part of indications of the special clauses of the contract (section 11) and consequently – except for the concept of compensation that every system grants to the insurer – specific clauses may be agreed upon.

The expression also has its reach regarding property but under another view. The assured value of the insurable interest sets out a second and different maximum limit. If the value of the damage to property suffered in the loss was superior to the amount of the assured value (amount of the insurance contract), it would correspond that the insured does not receive a compensation superior to the assured amount on which the premium has been paid.

There are other consequences derived from the compensation principle:

(1) In case of partial loss, that is, a loss of only a part of the property or properties covered, the amount of the salvaged property or the remains must be deducted from the amount of the damages caused.
(2) If the coverage taken out is at the new value or without deduction of the depreciation of the value of the interest on account of the course of time, it must be agreed upon that this would be balanced with the effective reconstruction or reposition of the property that is the subject of the insurable interest.
(3) The expiration in the matter of plurality of insurance on a same insurable interest or, if this was the case, the reduction on a pro rata basis of the assured amounts.
(4) The ones related to overinsurance included the nullity of the contract, taken out with the intention of enrichment.

88. Measurement of the Rendering of Services. Proportional Rule. Exceptions. As it arises from what has been stated, the loss or occurrence of the risk provided for in the contract implies damage to the insurable interest that is measurable in money. Thus, it is the measure and limit of redress that the insured must receive in order to satisfy his need to reinstate the affected economic relation.

From this compensatory principle, it can be concluded that, in reality, only at the moment of occurrence of the event of damage (loss in this type of insurance), the value of the insurable interest covered in the policy will be known. Such determination will be made in the policy by means of a number (assured value). This value, apart from the sense of maximum limit of possible compensation – non-transferable under any circumstances – has an approximate sense of the assessment of its value which the taker carries out. The premium has been calculated and paid taking into account the policyholder as a defining factor thereof, and that is why it is non-transferable; the taker, however, is the person that, at the moment of taking out the insurance, must know very accurately the measure of its interest, taking into account the cause thereof.

It must be pointed out that the significance in value can differ from the interest of the owner of property, to the interest of his privileged creditor (mortgage or pledge creditor), or to the interest of his tenant, to the value of the stakeholder.

It is possible that, in the habitual sense and without thinking of insurance as a whole, linked, technical field arising out of the commercial need to find solutions to the problems of the parties involved, the determination of the assured amount at the beginning of the insurance relationship would not be indispensable for the payment of a loss, as the compensation to be paid will have as limit the compensation of the insured, pursuant to the truly experienced loss (this refers only to damage insurance).

Yet, if we take into account that there are technical elements of indispensable significance to be taken into account, as the homogeneity of the assured amounts and methods of risk spreading (co-insurance, reinsurance), the indispensability of the collection of the premium at the beginning of the contract, or, at least, the certainty of its value at such moment, etc., we shall note that the establishment of the value attributed to the insurable interest is unavoidable, in order to permit these and other more complex things. These elements are important not only regarding the security of the business person but also regarding the assured community itself.

Among the more complex security means mentioned, we find the reserves or company provisions indispensable for the order and effectiveness of the insurance business. By establishing an assured amount, it is known as the last maximum limit to which the insurer could be compromised in case of loss, and, therefore, the loss impact that the insurer's economy could experience as a consequence thereof.

What must be clear is that it is very unlikely that the assured value turns out to be equal to the insurable value, as the former is a static value presumably existent at the moment of hiring the insurance, whereas the insurable value is essentially changeable, as it will suffer the changes produced in the values of the property of the corresponding kind, as well as the modifications occurred in those same interests. One example of this would be the decrease in value of the insurable interest of the creditor as time goes by in relation to the amortization of his credit.

Having clarified the reason for existence of the assured amount and the coexistence of such as from the loss with the value or insurable amount, it is necessary to analyse the manner of coexistence and the activity reciprocally influencing each other. As it has been expressed, very rarely the insured value will coincide with the insurable value although, in general, and very frequently, the approximations between one and the other are given by regulations, either by corrections of the former as notorious changes take place or by some special clause that automatically corrects the imbalances specifically determined.

It must be taken into account that, from all possible causes of the differences between the insured and insurable value by an increase thereof, the most habitual and the one we have long and sadly experienced in our country is inflation.[17] It is clear that the prospect of inflation requires the insured to take care of his interests and foresee the modalities or modifications of the contracts and to be alert of the real values of his assured interests in order to require the corresponding increases of the assured values.[18]

89. Underinsurance – Overinsurance. We shall distinctly analyse the different cases that may appear in relation to the two amounts referred to in the previous paragraph: (1) equivalence, (2) overinsurance, and (3) underinsurance:

---

17. The Argentine insurer market offered its products against damages in two different ways: (1) with variable index of the insurable value, pursuant to the increase between the price indexes existing in the month prior to the contract and the month prior to the loss; and (2) with an established increase of the assured value up to a maximum percentage from the originary one. In some very common contracts, such as motor vehicle insurance, via the Superintendence, obligations were established to the insurers with the purposes of indexing the policies and issuing the corresponding invoicing. Another type of corrective measure was applied by means of an agreement establishing the assured value by fixing the dollar as currency and fixing both the compensation and the assured amount in such currency.
18. At that moment, in May 2002, in Argentina, there were present the causes that inexorably led us and continue to lead us to a bursting inflation. The exorbitant unproductive public expense and the political waste of our governors and leaders are and will always be brilliant footlights foolishly attracting towards unwise and unrealistic paths. Thus, undoubtedly, a new path, a path that we have left many years ago, will be travelled again and the insurance contract will find the way to revalue its assured values.

(1) *Equivalence.* This will take place when there are no differences between values and, therefore, there is no specific situation, since the payment of the damage that will be carried out will be the same in all cases for the same value, which shall always be equal to the insurable value that – as it has been stated – is the same as the insured value.
(2) *Overinsurance.* This will take place when, at the moment of occurrence of the loss, the insurable value or real value is inferior to the insured value and, therefore, the amount to compensate shall, in turn, be that of the occurred damage, which, due to the described situation, in the case of greater intensity, that is, of the total loss, shall always coincide with the insurable value. In this assumption, were the taker paid a premium superior to the strictly corresponding to that real value, he shall not be entitled to any right to claim the reduction of the premium and, if it were the case, its return or partial release.

It should be noted that the amount or insured value has been provided by the taker, without the intervention of the insurer that has no interest in controlling such a subject, or will suffer any consequences on account of his decision. The determination of that value is the taker's prerogative since – as it has been stated – the price, that is, the premium to pay or to owe, must be determined among other factors in relation to its amount.

If there was an excess in the valuation or a depreciation on the insured value during the period that elapsed between the taking out and the loss in a way that, at the moment of its occurrence, the former exceeded it, the limitation of the compensation of the effective damage suffered plays the role of protecting the principle of compensation in order to avoid the unjust enrichment of the insured. This clear right of the property insurance taker, which may lead him to take out underinsurance on the grounds or circumstances he would have estimated and that would have influenced his voluntary act, must justly be considered as a true expression of the freedom of contract which does not influence at all the exact declaration of the risk, which has been previously appreciated when dealing with misrepresentation and aggravation.

Being flexible with language, the French Act of 1930 mentions in its section L 121-5 that it is a case in which the insured remains its own insurer, that is, that this situation presents the almost domestic feature of partial self-insurance that obviously does not exist with full rigour of the law.

The Argentine Act, in its section 62, establishes a regulation not expressly categorized as imperative, by means of which the insurer or taker may require the reduction of the assured amount or value, whenever such value was totally superior to the current value of the insurable interest. It is an exceptional provision intended to give a solution to both parties from their corresponding situation as: if the insured value was notably superior to the value that it would have as the insured value, if the loss occurred at a defined moment of the contractual relationship, the good faith taker would be prejudiced when paying a coverage to which he would not be entitled and the insurer would have the possibility of being prejudiced in case of loss, before the fraudulent attitude of the taker or insured.

In fact, regarding the taker, in principle, we have seen that he would not be entitled to require anything since the establishment of the assured value is his prerogative and, consequently, he would lose the same premium paid in excess of the value effectively 'guaranteed'.

Regarding the insurer, the noticeable superiority of the insured value by the insurable value does not permit it all alone to pose any case about it since his right is restricted to nullity in the only assumption that the contract would have been motivated by the intention of its counterpart of unjust enrichment with the excess. In consequence, the situation of not admitting the reduction would lead the takers to an agreement that would bring about great difficulties in the relationship.

The regulation in section 62 leaves it only to the good judgment of the quantification of both values, using the adverb 'notably' (which gives an idea of the importance of such difference). Thus, the solution of admitting the reduction of the assured amount although only for the case of the considerable superiority of the assured amount permits a just solution, even at a legislative level, as it would help to provide a simpler solution to problems that may arise.

In the case of reduction, it is obvious that not only the contract should be readjusted concerning its amount – for which would be needed the agreement of the parties, a third party, or the judicial decision – but also the premium should be readjusted.

(3) *Underinsurance.* This will take place when the real insurable value is superior to the insured value at the moment immediately prior to the occurrence of the event that derives in the loss.

The following items are to be taken into account: (i) on the one hand, the assured amount is the maximum limit of any compensation for the loss; (ii) on the other hand, the principle of compensation demands that the insured is compensated to the extent of the damage.

There is a problem in the assumption of assured values of less value than the real insurable values, both when dealing with total and partial damages. The solution established by the law would seem to be annoying in the case of partial damages. The matter to elucidate is related to how to pay the compensation to the insured, that is, whether the amount shall be established as in the other two analysed cases or the solution to be adopted shall be different.

Our Insurance Contracts Act (17.418), the same as the other legislations before it, establishes a guideline for the application of the principle of proportionality of the damage regarding both values (section 65, subsection 2) and calls this situation underinsurance, as it has been previously seen.

In other words: the assured amount establishes, under all circumstances, the limit of the commitment assumed by the insurer, not only regarding its amount but also regarding the proportion of the damage.

A simple example would suffice to improve the explanation. Let us suppose that there is an industrial machine, the assured value of which established in the policy is of ARS 100,000, but which, at the day of the loss, has a real value of ARS 200,000. If the loss took place, whatever the amount of the final damage established in the payment, this would constitute an underinsurance because the real insurable value of the machine in question is superior to the assured amount of the policy in the insurance contract.

The right of the insured to collect compensation would only reach the limit of the assured amount, but in relation to the proportion mentioned before that, thus conditioning it by the double incidence of the same factor.

In summary, in the example proposed, a damage of ARS 50,000 inferior to the insured value will not be established up to that amount, but only up to the percentage corresponding to the relation of the assured amount with the insurable amount, that is ARS 100,000 and ARS 200,000; ultimately, 50% will be considered, which renders a payment to the insured of ARS 25,000.

The compensation shall not reach but part of the amount of the damage, as a consequence of the insufficiency of the guaranteed capital. Thus – always in the case under analysis, that is, insured values inferior to the real insurable values – the compensation shall exclusively reach an amount inferior to the real insurable as the quotient between the assured amount and such amount is inferior to the unit.

According to what has been exposed, the result of dividing the insured amount (ARS 100,000) by the insurable amount (ARS 200,000) will render the usable value of 50% which, applied to the effectively occurred damage, shall establish the amount of corresponding compensation.

However, the explanation is equally possible that the compensation to be paid to the insured is the result of dividing by the real insurable amount, the result between the damage caused by the loss and the insured amount. Mathematically, this would be a relation expressed as follows: the compensation to be paid is to the damage as the assured amount is to the real insurable amount.

In an example that has the aforementioned parameters with a damage caused by the loss of ARS 50,000, we can appreciate that x, that is, the compensation to be paid on the denominator that is represented by the damage as ARS 50,000, is as the assured amount (ARS 100,000) is to the real insurable amount (ARS 200,000); that is: x = assured amount multiplied by the amount of damage, divided by the amount of the sum times the insurable amount. In summary, the mathematical operation is translated into x = 100,000 times 50,000 divided by 200,000 = 25,000.

It must be taken into account that this seemingly prejudice against the insured, a contract which assured amount is equal or superior to the one arising from the proportional rule, is not a penalty to such insured or taker, but it is the economic fact of an insufficient premium and a second supplementary insurance for the remaining value of the assured amount not taken out. This was so considered by the French Act of 1930 when sustaining that due to lack of insurance, the insured was considered his own insurer, which was no other thing but a fiction.

The reality is that, as it has been stated, there is an insufficient premium, for these are calculated on the total value of the insurable interest and, if the assured amount does not mean but a part of said amount, an alteration to the general and ordinary fund of premiums is produced. In practice, these are the cases where, due to an agreement, the proportional rule is left aside, as when all the damages either partial or total occurred are completely covered and the assured amount is not considered, then the premium to be paid is superior. That is to say that a higher price is paid for this exceptional situation; higher price is technically determined.

It is clear that in the universal application of the proportional rule as a consequence of underinsurance, it is not strange the commercial fight of the different interests, a conflict that has taken place throughout time.

90. Exceptions and Clauses – Absolute and Relative First Risk Insurance. Underinsurance, and thus the proportional rule, in matters of compensation turns out to be a rule liable of being freely repealed, and there are exceptions establishing its change in the assumption of partial damages. We are making reference to the clauses of absolute or relative first risk insurance.

In this matter, Act 17.418 in section 65, after establishing the principle of compensation in its first paragraph and the proportional rule at the beginning of its second paragraph, finishes by permitting the 'agreement to the contrary' that, in insurance business jargon, means first risk insurance.

First risk insurance means that, in spite of the fact that the assured amount may not suffice to represent the real value of the insurable interest exposed to risk, the insurer shall compensate partial losses as if that difference of amounts did not exist and for the amount that really arises from the occurred damage, always within the maximum limit of the assured amount. The origin of this repealing clause – contemplated by underinsurance – was presented in the insurance of a similar number of insurable interests, for instance, several buildings located in different places against fire risk. As the different geographical locations of the buildings made a difference that does not need to be registered when the insurable interests are not within an absolute vicinity, there was almost the certainty that there would not be more than one loss of fire affecting the same contract at the same time; thus, it did not make sense to establish an assured value equal to the sum of the values of all the buildings.

It sufficed that the assured value was the building of greatest value. Nevertheless, the proportional rule applied and applies when the assured amount that, as it has been explained, responded to the insurable interest of highest value turned out to be inferior to the insured value.

The relative first risk insurance, as this modality has been called – also known as first risk insurance with relative abandonment of the proportional rule – is frequently carried out over goods located in different places and on the basis of the declaration of such goods, that is, the declaration of stock (a declaration that has a function in the calculation of the premium).

When on the day of the loss, the insured had goods for a higher value than the one declared, the underinsurance for the case the damage turned out proportionally superior could be agreed.

Apart from this modality that is known as relative first risk, there is another one – even more beneficial – known as absolute risk, by which the insurable value is not even taken into account and the damage is compensated by the amount effectively occurred of the prejudice, up to the limit of the assured amount.

It is necessary to clarify again that, in both species, the premium turns out to be more important than the insurance under the proportional rule and that, even when the example provided *supra* is a real estate insurance against fire (relative first risk), any other insurable interest and risk can be subject to the modality, as long as it is agreed upon by the parties.

91. Appraised Value. The Argentine Act establishes another exception to the proportional rule emerging from the underinsurance situation. It is the clause of the appraised value (section 63) which admits that by agreement of the parties a determined amount of the value of the property (subject matter of the insurable interest) is established. In fact, the Act mentions the value of the property that the insurance refers to, and we know that, in property insurance, it is not a thing or property that is insured but the insurable interest that a person has over a property or thing.

This appraisal – that is carried out by agreement of the parties – shall be an estimated value that assumes that the agreed amounts shall be the value of the insured interest at the moment of the loss, except that the insurer evidences that it is notably superior – an item expressly provided for in section 63 of the Argentine Act – always in response to consequences arising out of the indemnity principle.

This value granted by a special agreement has not been common in Argentina in the usual contracts of property damage insurance, but it has been used with many restrictions since, besides the loss of profit insurance attached to a fire insurance contract, it is almost exclusively used in art pieces insurance or their collections, in which it is always very difficult to establish the insurable value after the occurrence of a loss.

The appraised value insurance – as our law calls it – does not necessarily require the appraisal of an expert; thus, it is preferable to the denomination of the accepted value or valued clause introduced by the French books of authority, although it is certain that, in some cases, for instance, works of art, the appraisal by an expert is a good prudent measure for both parties, as such appraisal establishes the real value of the insurable property interest beyond any sentimental value.

Whether this agreement is called valued clause of accepted or appraised value, what is important is the concrete and agreed stipulation that, on the one hand, implies a modification to the principle of proportionality and, on the other hand, brings about an important variation to the concept that has the declaration of the insured on the assured value, at the moment of entering into the contract, without the aforementioned agreement.

Let us remember that this declaration that the insurer rescues, to the effects of calculating the premium, and that is mentioned in the policy, does not bring about any certainty regarding the real value of the insurable interest or its existence.

These are not circumstances that, at the moment of the agreement of wills, must be taken into account by the insurer. The agreement of wills does not necessarily require the certainty of any of the two parties, as they will not have influence on the obligation of the insurer if the random event does not take place.

However, it is wise to think and believe that both agree with the declaration of the taker since the entering into the contract would not be otherwise explained. At the same time, it is correct to admit that this type of agreement, if the loss took place, may bring about benefits for the insured since the insurable value being determined from the moment of the agreement will not require further evidence in relation to it and, therefore, will constitute a very strong assumption of the insured's ownership of the insurable interest, whatever it was.

This situation deals with the assumption on the value which does not prevent – as we have seen – the questioning of the appraised or accepted value formulated by section 63 of Act and the more generic section 62, without mentioning the pathological cases in which nullity can be claimed.

Although the clause of accepted or appraised value does not modify any of the burdens that the insured must comply with once the event from which the loss could be estimated has taken place, it only influences the determination of the compensation. It is worth insisting on the fact that the insured is not released from his duties of evidencing the damage of the insured interest, as a consequence of a harmful event covered by the contract, pursuant to the determination of the risk expressed in the agreement of wills.

Notwithstanding what has been mentioned regarding the limits that form part of the compensation, there are payments that the insurer must carry out even above the insurable value or the assured amount. They are, to our criteria, additional expenses originating from the need to make a provision for extension of damages, such as salvage provisions (according to section 73 of the Insurance Contract Act) and judicial costs provisions (provided for in section 111). As it is certain that they are expenses and not indemnities to the insured and they have no connection with the insurable interest, it is clear that they do not constitute other exceptions to the principle analysed.

§4. Intermediate Conditions by Agreement of Wills

92. Overdraft and Franchise. Even though the two possibilities of payment of the compensation have been covered by law and the insurance business practice, since the course of business is characterized by the principle of compensation (proportional rule), which is characterized, in turn, by the appraised clause, it is still possible to establish intermediate conditions by agreement of wills of the parties that, on the one hand, have influence on the insured as it decreases the price of the insurance and, on the other hand, regarding the insurer, he is benefited by releasing him from responding in certain situations. These facts are those that only cause minor damages and that usually are in the different types of insurance that, altogether, cause the highest relative losses.

These means or guidelines to which we are referring, of an exclusively conventional nature, are called: (a) overdrafts and (b) franchises.

They are two typical institutes of the insurance sphere which, fundamentally, have as purpose to reduce the amount to be compensated to the insured in case of loss, that is, which economically limit the payment obligation of the insurer. They currently answer to denominations that in practice have different histories but only partially when it comes to effects or their purpose.

From that point of view – its origins, causes, and evolution – we can agree that we strictly speak of overdraft with the additional feature of being compulsory when the insurer obliges himself to maintain on him, a part of any damage, subject matter of the insured risk, in his exclusive charge or to his account. In other words, the insurer never covers the total of the price of the damages that may take place or –

with a terminology that is current but not technical or appropriate at all – the insured remains in all circumstances as if he was his own insurer.[19]

The specific reason for the compulsory overdraft lies in the fact of determining a greater interest in the insured so that the loss does not occur as, by means of a fixed amount or percentage on the total indemnity, he will always participate in the damage produced in every occurrence of the risk covered.

This participation will take place in each case, whatever the final amount of the damage to be compensated. It also carries the duty of not insuring the amount or percentage of the compulsory overdraft with any insurer.

Thus, beyond any economic benefit that this may bring about to the taker, due to the reduction of the premium, this implies – and we have made reference to this – the compulsory overdraft has as purpose the idea of protecting the possible light behaviour of the insured who knows that, whenever the loss occurs, the amount that he will receive will be always inferior to the one replacing the value of his insurable interest. In relation to the franchise, it is a modality of healthy administration of risk. The insured is not entitled to claim the compensations derived from minor losses in which liquidation expenses and other necessary expenses are of great significance, being sometimes equivalent to the amount to be paid for the loss itself. However, once the amount of the franchise has been exceeded, that is, when the insurer should take part in the loss to the effects of compensating, all the amount of the prejudice caused shall be in charge of him, without taking into account the franchise.

The custom and practice of the activity created, with time, two types of franchise: simple and absolute. The simple has just been analysed. Briefly: if the damages are inferior to the franchise, the prejudice is in charge of the insured. When damages surpass the limit of the amount agreed or the percentage or fraction established as franchise, all the damage caused is in charge of the insurer.

The absolute franchise, on the contrary, implies that, although the amount of the agreed franchise surpasses the damage caused by the loss, the effects of its inclusion in the contract continue and its amount will be deducted from the total to compensate. In this line, the absolute franchise is similar to the compulsory overdraft, but the great difference between one and the other institute is that they answer to different objectives; the compulsory overdraft cannot be subject of other insurance, whereas the franchise can, except otherwise agreed.[20]

Some concepts before concluding this subject: at the beginning of this paragraph, it was indicated that the two judicial creations being analysed have different denominations due to a historical reason. That has been motivated by the practice of the constant use of their names in the market in one or another way. There is no reference, in our legislation, to any of such significant creations or, even incidentally, some characterization thereof.

In our business, there has not been – but exceptionally – opportunity to establish a concrete difference between one and the other possibility. Nevertheless – as it has

19. Picard et Besson, *Le contrat d'assurance*, vol. I, 305 (Paris: LGJD Press, 1974).
20. Y. Lambert-Faivre, *Droit des Assurances*, 9th ed., 565 (Paris: Dalloz).

just been seen – the effect of the franchise and the compulsory overdraft are different, due to the possibility of insuring them or not. This is due to the different reasons of their uses.

The overdraft, as it has been stated in the preceding text with other words, deep down, attempts to deliver a new dose of morality to insurance, originating – because of the possible prejudice that a loss could cause in the amount to be compensated – a behaviour of absolute good faith, since, having to support such compulsory overdraft, the insured is forced by its own convenience to comply with his salvage duties and even with those that may possibly prevent harmful events, which could cause losses.

The franchise, on the contrary, has its emphasis placed on what has been explained about good company administration avoiding the participation in minor damages that would force liquidation expenses proportionally high in relation to the average expenses estimated for the statistical purposes of the calculation of premiums.

Another concept that would be indispensable to notice is the criterion that must be a priority in the application of deductions in some types of insurance, as, for instance, civil liability insurance.

In our country, there is no compulsory civil liability insurance up to now. The exceptions being the civil liability insurance related to the use of motor vehicles with a low insurable limit amount and the ones derived from work risks, both with special systems, thus dispensed with for the explanation of this item. The reason for this is that compulsory insurance does not exactly participate in the nature of the insurance contract but in social insurance where the public interest has a special weight that, in our opinion, is not legally an insurance contract but a regulatory requirement that, by using totally or partially the insurance technique, resembles insurance contracts only in the forms or the purposes of reaching a reciprocity.

As it will be later on analysed in this outline of insurance law in Argentina – when different modalities of insurance contracts are analysed – the civil liability insurance contract, as section 109 of Act 17.418 states, is an insurance covering the risk which assumes such liability in the person of the insured and not of a third party. It protects as liabilities insurance, the property of the insured and no other insurable interest.

The assured amount that is established in said contract has the function of being the maximum limit, up to which the insurer covenants to hold the insured harmless, and it is compared with the amount of compensation to pay to the damaged third party (liabilities amount in charge of the insured) to the sole effect of establishing whether the amount to compensate is absolutely or only partly in charge of the insurer (the limit of the assured amount, amount on which the taker has paid the premium).

With what has just been said, it is intended to explain that the proportional rule *supra* has no application, as it is not possible to establish with certainty the insurable value, one of the terms of the equation. The proportion between the assured amount and the compensation to pay brings about a special proportionality regarding supplementary costs. Such thing occurs with the judicial costs and expenses that are met by the insurer with the same particularity as performed in relation to the amount to compensate the third party according to the contractual agreement.

In this case of civil liability, if an absolute franchise was agreed upon, by which, in case of surpassing the amount to compensate – regarding the assured amount – a reduction of the sum to pay by the insurer took place, the injured party – being the third in the insurance contractual relationship – could not expect to go for the remaining part of the compensation, that is, for the amount of the deducted franchise against the insurer.

In summary, we would like to emphasize two ideas that have been stated in previous paragraphs: (1) civil liability insurance is not a contract to the benefit of others but protects the insured's property within the limits of the contractual coverage; (2) franchise is deductible from the compensation to be satisfied in order to hold the property of the insured harmless.

Lastly, it is interesting to point out that, the same way franchises and overdrafts are habitually agreed upon on the basis of set amounts or determinable sums, by a percentage or fraction of the amount of the loss, they can also be agreed on the basis of another concept that turns out translatable into such amount. In this respect, we are thinking of the case of insurance for loss of benefits, for which a deductible percentage from the benefits of the first days after the occurrence of the loss of the risk is usually agreed upon, to which the insurance for the loss of profit is attached.

§5. Alternatives of the Insurable Interest

93. Non-existence and Disappearance of the Insurable Interest. During the development of the aforementioned items, reference was made to the need of the existence of the insurable interest in property insurance at the moment of occurrence of the loss, since without this lawful economic relation, an essential element of such contractual species would be missing. As we are dealing with a property relation between a person and property, naturally, when the insurable interest does not exist, the subject creditor of the compensation that the insurer would normally have to afford would not exist either. However, there would be impossibility of payment, which would bring about the extinguishment of the obligation for the insurer.[21]

We have also referred to the existence of the insurable interest at the moment of commencement of the effectiveness of the contract, as well as during the period of occurrence of the aleatory event. Our law, as many others, has regulated this situation on the basis of certain effects that would cause the non-existence, disappearance, or transfer of the insurable interest.

Section 81 of Argentine Act 17.418 establishes the need of the existence of the insurable interest at the moment of commencement of the effectiveness of the contract. It must be understood as commencement of the effectiveness of the contract to these effects, such commencement that initiates the coverage of the risk by the insurer (commencement of the material effectiveness). In this way, it lacks significance, and, in fact, it happens in many occasions that, at the formal commencement of the contract (when the agreement of wills takes place), there is no insurable interest in the taker or in the person proposed as insured.

21. Giuseppe Ferri, *Manuale de Diritto Commerciale,* 729 (Torino: UTET Press, 1965).

With everything that has been said, what is intended is to clarify the possibility of the existence of the insurable risk after the moment of agreement of wills, as long as it was agreed that the coverage initiates later on. This happens, for instance, in the floating or unvalued insurance as well as in the expected profit insurance, always attached to another type of insurance, and which insurable interest is the benefit that the insured expects to obtain from certain activity that could turn out to be interrupted by a loss alien to the subject matter of that insurance. Effectively, as we shall see in the respective chapter, it is noticed that it will only appear when such interruption takes place that, ultimately, coincides with the moment of material commencement of the start of coverage of the risk for the insurer.

As it has been underlined, the aforementioned regulation does not legislate by the principle of insurable interest, but for the effects that are produced by the inexistence of the insurable interest at the moment of commencement of effectiveness and those effects are centred on the obligation of the payment of the premium, from which the taker is released.

Consequently, when establishing via consequence that it does not correspond to pay the premium, it cannot be conceived the existence of an insurance contract. The law only establishes one responsibility towards the insurer in order to satisfy his expenses incurred, plus an additional of up to 5% of the premium that corresponded. The law states the reimbursement to the insurer of these amounts, but it does so in the sense of establishing his right to collect by means of a payment, whatever is the means or form used, making a concrete reference to the expenses effectively incurred and to an additional, which limit is equivalent to the value of 5% of the premium.

To our criterion, although the law states nothing about the contract itself, it seems obvious that the contract ceases to exist since it lacks at least two essential elements: the premium and the rendering of services by the insurer. On the one hand, because of the inexistence of the interest (typical of contract nullity) and, on the other hand, before the lack of essential elements, the contract must be rendered invalid.[22]

Nothing is stated in the law about the case of fraud or bad faith, something unnecessary to our judgment, since it does not seem logical that a taker carries out such type of contract with fraud since he would be prejudiced at every instance. Yet nothing would be an obstacle to the fact that, if the behaviour was fraudulent, the penalty of nullity was accompanied by damages since section 81 is not of the imperative type (or not repealable), and it should be supplemented by the adequate and pertinent regulations of the general part of the law.[23]

When the insurable interest disappears, after the commencement of the coverage, the insurer is entitled to collect the premium according to the provisions of section 41 of Act 17.418. The contract will not be invalid from the beginning since at that

22. Isaac Halperín, *Insurance* (*Seguros*) vol. II, updated by Juan Carlos Morandi 776 et seq. (Buenos Aires: Depalma Press, 1983) and especially its notes.
23. In this sense, the regulation – as part of the science of law – is not speculative, since neither is it the law that as science is directed to the orientation of life. J. Llambías, *Treaty on Civil Law Obligations* (*Tratado de Derecho Civil Obligaciones*) vol. II, 372 (Buenos Aires: Perrot Press, 1975).

moment there existed all the elements and they only disappeared after the commencement of the effectiveness of the coverage. Thus, the Act in the second part of its section 81 regulates the situation indicated as disappearance of the insurable interest. In its regulation – as it has been already expressed – the law rescues another regulation that has been provided for, in the matter of aggravation of the risk when the contract is terminated due to such cause and because of the decision of the insurer.

The Act, when establishing the disappearance of the insurable interest – which, incidentally, is not done by an imperative but dispositive regulation and thus can be otherwise agreed – provides for different solutions regarding the premium according to the behaviour of the taker. Regarding the contract proper, the disappearance of the insurable interest brings about its extinguishment.

It should be noticed that without insurable interest, property insurance would lack an essential element since it would occur if the risk was missing, and thus it would be extinguished. The insurance contract could only continue its effectiveness if the insurable interest disappeared in the person that turned out to be insured but appeared in another owner of such interest, a situation that should be judged under such circumstances and regulations and even more, it is a matter of certain specifications in section 82 of Act 17.418.

This difference stems from the fact that the insurer is obliged to render the services or not, depending on whether he had received timely notification of the disappearance of the risk, as section 41 clearly states.

What would vary on a case-by-case basis would be the determination of the appropriate moment for the notification to the insurer, due to the variety of situations that could appear, as well as the different external circumstances influencing the possible causes of disappearance of the interest. This disappearance of the insurable interest must be considered of absolute permanence regarding the contract. It brings about its extinguishment for the future but not for the past. The Act when establishing provisions for the case of timely notification and fixing the debt of the taker for the premium proportional to the elapsed time (the elapsed time of the risk) does not render it void. Nullity, consequently, is less present in the assumption of failing to timely notify, as the Act punishes the taker with the debt of the whole premium for the period in course.

Section 41 of the Act, to which section 81 refers us, in its second item regarding disappearance of interest, is closely related to section 40, which, when referring to the risk, provides for some effects of its aggravation that are not applicable to the case of disappearance of the insurable interest.

In fact, if the insurable interest is construed – as we have sustained – as an element essential to the contracts of property insurance, its disappearance must cause some effect on it. Such effect is the one already mentioned: the extinguishment of the contract for the future but not from its beginning, as this fact would affect the legal relationship that, at the moment of the agreement of wills, counted on each and every one of the necessary elements to be lawful.

However, such penalty could be greater if a greater prejudice was verified. Besides, the indirect knowledge that the insurer may have about the disappearance of the insurable interest would play a role in the notification of the taker, since, to our judgment, what is important is not the way of accessing the knowledge of disappearance but the knowledge of the situation proper, regardless of the informative means. It is clear that these two last matters shall be matters to be evidenced.

94. Transfer of the Insurable Interest. Within the subject we have started this chapter with, it is necessary to consider a special aspect: the transfer of the insurable interest, and also the attempt to clarify certain questions deriving from provisions of Act 17.418 that have been already quoted. We are making reference to the provisions established by section 13 when regulating the policy and, after that, those of Article VII, Title I, related to the rights of the taker and of the insured in the generic third-party insurance.

There are several situations that coexist in order to elucidate the problems that may arise from the situation under analysis, transfer of the insurable interest (insured) and that we will attempt to individualize and analyse:

(1) In the first place, it must be individualized what is understood by transfer of the insurable interest (insured). Be it noticed that in two preceding occasions we have inserted between parentheses the word 'insured'. That was so because the analysis is regarding the insurance in full force and, therefore, the interest is the concrete element of a specific insurance. By transfer of the insured interest, it must be considered the assignment of this lawful economic relation that may exist between a subject and a property, a relation that, as it has been stated, does not need to be ownership, but which must be sufficient in order to determine in the interested party the will to prevent a loss that may cause detriment to the economic value that links him to that property.

(2) In the second place, it must be established whether the transfer of the insurable interest implies a transfer of the insurance contract, so that it is established whether the new owner is the new insurer, and analyse the effects of the existing regulations.

(3) In the third place, in light of the regulations – together with the rest of the regulations in force in our country – it must be understood some of the first regulations we have advanced under a distinctive construction, rather than what a simple construction of their letter would incline us to:

    (a) When the insurance is about the insurable interest of a thing owned by the insured, the transfer of property, that is, the sale of that thing, in turn carries the loss of the insured interest as this is sustained on the property right and once this right is lost, there is no insurable interest for such ownership without prejudice of having another insurable interest for another coexistent and different reason (mortgagee or pledgee, user, tenant, etc.).

When the right to the insurable interest derives from another cause than the ownership of a thing, the loss of such ownership – of the person holding the title of owner – does not bring about the loss of the right of the person holding the insurable interest derived from another cause as it happens in the cases of the mortgage property regarding the insured-creditor, from the pledgee in a similar assumption, or from the tenant of the sold real property.

(b) The hypothesis that matters to this part of the insurance contract is the transfer of the right that gave rise to the insurable interest and that has supported an insurance contract, thanks to such interest.

The first answer to the first question stated in the preceding item (2) must have a negative answer. The sole transfer of the insurable interest does not produce at all the transfer of the insurance contract that is attached to it. The owner of the insurable interest is free to assign it or not, but from there to oblige its co-taker, the insurer, to have a new counterpart in the insurance contract, a third-party alien to him or, in other words, to produce the effect of novation on the insurance contract, there is a great gap that can be tempered by certain special characteristics that, due to legislative policies, a legislator may introduce in the institute of novation.

The problem is that, still pending of occurrence the random event in an insurance contract, for the insurer, in principle, one debtor is not identical to another, although from the duties (burdens) standpoint that is not complied with, a penalty would apply and forced compliance could not be claimed. Without going any further into the subject, there could also still remain the obligation of the taker and, by extension, of the insured to pay at least a part of the premium.

The regulations of our Insurance Contracts Act contained this very generalized criterion that, although right, separates the voluntary change of ownership of the insurable interest from the change caused by death and, although it is not contemplated, the donation assumption of the thing or property on which the assured interest is laid, it is our thought that, as it is a voluntary, calculated, and foreseeable act, it must be regarded as not absorbed by testamentary succession but by the changing of interest regulated in the first part of section 82.

What is true is that section 82 requires the notification to the insurer whenever there has been a change in the owner of the insurable interest (transfer). This notification obviously cannot be prior to the event since the preparatory acts or measures of negotiation that may or may not end in the transmission of the insurable interest are not important, but the fact itself, that is, the moment when the insured interest on a property is transferred. This moment will depend on the provisions for each case provided for by law, regarding the intervening parts for its performance and not third parties.

That is why Act 17.418, in keeping with other precedents and even regulations after it, provides that the notification shall be carried out within seven days (if a longer period is not stated due to the type of regulation) and that the insurer could be released from responding for the loss in case of its occurrence after fifteen days as from these seven days (or longer period), as agreed. With this, the Act means that it is agreed, even when the notification of transfer of the insurable interest has been omitted, there is a term of protection for the new owner of at least twenty-two days from the moment when the change takes place.

It must be noted, the different existing system, when comparing – in order to solve all doubts – the regulations regarding risk and insurable interest. This is due to the fact that, for the effects of the rendering of services of the insurer, the transfer of the insurable interest only has effects on the risk or moral hazard and not on the specific risk being covered. It turns out to be a more legal than technical element, and, in many types of insurance, the moral hazard is every time less taken into account, as it happens in insurance of massive distribution.

Here, in the matter of insurable interest, the obligation of the insurer is not suspended or extinguished, and the pending occurrence of the random event is not of extreme importance either, that is, whether the loss takes place or not as long as the term of notification to the insurer of the assignment carried out is complied with.

As it has been previously stated, the transfer of the insurable interest is a fact; occurrence cannot be informed to anybody in advance. First, it is necessary that it takes place. After that, it is natural the notification to the insurer of the agreement carried out by the insured since the insurer is party to the insurance contract and alien to the mentioned agreement.

Therefore, our Act 17.418, as starting point, after the transfer of the insured interest has taken place, establishes the term of seven days in order to carry out the corresponding notification to the insurer, unless it was otherwise stated in the contract. (Let us remember that it is a repealable regulation, but only to the benefit of the insured.)

Once the insurer has been notified of the transfer of the insurable interest, it is obvious that he must count on a period to express his approval of the change. Nevertheless, the Act changes the criteria and establishes that it is the obligation of the insurer to expressly state his will in the assumption or rejection of the proposal. This is one of the cases where silence on one part is interpreted as acceptance.

Section 82 first part specifically obliges the insurer to express about the termination, within a definite term of twenty days. If he does not do so, he remains linked to the new insured; that is, he remains attached to the contractual relationship transferred to the new owner of the insurable interest.

Even in the event of termination, the insurer is obliged to remain as such, fifteen days as from his notification, as such is the prior notice he must give.

On its part, the acquiring party of the insurable interest is not obliged to keep the relationship of the insurance contract taken by its predecessor. He can, in the term of fifteen days as from assuming the ownership of the insurable interest, reject the acceptance of the insurance contract and notify such event to the insured.

The effects of this decision are immediate. It should be noted that Act 17.418 (section 82, second item) uses an inappropriate expression. The regulation in question tells us that 'the acquiring party may terminate' as if it was already a party to the contractual relationship, which is absolutely inexact, as the contractual relationship is just being established between the acquiring party and insurer, once the term of twenty days that the insurer counts on to express his decision has elapsed.

The effects of the omission of notification to the insurer of the transfer in relation to a possible loss after the transfer are more tempered than the ones of aggravation of the risk caused by one's own action. When the insurer is not informed of the transfer of the insurable interest in the term of seven days from its occurrence, the insurer continues with his obligation to compensate for all losses, which occurrence was within the following fifteen days. As it has been rightly stated, ultimately there is subsistence for twenty-two days as from the day the transfer of the interest of the obligation of the insurer has taken place. It is worth underlining that the knowledge of the insurer of the lawful transfer of the insurable interest has the same effects as the notification.

Finally, it is worth insisting on the fact of the different regulation section 82 establishes for transfers of insurable interests for testamentary succession or by compulsory sale. In the first assumption – testamentary succession – neither the heirs (legitimate or testamentary) nor the legatees are affected by the regulations that have been analysed. They inherit from the deceased person in the insurance contract, and a communication to the insurer only shows a good administration.

In the case of compulsory sale (we are always referring to the insurable interest), the regulations provided for are applied, but the terms must be calculated as from the approval of the auction.

In all that relates to the effects upon premium, the law follows the general rules. In principle, whereas the acceptance of the insurer was not reached to continue with the contract with the new owner of the insurable interest, the taker continues to be obliged, and the law appoints the acquiring party as joint and several co-debtor of such interest.

If the insurer does not accept the situation and terminates (directly rescinds) the contract, the obligation of the taker shall cease with the resolution and the amount of the premium shall be proportional only to the time of the risk elapsed (compare section 82, third and fourth paragraphs).

95. Transfer of the Interest in the Insurance for Account of a Third Party. There is another problem in Act 17.418 that tends to generate some kind of confusion. It is the regulation referred to the insurance for account of a third party, directly related to the possibility of issuance, in property insurance, of policies to the order and to the bearer.

In the case of insurance for account of a third party, there are some provisions where the right to collect compensation seems to be linked, in case of a loss, to the holding or possession of the policy, and section 13 of Act 17.418 directly establishes that the transfer of policies – to the order or to the bearer – transfers rights (of the insured) to the insurer.

This introduces, in my opinion, a confusing idea about the characteristics of a policy as document, and demands a very careful construction of the related regulations.

There is no doubt that the agility that modern commercial traffic requires demands a great modification regarding insurance policies and their role within the general theory of documents and, more precisely, their categorization as negotiable instruments. But in order to do that, many conceptions of the current books of authority and of Argentine legislation should change since, according to the most appropriate theses, negotiable instruments are not of free creation.

Even then, the use that the commercial custom would give to a document that has the characteristics and functions of a negotiable instrument should be very carefully considered since this is not a 'laboratory creation' but an instrument that must be useful for those utilizing it as means.

If we literally consider the text of section 13 of Act 17.418, we shall notice that it starts by equalizing the effects of the documents to the order of those to the bearer, wiping the slate clean of all the corresponding books of authority since the sole transfer of them would bring about the transmission of rights to the insurer.

A policy to the order, at least to bring about the transfer of a right, according to the current Act of documents to the order, would require the endorsement as legitimizing demonstration thereof. In no way would it be acceptable to mix both species of documents in one gender, causing the endorsement to disappear.

Yet, beyond the conceptual mistake of the Act in equalizing both types of policies, to our understanding, the effect of attribution of rights in relation to the insurer cannot be reached by establishing who holds a policy to the order, duly endorsed by the insured. Something of more significance is needed, as it is the emerging right of the attribution to such subject of the ownership of the insurable interest.

Act 17.418 in this respect quite disorganized advances on the general theory of negotiable instruments, mixing principles of legitimation – that is, the function by which it is attributed to a person in due possession – the possibility of exercising the literal and autonomous rights emerging from the document.

The lawful possessor of a negotiable instrument (the policy does not constitute one in our law) that is not necessarily the owner of the right is legitimized to demand compliance with the obligation. This obligation could be a monetary obligation or an obligation in kind (rights that emerge from a share of a corporation). At the same time, the document produces an effect of passive legitimation in relation to the debtor that is released when complying with his obligation to pay.

Therefore, in the documents to the bearer, the function of active legitimation is considered enabled regarding a person if, possessing the document, he presents it and exhibits it so as the person obliged complies with his obligation. In the documents to the order, the requirements, apart from the ones seen before, are the uninterrupted chain of endorsements and the evidence of identity of the person presenting them, which must coincide, also, with the last endorsee or be after a blank endorsement. Finally, the nominative documents also often require the registration of the successive transfers in the book of the issuer, an operation that is known as 'transfer'.

When the Act in its section 13 establishes that the transfer of a policy (document) brings about the transmission of the rights to the insurer, it is only validating a right of passive legitimation or, what is the same, the right of the debtor to be released if he pays to the person appearing as legitimated party, which is totally different from the active legitimation that produces on the debtor the obligation to pay.

Then again, the insurance policy that documents an insurance contract is not a document or negotiable instrument with an active legitimation function, but – though it possesses great affinity with negotiable instruments – it only renders an effect of passive legitimation, or, in other words, the payment carried out to the person that adequately and legitimately possesses the document releases the good faith debtor, who, nevertheless, may require of the assumed creditor the evidence of the ownership of his right.

Thus, in the case of a contract of property insurance, documented in a policy to the bearer, the good faith insurer paying to the person that shows the policy he possesses would be released, but he might as well require this person to demonstrate the evidence of ownership of the insurable interest. In this sense, section 13 of Act 17.418 establishes the demurrers and pleas in bar that can be entered against the holder of the policy. Among them, there are the ones against his person, the objective ones, and the ones that could have existed against the insured and other intermediaries since the manner of transfer of the insurable interest is via credit assignment, applicable even to certain kinds of endorsement (section 1456 of the Civil Code).

Finally, it is worth considering that, not being an imperative rule, section 13 and its modification, the substitution or non-utilization, is in keeping with the powers of the contractual agreement. Regarding the modification, let us remember the impossibility of creating by agreement of the parties a document of the category of negotiable instrument or of altering its characteristics and legal effects.

96. Insurable Interest and Life Insurance. Hans Möller, quoted by the Spanish Garrigues in this subject,[24] sustained that the insurable interest can only be significant in insurance against damages, whereas, on his part, Tulio Ascarelli – as recalled by Garrigues – and according to a work included in the Studi in tema di contratti, contrarily sustained that without insurable interest insurance would not be socially or technically possible since the beneficiary would become the perpetrator of the loss in order to profit with the compensation.

The two opposed extreme situations are sufficiently definite and clear in order to point out the profound differences that surround this subject, with the exception of the sustainers of the theory of compensation, according to the new formulation of Antígono Donati and also Viterbo and Butaro. These authors have denied in life insurance any idea of compensation, and thus they have placed it away from the aforementioned concept of insurable interest.

In order to save the moral note on Tulio Ascarelli's remark – regarding the temptation of the insured or the beneficiary to cause the loss – modern law has required in certain situations the written consent of the insured. It must be remembered that this is the title that has been denominating the person who bears the risk (*see*, for instance, section 128, third item, of Argentine Act 17.418). In the same sense, there appears section L 132-2 of the French Act.[25]

The inapplicability to life insurance of the concept of insurable interest, a typical element of property and things insurance, renders inapplicable the ideas that have been developed upon the effects of such principles. Thus, the assumptions of underinsurance and overinsurance are not present at all in life insurance, since in this type of insurance, the assured amount has as its only consequence to establish the amount of the obligation to which the insurer has committed in the case of occurrence of the risk.

In order to underline more cases of institutes of this kind in property or non-life insurance applicable to the species of life insurance, assessed value and third-party insurance can be mentioned. When the different types or species of life insurance are treated in more depth – which will be carried out *infra* – more considerations on the subject shall be made.

---

24. Joaquín Garrigues, *Land Insurance Contract* (*Contrato de Seguro Terrestre*), 2nd ed., 129, n. 8 (Madrid, 1983).
25. *See* 13th ed. of the Act (Paris: L'Argus Press, February 1995).

97. *Plurality of Insurance.* The plurality or accumulation of insurance is present when, as our law points out, more than one insurance contract with different insurers takes place protecting the same risk, the same insurable interest, as long as there is temporal coexistence. This situation is different, although with certain affinity, to the one of co-insurance, in which, at the same time, several insurers combine jointly to insure the same risk, generally for a very important amount to be afforded by only one insurer.

Plurality of insurance requires: (a) identity of the insurable interest, either regarding one thing or regarding a responsibility of the insured; (b) identity of the risk, subject matter of the different contracts; (c) plurality of insurers; (d) simultaneity of the contracts, that is, that all of them produce the same effects if the loss takes place.

In principle, the Act does not prohibit the possibility of taking out cumulative insurance, as long as the situation is notified to all insurers involved without further delay. This notification must contain the indication of all the contracts agreed upon, the assured amount of each of them, and, although the Act (section 67) does not say so, there is no obstacle to include the specific references to the existence of some clause conditioning the principle of compensation (proportional rule) – as the clause of first risk would be.

The omission of the notification to the insurers is punished with the expiration (section 67). The Act does not indicate to which expiration it is making reference, if to the complete set of rights of the insured, or only to the ones in relation to the insurers that have not been notified. The penalty of expiration of all the contracts would be too extreme and contrary to the nature of the protection of interest. Thus, in our judgment, the omission of the notification not provided on account of the lawful knowledge that the insurer should have of the situation should bring about the expiration of the rights of the insured regarding the contracts agreed upon with insurers that have suffered the omission, without affecting the obligation of paying the premium and, in case of a loss, the guideline of the second part of section 67 shall apply, considering those contracts as effective.

This consideration about effectiveness, in fact, tends to prevent conduct from the insured that may result in the prejudice of the insurers or of one of them in particular, as would be the case of the termination of certain contracts on the insured's will or even in the assumption of failure of some insurer (a case that would be classified as alien to the insured's will), every time that – as Halperín reminds us – the insured in such state or in a similar one with the same effects, would continue to be debtor, although his debt was restricted to bankruptcy currency.[26]

The intention of the Act arising out of the article entitled Plurality of Insurance is preventing that the insured attempts to avoid the regulations on insurable interest since it is related to the possible insurable value. Thus, the insured does not go away from the institute of compensation and turns the insurance into a source of profitability.

By means of plurality of insurance, overinsurance could be concealed, in violation of the related provisions, as it is established and punished in section 68 of the same Act. Therefore, and preventively, we are dealing with this type of regulation,

26. Isaac Halperín, *Insurance* vol. VII, 807, n. 116 (Buenos Aires: Depalma Press, 1983) (quoting Vivante).

which imposes the conduct of notification that, once complied with permits in case of a loss, the maintenance of the proportional rule as primary effect of the comparison – as we have seen – between the assured amount and the value of the insurable interest at the moment of such loss.

When a plural insurance is taken out for an assured amount superior to the amount of the damage consequence of the loss, the insured cannot claim a compensation superior to such actually experienced damage, and if, in order to carry out the plural insurance, there was the intention of unduly enriching himself, all the contract carried out in this manner shall be declared null and void.

Section 68 of Act 17.418 establishes the penalty of nullity in relation to the contracts so intended and, at the same time, for those insurers of the annulled contracts, the right to collect the premiums for the corresponding period of insurance. Apart from this, it establishes the express penalty of expiration of the right of the insured to collect the proportional part that would have corresponded to pay to the insurer or insurers of the annulled insurance since the intentionality provided for in section 67 remains effective.

If the insurance was agreed upon not acknowledging a previous one, the insured, with the intention of correcting or reorganizing the situation of plurality of insurance caused by his ignorance, may require the termination of the most recent contract or the reduction of its assured amount, with decrease of the proportional premium of the case, up to the real value of the assured amount.

The two cases that have just been analysed are mentioned by section 69 of Argentine Act 17.418, which admits the solutions indicated with premium deduction in the case of either termination of the contract or reduction of the amount, as long as it is adopted the conduct of acting 'immediately after having had knowledge of the prior insurance contract' and 'before the occurrence of the loss'.

Finally, it is worth mentioning the situation of plurality of insurance contract when they are entered into simultaneously. The concept of simultaneity must be understood in reference to the agreement of wills that took place in relation to the temporality of the moment (in a same day), considering this as the shortest space of time countable in civil terms. Time differences in the same day will not be taken into account.

It is clear that this reference is made in relation to contracts in which the insurable interest exists at the moment of agreement of wills since, if the insurable interest did not exist at that moment, the simultaneity would be extinguished at the moment of commencement of the material effectiveness of the contract. Refer in this sense to the beginning of this chapter, where the need of existence of commencement of the effectiveness of the contract (material effectiveness) of the insurable interest was established.

Act 17.418, in the last part of its section 69 referring to simultaneous contracts, agrees upon the ignorance of the taker and establishes a repealable regulation by agreement of the parties: the right of the insured to the reduction, on a proportional basis, of the assured amounts.

Two clarifications: the first is regarding the reduction on a pro rata basis; this is because we are dealing with the insurable value of the interest in question; the second is that this right of reduction can only be exercised before the loss.

Chapter 6. Technical Elements Used to Avoid Excesses

98. Co-insurance. This subject is frequently dealt with as a technical element, a contributory factor to the insurance economic activity, with the purpose of maintaining the homogeneity of assured amounts, and not to exceed the insurers' corresponding retention limits.

This last item, as we know, allows insurers to accept businesses for insurable interests, even superior to those that could be established for each of them, since they produce homogeneous minimizing effects on the assured amounts, retained as limit of their obligation to compensate, in the case of occurrence of the loss. Now co-insurance shall be seen from its legal aspect, as an admitted contractual form that resembles multiple insurance, although it is well differentiated and as it will be appreciated.

The appearance of this technical and legal modality was a means to avoid the insurance from becoming a speculative operation. It also was aimed at helping the commercial need of those that started to operate in business as professionals so as not to lose the important business they could not access. Otherwise, the payment of great sums of money would have brought imbalance to their business if they had assumed the great risks exceeding their economic coverage capacity on their own. It appeared in the first times of insurance, during the commencement of the business in the Mediterranean sea towards the end of the Middle Ages, when once the fights characterizing the late Middle Ages had been eased, the most influential port cities started to make incursions more organically into the insurance activity.

Those were the times when the basic principles were established for the development of the business as profitable means of exercising a type of commerce. The subject will be dealt with, starting with a reference to the name co-insurance. In this order of ideas, co-insurance is a way of taking out insurance or, in other words, a way of carrying out an insurance contract, in which the different insurers have agreed to satisfy the taker by participating with a defined percentage in the obligations that could arise from the loss – if it occurred – and by participating proportionally in their corresponding share of the premium to be paid by the taker. In both cases, what is habitual is not to agree to a joint and several responsibility.

In the day-to-day practice in the Argentine market – as there is no legal provision establishing guidelines or system – the way to proceed is the following: first comes the proposal of coverage of a risk to an insurance company; later on, this one will establish the convenience or need of co-insuring such coverage; then, there comes the adoption of an adequate conduct in order to determine what is called the reinsurance frame, that is, which companies of the trade will be offered to participate with a proportional quota share that is previously fixed in order to carry out the agreement of wills, together with the taker of the insurance.

The company that has been required and that, in turn, proposed the agreement to the co-insurers receives in general a distinctive name to differentiate it from the others as, although the obligations before the insurer shall not be faced jointly and severally, to this 'first' company is granted – by the other companies taking part – some powers in the tasks of administration for the collection of the gross premium or in the relationships with the insured as, for instance, the representation before the event of the notification of the loss and, finally, the representation in the payment of such loss. There is an old custom in the Argentine market of calling the 'lead' company the original insurance company proposing the co-insurance.

A sole policy that documents the co-insurance is issued by the lead company and in relation to the taker of the contract, establishing the quota by which each one of the different insurers will participate and assume their obligation regarding a possible loss. This copy of the contract is signed by each and every one of the insurers taking part.

It is possible that, responding to an internal organization, each insurer issues a policy, reflecting only his part of the contract, and keeps it in his documents without taking this public status and as mere support to his account-keeping. The communications, notifications, and requirements that the insured or the taker must carry out to the insurers will suffice if they are notified to the person representative of the lead insurer, establishing in the policy his representation to such effect.

In matters of maritime insurance, the Argentine Navigation Act, in its section 413, legally establishes the representation, even the judicial representation. It is necessary to clarify that our Act 17.418 does not establish any regulations regarding co-insurance. Thus, for Halperín, the author of the preliminary draft of 1959 and maximum precedent of the Act, co-insurance is a form of plurality of insurance. Notwithstanding that the name co-insurance is used in the sense we have been referred to in the legal language of many countries, in particular those with Roman-Latin tradition, and even when it turns out to be very common regarding other countries alien to this conception, as the United States of America, it cannot be affirmed that the term is a univocal term as it has been very well recalled by Muñoz Paredes,[27] since, in the United States of America, England, and some countries of Europe, the word 'co-insurance' also reflects the idea of a contract in which the insured could oblige himself to afford the damage caused by a loss jointly with the insurer, or assumptions in which many people (or interests) are covered by the same contract, or, as it happens in Spain, where reference is made to agreements between regional health assistance companies.

The legal feature that has certain affinity with the contractual modality we are dealing with is the one that has been mentioned as multiple insurance that, at the same time, we have denominated with the concept of plurality of insurance in order to adequate it to Act 17.418. Nevertheless, this affinity is only formal as it gives certain appearance of similarity in insurance on insurable interests, that is, property or things but not in insurance of the person, more precisely, life insurance, where the concept of insurable interest does not exist, as it has been seen and it shall be seen again when they are analysed.

Therefore, the lawful cumulative plural insurance has certain similarity with the co-insurance in the species of property insurance – as the element of the insurable interest – of indispensable existence in this species of insurance contracts.

In a truly witty phrase that has later on been profusely repeated by the German books of authority, Ehrenzweig in order to markedly differentiate both modalities said that, from the point of view of the insurers, the multiple insurance is a 'get

27. José María Muñoz Paredes, *Coinsurance* (*El Coaseguro*) 34, n. 14 (Madrid: Civitas Press, 1996).

together' and the co-insurance is an 'act together', in clear reference to the fact that the first is created by an initiative of the taker of the contracts, whereas the second has its origins in the insurers.[28]

However, it is necessary to take into account that the Argentine Act 17.418, when regulating on the plurality of insurance, does it so from the standpoint of property insurance, and the reference to the insurable interest is direct.

99. Co-insurance, Pools, and Clubs. It can be noted that, from what has been said up to now, the feature of insurance – by means of co-insurance – is basically a means of taking out insurance and not an end proper. It is the reflection of the collaboration among several insurers that covers the same risk, in different amounts that are established according to certain business guidelines, with the technical purpose of homogenizing the assured amounts.

It will not be overlooked by the reader that this business collaboration presents itself in day-to-day life with more frequency in certain companies among themselves than in relation to others, and, in consequence, it is usual that co-insurance agreements appear with certain specificity among habitually commercially related companies. The motivation can be different, according to the multiple cases that the ongoing operations may present. It is precisely due to such a repeating pattern of a community of commercial operations that the personal knowledge of the officers administering them, as well as the differentiation that specifically arises from the commercial/business aspect with reference to solvency, security, and trust, highlights, in the course of time, those relationships that could have been started slowly, as a business trial by the subscription of certain risks in a co-insurance.

Finally, the offering and even the acceptance of the subscription of the risks of the contracts that one of the insurers contributes to the portfolio and, surely, the reciprocal behaviour with others becomes something usual, automatic, or almost automatic reception, establishing with certain detail the obligations and rights in the co-insurance offered by each one of the insurers linked by this agreement.

The aforementioned agreement may or may not be established in writing, and it can even be made compulsory for the insurers, as long as the taker of the insurance proposing it to one of the linked parties agrees on the modality.

This way of operating commercially is very similar to the feature of pool, although the term 'pool' is used in the books of authority to define those that take out reinsurance.

In our opinion, there is no reason for any distinctive note that permits such exclusivity, except for one typical of reinsurance contracts stemming from their legal independence from insurance contracts, which it 'protects'. The taking out of reinsurance is free for the insurer regarding the election of the reinsurer since it does not need the agreement of each insured and, in co-insurance, the will of the taker is absolutely indispensable.

That is why reinsurance pools are formed by reinsurers, with or without a specifically typified association, and the insurers are obliged to assign to such pools their risks in reinsurance.

---

28. *Ibid.*

We do not see any clear difference between the co-insurance which we have been describing and the actions of the co-insurers' pool, as the latter does not have any difference in practice, with an insurance company that has as purpose to operate in co-insurance in an organic form, defining limiting guidelines.

The fact that a pool of insurers in order to subscribe risks in co-insurance turns out to be operatively established externally and publicly, and that the insurers, or only some of them, reciprocally assume the powers by means of their specific powers in order to subscribe on behalf of the pool members and with their mention, establish the proportions of such insurers, does not alter the situation.

In Argentina, there have existed some pools of co-insurance as, for instance, those covering risks derived from motor vehicle driving and others from aircraft risks as the one called Aircraft Insurers (Aseguradores de Aeronavegaci6n) which, curiously, acted in practice, as a sole insurance company, as if they have obtained the authorization of the SIN.

In reference to the clubs, we have just mentioned them in order to introduce their subject, but there cannot be any confusion regarding their operation and insurance. It is our opinion that they are a form of association, absolutely different from insurance and unmistakable with the subject matter of our purpose here. Clubs are associations or mutual associations, the purpose of which is the protection under such associative system of the club members that have suffered damages non-insurable by the maritime insurance contract or coming from important overdrafts, especially those derived from civil liability, always within the same field of maritime law.

They are the P&I (protection and indemnity) clubs which our already-disappeared official reinsurer, the National Institute of Reinsurance (INDER), inexplicably granted the reinsurance coverage.

100. The Legal Structure of Co-insurance. The problem that has been already mentioned in the legal structure of co-insurance is to elucidate whether, between the taker and the different intervening co-insurers, there exists a sole contractual relation with joint obligations or, on the contrary, whether there are as many contracts and obligations emerging among them as insurers take part.

It is worth pointing out that the books of authority of our country, in general, have avoided considerations of any type regarding co-insurance, especially the one mentioned under this title.

Also in Spain the matter has not been dealt with in depth, sharing our opinion is Mr José María Muñoz Paredes in the sense that, possibly, such circumstance has been due to the fact that the co-insurance has not deserved much attention from the legislator, surely because the field of action of this form of taking out insurance has traditionally been related to great risks, and thus it is alien to the types of risks with political ends of the given legislator.

The reality, before the evolution of customs and the extension of the field of co-insurance, sometimes because of the alterations and changes to the criteria to economically evaluate the concept of great risks and, sometimes, due to reconsiderations of technical order, makes it necessary to establish new concepts regarding co-insurance and attempt to review the conceptions that almost by gravity 'fall down' from traditions of great masters of other times.

The purpose of this introduction is to alert to the need of making efforts to think of constructions that we could reciprocally formulate, in order to solve these problems, as the existing precedents shall only guide our methodology and some possible conclusions.

In this sense, it is natural that the positions of those who have devoted to solving the problems set out may be classified as: (a) those who have conceived some sort of pluralist theory, that is, those that sustain that the contracts that exist when there is co-insurance are multiple; and (b) those that, on the contrary, have established a sole contractual relation.

It is not necessary that we clarify that, in this matter, the instrumentation of the agreement or agreements, that is, the existence of one or several insurance policies, has no relevance. The problem stems from the legal relation.

Among the ones of pluralist tendency, we can notice the presence of those who sustain the pluralism of legal relationships in the fact of non-existence of joint and several liability among the insurers as, due to the fact that association is always the rule, solidarity is only a possibility of reality; thus, they gather in pluralism due to positive provisions of the law of their countries that, as principle, regulate the obligations divisibly, that is, in the sense of generating independent obligations different from each other.[29]

At the same time, among the defenders of this pluralist position, there are authors that with less dogmatic postures and with full legal support have sustained – as grounds – that, as there is no 'person' in co-insurance, there is no contract between the taker and the co-insurance, but there are several contracts that create plural relationships among the taker and the co-insurers.[30]

It is clear that, between these two extreme positions, there are, apart from the ones synthetically explained, others that hold different principles in the intermediate ground, emphasizing the efficient cause of the contractual modality or the feature of pluralist acts tending to the creation of a sole contract.

In our opinion, there is no easy answer, and the regulations and the theory of simply joint obligations and joint and several obligations, as well as divisible and indivisible obligations, must be further analysed. Yet, the drawing of a conclusion of permanent validity in all cases is not very clear. On the contrary, we believe that a generalization is impossible, and the problem shall be to solve each case as, depending on the specifications of the contract, thus shall be the result.

In any case, it must be taken into consideration that: (a) co-insurance is not a type of insurance contract but a form or manner of taking out; (b) the obligations that generate the taking out of insurance in co-insurance are as many as there are parts

29. Rodrigo Bercovitz, *Divisible and Indivisible Obligations* (*Las obligaciones divisibles e indivisibles*), 507 et seq. (Madrid: Civil Law Yearbook, 1973).

30. Jean Bigot, '*Revue Générale des Assurances Terrestres*', *L'Argus*, 27 Dec. 1991, 3588 et seq., and *id*., 2 Jul. 1991. The article published in *L'Argus*, under the title '*Quel status pour la coassurance*', is even more fantastic, since the reasoning is very simple and he arrives at no other solution but to follow in a Cartesian style the consequences that stem from the fact that co-insurance is not a species of insurance but a form to insure, or in other words, to take out insurance. For further reading *see* René Rodiere & Emmanuel Pontavice, 677 (Paris: Droit Maritime, Dalloz, 1986).

involved; (c) the obligations assumed by the insurers are not joint, as neither the laws contemplate this typology nor the books of authority arising out of this type of obligation seem applicable.

Regarding the possibility of a special agreement, establishing the joint liability of the insurers, as it has been advanced, is a question merely depending on a theoretical possibility and of a lab essay speculation, as joint liability threatens the primary reason of co-insurance, which is the atomization of the distribution of the risk, to reduce the possible responsibility of an insurer to adequate technical limits. On the joint responsibility path, such responsibility would be increased when assuming the obligation of the other insurer or insurers.

Finally, it must be understood that: (d) the obligations the insurers assume are essentially divisible, both in nature and intellectually. In other words, in co-insurance and in relation to the obligations that the insurers undertake regarding the insured, we could consider them in the light of Argentine law as obligations of plural subject, as there is unity of subject matter and cause but, at the same time, a plural passive subject (debtor) that is simply joint and divisible, concerning either the energy of the denomination or the nature of its subject matter.[31]

From these general principles arise some consequences that are applied in day-to-day practice in co-insurance. For instance:

(1) The debt in the case of loss that each co-insurer assumes is agreed within the co-insurance frame, that is, the contract. If the terms and conditions did not say anything, the assumption of a debt would be in equal parts. In any case, it must be respected the consequences derived from an underinsurance or over-insurance if not otherwise agreed since the general system is not altered.
(2) Although there is a sole subject matter and a sole cause of the taking out, the relationships are multiple because their subjects are multiple, and thus there would be as many different credits and debts as relationships were constituted.
(3) The terms established by insurance law for the insurer to make a decision on the insured rights and the payment and, in order to file any demurrers, are independent regarding each co-insurer. The same happens to file the motion to dismiss.
(4) In general, except for some special regulations contained in the Insurance Act 17.418 regulating on a subject specifically, the regulations of the Argentine Civil and Commercial Code shall apply, which contain obligations with multiple subjects of the type simply jointly and divisible.

It is almost unnecessary to clarify that the same regulations apply regarding duties and obligations of the insured and the taker, and regarding the payment of the premium. The taker owes each insurer the part established in the co-insurance frame, that is, in the contractual agreement. What has been pointed out is no obstacle for, in order to simplify things, the lead co-insurer is granted specific powers by the co-insurers related to certain acts, such as the collection of the premium,

31. We agree with the theory of J. Llambías, *Civil Law Treaty* (*Tratado de Derecho Civil*), *Obligations II-A*, 369 et seq (Buenos Aires: Perrot Press, 1975).

the issuance or reception of notifications, and complying with specific duties, obligations, or positions that are provided for by several provisions of the Argentine Insurance Act 17.418.

There is no change in the nature of the obligations assumed, but in the granting of a specific representation for certain acts.

An important point that remains to be analysed is co-insurance in life insurance. Strictly, the principles are the same as the ones mentioned, as co-insurance is not a type or species of insurance but a form of taking out insurance. In life insurance, as it has been pointed out, it is possible to take out insurance under the form of co-insurance, with the simple and correct application of the same conditions, except for those mentioned that, due to their nature, belong only to property insurance.

A new final statement in order to solve any doubts: the co-insurance has been preferably explained in keeping with the customs and traditions existing in Argentina. There is nothing that prevents its transformation either on account of the lack of imperative regulations in this respect or because of the determining fact that, being a way of carrying out an insurance contract, the needs vary and change their expression.

101. Subsidiary Insurance. There is the possibility of taking out insurance with plurality of insurance, as long as one or more of the insurers involved respond only as a subsidiary, or when the damage experienced by the insurable interest exceeds a specific amount, always within the value of the insured interest as maximum.

The old Argentine Code of Commerce, in its section 521, in other words but in the same sense, established a regulatory principle equivalent to the one that has been just stated and that contains the last part of section 67 of Act 17.418.

Fernández,[32] when commenting on the aforementioned repealed section, reminds us of the assumptions of insolvency of the first insurer (thus, he describes it as insolvency insurance) or of a damage exceeding the assured amount (underinsurance) and at the same time reminds us that, on his part, Rivarola called it supplementary insurance.[33]

The Insurance Act 17.418 places the regulation within the section dedicated to plurality of insurance, as an exception to the prohibitive principle contained, generically, in the text of the two first items of the aforementioned section 67.

The situation to which he is referring as subsidiary insurance is not the same, since even when in subsidiary insurance there are certain similar elements partially present or equal to the existent in cases of plural insurance, there is a distinctive circumstance that prevents that the insured may, under any circumstances, avoid the criterion of compensation of the property insurance.

It is our opinion that the rendering of services in subsidiary insurance – which possible debtor is different – does not belong to the category of obligations with plural or multiple subject matters, and thus it cannot be included as alternative obligation and, less so, as optional obligation, as the Argentine Civil and Commercial Code does.

---

32. Raymundo L. Fernández, *Commented Commercial Code* (*Código de Comercio Comentado*), vol. II, 460 (Buenos Aires, 1950).
33. The quotation is from a traditional and excellent Argentine teacher of commercial law.

It is our belief that the rendering of services of the insurer emerging from the subsidiary insurance is of the category of conditional obligation since it does not deal with the election of a service but with the uncertainty of the existence of the compliance of such service originating the subsidiary insurance, being this uncertainty, the fact that establishes the external condition of the relationship.

In subsidiary insurance, there is a condition for its existence, the subsidiary responsibility of the insurer or insurers, that is, to replace or strengthen the main obligation of the originary insurer or insurers.

In other words, the subsidiary insurance is subject for its effectiveness to the condition of 'going to help' after the failure of the main insurer.

For Halperín[34] it is more about an insolvency insurance that, although our law does not provide for, in relation to which cases and how the liability of the subsidiary insurer would be judged, his silence or allegation of impossibility of payment would suffice since, due to the occurrence of the property damage, the insured would be in a much more serious need.

On the contrary, if the main insurer filed demurrers against the insured, the matter should be judged on a case-by-case basis.

34. Isaac Halperín, *Insurance* (*Seguros*), vol. II, 807 with commentary by Juan C. Morandi (Buenos Aires: Depalma Press, 1983).

Chapter 7. Insurance and Third Parties

102. Characteristics of Argentine Law. In many legal systems, this subject is significant, so much so as to be established as one of the two matters that drew the attention of the tenth World Congress of Insurance of AIDA, which took place in Marrakech from 11 May 1998 to 15 May 1998.

As from the Sydney Congress in 1994, the item required several clarifications, among those forming the Council of Presidency of AIDA, precisely because of the acquisition of diverse characteristics and positions of third parties, according to the contents of the different national regulations.

That is why even the terminology to be used included words such as 'beneficiary', of different meanings in different countries, which was of remarkable importance to the extent that the subject to be analysed by the host country in 1998 was 'The Beneficiary of the Insurance Policy'.

A very valuable source, in order to study in detail the existent situation of the matter in different countries of the world, is the compilation of national reports edited by the Association Internationale du Droit des Assurances in 1998. Another report worth reading is Professor Jérome Kullman's on behalf of the French representation of AIDA.

In this same monograph, in Part II, Chapter 1, when dealing with certain generalities of the insurance contract, reference was made to the different individuals taking part in the insurance contract, according to the roles they carry out.

The beneficiary in Argentine law, following the Latin-Roman tradition, is the person favoured or benefited by a contract or by an act of one's own or a third-party act.

In the case of insurance contracts, a beneficiary is the person that must collect the compensation, in the case of property insurance contracts or non-life insurance contracts, and the assured amount in life insurance contracts.

This does not alter the fact that, in property insurance contracts, in order to be beneficiary, it is an indispensable condition to be, at the same time, insured, that is, to hold the ownership of the insurable interest.

This effect that contracts in general – and insurance contracts in particular – produce in relation to those holding the relationship of beneficiary may take place when such individual is strictly a party to the legal relationship in question or when it is a third party.

The last assumption, that the person is alien to the parties, in the strict sense of such capacity, now passes to have a leading role as it is plainly related to the alteration of the principle of intangibility of the individual sphere, which may not be altered in any sense by an agreement among other people.

It is clear that this principle – respected with marked severity in the Napoleonic Code – would turn out to be excessively excluding regarding the person who, even having this third-party capacity, turns out to be the person benefited by the acts of the parties.

Those who in their national laws participate in the conception described in the previous paragraphs will draw the regulating conclusion that the intangibility of the rights of third parties, as alien to the effects of the contracts, is not applied with the same severity to the case of a promise in somebody else's benefit, since the contract is completely accepted and conceived as it is. Thus, the third party solely participates in the benefit, but not in any obligation that the parties would have imposed to it, except when such third party specifically accepted this last obligation.

It has been previously stated that, in insurance contracts, two other indispensable parties usually take part, as it is known, the insurer and insured. It has also been commented that this may be different in certain opportunities, without denaturalizing the insurance contract, as the insured may be left uncertain at the moment of the agreement of wills.

When starting the specific study of insurance called by Act 17.418 'for account of a third-party insurance', two situations must be pointed out:

(1) The first is that the generic denomination regarding the legal feature is 'insurance for account of a third party', which has, in turn, a concrete derivation, 'insurance for account of whom it may correspond', a scenario that provides a wider space and that is more utilized due to its versatility.
(2) The second situation is the subject that is profoundly linked to the corresponding insurable interest and, because of that, when analysing this topic, it is required to go back on certain common aspects frequently encountered.

To order the exposition, in first place reference will be made to the insurance for account of a third party of the species property insurance also called property, damages, and non-life insurance:

(a) In the property insurance for account of a third party, there is some sort of stipulation on behalf of and in the benefit of a third party. The taker does not invoke any representation, and he is not obliged to do so as, in that case, it would be a contract carried out by a representative, that is, on behalf of the represented party (ultimately, on the represented party's own account). In this property insurance for account of a third party, the stipulation is carried out by a person called taker or policyholder, as it has been seen, who will establish who the person insured is on whose behalf the contract shall be entered into.

Upon the occurrence of the loss, this third party shall demonstrate his insured capacity by means of the justification of his insurable interest, so that the insurance contract produces its benefit, the effects it was intended for.

Coming back to the beginning, we must insist on the fact that the independence regarding the relationship attached to the insurance contract concerns the individuals of the taker and the insured. The taker acts on its own but on behalf of another person or a third party that may be uncertain at the moment of the agreement of wills, but that may be specified and that is substantially determinable. This shall be seen with more detail when dealing with the insurance for account of whom it may correspond. It is worth categorically clarifying that this other individual or third party is not a commissioner or a consignor.

As a consequence of this lack of certainty of the insured at the moment of entering into the property insurance contract, the situation favours the possibility of transmission of the ownership of the insurable interest with less formality and without affecting the contract since, as it has been previously advanced, the identification of the insured, that is, the owner of the insurable interest in property insurance, shall be only necessary when the main rendering of services of the insurer is intended, that is, the payment of the compensation caused by the loss.

It must be clarified that there need not be any customary or legal power whatsoever in order to take out insurance for account of a third party. The reason why the taker acts in such capacity, that is, taking out on behalf of a third party, is not relevant to the insurance relationship.

Thus, on the same goods or personal or real property, different insured individuals may coexist or also have different insurable interests, although the risk/subject matter of the contracts may causally be the same in total or in a considerable part. This would be the risk, for instance, of damage to property by fire during the storage under the system of warehouse receipts and warrants.

This type of taking out is very common in certain activities in which the business person is liable for the property of others. Goods storage warehouses assume before their bailors the obligation of returning the goods in perfect state. As this obligation is compulsory in most of the assumptions, instead of insuring on their own account the economic liabilities caused by possible non-compliance as bailees, they insure on account of their lawful owners the goods subject matter of the different bailment contracts. The owners or managers of the warehouse act as takers of the insurance contract and the insured shall be those identified as owners of the insurable interest at the moment of occurrence of the loss.

In this example, besides, the taker may act due to a legal obligation that comes from the law of warrants, a commercial mechanism that has been recently resumed in Argentina.

The motivation of the taker to act in such manner does not matter to the effect of the insurance contract for account of a third party.

In a work in depth published many years ago,[35] in honour of Professor Garrigues, the insurance for account of a third party was differentiated from the insurance for account of whom it may correspond. The difference was sustained in the fact that in the former, the insured will never possibly be the taker, whereas in the latter, the taker could possibly be the insured if, at the moment of the loss, he has the insurable interest.

(b) The characteristic note of this type of insurance for account of a third party is that the interested party is someone different from the taker in his capacity as party, not in his capacity as person. In other words, the right to be insured derives substantially from the form of taking out performed by the taker or the policyholder,[36] joined to the ownership of the insurable interest at the moment of occurrence of the loss.

35. *Studies on Insurance Law* (*Estudios de Derecho de Seguros*), 259 et seq (Buenos Aires: Pannedille Press, 1971).

36. This is substantially the position of Garrigues expressed in page 71 of his aforementioned book, among others, in the preceding n. 51.

The legal nature of this specific type of contract is not exactly the same as in the 'insurance contract with stipulation in favour of another'; this is not only from our standpoint, under the provisions established by section 1161 corresponding to the Argentine Civil Code, but also from the standpoint of comparative law, since the ratification of such third party is not required at any point, as in the case of stipulation in favour of a third party.

This person effectively appears when he is invoked as insured, after the occurrence of a loss, but it is not strictly to ratify the originary insurance but to evidence his insurable interest, as it corresponds to do in all property and damage insurance.

However, the insurer may at no point – when the random event is pending unilaterally, except for the specific agreement admitted as generic by the Insurance Act in its section 18 – revoke his future promise, depending on the random event. In order to do so, without consequences of any nature derived from the insurance contract, he shall need to agree to the rescission with the taker or policyholder, without the need of requiring the agreement or ratification from the third party, who may continue to be uncertain.

Any assimilation intended, from a legal nature standpoint, to a commission or representation contract should be avoided.

It is a modern modality of contract, specific to insurance law, created from – as all commercial modalities – the usage and practice and, above all, the acceptance of its utilization in those practising it.

As new modality, its adaptation to the classic model of old forms regulated by law cannot be intended. It has, as it has been stated, its significant similarities with the insurance contract with stipulation in favour of another, but its differences are considerable, so as to make it fit within such sphere in an absolute way.

There is not even the possibility of a difference of gender or species, but it is about two genders of different modalities that may be linked only for explanatory or research purposes.

(c) Another distinctive note for insurance for account of a third party is provided by the fact that insurance cannot be arranged for the benefit of a person that is not the owner of the insurable interest at the moment of the loss. That means that if prior to the loss the appointment of a person as insured is clearly fulfilled but, later, it turns out to be that the person is not the owner of the insurable interest at the moment of the loss, the insurance shall not have the intended effect, as such holder is different from the person appointed insured.

Express reference is made about the exceptions to the assumptions of automatic transfer of the insurable interest – as it would be in case of heirs or the specific case in section 23 of Act 17.418, where transfer is made to the taker as long as the requirement of being in possession of the policy is fulfilled – as we shall see right away.

(d) Some specifications regarding the special situation of the taker and the insured appear in this modality of insurance contract. In all that has been analysed, reference was made to all the assumptions in which Act 17.418 places in the hands of the taker and the insured the compliance with obligations and burdens. To the ends of remembering the points, a list has been made: items of precontractual burden of information, misrepresentation in relation to section 10 last paragraph, obligation to pay the premium and payment by third parties and by compensation (section 27), aggravation of the risk by the taker's own or third-party act, and notification of loss.

Nevertheless, in the insurance for account of a third party, important innovations are made that deserve comment. As significant matter – in which the law is not very clear – there appears the matter of knowing exactly if any right on the compensation that the property or damage insurance brings about corresponds to the taker, which benefits the insured if the loss takes place.

Some paragraphs ago, it was mentioned section 23 as specific assumption of the granting of the right to claim compensation. Now, examining its contents more closely and comparing its two paragraphs, objections will be portrayed.

The Act in the first part of section 23 states that the taker may dispose in his own name of the rights arising out of the contract if he is in possession of the policy. With this expression, if accepted literally, a shocking exception to all the system supporting property and damage insurance will come to be introduced in our law, which is the lack of importance of the insurable interest – that has been expressly stated as an indispensable element in this type of insurance – and, subsequently, the absolute alteration of the consequences of the adoption of a universal and traditional principle incorporated to our law will follow.

Thus, the taker of an insurance for account of a third party, in the literal construction of the text of section 23, would not need in order to 'dispose in his own name of the right arising from the contract' of any other thing but the possession of the policy, which by itself does not establish the capacity of ownership of any insurable interest, and less so the concrete ownership referred to in the contract. Thus it is our opinion that the regulation contained in this first paragraph of section 23 must be interpreted otherwise and not literally.

The regulation that we are seeking, as appropriate, arises out of the second part of section 23 as, besides disposing in his own name of the rights arising from the contract, the taker is granted the right of collecting the compensation, but the insurer is empowered to require the evidence of acceptance of the insured, except for two circumstances that shall be analysed later on.[37]

In the first place, it is not possible to notice that the right to collect compensation turns out to be a plus over the expression 'the rights arising from the contract', that is, that this turns out to be a right alien to any other right arising from the contract, as collecting the compensation is the fundamental right agreed in a property insurance contract.

In the second place, the generic observation of granting to the policy qualities alien to the probatory document is sustained. We are specifically mentioning what

37. Section 23 of Argentine Act 17.418 states 'When in possession of the policy, the taker may dispose in his own name of the rights resulting from the contract. He might as well collect compensation but the insurer has the right to demand that the taker previously evidences the consent of the insured, unless the taker demonstrates that he took out the insurance by mandate of the latter or by virtue of a legal obligation.'

has been already pointed out in relation to the insured interest and, more seriously even, the change of this element by the possession of policy since this would grant the taker a substitute of that insured interest, which would be unacceptable as it favours a speculative traffic of insurance by turning it into a game.

It is not noticed, even coming back to the theory of titles of active legitimation, any aptitude of the insurance policy to actively legitimate the creditor. Another would be the matter in relation to the passive legitimation. Yet, in this case, we are not dealing with an assumption of passive legitimation, but a typical case of active legitimation as the literal construction would grant the right to claim the collection, without the need of demonstration of the insurable interest.[38]

Finally, the beginning of section 24 of Act 17.418 announces another topic very clearly, when stating that 'the rights deriving from the contract correspond to the insured if he possesses the policy'.

Everything leads to thinking that the literal construction of section 23 not only would take us to a contradiction in terms but also would violently clash with other regulations of the same Act and, above all, with regulations of a more generic nature that portray the right of the insured proper. The adequate construction of this regulation, in order to grant it functionality, is to consider the reality in which it may take place.

In this sense, the claim to collect the compensation on the insured's part in the insurance for account of a third party must go together with the demonstration of the ownership of the insurable interest at the moment of the loss. His right will be placed between taker and insurer and, obviously, it cannot exceed what has been agreed in the contract. Thus, he will be subject to the demurrers that the insurer may file against the taker, inclusively those related to non-compliance with burdens – such as declaration of status of risk, causing of loss, tardy notification, etc. – as well as other personal defences.

The insured could never be his own taker in the insurance for account of a third party since such a situation would not be other than the existent in an insurance for one's own account, distinguished behind the appearance of an insurance for the account of a third party, a fact unknown to the insurer.

It should be noticed that one situation is when the contract is about an interest that could never belong to the taker or that would always be alien to the taker, and the law has provided for it in answering to certain needs related to its use and application (such is the case of insurance for account of a defined third party); another situation is when a contract refers to an interest that may even be an own interest, but which shall remain uncertain up to the moment of claiming the compensation (insurance for account of whom it may correspond). May it be noticed that the position of the taker regarding duties and obligations is different from the insured's, as from the very same moment of entering into the contract.

---

38. Morandi, in the work mentioned in n. 52, wisely and knowledgably arrives at a solution on the literality of the text of s. 23. For that, he makes a difference between the idea of disposition of the rights of the contract and the concept of ownership of those rights, as if it was a negotiable instrument and an acquiring party *a non domino* (who has no title). The solution in my opinion is wrong, as it has been determined by the whole s. 23.

If the insured, that is, the owner of the insurable interest, is a third party or the taker in the insurance for account of whom it may correspond, he will be entitled to claim for payment as such to the insurer. The requirement of possession of the policy of section 24 or of the taker's consent is not established due to the nature of negotiable instrument or active legitimation of the policy, but simply due to the right of the taker to collect the gross premium of the insurance contract from the insured or from the compensation that will be received and, consequently, the possibility of not having delivered to the insured party such policy, in this case, would play a role of document of passive legitimation.

What is more, the Act, in section 25, proposes a guarantee for the taker that seems to be more extensive since it refers to all that corresponds (to collect) as a consequence of the contract (without referring or specifying if it is regarding the insurance contract, for example, other expenses), or a base contract which made him take out the insurance coverage.

If the insured does not exist as such, by whatever reason, the insurer will be released by the non-existence of the creditor or of the owner of the insurable interest, which takes us to the non-existence of such person, as there cannot be insurable interest without a person to which such right belongs.

However, it is possible to think that the Act in section 23, in its second part, has not referred to the taker as a party, but as a person, and without expressly stating it, has attributed it the capacity of representative – with or without mandate – of the insured, since neither the final reference to the demonstration of the mandate nor the legal obligation to contract is explained as, in this case, the insurance contract for account of a third party would turn out to be a contract for one's own account or by obliged legal representation of the insured.

Summarizing: Section 23, as it is conceived, is not possible to be applied literally because of the following reasons:

(1) The possession of the policy does not release the taker from his burden or duty to evidence – if it is the case of insurance for account of whom it may correspond – his joint capacity or condition of insured, that is, of owner of the insurable interest established in the policy. If it was not insurance for account of whom it may correspond, the taker could never be the insured, although in the construction of the contractual type, it is possible to discover that the true nature is the one for account of whom it may correspond.

(2) The possession of the policy could make other things be assumed that are alien to the insurance contract as, for instance, retention of such by the taker, in guarantee of credits arising from the same insurance contract (reimbursement of premium payment that was made to take out the insurance, expenses incurred by the notification of loss or its investigation or payment), or which may arise from the contract that motivated the taking out of the insurance for account of a third party.

(3) Possession of policy by the taker does not have any effect in his favour of legitimation in order to collect compensation, nor to the ends of exercising its specific rights as taker as long as the insurance contract may be evidenced by

other means of proof, pursuant to section 11 of the Act. It is clear that its possession by the taker is demonstrative of such capacity as taker since the policy – which is not false – naturally instruments the contract.

(4) The taker, as such, has no rights to demand the payment of compensation (that is, the payment of the rendering of services promised by the insurer), and the insurer can file the corresponding demurrers. If, to its capacity as taker, it is added its capacity as attorney-in-fact, its performance would not only be taker but also representative. If the taker states a legal obligation for the taking out of the insurance, this legal obligation must be restricted to the ones arising out of the laws for every person administering property belonging to another or being demanded, in his capacity as representative by law, to act in that manner.

The last expression of section 23 cannot be interpreted in a generic way since it would be, again going round the same circle, originated in the principle of insurance for account of a third party and that the books of authority have summarized as the insurance opposed to the insurance on one's own account and, further, a customary or legal representative does not act on his own but on behalf of the person he represents and, consequently, it should be an insurance on the represented's own account, in which the rights are different from the ones corresponding to such discipline.[39]

(5) Obviously, the consent of the insured is valid, coming from an express act at that specific moment of the agreement between taker and insurer, from the beginning authorizing the taker or a third party to collect, but such 'collector' will act not based on a right emerging from the insurance relationship but from this agreement (and the feature of taker as such will not have importance). Only the generic name individualizes him as authorized person. It should be taken into account that it is important not only the right to collect but also the right to pay and to pay in a correct way as the person who pays wrongly to the inadequate person pays twice and the policy, and its 'possession', does not actively legitimize in this respect.

Previously, the analysis of certain specifications of this type of taking out was started, specifications which will continue to be analysed now.

Section 24 of Act 17.418 starts repeating a basic concept, by adding a concept that does not strictly refers to the law of the insured as such, but yes to the safeguarding of certain rights, alien to the insurance contract but of undoubted weight in the linked relations between taker and insured.

It is easy to imagine that the reason of being of the insurance for account of a third party in its two established modalities (insurance for account of a third party

39. As summary of these books of authority and of the principle, *see* Morandi's work referred to in n. 12, where in page 261 and books of authority he quotes, he sustains that 'the insurance for account of a third party is the reverse side of the insurance on one's own account and the criteria to differentiate one from the other has its grounds on the ownership of the insured interest, i.e., it depends on whether the interest belongs to the taker or to the third party'.

and insurance for account of whom it may correspond) has its origin in motivations alien to insurance properly. Yet, these origins are very tightly related to the commercial operation, natural recipient of such and which insurance has constantly supported since it has permitted the support of business, companies, and even modern life, all of which would not be possible if insurance had not been discovered or invented.

No matter which author we may choose to support this topic, the possible origins of these modalities are found in the maritime sphere first, Ordinances of Barcelona of 1435 (*Ordenanzas de Barcelona de 1435*) and then in land transport,[40] always very closely linked to the maritime or land transport contracts, according to the case.

Thus, it can be stated that the insurance for account of a third party derives from a legal relation, prior or simultaneously causing it, whether by protection of the policyholder or by protection of the insured (co-policyholder of the taker in the other contract). At the same time, although the insurer is concealed and he may never have any significance, it could be that it derives from an underlying legal obligation. It even could be originated in a unilateral act of the taker, for no consideration (gratuitous) without any of this having influence on the insurance, except for the fact – as it has been expressed – that the circumstance is not known.

In this line, it is not strange that Act 17.418 of a strong regulating nature would have provided for a regulation – as the one contained in section 24 and, above all, section 25 – evidencing that the governing principle is not the protection of the insured or the insurer, but the policyholder and even because of relationships alien to the insurance contract.

If we go through the most recent legislative precedents of Act 17.418, we shall notice that in the preliminary draft Halperín, sections 21 and 22, the only ones referring to the insurance for account of a third party have a structure and letter similar to the ones in force, although with a greater mixture of regulations due to the smaller number of sections dedicated to this matter and without reference whatsoever to the purposes article.

In another bill, the one of the Commission of 1969 – where text in this part is identical to its structure and sections 21–26 to the current Act – in the purposes article, the matter is laid in support of the policyholder and the problems alien to insurance, although without expressly mentioning it.

Thus, the possession of the policy (we understand as with right of title and not *a non domino*) is required for the protection of the insured regarding his possible credits against the insured or his assignees.

(e) Finally, we will refer to the right of retention that for the same credit reasons – which have been previously pointed out – the Act grants the taker. The right to recover the payment of the premium that could or should have made to the insurer, according to his primary obligation as taker and that implies a specific power of the insurer to compensate (section 27), is privileged with the right to retain the policy during the reorganization proceedings to avoid bankruptcy or bankruptcy proceedings of the insured, granting him the preference to collect over the other creditors.

40. *See*, for instance, Garrigues, work quoted in n. 11, at 70.

Despite the fact that the law does not indicate to which contract it is making reference, we deem that this preference and the retention privilege granted are over the credits related to the insurance contract.

As last point, reference should be made to the aforementioned derivation of the taking out for account of whom it may correspond, in other words, for account of the person who turns out to be the insured and, therefore, the owner of the insurable interest. In some previous paragraphs, certain comments have been made, but it turns out to be very important to take into account that, in property insurance for account of whom it may correspond, as the insured/beneficiary is left uncertain, it is implicitly permitted that the policyholder may turn out to be the insured.

To support this, it is only necessary to take a look at the second part of section 21 of Act 17.418, where this is expressly admitted by using the adequate expression.

Once we have accomplished the purposes stated for paragraph 102 of considering in a separate way the insurance for account of a third party and for account of whom it may correspond in the type of property insurance, now it corresponds to deal with this modality on behalf of a third party in life insurance. Although it has its own characteristics, the feature of the policyholder, different from the insured and, in turn, different from the beneficiary, is admitted for insurance of the person, in the terminology used in Argentina.

Nevertheless, going into details, in life insurance over one's own life, the policyholder always causes a taking out for account of a third party since the beneficiary can never be the taker, but always a party or a different person. The risk/subject matter of the contract – synthetically the death of the insured – will never be an economic benefit coming from the payment of the services to the person undertaking the insurance or the person of the insured, but the payment shall always be to a third person, the beneficiary.[41]

However – and though this is not an undisputable part of the subject to be dealt with – it is worth making reference to the fact that, in some life insurance, there may exist even a fourth party: the strictly benefited, whose attributions and obligations shall be analysed, as it has been advanced, in the part of this monograph devoted to life insurance. A clarification needs to be made: in life insurance, the person of a third-party policyholder, alien to the person of the insured, may exist, but it is not strictly the policyholder as it appears in property insurance or non-life insurance for account of a third party.

103. Reference to Argentine Law. After having analysed the general matters and the individual matters referred to in the contracts for account of a third party and for account of whom it may correspond, it is appropriate to make certain comments arising from the analysis of the Argentine Insurance Contract Act No. 17.418.

In the first place, it is essential to be clear on the fact that, even when certain creditors or the insured may have some preference on the collection of the compensation corresponding to its debtor, in no way is it possible to consider them beneficiaries of the indicated compensation and turn them, in consequence, into direct creditors of the insurer.

---

41. *See* Joaquín Garrigues, *Land Insurance Contracts* (*Contrato de Seguro Terrestre*), 2nd ed. (Madrid, 1982), 70, n. 31, although with argumentations we do not completely share.

In Argentine positive law – as in many others of the same orientation – privileged creditors of guarantees secured by mortgages or pledges may exercise a special right consisting of the insurer not paying the compensation corresponding to the debtor, in order to reserve such corresponding amount by means of a judicial consignment, so that the Court decides on the opposition that such creditor may file.

Section 84 of Act 17.418, as it has been previously indicated, facilitates the registered mortgage and pledge creditor, the exercise of his preferential rights, by means of the simple remedy of notifying the insurer of the property affected by the privilege, precisely the existence of such privilege. Before paying the compensation, except for the case of repairs carried out or to be carried out with the insurer's participation, it shall be informed to the creditor so that he files the opposition of the case, opposition that can be decided on by agreement between the parties.

In the second place, an insured of a contract of property insurance who has suffered a loss that must be compensated has its own right to assign to a third party, absolutely alien to the contract, such compensation that it will be entitled to collect. This credit assignment of the insured to a third party turns him into a creditor of the insurer because the effect of the assignment is to place the third-party creditor assignee in the place of an insured assignor.

It is important to point out that this is a person who has access to credit in his capacity as assignor but not as original beneficiary. His entitlement to the amount paid by the loss is not as insured-beneficiary, but as assignee of the insured. Therefore, he cannot be considered a third party to the insurance contract but, at most, a third party in the insurance contract, whereas his entitlement to the collection of the compensation is alien to the relationship arising from and by virtue of the insurance contract.

In the third place and, at least, in relation to civil liability insurance contracts, the injured third party may not be considered beneficiary to the compensation.

According to section 109 of Act 17.418, the civil liability insurance contract is a contract whose beneficiary is the insured as, pursuant to the aforementioned rule, the obligation of the insurer is to hold the insured harmless and not a third party since, under any circumstances, he is the injured party by the foreseen event.

When analysing this type of contract, it shall be seen that a moderation of this precept is posed by the possibility of the guaranteed subpoena of the insurer, but neither such subpoena nor the determination of an Act of social type, which could declare the injured third-party beneficiary of the compensation to pay, shall change the current situation in the contract.

Chapter 8. Termination of the Insurance Contract

104. Generalities about Its Duration. Even when Act 17.418 attempts to establish via assumptions a legal term of duration for the effectiveness of the insurance contract, in reality the nature of the power to establish the time of effectiveness is indisputably consensual since said decision is the essence of the agreement of the parties.

The assumption of the Act that has been mentioned in the previous paragraph and that section 17 contains, under a title which states that the regulation refers to the temporal extension of the insurance, is a supplementary provision because, in the first place, the law does not establish in a compulsory way that the term of duration must be fixed in any specific manner, as it would be by means of an established term or with a reference to one or more specific guidelines, and, in the second place, it is a term in which the insurance contract establishes the existence of the coverage of the risk and not a term for compliance with the obligation of the insurer.

It must be present that, in an insurance contract, the most significant obligation of the insurer is to take care of the loss in case of its occurrence, but the lapse of such occurrence cannot be unspecified, since, technically, there must be a correspondence between the covered risk and the time of that coverage, with the premium paid by the policyholder.

Thus, the presumption *juris tantum* (of law alone) of section 17 Act 17.418 regarding the term of risk coverage on the insurer's part is of one year when the parties would not have agreed so, a situation that would take place only by evident mistake.

This year of duration also supplementary, pursuant to the regulation established, is, at the same time, susceptible of a correction when the nature of the risk requires a lapse of coverage different to one year, to be established. This is so to such extent that section 19 – which follows in the order of the Act – underlines the matter as reserved to the agreement of the parties to the contract (policyholder and insurer). No other thing is sustainable since, in the second part of the mentioned section, the taking out of any insurance contract by any unspecified time is authorized.

Confirming this concept of freedom of contract, it is worth mentioning the law frequently used by the parties, establishing durations by means of parameters linked to other types of causes, as it happens with transport insurance contracts that arrange duration only for one or two trips.

In order to complete the ideas arising out of the subject in question, reference should be made to some sort of precept attached to section 19 of Act 17.418, referred to the possibility of rescission of unspecified term insurance contracts, as legislative policy preventing the incoherent captivity within the contractual relationship. Nevertheless, as the provision solves the matter on the basis of termination of the contract, it is better to leave if for the next paragraph.

For reasons of uniformity and for the estimation of the premiums of the different contracts, mainly on the basis of an annual period, the habitual duration of the different types of insurance contracts is stipulated in the policies in the term of one year. Also, due to generalized customs accepted in the insurance business, the indication of this is notably marked in the texts of the policies, fixing the dates of commencement and ending of the period of the contract.

In Argentina, there was an additional custom that, when incorporating Act 17.418 modified for the insurance contract, the way of calculation of the terms used by the Argentine Civil Code as, pursuant to what is established in section 18 first part, the commencement and termination is twelve hours from the days agreed upon, instead of the zero hour, that is, the commencement and termination of a day.

105. Termination of the Insurance Contract. The period of coverage of the insurance contract, point that has been considered up to now in this chapter, as well as commencing and finishing, pursuant to the agreement of the parties, is susceptible of being altered both by another agreement of the parties and by other reasons.

In summary, to the effects of termination of the insurance contract, the following can be considered: (a) normal accomplishment of the term agreed upon or the altered reduced term agreed upon by the parties; (b) unilateral rescission of the contract without expressing cause, by any of the parties, even in case of the contract agreed for an unspecified term; (c) unilateral rescission by any of the parties, when a loss occurred that caused only partial damage.

Different hypotheses extracted from the legal text shall be analysed below.

In the first place, reference was made to the ending of the term of duration by the normal course of time. At the moment the parties establish, either because they arrived to an established day or by the compliance with the determining event – as it would happen in the transport contract by trip – the arranged coverage ends and is rendered ineffective for the future.

In the second place, it was advanced the grounds of termination of the insurance contract by agreement of the parties by reduction of the agreed term. As the duration term of the contract depends strictly on the right of the parties, as a rescission is possible, it is also possible to make an alteration of the term originally agreed upon.

In the third place, it has been mentioned as cause of termination of the insurance contract that there can be unilateral rescission by any of the parties. In order for both the insurer and the policyholder of the contract to exercise that right, it is indispensable that this power is established in the agreement, as required by section 18, second part, of Act 17.418.

If that was so agreed upon and the insurer exercised that right of unilateral rescission, a prior notice of fifteen days must be given and, further, the corresponding premium has to be reimbursed, proportionally to the term of effectiveness not elapsed.

If, on the contrary, the person that terminates the contract is the policyholder, the prior notice to the insurer is not necessary, but he is entitled to the premium accrued for the term of risk covered, pursuant to short-term rates that, as it is known, are superior to the ones that would emerge from a proportionality of time.

Although the law does not explicitly state anything about it, it is obvious that when the role of policyholder corresponds to one person different from that person exercising the role of insured, the rights of such person should be contemplated.

Besides, this unilateral power, even when not expressly agreed upon – and with the exception made for life insurance contracts – has also been recognized by section 19, second part, of Act 17.418, for the unspecified term contracts in which, nevertheless, it is possible to waive them for five years.

Finally, it was mentioned as grounds of termination of the contract the unilateral rescission by any of the parties, before the occurrence of a loss determining a partial damage. This power can only be exercised up to the moment of payment of compensation for the partial loss. It is a right mainly granted to the insurer before two hypotheses related to moral hazard or, in other words, suspicions that are not evidenced. It is the assumption of a doubtful or suspicious loss and a wrongly appraised contract for a higher risk than the one estimated.

Finally, to finish this chapter, it is worth remembering that reference has not been made to other means of termination of insurance contract, as are the occurrence of the loss, nullities caused by misrepresentations or false declarations of the insured, or the rescission that may come from the aggravation of the risk.

The cases considered in this chapter are related to the term of effectiveness of the coverage, without affecting the correction of the contractual relationship regarding technical aspects of the insurance. Examples of this would be the assumptions of misrepresentation, occurrence of the loss or aggravation of the risk, or even assumptions affecting the will of the parties, by vices of the will or the nature of the contract, due to the disappearance of an essential element.

Part III. Property and Liability Insurance

106. Generalities. The third part of this monograph about insurance contract law in the Argentine Republic and which starts to separate the different species that may appear within its territory must be preceded by some general comments intended to enhance the understanding of the characteristics of our legislation.

The economy of the insurance contract is inseparable from insurance contract law, as evidently it characterizes the law ordering it and, in order to explain such law, it is indispensable to take into account the interests that have had influence, such as the richness of the environment in which the commercial activities have taken place.

In the old Commercial Code originally drawn up for the Province of Buenos Aires alone in 1859 – and after the National Organization of the Country in 1862 by Act 15 declared Code of the Nation and later amended by Act 2637 – there were about sixty sections that referred to the insurance contract.

When contemplating its principles not only from the standpoint of the times when it became effective but also considering these were the initial times of the Argentine Nation, as such were of extraordinary modernity and strength, typical of their authors, Mr Dalmacio Vélez Sarsfield, Esq. and Mr Eduardo Acevedo, Esq, it must be remembered that the former also was the author of the Argentine Civil Code.

With its commerce in the dawn of its strong expansion, at the beginning of the twentieth century, Argentina lacked an insurance interest of importance, coming from the strictly local environment, and thus the insurance companies that established their business in the country were logically those that, from foreign markets, could see the convenience of the possibilities of the development of the new traffic and thus brought their legal experience (that came from the insurance regulations and contracts used in their operations) following the style and tradition of their origins, with the scarce differences that certain regulations of our law imposed, as our law was very similar to the existent in Europe, from where it had got its inspiration.

The commercial influence, which meant the constant presence of insurers of the aforementioned orientation and, in general, the seriousness they showed in their businesses, determined that the market was practically left captive in the monopoly of certain insurance companies which satisfied, during many years, the needs of insurance that the external and internal transactions were requiring every time more.

The eagerness shown for Statism – as policy awoken in our country by different factors, among them, the influence from European nationalism starting before the war of 1939–1945 – was later deepened by the advent of considerations of a social democrat and socialist nature, developed in that same scenario, as a consequence of the Beverage report and before, in the Roosevelt era in the United States of America and the economy of John M. Keynes.

It was then that, with inconceivable excuses, always present in Argentina, it started to appear the tendency to confiscate business capital with several excuses, but with the senseless objective of turning the State into a business administrator, a purpose for which it was not prepared and of which no solid precedents could be put forward in the public aspect.

In this way, by means of laws enacted by the Executive Power that during ten years counted on the systematic collaboration of a legislative power politically dominated by the same governing party, these activities regulated by the State started to be created; the State reaching its intervention in absolutely uneven tasks, as the exports of agricultural products to the commercialization of reinsurance and of insurance itself.

In these two last trades – that were maintained separate in theory – the State got to the point of constituting a destroying monopoly, the worst consequence of which has been the ignorance into which the existent market was submerged. The market, being or not ashamed of such behaviour, devoted to the activity of brokers of the official reinsurer, the NRI, of which only sad memories remain (plus the many losses generated in an activity that, seriously exercised, could not have, in environments like Argentina, determined the prejudices it did during the long years of inflation which, in turn, was produced by wrong government policies).

It is not necessary to be too shrewd to imagine the unscrupulous management that the State made use of in the years that follow, which continue to be prejudicial in the many decades that followed and that took our poor country to the situation it finally arrived at and that conditioned the failure of the apparent accomplishments that were achieved near the close of the twentieth century.

Nevertheless, in this end of the century, in the matter of insurance activity, the ending of the State privilege was achieved and the unlimited opening to the reinsurance world became possible, a fact that altered dramatically the shape of business – that had severely been damaged – by permitting the unlimited entering of foreign capital with which the substantial modernization of its operations was achieved.

The Acts that have been modified towards 1968 had the influence of the winds blowing in the world since 1950, maintaining, nevertheless, some guidelines, thanks to the scarce local movement of the local insurance – which extension did not surpass 2.5% of the gross national product of the country, a not very considerable sum. To this was added the inexistent importance granted to life insurance, by virtue of the huge inflation undergone for almost forty-five years and that, after ten new years, has come back to being a predominant factor for the destruction of the commercial movement.

107. The Insurance Contract Act. In these paragraphs with which we have wished to precede Chapter I of this Part, it is worth mentioning the consideration of the species of insurance contracts that are possible in our Argentine law, so as to make reference to the ones that shall include our work.

With severe method mistakes in Act 17.418 – as it was exposed in the book *Insurance Law and Other Related Businesses* (*El derecho de seguros y de otros negocios vinculados*), the mentioned Act has gathered – as it has been advanced – the theoretical positions of their generational times, as well as the experiences that started to translate into regulations and later on constituted the basis of the current communitarian regulations.

Act 17.418 of the Argentine Republic, known as the Insurance Contracts Act, has 158 main sections about this subject; then it devotes, in its Title II, four sections to reinsurance; and finally in its Title III, devotes two sections (Numbers 163 and 164) to the transitory and final provisions that do not alter the essence and supremacy of the ones numerically preceding:

(a) The structure of the Insurance Contracts Act, generally speaking, in order to be able to offer a plan of its system, starts with a general part regarding the insurance contract, which includes items referred to its formation, misrepresentation or false declaration of the risk (sufficiently analysed), policy, insurance for account of a third party and for account of whom it may correspond, aggravation of the risk, notification of loss, insurer's rights, and compliance with its obligation and statute of limitations of the emerging acts.

In Chapter II, with reference to property insurance, the Act regulates some general rules, among them the compensation by the insurer, by virtue of the damage and the assured amount, the prefixed amount of the assessed value, the effects of overinsurance and underinsurance, the plurality of insurance, the penalties for noncompliance with the duty not to cause the loss or increase the damages, as well as the scheme pertaining to the salvage burden and damage verification.

Finally, in the general part of this chapter about damage insurance, the Act establishes the effects of the change and disappearance of the insurable interest. Between sections 85 and 127, there are regulating references to certain specific insurance, among which it can be pointed out, as from section 109, those of civil liability.

Although it is possible to make some criticism to the fact of the restrictive nature of these references, it must be taken into account, as it has happened in these last two paragraphs, two things: (1) that when the Act was issued it was a regulatory body that organically and originally legislated on insurance (matters on which there had been only isolated legislative activity and the existent contracts of different types were of great age and of certain harmful practices that did not adequately protect the insurables); and (2) the types of contracts mentioned in the text were those that, at the time of the bill and the Act, were the most frequent and governed the business of our country, in which, since 1945, the private impulse had been reduced in production and commerce. In our opinion, it was after those years when new modalities derived and new problems of civil and commercial life appeared.

Act 17.418 in Chapter III makes a diversion, leading us to think that in the following regulations the Act would conveniently deepen into the species of property insurance and insurance of the person contracts. Nevertheless, the principles of the Act regarding the treatment of insurance of the person leave much to be desired, as it centres almost completely on life insurance, which modern evolution had started to have its influence.

Starting in life insurance, the Act limited to rehearse some regulations on the contractual forms in use at that time, forms among which were not or did not have sufficient history or support, forms very much used nowadays.

Despite these drawbacks, it is necessary to acknowledge that the legal regulations contained in Regulation 17.418 do not bring about any impediment, in order to take out new existing modalities in the commercial practice or modalities that may exist in the future, as there is no prohibitive regulation following the principle arising from the National Constitution and the Civil Code.

(b) The regulations of Act 17.418 for the time of their appearance had a markedly regulating tone, a product of the influence of the author of the preliminary draft, preponderance that implied the protection of the insured.

In this sense, it is worth analysing section 158, which precisely points to dividing the regulations of the Act into two of the three types known, according to the old classification of rules: imperative, dispositive, and interpretative regulations.

In this regard, section 158, under the subtitle 'enforceability of the rules', states that regulations are, according to their letter or nature, totally or partially unchangeable, leaving the resolution of the problem either to the Act itself (when this has been provided for) or to the jurisprudential construction (when there is silence in the Act and the nature of a specific regulation has to be investigated). Immediately after, section 158 mentions five sections that cannot be modified by agreement of the parties, that is, which belong to the category of unchangeable sections or, in other words, to the category of imperative regulations, that is, those of public order, compulsory, and on which the autonomy of the will cannot advance.

Later on in section 158, the existence of other changeable regulations is pointed out, but only to the benefit of the insured. These dispositive provisions (as they are not imperative) can be left aside by the parties, by application of the principle of autonomy of the will, agreeing something different.

Having made these clarifications, for which evidently the most significant is the one derived from the influence of the times when Act 17.418 was issued and the need for an adaptation, we shall continue to consider some insurance contracts. These insurance contracts in Argentina are the ones that enjoyed the greater market and, thus, counted on the greater experience. Nevertheless, it is worth reminding that, in the drawing up of the policies documenting the contracts, although there are no provisions establishing the obligatory nature of specific texts, during the time of the passing of Act 17.418, there was a great regulating activity on the part of the SIN. This body, with the complicity of the insurers of the time who, we repeat, were compelled by the statistic policy of the government, proceeded to pass without any legitimacy whatsoever uniform texts of policies that were incorporated into the market, as if they were regulating Acts. In reality, such texts did not mean anything but copies of the sections of the Act.

Chapter 1. Fire Insurance

108. Fire Insurance. This insurance contract has always been the paradigm taken into account as model for regulating the individual agreements of every type of contractual species of property insurance. In Act 17.418, it appears in five sections forming Article VIII of Chapter II of property damage insurance. Such five sections are not regulations of imperative nature as they are provisions that, normally, by commercial agreements, are included in the clauses of the policies.

Even when these policies documenting the contractual agreement in this species of contract specify as covered risk the material damages caused by the direct or indirect action of fire, lightning, or explosion, then it is clarified – to the effects of insurance – that fire is all combustion originating a fire or point of origin of fire. With this, despite the tautological mistake, the effect of emphasis is reached as not all combustion implies fire, but solely that producing fire.

However, it is as well indispensable to state that in the Argentine market, it is possible to insure other risks as additional to fire by means of premiums corresponding to those other coverages that may or may not be individualized in the policy.

We have attempted to follow in this monograph, whenever it has been advised or demanded, the preestablished scheme of other monographs that have preceded it in time of publication. In this line, we have opted, in order to achieve a similar system to those, to start referring to the persons that can be the insured of this type of insurance.

According to what has been stated in relation to the insured in property insurance contracts, the only possible insured are those who own some insurable interest.

In this sense, in the first place, it must be pointed out the importance of the owner of the property in relation to this type of insurance, regardless of the type of property we are dealing with, that is, if it is personal or real property.

Yet, as it has been well established, apart from the right of property, there are different rights which may be involved. We are referring to third party's rights that may be affected by the fire, in neighbouring real property or in movable property or goods deposited nearby.

Moreover, the condition of insured is possible for those that hold other kinds of rights on the thing as use, usufruct, possession or easement, mortgage, pledge, or antichresis.

Subjects to insurance can also be – always in relation to their insurable interest – whoever is lessee, bailee, or user of property.

It must be taken into account the dimension of the insurable interest that each one may protect from damages by occurrence of the risk covered, as it is not the same the insurable interest of an owner than that of a lessee because it is precisely the difference between one and the other that permits several insurance contracts, without affecting the matter previously studied under the heading plurality of insurance.

With this having been said, it must be reminded that the insurable interest is an indispensable requirement, in order to enable the person to be insured, and thus to be the original recipient of the compensation to be collected in property insurance contracts, as is the fire insurance contract under analysis.

In certain species of plural coverage – which currently are used for certain risks such as theft and larceny of the movable property of a house – it is taken into account a feature similar to 'householders', which are referred to as beneficiaries of the compensation of the owners of such movable property, as long as it is property of relatives or maids living together with the insured.

The wife of the owner, besides, may have another right emerging from the insurance contract, as her legal situation is different from the one that has just been commented on; if this was the case, she could claim by the fact of the marriage institution the right arising out of the marital property of the insured.

The analysis of specific matters that has started in preceding paragraphs, with the capacity of insured as indispensable in order to benefit from the payment of the compensation, must be continued now with the special description of the risk covered. When entering into an insurance contract, it must be established the location of the risk in the space. This indication of place where the risk is or must be located is absolutely necessary so that, in the case of occurrence of the foreseen generic event, it is considered a possible loss.

The object on which the insurable interest is, which in plain language is known as 'assured property', must be described with enough detail to individualize it without further problems. In this sense, it must be very clear that there are no usual insurance practices in Argentina where reference can be made to 'the domicile' of the insured, but the address where the insured is must be included.

When the insurable interest is on individual movable property of the insured, these shall be those as detailed in the insurance contract or in the furniture located in the dwelling of the insured, in the way indicated *supra.*

In reference to the multiplicity or plurality of the risks to be covered by the same contract, pursuant to the current trends in all the countries – and for some years now in Argentina – the custom has been followed of concentrating different coverages in only one contract, even in the generic risk. This is so because they are tightly linked, as they refer to the same insurable and the prejudices that they may experiment arise from different hazards to which the different property or the property protected by the insured is exposed.

The case to which reference is made is the contract of homeowner's comprehensive insurance, which sometimes has the additional term of 'family', without this implying any connotation in relation to the determination of the insured within the members of a concrete family group. This word has a linking connection that is the possibility of suffering a loss in certain property, physically located at the same location.

As usual, the risks covered by the homeowner's comprehensive insurance are: fire; lightning; explosion; material damages by public riots, strike, and lock out; vandalism; terrorism; and malevolence. Also, aircraft and/or land vehicles impact, hurricane, cyclone, or tornado, with additionals for cleaning expenses and rubble removal, as well as accommodation expenses due to the bad condition of dwelling.

However, it covers the risk of burglary and theft of the movable property and, in an annex to the contract, it is established the coverage for personal accidents upon the case of death or permanent disability of the insured.

Lastly, the policies documenting this contract also establish the additional coverage for glass breakage or mirrors placed vertically or obliquely in a particular dwelling to which the insured interest refers, in that same contract of fire and others.

109. Range of Covered Risk. Coming back, we would like to remind the reader again that, in our country, Argentina, Act 17.418 has not analysed aspects related to the extension of the risk and thus the coverage that each contract specifically may include.

Only exceptionally, as we shall see later, in the assumption of the civil liability insurance contract, the Act actually limits the risk concept and extension due to legislative policy reasons. The reason for this would be either the novelty of the subject or the fact that, from its very origin, such contractual species had given rise to construction conflicts, forcing the indispensable establishment of the legal choice.

This has timely been stated as it constantly happens that contracts establish inner guidelines, acting as additional conditions to Act 17.418, in keeping with Argentine law, which widely admit these contractual agreements, except when they affect public order, morality, and good customs. These guidelines, the product of the freedom of contract, obviously do not have the stability, immobility, or invariability that corresponds to legal precepts; thus, it is impossible to analyse them individually. In this sense, it must be clear that the description of the risk must be as precise as possible. This means that, apart from having a positive description by means of cause, space, and temporal parameters, it could be required in many opportunities a limitation by the negative form (as it would be the express exclusion) and which shall always have the same significance as the positive expression.

The exclusions of coverage may be equally referred to descriptions of a cause, space, or time including factors of the origin of the events causing damages or the damages proper.

Chapter 2. Loss of Benefits Insurance

110. Perspective of This Contract from Act 17.418. For different reasons, our Act 17.418, even when not dealing directly with this insurance contract, made some brief and incidental references to it. Section 61 does not include, when stating the regulations of the principle of insurance compensation, the loss of profits from interruption of business, except for when it had been specifically agreed.

In our opinion, following the fundamental element of grounds for the limitation of the covered risk, the legal prescription, respecting the dimension that the policyholders wished to grant to the obligations undertaken, only provided for the agreement of wills to determine the risk. Later on, section 88, when referring to fire insurance, contemplates the possibility of such compensation, although it limits the possibility establishing it to an agreed value.

The reasons for such absence of regulations, as well as the presence of the brief incidental references aforementioned, are due to the fact that this type of contract represents a novelty in insurance law in many countries.

It is important to notice how the not so convincing section 61 stumbles when compared to section 88 which is also vague, bringing uncertainty to specific aspects of the legislation, its application and effects. Yet far from aiming at criticizing the contents of the Act, these are just notes aimed at considering the advance that in this matter the insurance law in our country achieved during those years of the passing of the Act. Mainly thanks to the criterion assumed in the preliminary draft by Halperín who, in spite of referring to the matter of the loss of expected profit, within the section provided for fire insurance, from our interpretation, meant to extend it to other property, considering that fire insurance was the archetype of property insurance in those times.

It must be noticed that the prohibition to insure the expected profit by means of an agreed value, in the line we are discussing, which the preliminary draft we are dealing with states in its section 90 is of a generic order, and it is not referred in particular as fire insurance, as it is wrongly posed by section 88 of Act 17.418 and its precedent, the bill of the Commission of 1961.

Although the novelty of the subject may have caused problems during the drawing up of the model, used by the authors of Act 17.418 and even when the Act itself was drawn up, it must be present that, in the reality of commerce, such demand was starting the phase of forcing the appearance of regulations ruling human behaviour in business aiming at satisfying the needs of the positive right of not only relying on the agreements of the parties (which many times were not feasible). This tendency to concrete dispositive rules had been strengthened in the years that followed, and today we can talk about a new species of insurance contract.

111. Appearance in the Market, Development, and Denomination Used. This variety or type of insurance generated much controversy since there were voices raised against its acknowledgement due to the possible enrichment without cause of the insured, mostly as this meant compensating a prejudice that could not be measured, to the extent that its dimension was not measurable in advance.

This type of insurance provides us an interesting perspective of the underlying opposing positions that have always been confronting in relation to the development of the economy and of the regulating law of the human activity, especially when insurance is specifically placed as a function of the economy at the service of the human activity.

Beyond the use of this type of insurance as a tendentious argumentation in defence of the unitary concept of insurance, it is important to take into account that both the books of authority and the legislation have been contrary to the acknowledgement of this type of insurance contract as, historically, there has always been an aftertaste of the fight that since time immemorial existed between insurance as a means of covering needs caused by damage and gambling.[42]

Not being recognized at the beginning the total value of things and the value of the goods transported, the insured and carriers were obliged to retain – without insurance – a tithe of such amounts, to awake interest in the conservation of such goods.[43] In this perspective, less likely was the possibility of insuring any expected benefit.

Nevertheless, the Indies path took those that commercialized with the colonies, to exert sufficient pressure on the vessels and their owners, to gradually change their criteria and the almost dogmatic considerations of the Ordinance of Colbert of 1681 did not have other effect than the local.

As time went by, it would seem for the scholars that in the nineteenth century, in Spain, there appeared the legislated possibility, annexed to fire insurance by means of specific agreement, of insuring certain prejudices, arising beyond the damages directly caused by fire to things. At the same time, from 1829, it was admitted the surplus value of the goods at the place of destination in maritime transport.

In the perspective of the mentioned background, this would turn out to be the beginning of a change, from the surplus value to the expected benefit.[44]

We always insist on the undisputable value of the behaviour of merchants and of individuals linked by the commercial activity, in order to observe the day-to-day reality and extract from it, in a beneficial manner, its consequences and needs of regulation of their conduct. In this decade of 1820, the claims of those that had been suffering for some time due to the impossibility of covering the risk of the losses arising from the stoppage or standstill of the company's effectiveness started to have effect. These were sometimes financially prevented – on account of the halted company benefit – from paying the interest of a loan or from taking loan money for the development of the business or from investing in their production or purchasing goods.

42. Cf. Francisco J. Tirado Suarez, comments to ss 63 et seq., of the Spanish Act of 1980, Insurance Contract Act, vol. XXIV, 325.
43. 'By no title or case, insurance could be made out of imaginary profits, teachers or sailors wages or freights that have not been complied with effectively, on pain of nullity; except what is expressed regarding the profits of the commerce of Indies.' *See*, Act XI and Act VIII of the Ordinances of Bilbao of 1737, which refer to great risks and other factors that ordinarily determined profits, superior to the ones obtained in the European market.
44. Joaquín Garrigues, 308 and 309.

These claims, rejected by courts, since the risk was not accepted as covered by the insurers who had insured the fire risk of those same goods or the premises,[45] helped, at least, to show the path that would lead to bridge the final gap.

The first of these cases had been *Wright v. Pole* in 1834. With no success – as it was not an agreed-upon risk of the fire insurance taken with the insurance company Ship Inn – the claim attempted was for an important additional amount to the material value of the emerging damages from the fire, by virtue of the loss of the clientele suffered whereas the Inn (such was the type of business involved) was being rebuilt.[46]

As a consequence of this legislative appearance, the books of authority started to accept this new modality as a new species of contract, but under the need of an express agreement in this respect, agreement that seemed extraordinary, without noticing that, for other species of risk, the concrete agreement was compulsory, since at that time a contractual agreement had started to be compulsory for the existence of insurance.

Generally speaking, in this very brief outline, it is feasible to notice the role that, once again, economic reality had on the expression of the merchants who, due to mere theoretical ideas, saw themselves prejudiced for not being able to cover the risk of losing the benefit that they logically expected, on account of their operations of forwarding goods to very long distances for their commercialization, taking much more serious risks than the habitual ones.[47]

There was also another economic reality to definitively prevent the abuse of theoretical ideas only generated in labs and confronting objective reality. This other reality was the one related to the agricultural insurance that covered the crops against the climate adversities, which was no other thing but an insurance of expected profit.[48]

If such insurance was accepted, there would not be any objections for other similar ones, but this one answered to a damage generated from a loss of profit of other kind.

In the preceding different paragraphs, there have been used with certain discretion the denominations of insurance of expected profit and loss of profit. Nevertheless, it is possible the use of the expression insurance of probable benefit.[49]

---

45. It is of utmost interest to go through the work of the Spanish Francisco J. Tirado Suárez, *Legal Summary of Interruption of Business Insurance* (*Sinopsis jurídica del seguro de interrupción de empresa*) Madrid: Revista Española de Seguros, 1976, nos 7 and 9, 30, 37 et seq. Also his monograph, *Loss of Benefit Insurance by Interruption of Business* (*El seguro de pérdida de beneficios por interrupción de la empresa*) (Jerez de la Frontera, 1976).
46. Chartered Insurance Institute, *Engineering Insurance* (*Seguro de Ingeniería*) (Madrid: Mapfre Press, 1977).
47. Joaquín Garrigues, *Land Insurance Contract* (*Contrato de seguros terrestre*), 307 (Madrid, 1983).
48. *Ibid.*, 308.
49. Tulio Ascarelli, '*Sul concetto unitario del contratto di Assicurazione*', *Studi in tema di contratti*, 368 et seq. (Milan: Giuffré Press, 1952). The great Italian master, noticing the need of separating from the narrow concept of the books of authority that rejected the reality of the acceptance of the regulations of this insurance and, at the same time, supporting its unitary concept, presented distinctions between loss of profit *lato sensu* and loss of profit *strictu sensu*, or expected benefit. The textual words were: '*Meno frequentemente vi en messa in rilievo la distinzione, nell'ambito del lucro cessante lato sensu, fra il lucro cessante stricto sensu e il beneficio sperato.*'

As it has been previously stated in the first item corresponding to this insurance contract, our Act 17.418 has used the name of loss of profit insurance in line with the Argentine Civil Code, when in its sections 519 and 1069 it refers to damages and interests.[50]

Evidently, terminology is not important, but the exact concept of this type of insurance is. We can specifically point out that we are dealing with the protection of a risk coming from the effect of the absence of a result of expected profit in business. Therefore, it responds to certain idea of a profit that ceased to be obtained, as consequence of the occurrence of the risks established in the insurance contract.

To make it simpler, it could be said that the direct damage by the aggression derived from a specific event is not the specific object of the insurance under analysis, but that such subject matter of the contract is given by the tangible and measurable risk of the property, damage that would turn out from not effectively receiving the expected income.

Generally, this type of insurance has been considered within the broader type of damage insurance, although some authors have advocated placing it as property insurance (*tertius genus*) instead of insurance of things or strictly damage insurance.[51]

Precisely for being an insurance of the property type – a broader denomination than insurance of things – it should have been agreed that this insurance would protect a loss of property, loss that will be produced by not reaching the foreseen or considered profit.

In this is laid on the problem that this insurance of expected profit does not cover the concrete loss of a thing and the damage undergone by such thing (rectius: the insurable interest held on such thing), but it protects the property damage caused by the lack of income or the lack of certainly expected profit or the damage that determines property loss by a negative expression. Something comparable in its nature to the risk covered by civil liability insurance.

It has been very strongly sustained during the years of discussions on the possibility of the loss of profit insurance – a subject that nowadays is completely settled – that the concept of loss must be understood as extended from the failure of the hope of increasing the property.[52]

This matter, in our opinion, is not a problem today, as the risk of loss of benefit or of expected profit is not a 'forced' concept of compensation for the modern books of authority, but is a way of contemplating losses which could be experienced as a consequence of unfortunate events.

---

50. Section 519, referring to non-compliance with an obligation provides for, that they are called damages and interests; the value of the loss that has been undergone and the profit that has stopped to be collected by the creditor of the obligation, by the non-compliance with such obligation in due time. At the same time, s. 1069, in relation to illicit acts, provides for damage that includes not only the effectively suffered prejudice, but the profit from which the damaged party has been deprived by the illicit act and that the code calls by the words 'losses and interests'.
51. Joaquín Garrigues, *Land Insurance Contract* (*Contrato de seguro terrestre*) 2nd ed., 310 (Madrid, 1983).
52. *Ibid.*, 312.

When Professor Garrigues took this matter into consideration for the last time in his *Land Insurance Contract*, which has been many times quoted in this monograph, there was still a long way to go, and even the Act of 1980 of Spain could conciliate matters apparently differently, maybe because of the confusing mixture introduced by the regulations of sections 65 and 66 of the Insurance Contract Act of 1980.

In the aspect under analysis, our opinion is that the insurance of expected profit or loss of benefit must not necessarily refer to another contract, but it is a risk with its own characteristics, and it is a risk included within the insurance of damages or property. The term of compensation is the one specific to name this coverage.

The loss experienced as triggering the guarantee offered by the insurer by the contract in question is, in our opinion, the correct one and does not introduce any confusion as the expected profit that did not get to be produced because of the occurrence of a possible future and uncertain event is no other thing than a loss, without any doubt of special features, but loss after all, which can be compensated by means of a precise and stipulated insurance.

112. Possibilities of Risks and Insurable Interests – Value at Stake. The Spanish Act of 1980, which has obviously taken place after ours, may serve us as orientation regarding the general system of this type of insurance.

In some opportunities, to ease the organized study of the whole problems of our law,[53] the analysis may be referred to foreign regulations.

If we took as a generic immediate item the law arising from the policies documenting the most common contracts in our sphere, we would gain neither precision nor celerity to the ends of this monograph.

It is clear that we must always confront the most usual contracts, due to the specifications they can offer regarding others of the same or different species.

It must be noticed that, in the preceding paragraph, we have chosen the Spanish law for the organized study of the subject, but not with the criteria of thinking that the laws must regulate, excluding the agreement of the wills, above them.

It must be remembered once more that freedom of contract is our governing principle in the matter of contracts, except express provisions of the laws, as the one in general contained in section 21 of the Civil Code and the one, in particular, contained in the regulations specified in section 158 of Act 17.418.

In this sense, we deem it indispensable to start by the idea of insurable interest in relation to value, continue with the intensity of the loss and the modalities of valuation of the compensation to be met, to later penetrate the assumption of different insurers who have claimed the payment of related risks.

Some paragraphs ago developed the idea of risk with an insurable interest closely related to the protection of the actually expected future value, by virtue of the benefit that the concrete activity causing the expectation would produce.

---

53. In Act 17.418, this kind of insurance is not specifically legislated, without this constituting an obstacle for the incidental introduction of some precepts referred to the type, as is the case of Art. IX (Agricultural Insurance) in s. 92, which determines, as dispositive regulation, the way of calculating the value of the lost proceeds.

In other words, the greatest value that would be incorporated into the property of the insured if the loss did not take place, as consequence of the sale or usage of the property, subject matter of the insurable interest protected by the insurance contract under consideration.

It is very clear that, since the moment that the concept of insurance of profit or expected profit is appreciated, the concern or difficulty that started to exist for the development of this type of insurance has been the amount of such loss.

Something occurs in this insurance – that is different from everything that used to happen and that happens with other insurance – with the defined things that are subject matter of the insurable interest. In those types of insurance, the values, at least with certain proximity, were plausible of being justly appraised from the very first moment, except sporadic or unforeseen circumstances.

In this insurance, as it also happens with civil liability insurance, the value not registered in the property of the insurer will only be established after the loss, as the loss that will be experienced shall constitute the value of the damage to be considered. It is not that the value of the interest turns out to be the property value when occurring the loss,[54] but such value is the property loss that may and must be considered as generically included in the concept of value of the thing property.

The hope, more precisely the expectation, of profit is frustrated when the property truly has not had the increase that was expected to have and towards which the will of the insured was oriented and, in consequence, there appears the obligation to compensate the insurer as it is then when the loss occurs which consequences were intended to be protected by 'transferring the risk'.

Besides, it is fundamental that, in order to speak of loss of profit or loss of economic profitability, the business we are dealing with is susceptible of getting an economic benefit or, in other words, a positive economic outcome.

No mention is made of the requirement of the lawfulness of business as some author has advised to remember,[55] due to the fact that we consider it unnecessary to repeat fundamental principles of contracts since this condition is provided for in the extremely important section 953 of the Argentine Civil Code.

As a summary of what has been exposed, it can be perfectly stated that the risk is the loss of the expected profit or the loss of the profit from interruption of business or the expected benefit, terminology that has been applied to the denomination of this species as previously seen.

It must be appreciated that what is required is that, conceptually, the property does not get to receive the increase that was expected as a consequence of the loss, consequence or consequences that may be established in the contract, either in a specific manner or directing the contractual attention to the adequate causes of the

54. This, with a criterion that we do not share, is the opinion of some individuals like Joaquín Garrigues, in his quoted work, 313. Although there is no erratum, it is our opinion that there must be certain confusion in the edition of the book in relation to the idea that author Joaquín Garrigues attributes to himself with the sentence 'in the insurance of loss of profit, the interest would be the relation that joins the insured with his property and the value of such interest shall equal his property, at the moment of occurrence of the loss'. Joaquín Garrigues, *Land Insurance Contract* (*Contrato de seguros terrestre*), 2nd ed., 313 (Madrid, 1983).

55. José L. Ruiz Sánchez, *Expert Opinion in Private Insurance* (*El peritaje en el seguro privado*) (Madrid: Montecorvo S.A. Press, 1985).

loss pursuant to the cause provision formulated by our Civil Code (its most influencing principle) and the habitual jurisprudence of the courts both Provincial and National.

The principle of adequate cause, however, is the one that most prudently permits us to apply the technical scientific bases of statistics and its experience, prudence that must indispensably guide the specific solutions.

In order to summarize the idea again, although the damage attempted to avoid will be denominated loss or, ultimately, a guarantee of the insurer will be agreed which is not on a specific profit but on preventing the consequences of an unattained profit, or that the contract is about the lack of realization of a potential profit; the insurance contract in question must be considered as property damage insurance since the expected profit shall always bring about an increase in property and, on the contrary, the lack of increase in property shall be translated into a clear damage.

This is the adequate concept of damage, strictly linked to the concept of 'lack of increase in property' that must be taken into account, pursuant to section 61 of our Act 17.418, when legislating on the obligation to which the insurer is subject in property damage insurance.

In section 61 of Act 17.418 and in its domestic precedents, the expected profit has been expressly mentioned, in order to remind us of the fact that it was not included per se in the compensations to be paid by the insurer of damaged property, but that it could be a matter of risk to be covered if it was so agreed.

In this sense, the regulation mentioned inspired the identical regulation in the same section 61 of the preliminary draft of the Commission of 1961 and section 57 of the preliminary project of Halperín of 1959, all of which gathered the teachings of the old Argentine Commercial Code (section 492) and section 14 of the French Act of 1930, among other similar regulations.

In conclusion, it is a good decision of our law, at least the incidental mention that is made to the expected profit insurance and a true guideline towards the definition of the concept as insurable. More so, when thinking that at the moment Act 17.418 was finished, it was a period when the insurance contract was not of frequent use in the existing commerce or industry in the country.

There is, in the whole exposition that has been carried out, an underlying idea that comes from the need of the existence of an insurable interest in the property insurance contract, as it is demanded by section 60 of Act 17.418, interest that, as it has been mentioned before, turns out to be affected upon the production of the future and uncertain event, which would determine the occurrence of the risk or, in the legal mirror, its contrary, the loss.

The expected profit is not produced or, in other words, the loss of the benefit occurs as the facts that have been foreseen taking place. Now, the magnitude or extension of such loss of benefit only would be appreciated when establishing its true dimension after a correct appraisal thereof, after the evidence of the case.

113. Different Contracts. In this idea that is attempted to be conveyed of insurable interest, it is important to mention and describe the different species of risks which, by means of this insurance contract, are usually covered in the insurance markets.

They are insurance for frustration of expected profits, or for money losses coming from events occurred in relation to work, or due to the suspension or privation of employment, or by property drawbacks derived from bad climate,[56] or by disposal of lease, or indirect commercial or even not related to commerce disadvantages, or by temporary professional disqualification, or by interruption of the business activity.

In policies by means of which the most prestigious insurers operating in our country document the fire insurance contract, it is commonly agreed by independent coverage that corresponds to the lease expected profit that the real property affected by the covered loss will not produce.

One characteristic that the lease loss of profit requires is that: (1) the building is condemned and in consequence, it was impossible to rent, and (2) the building or damaged part would have been occupied the day of the fire or within a month before such event.

The amount to pay due to the loss – as it is a compensation – the expected profit or, more directly for the case, the loss of lease rent shall be extended during the time necessary for the repair of the building or, if that was the case, for the reconstruction, with a maximum limit in the time of rehabilitation, if they have acted with due promptness and with the maximum limit in the amount of compensation of the assured amount by the risk 'fire'.

Another clause that, as additional to the coverage, is usually attached is to cover the loss of profit from interruption of business. It is present, as well, in the taking out of the risk covered by fire and risk of goods insurance.

As it has been stated, the fire insurance contract that – in order to clarify the following concepts could be called 'principal' insurance contract – permits in the case of goods, by means of a specific agreement embedded in a clause to be expressly agreed, the insurance guarantee of up to 85% of loss of profit, according to a stipulation of the contract and that the insured could claim for a loss affecting the principal contract.

This coverage limited to 85%, in our view, of loss of profit from interruption of business or expected profit is the application of an overdraft, the role of which is to maintain alive the interest of the insured in avoiding the occurrence of the loss.

In policies documenting the coverage of the expected profit, as additional clause to the fire clause, the denomination of overdraft is not used, but, when analysing it, it can effortlessly be noticed that when limiting the compensation payment to a percentage of the total of the experienced loss of profit – according to the proceedings that we shall be shortly analysing – it is this very adequate instrument that is being used, which collaborates with the ethics of the behaviour.[57]

As we have remembered in previous paragraphs, the difficulty to determine the expected profit comes from the need to define the concept of such damage, which is not as objective as a concrete thing and, for that reason, the requirement is to start

56. Insurance contracts that ultimately have protected the loss of benefits coming from the suspension or final cancellation of shows in the open air, as a consequence of bad climate conditions, have been carried out in several opportunities.

57. For a better analysis, it is important to have at hand the text of any of the specific clauses with which this risk is covered in our market. Nevertheless, it would be impracticable to insert such text in this type of work.

by establishing what the loss of profit from interruption of business will be the subject matter of the risk specifically covered.

Thus, the significance of establishing this and the reason why the policies of this kind of insurance contain definition clauses establishing not only the steps to find the loss of profit that should be taken as basis in order to compensate the loss but also the meaning of some indispensable concepts.

In this sense, we depart from the criterion with which the work must be carried out and, therefore, as method of work arriving to the governing concept of loss of profit or expected or unrealized profit, the idea of finding a quotient is achieved when relating 'cash value of sale' with the manufacturing or acquisition cost, both referred to goods, subject matter of the insurable interest of the principal insurance contract.

In order to achieve this relation, it is necessary to continue with the definitions: (a) cash value of sale, (b) manufacturing and acquisition cost. It is pointed out that the first is the cash sale price at the day of the loss, net of VAT, gross income, and any other tax which may be levied on the sale. The concept includes contributions. Regarding the second element that is required in order to create the aforementioned relation or percentage, that is, the 'manufacturing or acquisition cost' of the goods in question, it is equal to the same value that would correspond to compensate the principal contract, that is, the value of the compensation that would deserve to be met by virtue of the risk covered by the insurance contract, without including the value that would increase the clause of coverage by expected profit.

As it has been previously stated, it is established as loss of profit the compensation of only the 85% from the result of the aforementioned relation, upon the compensation that would have corresponded to the principal coverage and with the limitation that could arise from the assured amount, specifically agreed upon, corresponding to the coverage resulting from the specific clause of expected profit.

Finally, and so as to know where to find this regulation in the body of risk policies, it is customary to attach it to the risk of fire by an additional clause that may be called 'Clause of compensation for the goods affected to the loss per value of sale'. This denomination does not provide with accuracy the correct and prompt idea of the reality of such compensation because it misleads the reader (without purpose) from the true risk it covers, that is the loss of profit that, however, is expressly mentioned in the contents of the stipulation.

In fact, the compensation per value of sale implies the coverage of the expected profit, as the benefit considered to exist with the occurrence of the sale is the foreseeable profit which, when not receiving it by the loss of goods, is transformed into loss of profit.

Continuing with this type of insurance, reference can be made to a third case of expected profit or loss of benefit or loss of profit, which is the risk emerging of facts from different origin, that may prevent the realization or affect the massive attendance at sports events, artistic shows, or shows of any other nature.[58]

58. Many years ago, maybe twenty years ago, one of the most eminent insurance companies of our country took out the first or one of the first coverages to which we are making reference. It was the coverage of a company that brought to our country a very well-known but controversial foreign musical band in relation to loss of profit for suspension or ending of shows, as consequence of certain events, obviously alien to the parties.

A fourth assumption is the insurance protecting the loss of profit, due to the suspension or cessation of activities on account of bad climate conditions. It is very common that in countries where tourism is very much developed, the risk of a lower entrance of tourists is protected by those individuals organizing an event, or who are in charge of accommodation or lodging and restaurants, as consequence of specific facts as rain, which may prevent the usual attendance of tourists expected in a region.

114. Insurance for Loss of Benefits for Interruption of a Specific Business. In the insurance field, according to the most influencing custom, 'loss of benefits' insurance is the most common expression to cover specifically the insurance related to the interruption of business.

It is conceptually similar to the aforementioned expressions 'expected profit' or 'loss of profit'. It means that there are equal notions related to different species of the same family as one grants the general image of loss of profit insurance and the other describes one of its components.

Thus, when seeing or hearing the expression 'loss of benefits', it must be carefully considered without prejudices to which of the expression we are referring. This difference is made in order to draw attention to this possible confusion, and also to attend to the different items that may form part of the compensation.

It is necessary first to take note of the business carried out by the insured company, which procedures it uses in the elaboration of its products, the dimension of the utilized technology, the situation of the company for the assumption of constituting a legally related company and establishing the dependence or independence from another company outside or inside the market, as well as other details related to its inner structure, dimension of its payroll and directives and circumstances and opportunities of the commercial or industrial management.

The insurance of loss of benefits that we are analysing has been referred to by the market of Great Britain, the commercial net benefit plus the fixed general expenses or the constant assured expenses, ultimately, to the benefit of the gross commercial amount, having to be established a system or procedure in order to fix its corresponding amount. This insurance also has been known as loss of exploitation.

This gross commercial benefit criterion constitutes the essential information to establish an underinsurance or overinsurance since it conveys the assured value to be provided by the insured, by means of the addition of the expected net benefits and the expenses he incurred in order to obtain them.

Let us remember that the assured amount in this – as in any property insurance, even civil liability insurance – does not have any relationship with the damage. It is related to the maximum to compensate the insured and to the assured value in order to apply the proportional rule. Besides, commercially and technically, its function is to establish the premium.

There is no legal authorization needed by our law to validate a contract and, requiring for their effectiveness only compliance with the existence of their essential elements, it is not necessary that the law specially nominates this type of insurance. This is more so when, as it happens with this species, the regulations do not have nowadays any unchangeable characteristics or solely changeable characteristics in favour of the insured (section 158).

What has just been stated is also valid in relation to each and every one of the contractual features that our law and the foreign laws contribute, and which may have this same profile, as it is the parties who have the freedom to define the contractual subject matter within the guidelines of our civil law in reference to the lawfulness, agreement, consent, discernment, freedom, etc.

As variations to this coverage of expected benefits, there can be considered:

(1) An insurance contract 'annexed' to another, with different coverages, but linked in such a way that it may be estimated that the first depends on the other in regard to the occurrence of the risk. This variation implies markedly that they are considered supplementary to the property insurance taken out so that, in certain occasions, the corresponding compensation is calculated as a percentage of the one corresponding to the 'principal' compensation.
(2) An insurance contract independent from another or, in the words of some authors, which does not require of another contract to determine its shape, the risk covered and the insured risk. For instance, it would be an insurance of expected benefits with an only and exclusive subject matter, with the possibility of agreeing separately and with no relation, the specific and concrete damage of the property, making one contract conditional to the other, whose total or partial damage will interrupt or diminish the manufacturing, generating the loss of the expected benefits.

Within this type of insurance of loss of benefits by interruption of business – the taking out of which is independent from the insurance that could be agreed upon for direct damages of certain property and for different risks – there are, on the one hand, the loss of benefits for interruption or decrease of business upon cause of fire (remembering that within this insurance there are other risks included apart from fire) and, on the other hand, the loss of benefits for the interruption of business on account of damage to the machinery.

Other less frequent insurance in our business – but habitual in other more modern and booming markets – would be the coverage regarding the risk of interruption of business in electronic companies for damages in its information technology structure, either related to the material part, machinery or hardware or the part related to the programs and remaining software.

Finally, – and to the end of providing more examples of insurance cases – there is the loss of benefits by interruption of business due to strike. Without entering into the discussion of the lawfulness or unlawfulness of strikes, their possibility is stated in section 279 of the Argentine Civil and Commercial Code.

115. Appraisal of the Loss of Benefit for Interruption of Business. The loss of benefits is not restricted to the cases of absolute absence thereof, but it is referred to its diminishment. As corollary to what has been stated, comparison of the values is required that may permit to establish whether there was a decrease or not and in the affirmative case, its magnitude.

It has been mentioned *supra* the land transport insurance due to its customary rule of payment of losses occurred to goods, on the basis of the value of sale they would have had at their place of destination. That is to say that they are appraised on their purchase price (or manufacturing price added to the expected profit, since commercially, in the purchase price at destination, the expected profit is considered included).

With this, it can be stated that the profit or benefit expected could have a supposedly adequate valuation due to its reality in the case just quoted of transport but that, in the other assumptions, such loss of profit would not be anything else but a probability that, no matter how well applied the calculation is, it will always be an imaginary value.

As probability of expected profit, it must be defined the criterion to adjust it to what could have been, as from the fact bringing about the event that produces the interruption of the business activity, with consequences of total or partial loss of those expected benefits.

It is indispensable for this type of contract to clearly establish the temporal factor of compensation, that is, the time during which the insurer will meet the lost benefit.

At this stage of our analysis, it is pivotal to consider the systems or methods used to determine the loss of benefits for interruption of business. Notwithstanding the possibility – as it has been said – of exploring some contracts by virtue of the text of the policy.

The starting point would be to make it clear that such losses may come from two sources: diminishment of the income or increase of expenditure, since one way or other and, in a generic form, it can be anticipated what is obviously known regarding benefits: they are the difference between the value of cost and the price of cash sale produced.

As a confirmation of what has been exposed, it must be noted that, in the idea of diminishment of income, it is included the decrease of sales or production with direct influence on the amount to be collected since, usually, in well-established industries or commercial companies, in order to take out this kind of insurance it is considered that profitability turns out proportionally direct to the volume of the industrial and commercial movement.

It is also understood that, in the idea of decrease of income, situations – alien to the business itself – are included as, for instance, the ones coming from general economic situations or losses of the market caused by foreign factors.

However, in the concept of increase of expenditure, there are included the greater costs derived from acquisition or manufacturing price increase, fixed expenditure of administration or general expenses, and expenses incurred during the interruption in order to resume normality, which could easily be assumed under the characteristic of salvage expenses.

The suspension or interruption of the production of a company usually generates disarrangements in the harmonic relation that all companies must attempt to achieve among income and outcome or production and maintenance costs.

Let us see, then, the methods applied in order to establish the benefits lost due to the interruption or diminishment of business productivity, adding in a very simple way to what shall be analysed that, in this respect, the custom or the mechanism used by the English and American insurance markets, have imposed.

The first matter elaborated throughout time and finally adopted by contracts – with the texts nowadays in use – has been to determine whether the loss of expected benefit was conceived as net benefit or gross benefit.

In order to provide further clarification, there are definitions commonly accepted in the insurance thought and language.[59] They are:

(a) Gross benefit: net benefit plus fixed expenses that should be insured, or the total of sales less variable expenses.[60] These two last ways of achieving gross benefit should have the same result, except that, in the first assumption, all fixed expenses were not insured.
(b) Fixed expenses: an expense that the company will have to afford under any circumstance, that is, in full production or in full stop; as such expenditure does not change, it does not vary. Within this concept of fixed expenses can be pointed out: interest on loan money borrowed by the company; the leases to pay on real or personal property for the use of the company; taxes; rates or contributions corresponding to property of the company; publicity; insurance premiums; tax rebates to be paid to the payroll of the stable personnel and of the personnel under contract; expenses accrued by maintenance of property; expenses corresponding to certain special contracts such as patents and trademarks, etc.
(c) Business activities: the amounts paid to the insured for property sold or delivered from the specified store of the insured and the work carried out, including materials supplied and charged independently.
(d) Net benefit: the commercial benefit of the activity of the company, without including income or outcome chargeable to other concepts such as, for instance, the equity account, from which fixed expenses and the necessary amounts are subtracted to cover devaluation.

116. Characteristics of the Insurance of Loss of Benefits Taken out Exclusively.

We have been analysing the insurance for loss of benefit for interruption of business activity as autonomous species and, at the beginning of this chapter, as supplementary to an insurance contract of a different species as, for instance, fire insurance or engineering insurance.

Although Act 17.418 has made no reference to the contract of insurance under comment[61] in its section 88, when legislating on fire insurance it has compiled provisions similar to the Acts of Austria (section 77) and Germany (sections 89 and 90) which, in turn, were the basis of section 90 of the preliminary draft Halperín, the main source of current section 88.

The reason of this regulation, which prohibits to agree the loss of profit by means of an appraised policy,[62] comes from the mistake of conceiving that, in this way,

59. The expression 'insurance thought and language' is meant to refer to the way of thinking and current and accepted language for insurance companies and insured business people.
60. These two ways of making such determination have been called, respectively: addition method and difference method.
61. *See* the beginning of the first item of this contract.
62. *See* the quoted reference in preceding n. 77.

violations to the principle of indemnity could be avoided in this type of insurance, forgetting that this type of insurance contract of accepted value does not mean a permission for the unlawful insured's enrichment.

It is remembered that the most significant commercial utilization of this type of insurance is, as it has always happened, in the field of insurable interests of difficult appraisal.

Even when, to our opinion, section 88 of Act 17.418 is a dispositive regulation or changeable under the terms of section 158, for those placing it in the contrary sector, that is, an unchangeable regulation, it would be indispensable to notice that such thing could only happen, to follow the letter of the Act, when we are dealing with an insurance supplementary to the fire insurance and not when it is an insurance supplementary to another insurance contract, different from the fire insurance or when the coverage of loss of benefits (loss of profit) has been instrumented by means of an autonomous contract.

Although it may seem illogical, this comes from the letter of the Act and the clear sense of the words at the beginning of the aforementioned section 88 of Act 17.418.[63] And it has been qualified as illogical because the precedents of this subject, of the Austrian and German Acts, and the preliminary draft Halperín, precisely limit the possibility of agreeing in advance and by means of an appraised value, the amount of a compensation by loss of profit in order to avoid frauds that could be possible in insurance contracts of expected benefit of autonomous nature,[64] that is, those contracts that are mainly affected by a value appraised above its real value.

However, those that consider that the aforementioned section 88 of Act 17.418 is an imperative precept and thus unchangeable in the benefit of the insured, it is reminded that the penalty of nullity that would correspond according to law, would be impossible to apply due to the principle of conservation of legal businesses,[65] since, if the assumed nullity was so declared, it would not bring about any benefits to the insured that suffered the loss. Nor would it benefit an insured suffering a loss that the specific clause of the assured amount was declared null and void because then he should register the amount of the damage occurred as loss of benefit or loss of profit.

Thus, concluding this matter of application of section 88 of Act 17.418, it is our opinion that it contains an inapplicable provision because: (a) in the broadest sense of the assumption, as the clear and express letter of the law relates it to fire insurance, its nullity could be explained solely in the case it refers to an insurance of loss of profit annexed to one of fire, and (b) the nullity derived from the regulation having been violated due to taking out an annexed insurance of expected profit with an accepted value, far from benefiting the insured would prejudice him, as it has been seen.

---

63. Section 88 of Argentine Act 17.418 starts referring to fire insurance in particular, which emphasizes the position as such reference was not indispensable since such regulation is included in Art. VIII (fire insurance).
64. Francisco J. Tirado Suarez, *Insurance Contract Act* (*Ley de Contrato de Seguro*), vol. II, 405, n. 10; 409, n. 21 (Madrid: Derecho Reunidas Press, 1985).
65. It is worth remembering the Latin aphorism usually learnt during the undergraduate studies at law school: '*utile per inutile non vitiatur*'; 'what is useful is not vitiated by the useless'.

Chapter 3. Transport Insurance

117. Problems of the Speciality. Considerations Concerning Types and Legislation. It is usual that when dealing with this species of insurance, both in the theoretical and the legislation aspect, the considerations about the insurance of maritime shipping are separated from land transport insurance.[66] This separation has also been carried out regarding transport and commerce and, in consequence, between the law of transport as a unity and commercial law.

It is not the purpose, in this instance, to sustain positions about the autonomy or dependence of navigation law because they have sensibly been removed from legal literature during the twentieth century, above all since – with clear evidence – Georges Ripert[67] pointed out the subject matter of such law and specifically underlined that navigation law is an original law with the characteristic of having a very specific time and space.

It is simply important to make some considerations about an existent and very special reality; to attempt to establish the reasons that throughout time have managed to influence a tendency to convert everything related to navigation, maritime insurance, and the law governing them, into something almost esoteric. Maybe some influencing factors have been the environment where this business has developed in a concrete manner, the sea. This environment, due to its mysterious, dangerous, and, above all, fundamentally cosmopolitan characteristics, has been the cause of encouragement of lack of information of the population and merchants in general about the peculiarities surrounding it, not only during the maritime voyage but also at the ports.

The popular lack of knowledge about the activity in the sea, its commerce and its adventures has not been a matter of concern, either for the people involved in the business or for those alien to the business. For the former, it is logical to reserve their knowledge without sharing it; for the latter, it has not been indispensable or easy for them to reveal its secrets.

Additionally, the situation arising from the singular interests, first of each territory and then of each nation and country have contributed to this problem. From time immemorial, those without great extensions or riches but with important maritime territory have been naturally destined to develop their efforts, in order to improve everything that was related to the sea, to its exploitation and use, that is, everything that was centred in transportation and commerce by sea. This was because they depended on it in order to compete with other countries of greater extensions or of more powerful manufacturing of goods, but for which transport they used more known and less complex land transport means.

These countries – which we can define as maritime countries – started to create a series of analogous customs that responded to their interests in the same way they established a series of legal regulations in order to regulate those customs that were

66. Garrigues, for instance, tells us in the chapter devoted to land transport insurance that the maritime transport is not a study of 'this place', referring with this expression precisely the book and chapter that determined this note. Joaquín Garrigues, *Land Insurance Contract* (*Contrato de Seguro Terrestre*) 2nd ed., 293 (Madrid, 1983).

67. G. Ripert, *Droit Maritime*, 4th ed., vol. I (Paris: Dalloz Press, 1950).

similar in all those countries devoted to the activity in the sea. This was due to the similar characteristics, yet they differed in their inner practices and experiences – as their manufacturing forces were not linked – and all that belonged to the sea was created separately and evolved separately[68] inside them.

Thus, it was a habitual action to start attributing to the captain of the vessel very extensive powers until reaching the empowerment of his figure with unique characteristics that coined the saying 'the first in the ship after God'. It was also a common practice to classify the vessels according to certain qualities that started to be gathered under common denominators, in a way, rehearsing different frameworks for the vicissitudes to which navigation was subject.[69]

This special environment to which reference was made *supra* and the customs that every time started to more deeply root got to the point of introducing historical characteristics markedly different from the ones commercial law established as a consequence of transactions commonly carried out in towns in the course of their habitual activities, or to cover day-to-day simple needs in a way, alien to the maritime life and means.

This has been so much so that it can be affirmed that navigation law not only has not originated in commercial law but also has been exactly the opposite or, at least, that both laws, though with similar ends – ordering the relations of commerce – shaped their expression independently, reserving some institutes, in priority, for navigation law.[70]

Let us remember finally that, although autonomous, they are two branches of the law with the same interdependence and connections existing among each and every one of the several and multiple divisions of the law.

Maritime law that, besides other institutions, regulates sea transport and maritime insurance has had a precise influence on public law, as the states were not able – and it was not convenient to them – to take an interest in its evolution and the advance of commerce by sea. Over the course of time, maritime security required more attention, both in the aspects related to devices destined to render services and as the men themselves render services on the ships, in order to provide them with greater protection in the different aspects at stake.

It can be clearly noticed that navigation law also refers to, however, sport, scientific, and leisure transports that have equally demanded the contemplation of their security, from the construction of nautical elements that are utilized to the regulations pertaining to their circulation.

The influence of public law has been significant, much more than common law and even commercial law, as navigation law has sacrificed always private interests to the general interest, although this general interest many times would have been placed in the same line as private interests, connected to the maritime activity.

Lastly, in order to reach an extensive and fluid knowledge of navigation law and concretely sea transport law and of the insurance related to them, the characteristics of its customs – as it has been mentioned – the law itself due to the contents of some

68. A. Scialoja, *Sistema del diritto de la Navegazione*, 3rd ed., vol. I (Rome, 1933).
69. It must be remembered that these facts may be considered as the beginnings of the task to unravel both the frequency and the intensity of the risk.
70. *See* author and book quoted in n. 87.

exclusive institutions as for example general average, surrender,[71] bottomry and others coming from the public environment not referred to the commercial activities, but solely aiming at the uniformity of certain laws to give certainty to navigation, have constituted great obstacles. The reference is directed to the property of the ship, to the jurisdiction over it, to certain rules of the art of navigation, etc.

These situations, born under the protection of the singularities of the environment of navigation, due to the traditional characteristics of the maritime law, were maintained throughout the centuries, keeping very old regulations without further modifications, despite the advancements that those centuries had brought to science and techniques.

In France, in spite of being a country with very important coasts, two of which on fundamental seas to humanity and that, from many centuries now, has been constituted as territory leader of a group of the most culturally, scientifically, and commercially developed countries – in the words of Georges Ripert – a professional environment, almost separated from the rest of the country, has been formed.

In Argentina, that only appeared and was born politically in the nineteenth century and that has many times suffered severe problems of organizations with negative consequences, in particular in the aspects of production and foreign and economic trade in general, it seems obvious that the enigma about everything related to the sea and the transport by those means and the insurance protecting the maritime insurable interests turns out to be much more extended, reaching an avalanche of regulations and technical rules which appeared in the last decades.

This situation has not tended to change at all in the current times because, as it has happened in the past, almost defensively, those already initiated reduce the spaces for the transmission of knowledge in order to prevent those alien to them from getting such transmission. This negative attitude is impossible to avoid effectively as, first, there is no unlawfulness attached to it, and, second, it is a speciality that requires a permanent update and thus a close connection with the constant corresponding reality. This could not be possible if there is no relationship with shipowners, insurers, or at least habitual carriers of significance, permitting access to the different problems of the practice of this speciality.

Due to a matter of certain specificity – although much less important – the insurance of maritime transport has also been reserved as something mysterious or difficult. This situation was intended to be extended to land transport insurance and land transport. They do not constitute either scope for the just initiated. Yet, it is indeed full of obscurantism in the exact sense of the word, that is, of opposition to the spreading of its knowledge among many, since that would go against important interests, traditionally restricted to a few, as if we were dealing with corporate profits.

In order to finish with this introduction, we think that, although the transport of things or people has a generic objective – as it is to get these individuals or these things closer to distant places in order to permit them the access to other places,

71. This term comes from the French '*delaissement*'. *See*, G. Ripert, *Compilation of Maritime Law* (*Compendio de Derecho Marítimo*) 451 et seq. (Buenos Aires: Tea Press, 1954) as well as translator note of the mentioned page.

where some advantage is expected and strictly in the transport of goods to facilitate commerce – it is not feasible to arrive at the possibility of unifying legislatively the contents of the laws regulating them.

This impossibility comes from the unattainable equality of the elements surrounding one and the other and from the huge difference between means and places, by means of which maritime and land transport have been developed.

In this same situation of inaccessibility, river transportation is included – more so if it is interior – and air transport, which may have and has excluding regulations that are exclusive to them.

Thus, transport insurance shall not be studied as a unique entity in the analysis that follows *infra*. On the contrary, although the characteristics in common shall be analysed together, it will be considered separately, in most of the cases, the land transport insurance contract and the maritime transport insurance contract.

It will be also attempted to partially follow the criterion established in the seventeenth century which could affirm such singularity for the times that followed.

We are referring to the one adopted in France by means of the two great regulations related to commerce: the Ordinance of 1673 of land commerce and of 1681 called Ordinance about navy that was – with no doubt – a navigation code which contained specific provisions about insurance in Book VI.

In summary: The insurance contract in relation to maritime or air transport should be dealt with in monographs devoted specifically to such aspects – and more in keeping with the different Acts of our country – it shall be dealt with in this monograph only with the insurance contract referred to land carriage.

118. Land Transport Insurance Contract. The Argentine Act of Insurance 17.418 includes some regulations about land transport insurance contracts; in its Title I, Article XII, Chapter II referred to property damage.

In two of these sections, section 121 in its second part and section 123, is mentioned the right to take out insurance of any type of risk for transport vehicles or transported goods and also for transporters' liability as well as the interval of coverage.

This position regarding land transport insurance did not mean that the tendencies of the times of abandoning the criterion of universal coverage of risks of transport to open to the principle of plurality or individualization of risks were being followed – as the legislations that had already appeared in the twentieth century had started to impose – when adopting the custom of commercially developing, by means of the coverage granted by the policies instrumenting contracts. It solely expressed the position of looking for and obtaining the State's intervention for many commercial activities, in accordance with the political tendencies that were developed in Argentina and that constituted the interventionism of the State that we have previously mentioned.

The item about the individualization or generality of risks is a current topic, as, frequently both in the language used in the insurance scope and in certain abbreviations in the expression and writing, this matter of transport of goods insurance is referred to under the title or generic denomination of this type of insurance in the same way we speak about motor vehicle insurance.

In no way an attempt is being made to refer to the risk or risks covered, as if they were included in a whole or, ultimately, and with the use of our imagination, an insurance contract of some type covering ‘all risks’. In other words, one thing is the general title of the contract (transport), and another thing are the risks that it may cover or that are usually covered by any of these contracts, as is indicated in the specific conditions of the policies documenting them, in accordance with the applications filed by the policyholders.

It can be seen that clause 2 of the general conditions rules of the policies – in use in our country – specifically mentions the coverage of risks indicated therein and refers to the event of transport as the lapse of effectiveness of the contract.

What has just been mentioned is to such extent true in relation to the use by extension of the name ‘transport insurance’ that even in the judicial judgments – and with the same innocent intention that any person could have – it is habitual to refer to ‘risk of transport’ when, in reality, mention is being made to one or some of the specific risks that could occur during the lapse and trajectory of the transport.

Truly, the risk must be established affirmatively, and the exclusions, obviously, when they are connected to covered risks, must also be affirmative. The exclusions do not necessarily need to be mentioned when the risk is not covered.

Land transport may be carried out by different means covering the trajectories by land proper, such as railroads, motor vehicles, or vehicles drawn by animals either in the interior of the country or internationally.

Land transport insurance is an insurance of damage to property, although it is a subspecies with independent features. As a subspecies of the insurance of damage to property it has a direct relation with the indemnity principle and, consequently, with the insurable interest.

In the matter of maritime insurance, the regulations to be applied are the ones contained in Act 20.094 for generic use in the sense that section 16 of the Civil Code admits the supplementary application of regulations.

Despite the exceptions that the advances of modern techniques of communication and surveillance systems may determine, also during the interval of transportation, there is certain independence from the means used and from its maximum responsible person as, saving the distance between the different motor vehicles serving land and maritime transports – as well as the different possibilities in communication of one and the other – there is a sort of self-government in land transport in relation to the means intended for such activity or to the specific responsible thereof, beyond the control that may be exercised from general operative centres, as it would be the stations of the train service or trucks or buses, etc.

Expanding this item, the distinction among risks that may be covered in the land transport insurance contract is not of legal consequence, as our Act 17.418 does not establish different or specific consequences for each and every class of insurance, as it has been generically and unnecessarily established in its sections 121 and 123.

It has been already pointed out the previous tendency to establish the principle of universality of risks, that is to say that, instead of insuring one or several specific risks, the total of risks subject to carriage of things, as consequence of the transportation event, is insured.

In other words, all risks that could happen during transportation are insured, which was considered one work; that is, the transport was considered a sole task: the carriage of things from one place to another.

From there that the idea of transport, in the first place, included a longer lapse than the strict trip, as it referred to the course of time and space during which the things to be transported, after being delivered to a transporter, had to remain under the absolute control of this individual until they were passed to the consignor at the agreed place and, in the second place that, due to the fact of such control, holding or availability and due to the criterion regarding the task undertaken, risks were estimated as coming from transport and not from other cause as fire, theft, etc.

For better clarification, it was not, for instance, that the subtraction with violence of the goods participated of the nature of the 'theft' but that, when this occurred during transportation – the interval during which it was unknown what could happen – the significant fact was precisely that the transport was not carried out with correction.

In the case of maritime shipping, it was conceived the thought of the existence on the hands of the transporter, of an obligation of result; thought that, later on was also translated into land carriage.[72]

In reality, during transport, there are combined activities of different nature as, on the one hand, things or people are being transported and, on the other hand, there occurs either a contract of regular storage in the first case or an innominate contract of protection and security if the transport included people, which clarifies the understanding that the transport contract attaches some obligations of one and the other.

It has been sustained the legal and economic freedom to carry out insurance contracts via land, including an absolute variety of risks, without the need of regulating their names or ends. It is in the interest of commerce to establish the specificity of those risks and their limitations, as we are dealing with insurance protecting insurable interests or the insured during their transport and their agreed extensions.[73]

Finally – and though it is a matter applicable to all types of insurance – it is valid to state that, even when the specific or concrete risk covered is established in each insurance contract (grounds of the risk), it is undoubted that the name that legally can be granted to some type or class of these contracts (for instance, fire, liability, life, accidents, etc.), generically marks their legal position, as it is required on several grounds by controlling Act 20.091.

119. Risk and Insurable Interest in Land Transport Insurance. Every risk that is agreed upon, as we are dealing with a subspecies of insurance within the type of damage to property, shall have the characteristic of compensatory insurance. As a consequence of this, the insurable interest is one of its indispensable elements; without its existence, the land transport insurance contract would not exist.

---

72. Giuseppe Ferri, *Manuale di Diritto Commerciale*, 2nd ed., 655 (Torino: Utet Press, 1965). For Ferri, as it has also been for many others for a long time, the purpose of the rendering of service of transport is the result of an activity to one's own risk, activity that is within the category of contract for work, being characterized by the particularity of the promised result that consists in the transportation from one place to another of people or things.
73. Argentine Act 17.418 has not established expressly as compulsory any regulation that brings about the principle of universality in this respect.

As in the remaining property damage insurance, the insurable risk that is ordinarily evidenced is the owner's, as this one is the usual insured, but the possibility of other intervening insurable interests and other insured, different from the owners, has been already commented on, always taking into account that such insurable interest, above all, would really mean the conservation of the transported things.

It is worth considering the importance arising out of this type of insurance, the contract for account of a third party, by virtue of the urgent matter that in the world of commerce is respecting the need of a rapid way to transmit rights over things that are the subject matter of commercial traffic.

The transfer of the insurance contract does not bring about the transfer of the insurable risk, but once transferred the right in a legal form, the insurance for account of a third party or the insurance for account of whom it may correspond shall be effective regarding the passive legitimation of the holder; thus the celerity of the operations does not have a solution of continuity.

This way, the value implied in this modality of contract is increased in the land insurance contract, as also the floating or unvalued insurance is revitalized due to its invaluable function of speeding the coverage of goods, insuring them beforehand, although they would be regularized only with the successive declarations of unvalued insurance.

In order to provide a list of insurable interests in relation to a current assessment of their classification, attention should be drawn to: goods, means of transport, and finally, other objectives:

(a) *Goods.* Not all the goods are susceptible of being subject matter of a land transport insurance contract, as not all of them are aimed at being transported in the same way. The reference is not linked to the legal possibilities, but to the technical and commercial convenience, due to the excessive danger that the assumption of the risk implies. We must take into account the fact that the carriage of certain types of goods can only be instrumented by agreeing expressly – with an express statement – the type of things to be transported in order to disclaim or assume the responsibilities of the case. In this line, inflammable, corrosive, explosive, or hazardous materials are involved, and it is required – due to the evident link between transport and insurance contracts – a specific agreement. It can be considered an extension to this, radioactive goods or material, subjects on which there are regulations locally and internationally, for a possible insurance coverage.

From another point of view – and following what has been mentioned *supra* – due to the specific quality of the goods to be transported, there are technical impossibilities of assuming the risks in the case of money, jewellery, and commercial papers, which, in the same way as in fire insurance, require a concrete value to be notified since each object is subject matter of the insurable interest. Thus, for these assumptions special agreements are required.

There are other goods that, due to their nature, need to comply with certain supplementary conditions, in addition to the usual ones which imply a greater price in transport and in the corresponding insurance as, for instance, it is the case of live animals and of organic matter, be they for alimentary purposes or not.

The terms and conditions of the policies documenting the contracts of the type under analysis determine a subdivision in the class of goods that have been traditionally established by transporters and individuals linked to the activity.

In the case of different types of insured goods, when the coverage is due to the risk of robbery with violence over people or force over things, besides a different premium, it is a common practice, to establish an overdraft of 5%–20% of the amount to be compensated – in keeping with one or another type of class of things. This clause expressly states the prohibition of insuring such overdraft and the independence of such deduction coming from an underinsurance or any other that was agreed upon.

There are also goods of a heterogeneous nature, as they constitute a group of connected things among each other by different circumstances. This happens with carriage for different kinds of things: the corresponding insurance for furniture of a house, as consequence of a removal and the so modern container carriage and insurance.

(b) *Means Employed.* It has been advanced that, according to the means employed, land transport can be carried out by motor vehicle, by animals, or by railway. Regarding transport insurance contracts it must be excluded those referred to motor vehicle means as, according to the customs followed, the risks corresponding to the cab of the carriage, including the parts of the vehicle that are necessary to contain the goods transported according to their nature (e.g., tank truck for liquid products) are covered by motor vehicle insurance, different from the land transport insurance contract.

These coverages exclude damages habitually caused by the goods themselves from the moment of loading to downloading, both included.

(c) *Other Objectives.* Leaving aside due to its absolute insignificance nowadays the transport by animals, it deserves special consideration the insurance of non-motor rolling material destined to the transport of people or things for the damages that could be experienced during their specific functions, as well as those that such material could cause on people or transported goods.

The policies documenting the carriage insurance establish their provisions under which an agreement is reached and that, besides, establish the limits of the case.

Up to now, nothing has been said about passenger insurance. This is due to the fact that, in our system as in other parts of the world (e.g., Spain), by means of special Acts, the transport of passengers has been regulated, through different mechanisms, which practically cover the total of the means used.

In the matter of transport of people by motor vehicles, the insurance contract of that type has been traditionally the one in charge of granting the coverages of the case, either by means of a liability insurance contract or by means of a specific passenger insurance, which characteristic is to be a special social type coverage, aimed at collecting a premium included in the cost of each ticket, automatically paid by each user of a means of transport (buses or motor vehicles) adhered to a collective or group system that has been designed.

Truly, this insurance has worked as a subsidy to the means of transport by the passengers themselves. Its mechanism – in order to claim a compensation as a consequence of an accident – has been a channel for fraud since the basis for the possibility of a claim is to have been passenger to the vehicle at the moment of the accident, and such events have always been evidenced by simply showing a ticket, without the possibility of avoiding an unjustified use, possession, or holding thereof.

The risk in passenger transportation is insured by the same insurance contract covering civil liability with respect to third parties (non-passengers).

120. Some More Information about Risk. Regarding transportation, as it is widely known, there are many changeable concepts in relation to the responsibility for damages that may have been caused to individuals or things during its performance, as well as the civil liability with respect to damage to a third party.

This contractual or extra-contractual liability has determined insurance coverages of different kinds that, however, have been caused or influenced by the person that turns out to be the insured.

In our law system, the old Commercial Code introduced a principle that states that, in the matter of transports, business people must prevent the deterioration of the effects that are being transported, and from section 162, it starts to establish precepts establishing the same role for the transporter[74] until reaching the extraordinary concept of section 184, where it is stated – although mainly referring to injury or death of a passenger occurred during the transport via railway – the principle that the jurisprudence of all courts in the country have interpreted as compensation of damages and that has been linked to all the transport industry, regardless of the means of transport.

However, it is feasible in certain assumptions, to apply sections 1109 and 1113 of the Civil Code regarding civil liability and, from the international scope, Act 24.449 about transport on roads in the country as of 22 December 1994 and enacted 6 February of the following year, where it is ratified the application of treaties, as the one of Paris in 1926, Washington in 1943, and Geneva in 1949.

Regarding railway transport, there is the Act in full force No. 22.647 with its reglementary Decrees 747/88 and 114/91, ratified the regulations of the Commercial Code and emphasized the talent of its author Mr Dalmacio Vélez Sarsfield when providing in section 204 that: 'The regulations or provisions of the companies that would have offered services to the public, excluding obligation and responsibilities imposed by this Code shall be null and void.'

It is worth remembering that, due to its importance and use, the insurance existing in certain countries, covering the risk of loss of profit or loss of benefit of the drivers of motor vehicles who, by punishable offences, are sentenced not to drive for a shorter or longer period of time.

74. This section that has been applied analogically to passenger transportation by other means of transport besides the railway states, however, the full compensation for damages, prohibiting any agreement to the contrary.

The professional driver sentenced with this prohibitive sanction, which bans him from driving a means of transport – which may include the withdrawal of the driving licence – not being able to continue with his habitual job, loses income (either wages, commissions, or any other kind of remuneration) and the insurance covers such loss.[75]

Another point to mention is the civil liability insurance contract in the matter of transport, a point that has been already mentioned. In order to limit this subject, it is important to establish the independence that this contract has in relation to the specific transport insurance or any other contract that may exist in reference to passengers and the possibility of their coexistence. What is intended with this explanation is to clarify that, in case of concurrence of insurance contracts, if a load is damaged due to a risk covered during a transportation, the owner of the insurable interest has the possibility of exercising two types of claims against the insurers from any of the two existing contracts in the example that has just been mentioned.

All that notwithstanding, the rights against the transporter by application of the responsibility derived from the contract of transport proper, contractually or extra-contractually. One of such claims would be against the specific insurer of the load damaged as a consequence of the carriage insurance contract, and the other claim would be brought against the insurer by civil liability of the transporter or any other person civilly liable for the damage. Naturally, the actions will not be able to accrue compensations but only up to the amount of the damage.

In the insurance practice of our country by the most prominent insurance companies, liability coverage as supplementary clause to be annexed to the carriage policy is limited by the claim, which could only be carried out by the insurers attempting to recover the payment that they could have previously performed to their damaged insured during transportation, on account of certain specific risks. It is also limited by the amount of the claim up to the amount with which the owner of the goods could have been compensated, excluding certain risks such as larceny, pilferage, failure to deliver, and disappearance of the goods when it is accompanied by disappearance of the driver or when the latter was involved in the event.

121. Surrender. In this paragraph, it shall be seen a typical institute[76] of the maritime law that has passed to insurance law: the abandonment.

Our Insurance Contract Act regulates the matter primarily in section 74, rejecting it generically for all types of property insurance. Later on, Act 17.418 by means of section 124 accepts it for the case of transport insurance contracts. We shall begin by defining the right of abandonment in order to differentiate it from the other alternative rights, nominated with the same name in the laws of some countries.

The abandonment in maritime law that originated the abandonment in insurance law has nothing to do with the abandonment of French law, meaning resignation or

75. Antigono Donati, *Trattato del Diritto delle Assucurazioni Private*, vol. III, 277 et seq (Milan). For Donati it is a loss of profit insurance.
76. Once again, the words 'institution' or 'institute' have been used in order to denominate, as many other individuals do, a group of regulations related to the same subject or the same substance, subject matter of the legal body of laws.

assignment of vessel to creditors.[77] Thus, to denominate it in the law we are dealing with, it has been called surrender,[78] and abandonment is reserved for the corresponding maritime right as explained.

The 'surrender' is a very old practice, by virtue of which was established a sort of benefit for the insured who, due to the lack of news in cases of lost vessels, was not compensated because of the impossibility of irrefutably evidencing such loss. With this custom of granting the insured the right of surrender, the insured was benefited because the loss of the vessel in fact was a loss for him by means of this absurd subterfuge.

As time went by, the protection was extended by a random convention to the total compensation of the insured by means of the complete assignment of the insured interest.

Briefly, it can be commented that the surrender or the abandonment of the right of insurance is a technical instrument of payment of damage. Evidently, this was finally the result of a conflict of interest because insurers restricted the subject first to major events, as consequence of risks common to the sea, as in this subject, then and now, is always more taken into account the intensity of the loss than the quality of the risk from which it arises.

Lastly, the surrender has passed to the law of our day by the Colbertian Ordinance of 1681 which has been discarded today for land insurance cases, including the type of the transport trade.

Nevertheless, as it has been seen in our Act 17.418, the agreement to the contrary is possible, thus reaffirming the dispositive characteristic of the legal provision.

In summary: in our law, surrender of the property, the subject matter of the insurable interest, is not imposed on any of the parties of the insurance contract, and only an express agreement would allow the insured to exercise his right of assigning the insurer the ownership of the property, collecting the total of the compensation which would mean for the insurer to become the owner of the title thereof.

With what has just been said, it is natural that the surrender could only be agreed upon when the insured turned out to be the owner of the insurable interest, as he would be the only person entitled to carry out that indispensable transfer of title.

It has been mentioned in this item that, despite rejecting the law of surrender in general for insurance in contracts of transport, except agreement to the contrary, there is a provision for one case according to section 124 that is transcribed below due to its importance for the matter.[79]

122. Coverage for Time and Trip. In the matter of land transport insurance, the temporal limitation of the insurance contract, that is, the lapse of effectiveness of the carriage that is hired, has different ways of expression.

---

77. Georges Ripert, *Compilation of Maritime Law* (*Compendio de Derecho Marítimo*) 709 (Buenos Aires: Tea Press, 1954).
78. This word is translated by Pedro G. San Martín from the term '*delaissement*', which Ripert includes in the book quoted in the previous note.
79. Section 124: 'When it is being dealt with land transportation, the surrender shall only be possible if there is effective total loss. The surrender shall be carried out in a lapse of 30 days as from the occurrence of the loss. For the means of transport by river and interior waters, maritime insurance regulations are applied.'

Time can be determined by means of specific dates, as it happens when in the contract the date of commencement of coverage and the day of ending of coverage is established.

The transport insurance contract can be agreed not only by a definite time but also by trip, that is, according to the lapse of duration that a specific trip may have.

The subject has been legislated by section 123 of Act 17.418.

The commencement and ending of coverage, regardless of the type of contract that is carried out, either by time or by trip, shall be habitually fixed in contracts that are carried out in our country by establishing in a general clause, said term of material duration, by means of a specification that shall be different in the assumption that the transportation was carried out by the insured or by a transporter.

If the transportation was carried out by the insured proper, that is, the person who has the insurable interest of the load, the commencement of the coverage would start at the moment in which the vehicle destined to carry out the transportation is put in movement to start the trip, provided for in the contract, logically, once the goods, subject matter of the insurable interest, are on board such vehicle.

The insurance, thus commenced, would be effective during the ordinary course of transport, ending with the arrival of the vehicle at the final destination, in keeping with the contract. Included in this clause, in the ordinary course of transport, are stops, stays, and normal transfers.

If the transportation was carried out by a transporter alien to the insurable interest on the load, the situation would change.

The commencement of coverage is established when those goods that are the subject matter of the insurable interest are received by said transporter, and the ending of the coverage is agreed upon in the insurance policy when these transported goods are delivered at the final destination, such delivery having to be fulfilled fifteen days from the arrival at the forwarder's deposit. In this assumption, the coverage extends during the ordinary course of transportation where stops, stays, and normal transfers are included.

The expression of this clause 'ordinary', which means 'habitual', is very significant, as it renders a broad meaning to the coverage and provides a sensible term within which the trajectory of the transport will be assessed. Thus, all stop or stay or transfer, under normal circumstances, shall be a normal part of the transportation as they are part of the process of transfer of the goods.

The interruptions taking place out of the insured's or transporter's control which lasted more than five days will be excluded, as from their corresponding commencements, except when the extension of the trip responded to the occurrence of a risk covered by the policy.

In some parts, it is usual to add some conditions to the policies in order to complete the extension of the ordinary course of the trip with a maximum term of coverage. If once such term has elapsed, the trip is not resumed, the final termination of the transport insurance contract takes place.

From what has been observed in the previous paragraphs, it turns out that the policies documenting in our country transport insurance contracts which, for specific reasons of our market, have taken texts similar or practically identical to the conditions regulating them, follow different guidelines in connection to the different situations that a cargo may undergo, whether its transportation is the owner's responsibility or not.

123. The Own Vice. The institute of own vice of our Act 17.418, which, with fidelity to its model, regulates in almost an identical way as the French Act of 1930, has been from its beginnings full of variations for its correct formation, construction, and definition.

The own vice appeared as grounds of reaffirmation of exclusion of the responsibility of the maritime carrier and, after being accepted its accidental and natural division, it was recognized as possible theoretical risk to be separately covered and finally, as legal basis of exclusion of risk.

Act 17.418 analyses the matter in section 66, when legislating about property damage in general and, later on, in section 127, when specifically dealing with transport insurance.

The precedent of these two regulations had been two other regulations of the French law of 1930, sections 33 and 44, later incorporated as sections L 121-7 and L 122-5 of the *Code des Assurances.*

They are placed as matters of maritime law, specifically after the Convention of Brussels of 1924, when the formula of English and American law of the end of the nineteenth century on responsibility of the transporter was incorporated.

This responsibility was attributed to the transporter when he did not exercise due diligence in compliance with his obligations in order to put the vessel in a good state for navigability before an expedition or the commencement of a voyage in each one of the stages of the route (the so-called due diligence of the Anglo-Saxon law which, later on, was extended to many activities, although obviously changing the type of obligation to fulfil).

This duty in the maritime transport of cargo was solely and especially linked to the behaviour of the shipowner, but it was not related to any other safeguarding principle of the freighter or consignee of the cargo. Thus, once accomplished the duty of the burden of navigability in a sensible way, the transporter was not liable for any damages that could occur to the goods and that would not have been caused by having omitted 'due diligence' or having made certain mistakes while carrying it out.

The maritime transporter then was not the responsible party for any damages or latent defects of the vessel not detected during the reasonable due diligence, duly carried out. More so, the transporter was not liable if the damages of the goods came from a specific defect thereof, as in no way could such defect be attributed to the person acting with reasonable due diligence. Further, there was also an assumption of culpability on the carrier if the goods had a defect.

The own vice derived from the same nature as goods, and it was inseparable from them. It was not a defect that could become evident during transportation, on account of it or of the transfer.

The own vice – that is not very simply determined – had its most adjusted definition maybe when it was characterized as a pathological condition of the goods, a condition dependant either on an intrinsic originary defect or a natural defect of the goods, as long as, in the cause of the damage produced, there was no culpability on the transporter or his agents.[80]

For maritime law, the classes of own vices ruling out the responsibility of the transporter were, for instance: excessive humidity, which could remain in the baling of cotton and that encouraged spontaneous combustion; excessive maturity of the fruit embarked during the beginning of the spring; decrease of volume and weight during the route of transport by usual evaporation of liquids or humidity of grains.

The French law of 1930 has been the first body of law of significance that installed a regulation about the own vice, referring to the natural defects of one thing, thus there was no insurable risk since it was not an uncertain event but, on the contrary, its future occurrence was undoubted. Later on, the books of authority noticed the possibility of accidental defects, which could be distinguished from the natural defects commented on, and, although the latter could not have been subject matter of insurance for the almost true occurrence of the loss, accidental vices – as they were truly contingent – could actually be the subject matter of a risk to cover.

Thus, it was ruled that the accidental defects were the ones unknown about a thing (latent defects) but which not necessarily would appear in others of the same species. (These defects are derived from bad formation or bad manufacturing.)

One of the classic examples was the cracks in the steel of a machine that affected the structure (*paille*),[81] but did not repeat in other similar machines, as a result of a better manufacturing.[82]

Thus, these malformations or bad manufacturing constituted vices or accidental, abnormal defects and due to their uncertainty, for the condition of unforeseeable and the characteristic of doubtful, they were liable to be covered by insurance as they would not inevitably occur. Ultimately, due to the transformation occurred through the different books of authorities and experiences, the own vice, in reality, became an accidental, latent defect, different from natural defects of the thing, as previously seen in maritime law.

This transformation was caused by a matter that, far from being legally significant, came from a legislative policy derived, in turn, from economic pressures of a sector on the regulation on insurance. Thus, when deciding about the construction of the agreement of the parties, the risk representing the own vice was excluded from the coverage, except when an express agreement of the parties took place.

The Argentine Act respected the method of its French model since, besides practically providing its text and criterion, also adopted its considerations and, on the one hand, dealt with the matter in a generic way for all property damage insurance – as section 33 of French Act of 1930 did – and, on the other hand, legislated on the

80. Simone Osvaldo, *Compilation of Navigation Law* (*Compendio de Derecho de la navegación*) (Buenos Aires: Abaco Press de Rodolfo Depalma, 1996) (*see* judgment of the Italian Cassation Court, quoted by Osvaldo).
81. In reality, the French authors quoted in this monograph to compare the institute of own vice in our legislations literally mention a '*paille*' in the machine. Even when '*paille*' is translated as straw in Spanish, it is also translated as crack and hair in the dictionary Larrouse, ed. 1967, 526. A crack in Spanish is defined as a defect in the blade of the sword consisting of cracks in the steel that are discovered when folding it.
82. M. Picard & A. Besson, *Les Assurances Terrestres*, vol. I, 321 (Paris: LGDJ Press).

point in a particular manner when referring to the fire insurance with section 44, after section L 122-5 of the Insurance Code.

This matter of own vice has been so full of obstacles and entanglements that our Act[83] mixed in one of its sections, section 127, the own vice with deteriorations of the thing (that is, the insurable interest) and with other absolutely different grounds as it could be those derived from negligence, error, or malice of the carrier and other objective ones.

The damage to the goods caused by intrinsic nature (natural own vice) or those caused by decrease or spillage (also natural own vice) is very different from those coming from bad conditioning and packing in which, at least, recklessness from the carrier could have taken place, without prejudice of the negligence derived from the action or omission of the transporter.

In the same way, the connection made between contracts of adhesion and the crisis of contract has influenced the matter under consideration, establishing certain regulatory determinations about coverage and restrictions to the freedom of contract, with non-guaranteed damages, except where there is agreement to the contrary.

The French law had contradictions when intending the application of contrary principles, exaggerating the realities that existed until then. On the one hand, we are before a postulate of its purposes article about the limitation of the legislator to impose on the insurer certain guarantees regarding one or another risk.[84] On the other hand, its section 12 (L 113-1) determined a need for the determination of the extension of each and every risk exclusion, in a formal and limited way, without admitting vague clauses.[85]

It is our opinion that, beyond those very first moments, when the responsibility of the transporter and the incorporation of the institute of insurance started to form commercially, any reference to the own vice should have been legislatively suppressed since, if it is or it was considered a risk, even a non-habitual or common risk, any reference in the law was unnecessary since, for being a risk, it required and requires a clear description for its coverage, that is, for its inclusion as covered risk.

The negative determination of the not covered risk is not urgent; far from it. It is advisable though, said determination or the specific indication of coverage exclusions when it implies a more precise clarification of coverage, but not when it may imply confusions. More so, when the transport coverage has ceased to be universal or all risk, as pointed out in the first part of item 2 of this chapter.

83. This subject has not been privative of the Argentine law since it has been introduced by other prior and posterior laws as the French law of 1930 (ss 13, 33, 34 and the decision of Argel of 10 Jun. 1965) and partially the Spanish (s. 44).

84. Besson & Picard, *Les Assurances Terrestres*, vol. 1, 64 (Paris: LGDJ Press, 1975): '*il ne dépend pas du législateur d'imposer à l'assureur la garantie de tel ou tel risque*'.

85. The authors – particularly those quoted in the previous note and the following note – remember that this regulation of s. 12 had not been introduced to the preliminary draft and that it appeared in the parliamentary discussion; thus is suggested the intervention of political reasons for electoral purposes.

124. The War. We would like to point out the fact that, when dealing with certain coverages in particular as, for instance, life and land transport, advantage has been taken in order to analyse certain exclusions of risk of other motivations expressed by law that could have been commented in the general part of this monograph.

The scheme decided, in order to write about insurance contracts in Argentine law, was chosen following what we thought the best way for its study; thus, we have left them for the second part of this monograph, even when we know they are generic matters, as we believe they are much closer to specific insurance.

This has happened with own vice and war. Although this could be a reprehensible mistake, we consider that it will not end in a drawback for the structure of the monograph, more so when this second part is included in the edition.

To begin with, it can be established that in a similar manner to what occurred with the own vice of the insurable interest – where it was assumed what the will of the parties would be and thus, it was excluded from the coverage in the same Act – the legislator has also speculated with the negative position of the parties in order to include in the agreement the risks of war.

However, it is important to take into consideration that this 'risk of war' is a relative and variable concept according to the conditions, even the political conditions, of such wars.

In this sense, it must be pointed out the great differences that have existed between the different wars that took place in the last sixty years, both in regard to its territorial extensions and their durations and, obviously, their effects.[86] Due to these circumstances, such risks have or may have truly great variations both of frequency and intensity, irregularities that do not permit calculations given their useless statistics for subsequent wars, as a consequence of these variables that take place in time.

The similarity with own vice regarding the assumption of the will of the parties, commented at the beginning of one of the previous paragraphs, is the fact that both risks come from maritime law; pursuant to an old practice, they are unforeseeable, they are impossible to resist by ordinary means and the reach of commerce and, precisely, the argumentation that supported exclusions which have been just analysed derived from that technical scope.

This is true especially for those coming from the risk of war, as they do not have sufficient dispersion, in order to economically enable compensation. Moral support as exclusion of intent, at the same time, contributed to strengthen the idea of its elimination.

In this line, it is not understandable the motivation that could have had the law in our country when gathering under the same article, entitled causing of loss, circumstances so different that should not have been gathered (as negligence and malice of the insured and international war or public riot). It is our conclusion that the French precedent excessively influenced the preliminary draft of 1959 and 1961, above all,

86. Jacob Nicolás, *Les Assurances*, 2nd ed., 233 and 93 (Paris: Dalloz Press, 1979). The opinion of Jacob enlightens us with some of the reality about this point when saying that '... *cette notion n'est pas en effet la même dans la loi du 22 Juillet 1919 et dans celle du 22 février 1940–14 mai 1941, ni dans la jurisprudence des deux guerres*'.

because of the profuse and contradictory jurisprudence existing as a consequence of World War II,[87] and almost immediately after the war nominated French-Indochina war, of which stories about Bien Dien Phu as well as about the award-winner nurse Geneviéve are still remembered.

The situation is regulated by insurance contracts by means of the uniform text of the policies, text truly imposed, although unfairly, by the SIN, as from the very first moments of Act 17.418.

In these policies, towards the first years of the decades of 1970s and 1980s, it started to be introduced compulsorily and by resolution of the Superintendence, the clause of coverage exclusion denominated as clause of coverages interpretation contained in the general conditions.

This compulsory text, with the purpose of interpreting a clause that forms part of the 'general conditions', is simply about granting precision to something that traditionally constituted the study of scholars linked to the reality of insurance and, further, as determining factor, there was a political need to resolve a severe situation that terrorist attacks by guerrilla rebels who had made their appearance in the country at that time had given rise to.[88]

What were the damages caused by the civil or international events of war, mutiny, public riot, as it states section 71 of Act 17.418? This has been the question not only in our sphere but, and with more concern, due to the experiences suffered abroad. Not even as a consequence of the war of Malvinas in 1982, of the military revolutions that took place over several years, or the terrorist guerrillas unravelled all over the country during the decades of the 1960s and 1970s can answer that question; in our jurisprudence they are only isolated cases. Nor can the inner books of authority serve as guidelines. In this line, it is worth remembering the political influence that had in our country the governments of Perón before and after 1955 and the several military governments until 1989, which conditioned many judgments of the Courts.

That is why we have deemed it convenient to resource both to foreign jurisprudence and foreign books of authority, especially those coming from countries where legislation has served us as precedent. The question went around several related matters, the main ones being the causal influence that a war or the state of war may or may not have over occurred damages.

125. Other References to Texts of the Policies of Insurance Contracts of Land Transportation. To achieve a better precision in the preceding title, it should be read as 'content and meaning of some of the general terms and conditions more commonly used in the Argentine market'.

---

87. Paul Sumien, *Traité Théorique et Pratique des Assurances Terrestres*, 7th ed., 1045, 1st (Dalloz Press, 1957).
88. The matter of reference are the terrorist attacks with explosive devices causing fire in several local *Minimax* supermarkets installed at that time in the City of Buenos Aires. Without further comments, it can be remembered that, during one or two nights in a row, there were explosions of great magnitude in such stores that, together with the fires, caused great damage. The question was whether they ought to be covered or not, for being events that had just started in Argentina and that showed a specific kind of behaviour.

The reason of such statement is to make some clarifications that we deem important as the insurance contract of land transport is a typical case of regulation by agreement of wills, in which the law solely has dispositive rules since there are no preventions seen in other insurance contracts, by the different position that the parties assume:

(a) In transport insurance contracts, a general clause is included that, when making reference to the owner of the insurable interest, would seem to accept his change, that is, the assignment of the insurable interest with effects regarding the insurance contract, without the need of an express intervention from the insurer.

We are referring to the fact that, under the denomination of the change of owner of the insured interest or the taker, it is established that the insured is released from notifying the insurer of the change in the insured interest, but the taker must notify without delay to the insurer the change of carrier, transporter, or consignee, whenever he is invested with any of these capacities.

Even when it is not expressly stated, the text used for this clause brings about the sensation of referring to the fact that, before the assignment of the insured interest, the insurance shall be also transferred to its assignee.

Nevertheless, that is not so. The insurable interest is assignable in Argentine law, without that implying the transfer ipso jure of the transport insurance contract, which may protect the property subject matter of the insurable interest.

In the case under analysis, there is another case in the policies documenting the transport insurance contract in our country that establishes the favourable agreement to the trade, on account of its broadness, which is the insurance for account of whom it may correspond.

Then the condition we are referring to in this brief paragraph, instead of being related to the transfer of the transport insurance contract, as a consequence of the transfer of the insurable interest, is closely related to the situation emerging from the contractual form of the insurance that, leaving uncertain the person of the insured when agreeing that it would be for account of whom it may correspond, it unavoidably requires the appearance of such in order to claim the payment of the loss, without such appearance having to be prior to the mentioned loss (clear doctrine arising from section 22 of Act 17.418).

With reference to the taker of the transport insurance contract, whose rights have been considered when dealing with the subject of the taker in general, the clause under analysis demands the burden of informing 'without delay' to the insurer the change of carrier, transporter, or consignee, in the assumption that the taker proper also was invested with some of these capacities.

This duty, on the hands of the taker under specific circumstances, turns out to be logical in order to guarantee the insurer that the existence of his person shall not be altered when the concrete transport is indicated with some of these qualities of significance for the transport or for the compliance with the obligations imposed by the established trip. It is very important to remember the concepts mentioned about insurable risk and its transfer, as well as the regulations contained in Act 17.418 in sections 81 and 82, as it is precise not to misinterpret these regulations. The law in itself provides a conflictive disorder when mentioning section 82 as a repealable regulation in favour of the insured, without the necessary certainty of making an exception to the precept contained in the first paragraph, in relation to the importance of the notification.

(b) Another clause that usually appears in order to reduce risks in some way and, consequently, to cut insurance costs is to agree on the application of a franchise that will be deducted from the amount of the compensation to pay in the case of a loss. Contractually, this clause is known as 'optional franchise', although, in our opinion, the reference should be to an overdraft and not to a franchise.

The expression of option, though, is correct to the extent that only by means of a special agreement of wills can a reduction on the amount of real compensation to pay by a loss be established and collected by the insured.

The matter of the terminology used at the beginning of the first paragraph of this item (b) is not certainly inflexible but, at least, is harmonic, according to the meaning of one and other word as it has been previously stated. In general, when this particular condition is introduced, it is done by a text in which it is expressly established that, under no concept, the percentage or the agreed fixed amount could be insured to be deducted from the compensation to collect, with the additional item that this duty of the insured is extended to other individuals related to the business, as it could be the owner of the interest insured (that is, the owner of the property on which is the insured interest).

This way, the absolute of the franchise determines the legal effect, equal to the overdraft, and it is this reality – as it has been previously mentioned – the one that calls for this situation, beyond the inadequate nomination of franchise.

In other words, the reason of the agreement in question stems from obtaining a reduction in the compensation to pay by the insurer and link up that saving with an interest of the insured, in that both the possible loss and its consequences turn out to be of less importance due to the fact of having to support part of it when paying a lower premium.

(c) A third clause that appears convenient to highlight is the one generally denominated 'clause of modification of quotation or conditions' which appears as a general condition of transport insurance contract policies. The word 'convenient' has been used, as this clause indisputably refers to a modification in the contract that could not take place without the agreement of the parties or, in the insurance contract case, without the nullity by misrepresentation (pursuant to sections 6 and 7 of Act 17.418), or without an assumption of aggravation of risk.

The aforementioned general condition implicitly establishes that the insurer would make use of his right to rescind – provided for in the policy and under the same conditions – in the case of modification of the quotation or quotations.

It is evident that the taker of the insurance can challenge the intended change through the insurer. On our part, we interpret that such challenge – which notification is of a receptive nature – must be simply considered as the termination of the contract since the rescission starts with the modification of the contractual terms.

Chapter 4. Credit and Caution Insurance

126. Absence of Regulations. Our Insurance Contract Act 17.418 did not devote any of its regulations to credit insurance. Notwithstanding this, it is important to mention that, at the time of its appearance, it was known in commerce locally and worldwide. It is not strange, either, that no reference is made in our law to the surety bond which has been linked to the credit.

It is our thought that the law scholars of half of the twentieth century did not consider it necessary to mention such institutes as the risks covered by means of both contracts, given their lawfulness; that is, they were legally admissible without the need of any specific legal suggestion whatsoever, and because they could have well expected a broader utilization and management of such institutes in order to better determine the most convenient guidelines in their respect. From another perspective, it could have seemed inadequate to submit to legal provisions, legal acts that had adverse individuals to be gathered in one act and thus consider it an authentic insurance contract.

The origin of the credit insurance contract is a bit curious, but it has been studied as an insurance subsidiary to cover those losses from the insurance contract that could not have been satisfied by the corresponding insurer. It was typical of a time where there were only isolated merchants that carried out separated insurance operations, without having the modern technical basis and instruments, and thus additional guarantees to the primary insurer frequently were required to back up his payment in case of loss, and thus control in some manner the deviation that could suffer its solvency.

The years passed, having appeared those technical means mentioned and starting the control of the insurers by the State, especially relating to solvency, and giving shape to the business as an independent insurance, when some objections coming from attacks produced against the legality of the specific insurance activity of the newly born credit were heard. This obstructing doctrinarian attitude was not alien to the conflict of interests that could be awoken in bankers because of the commercial displacement that the appearance of insurers in the commercialization of products that habitually belonged to their sphere would mean to them.

Some arguments about effectiveness were posed, but without convincing legal support, the credit insurance contract failing, for not keeping its random and fortuitous characteristic that should be the risk.

These considerations did not take into account that, when the creditor is the taker/ insured, there is no possibility, except a specific fraud, to have influence on the occurrence of the loss, which, if occurring would be caused by the debtor, alien to the insured.

To sum up, the unity in treatment that often has been followed by authors responds to a traditional reason or custom or comfortability before the commercial attitudes mentioned *supra,* but not to an insurance notion with grounds since the generic risk in credit insurance proper is the insolvency of the debtor – who is not the insured – and in the security bond, the generic risk is non-compliance with the obligation of the taker in a third-party contract, a contract where the taker could never be the insured.

In this chapter, as it can be inferred from its title, credit insurance contracts and security bonds shall be analysed.

§1. CREDIT INSURANCE CONTRACT

127. Introduction. Leaving aside the reference made to credit insurance in the preceding paragraphs, in order to differentiate it from the specific characteristic considered in this part of this chapter, the insolvency of the debtor can be pointed out as the general predominant characteristic in the credit insurance contract proper. This rendering of services causes in reality, due to the practical consequence that, habitually, there appears a speculative attempt to transform the risk into something different than the insolvency of the debtor, as it would be the simple non-compliance or arrears.

Our Insurance Contract Act, as it was mentioned, fortunately did not introduce any individualized regulation for this species of contract, nor provided any generic idea of the risk. Yet this apparent silence of the law has not brought about any inconvenience in order to correctly determine the risk to cover, as the notion of insolvency, besides coming from a stable legal interpretation, has also a constant and similar construction for the books of authority that is very similar in the countries with the best legal production of the world.

In order to ratify what has been exposed, it is appropriate to remember the definition of insolvency established in the twenty-first edition of the Spanish Royal Academy: 'the incapacity of paying debts'; that is, insolvency is a situation equivalent to property impotence to face the obligations to be afforded. The same definition provided by Act No. 24.522 of the Argentine reorganization proceedings to avoid bankruptcy, in its section 1, when establishing as assumption for the reorganization proceedings to be approved, the state of suspension of payments.

In this, there is logically homogeneity between the mentioned expressions and the terminology adopted by the Italian law when mentioning the '*stato de insolvenza*' to interpret such idea.[89] In the same line, authors Mauricio Yadarola[90] and Raymundo Fernández[91] agree with practically all the judgments passed in Courts in Commercial matters.

It is important that the idea of insolvency is always related to a dynamic aspect of the company, not corresponding at all to assimilate it to non-compliance with an obligation since, due to the many meanings of this word, a debtor may be in arrears for failing to comply with his legal obligation on time by other causes without falling into insolvency or suspension of payments, as his property is capable of

89. *See* fifth section of the *Legge Fallimentare* of 16 Mar. 1942, contained in Royal Decree 267.
90. Mauricio Yadarola, '*The Technical Scientific Concept of Suspension of Payments*' (*El concepto8 técnico científico de cesación de pagos*), Journal of Argentine Jurisprudence, vol. 68, 81 et seq. Books of Authority.
91. Raymundo Fernández, *Grounds for Bankruptcy* (*Fundamentos de la quiebra*) 29 et seq (Buenos Aires: Compañía Impresora Argentina Press, 1937).

affording it. In other words, as it has been expressed by Pablo D. Heredia,[92] non-compliance does not mean suspension of payments since this situation is related to a specific property status, whereas this is a fact simply revealing that such status and its effects must be considered in relation to the whole commercial business. This last author supports his opinion on the Honourable Justices of the Commercial Court of Appeals of the Federal Capital City in a comment registered in the book and place mentioned in the preceding note.

Summing up, it could be concluded that insolvency evidences two characteristics: (1) durability, that is, it is not transitory or even contingent; and (2) completeness, that is, it is not partial to a sector of the activity of the debtor, but it affects him significantly, regardless of the amount of the non-compliance.

128. Credit Insurance and Its Types. When studying its grounds, we can note that this type of insurance arises as a new alternative to the commonly constituted guarantees.

Property insurance implies the distribution of the damage that may possibly occur to a number of individuals – as a consequence of having suffered the same risk – among a greater amount of people included in the same group. In credit insurance, this original technique is present in the institute, and it implies a substantial difference in relation to the grounds of other guarantees.

This insurance has the characteristic of granting coverage to the creditor – that is the insured – by virtue of its insurable interest. The insurer assumes the risk of non-compliance with the payment of the credits the insured has granted but, as it has been said, since it is an insurance contract or a contract in the benefit or for account of an appointed third party, the taker of the contract and, at the same time, debtor of the obligation could never be insured. In other words, this contract would never admit the form for account of whom it may correspond.

This contract has been conceived in order to provide coverage to industries, merchants, etc., against the losses that, as creditors, they may suffer due to the insolvency or suspension of payments, under certain circumstances, of the purchasers of their products, in exchange for a determined premium.

Briefly, it should be mentioned the two possible types of credit insurance in order to analyse them. In such sense, under the denomination of credit insurance in the broad sense, there is, on the one hand, credit insurance proper and, on the other hand, the security bond; finally and as species of the former, there is exports insurance.

The specific credit insurance contract or credit insurance contract proper – which we have been referring to – is characterized by the risk of the insolvency of the debtor on account of property loss caused to the creditor, that is to say that, ultimately, it is the non-compliance of the debtor due to its suspension of payments. Thus, it is a general and permanent situation of the property of the debtor.

92. Pablo D. Heredia, *Exegetic Treaty on Reorganization Proceedings Law* (*Tratado Exegético de Derecho Concursal*) 217 (Buenos Aires: Ábaco Press of Rodolfo Depalma, 2000).

In other words, the coverage corresponding to this insurance contract, as it is commonly agreed and, pursuant to the generic risk, is the compensation of the insured-creditor of an insolvent debtor, that is, a debtor that is under suspension of payments.

The risk in the credit insurance contract proper or strict credit insurance contract in no way is the mere non-compliance with an obligation, though this fact, as it also happens with some other facts, may show the state of suspension of payments or insolvency of the debtor by virtue of the impotence of its property to afford the generality of its debtors.

Following this criterion, the insurance related to credits granted in a general sense has been included, that is, as the 'assets' side of any legal relation, before the 'liability or debt', which could consist of the demand for a behaviour of the debtor to perform an act to deliver or not to deliver.[93]

Concretely, the credit insurance in a strict sense is that contract by which the insurer, by means of the collection of a premium covenant to compensate – in the way established by the contract – the damages that may be caused to the creditor (insured), because of the non-compliance of his debtor, determining factor of his insolvency.

As it will be seen later on, it can be sustained that the most marked difference between the two classes of credit insurance that have just been mentioned is the purpose of one or the other and their specific subject matter.

In this line, in credit insurance in the broad sense, in turn, all the hypotheses of unpaid debts are framed. The ones generated by the debtor's insolvency – no matter their exteriorization – and the assumptions of unpaid amounts as a result of simple non-compliance. The characteristic being that, while in the latter – equally known as security bonds – the purpose of the contract is the redress of the damage, derived from the mere non-compliance with an obligation assumed by the debtor pursuant to the insurance taken, in the credit insurance proper, the purpose of the contract is to compensate the loss suffered by the insured in his capacity as creditor by non-compliance with payment of the obligations assumed by the debtor and originated by his insolvency, whatever its determining cause.

At the same time, regarding the specific purpose of one and the other contract, in the security bond, the subject matter is the risk of the property loss, caused by non-compliance with a debtor's obligation, whereas in the strict credit insurance, the subject matter is the risk of the property loss caused to the creditor by the property impotence to afford the obligations undertaken by the specific debtor, determining the non-compliance or non-compliances.

Thus, the concept of insolvency in the credit insurance in the strict sense has a predominant and conditioning role, a fact that does not occur in the security bond.

In consequence, even when in the corresponding cases, the mere non-compliance shall have its origin in the state of insolvency of the debtor, such thing will not be of significance at the moment of analysing whether the requirements to consider the risk occurred verify or not when dealing with a security bond.

93. F.J. Tirado Suarez, *Insurance Contract Act* (*Ley de Contrato de Seguro*), vol. II, 417 et seq (Madrid: Journal of Private Law Press, 1985).

From now onwards, in order to avoid unnecessarily changing the denomination of one or another insurance, they will be called by their specific names; security bonds or simply credit insurance.

129. The Risk in Credit Insurance. Closely related to what has been mentioned before, from the rigorously disciplined point of view of insurance, it is worth pointing out that the risk, as purpose of this insurance contract, does not imply either danger or exposure to something harmful. In relation to damage, this being a property insurance contract, there appears the insurable interest which is protected, and that is the essential element standing out and which – maybe – is more involved in this contract than in any other property damage insurance contract, in an impression of danger, loss, or detriment.

This is due to the fact that, in any credit operation, the risk is the failure to timely pay the debt, acknowledging as generators of this non-compliance both external factors that escape the possibilities of the creditor's control – and many times, the debtor's control – and inner factors that depend on the degree of efficiency of the latter to administer his business and interests in general.

In this chapter – as it has been previously done with other types of insurance – some details related to the risk and loss, in the matter of credit insurance will be analysed. Previously we have been talking about risk as subject matter of the credit insurance around the insolvency of the debtor, that is, a factual situation of his property that brings about the suspension of payments, carrying the impossibility of complying with his obligations by ordinary means in relation to its creditors. In this sense, we would like to stress the importance of the use of the adjective 'ordinary' as the non-compliance with an obligation not associated with exceptional circumstances – as it is assumed are the ones around insolvency – would not form the assumptions of property impotence that the risk of insolvency requires.[94]

In this order of ideas, it is important to remember that we are not dealing with special or specific demonstrative assumptions of the insolvency of the debtor, invoked by the insured-creditor, because it is not a judicial declaration of bankruptcy or the acceptance of the filing of reorganization proceedings to avoid bankruptcy of a debtor, but we are dealing with the establishment or ratification of a fact that is very important to the parties to the credit insurance contract (private contract of great interest to them but without the importance that the general principles of bankruptcy law establish for the aforementioned judicial resolutions).

The confirmation at first sight of the corresponding state of insolvency has to be justified with a reorganization perception of the problem so that, with a modern and current criterion, the promised coverage is triggered. As previously stated, pursuant to the books of authority,[95] the risk covered is not so much the insolvency of the debtor but the loss suffered by the creditor due to the insolvency, the latter understood as the property impotence to pay.[96]

---

94. *See* Court of Appeals in Commercial Matters of the Federal Capital City, Room A 24 Apr. 1989 in '*Canelli Miguel Angel on Bankruptcy*'.
95. Joaquín Garrigues, *Land Insurance Contract* (*Contrato de seguros terrestre*) 330, item II.
96. In this matter, it must be pointed out that, in relation to the suspension of payments directly related to reorganization proceedings, prevention demands anticipation in order to detect the facts that form

Although the nuances of the law are sometimes difficult, in order to reach a true explanation and, above all, to determine the focus of the problem and find its solution, in this opportunity there is no other contingency than to resource to the acuteness of perception. In the previous paragraph, the preventive perception was applied over reorganization proceedings law; now, it might as well be applied over a mere individual contract.

Due to the constant evolution of commercial facts, not so long ago the principles that supported the basis of the existing regulatory reasoning started to rapidly change, due to the principles that were being established in our modern world. In these times of change, the salvage of companies with difficulties adjudged as rescuable became an issue, apparently with the purposes of preserving employment.

Demonstrations of this tendency have been the reorganization proceedings of insolvency: the Edwards Act of 6 January 1978, aiming at the reorganization of a company; the Portuguese Company Recovery Act of 1986 repealed by Act 132 of 23 April 1993; and especially the French Acts 148 of 1 March 1984 and 1998 and 1999, both of 25 January 1985, with the modifications brought about by Act 475 of 10 June 1994.

Not overlooked in this synthetic list are some of the precedents of the tendency towards a different consideration in the matter insolvency: the Spanish precedents from which the conceptions of final insolvency as irreversible circumstance and provisory or insolvency assimilable to guilty non-compliance. In this line, it should be noted that insolvency – as a situation of property impossibility in order to face assumed debts – the same as in reorganization proceedings law, needs external evidence in order for the situation to be taken into consideration: either the already occurring property impotence or the potential property impotence. That is to say that the exteriorization of certain assumptions shall be taken as verification of insolvency assumptions.

This revealing facts of the insolvency risk may vary and may be established in the terms and conditions of contracts; thus, even when dealing with arrears in the payment of a credit linked to the credit insurance, if it is so provided, risk verification shall be accepted. Thus, and to the extent it had been established in the insurance contract as one of the assumptions, evidence of insolvency, the failure to pay on time and completely a credit could be confused with such non-compliance that, in turn, would cause other non-compliances.

In summary: (a) insolvency is not a concept similar to non-compliance in the credit insurance contract, as it has been developed in the reality of business as we know it; (b) insolvency, in recent times, has adopted a turn regarding non-compliances indicating the need to prevent the disappearance of the debtor company; (c) insolvency in any of both expressions requires evidencing facts; (d) these facts that would evidence the situation of credit, related to the credit insurance contract, must be established in the contract proper; (e) such contractual expression may contain, as guideline of insolvency, a mere non-compliance that cannot be taken as a synonym of insolvency.

---

the irreversible economic situation. In this regard, it is illustrative of this point the one made by Pablo D., Heredia in his book *Exegetic Treaty on Reorganization Proceedings Law* (*Tratado Exegético de Derecho Concursal*) 223 and 224, item g.

130. Partial Down Payment. There is a clarification due since, in the world of business, the convenience of not imposing rigorous terms to declare insolvency opened its way. The reference is made to certain clause that fixes a term as the event of provisional or conditional insolvency is declared (generating the right of the insured to collect from the insurer a part of the compensation).

This possibility has been incorporated in some regulations, for example, the Insurance Contract Act in Spain, which section 70, after having established as examples certain assumptions, finally imposed this down payment.

The parameters of the Spanish law are quoted in order to enhance comprehension.

Such regulations expressly establish that insolvency must be in the first place 'final' (section 69), and later, it establishes four cases in which insolvency shall be so considered (section 70): (1) when it has been so declared by final judicial judgment; (2) when it has been judicially approved an agreement where it is established a reduction in the payment of debts; (3) when the judicial order to collect money owed or for execution has been summoned without resulting from the attachment enough released property to meet the payment; and (4) when the insured and insurer have agreed to consider the credit a bad debt.

In its last part, section 70 of the Spanish law makes a statement that contradicts the principle sustained by the Act when expressing: 'Notwithstanding what has been mentioned, after six months as from the insured's notice to the insurer of the failure to comply with the credit, the Insurer shall carry out a down payment of 50% of the agreed coverage to the insured provisionally, with the balance to be paid later.'

As it might be observed from the last part of this section, the final insolvency is left aside to get closer to the lack of payment, typical of the security bond.

Also as hypotheses of insolvency there have been used the cases in which the insured and the insurer agree to consider the credit uncollectible or that the legal proceedings or the collecting formalities are too expensive resulting, ultimately, in the express acceptance of the insurer of the occurrence of the loss.

In our country, even when there is no regulatory act of credit insurance where it is specified each one of the admitted assumptions of insolvency, there are interesting regulations in this respect, such as the Communications of the Central Bank of the Argentine Republic, where the clients of the Bank are classified according to their general situation and the possibilities of facing the debts assumed with the institution. In such communications is established the obligatory nature of a detailed property analysis of the client to later classify him according to the guidelines established by the communication. Within the classification of these communications, it is important to the effects of credit insurance to point out the situation of those clients which the indicators established by the Central Bank evaluation as 'with high risk of insolvency' and 'bad debts'.[97]

This can serve as contractual guideline – or even construction guideline – under very special situations, in order to establish the occurrence or not of the risk provided for in the contract of credit insurance.

97. 'Communication A 2216 (BC)', Circular of the Office, Records of Argentine Legislation, 9 Jun. 1994, 44745–4754.

131. The Parties and the Influence over the Risk of the Events of Their Own or Third Parties. As it could be noticed when appreciating the risk assumed by the insurer, there is a differential note in the most common insurance contracts: the influential presence that human behaviour can exert.

In general, in credit insurance there is a relation among the risk effectiveness and the individuals' behaviour that is highlighted when drawing a parallel between the two. In this line, it must be distinguished – due to its influence in this insurance as inherent to a human characteristic – the unpredictability of his behaviour, and thus the difficulty which that fact carries for the insurer at the moment of deciding the reach of the coverage he is willing to assume.

Nevertheless – and despite the fact that, in general, there is a link between human behaviour and risk – not always the occurrence of a risk is the result of a fact performed by people whose behaviour and situation were assessed in order to determine the coverage, but the origins could be many, for example, political factors, catastrophes, etc.

In credit insurance, both the behaviour and the property situation of the debtor turn out to be absolutely important since, ultimately, this is what would be analysed at the moment of establishing if we are effectively before the occurrence of the assured risk.

What has been said finds support in the fact that, during the normal and ordinary course of business, the behaviour and the decisions by each business person with decision-making power will be the key factors of the success or failure of the companies he is in charge of. Thus, in some frequent occasions, these absolutely personal circumstances may decisively influence the state of insolvency that the risk assumed may produce.

Notwithstanding this, and as it was previously advanced, not always the effective occurrence of the risk is the consequence of an event caused by the debtor, but it can also be caused by third parties. A clear example of these events, alien to the debtor with an evident influence in the contingency of the risk, would be the passing of regulations that may regulate in a different manner a state of things given at the time of taking out the policy, which may in turn, bring about a difficult economic financial situation for the debtor. Examples of this would be new provisions intended for the protection of the environment, extension of the responsibility in the matter of products, systems of toxic waste and protection of consumers. Not to mention matters of monetary and economic policy, which may vary during the lapse of the insurance contract's effectiveness and have a marked influence on the generation of the occurrence of the assured risk.

As a consequence of what has just been exposed, it appears necessary to make a comment on the term 'parties', included in the title of this part, and the connection that the commented influence may have, by virtue of section 70 of Act 17.418 on, for instance, civil liability. In the first place, it must be taken into account that, for the credit insurance contract under consideration, the position of the insured, owner of the insurable interest shall be creditor in relation with the credit of the contract. Thus, it would be impossible that he could cause with malice or gross negligence the loss, that is, the occurrence of the risk contractually provided for. The insolvency of the debtor thus cannot be caused independently.

In the second place, if the insured was the debtor and, in consequence, it was sustained contrarily and wrongly with the aforementioned position that the insurable interest is on his hands, as the intent is not to damage him with impoverishment deriving from his insolvency, the causing of the occurrence of the loss contained as precept in section 70 *supra* would need to have the characteristic of malice or gross negligence, which would take it to extreme levels, much easier to be evidenced.

In the third place, the taker – that is the other party to the risk insurance contract – except for the insurer that to this effect appears as insignificant, will always be someone different from the debtor, since if it was not so, the consequence would be the inexistence of the contract because the risk as future, uncertain event, alien to the will of the parties, would turn out to be something impossible to admit, since the taker that, at the same time is the debtor would be the owner of the situation.

To what has been said, it should be added that the burden of salvage would be subject to the uncontrollable arbitration of the taker of the contract, debtor of the obligation linked to such contract and interested party thereof.

Finally, in the fourth place, the beneficiary of the credit insurance contract, the creditor of the linked obligation, would turn into the first case seen *supra*, to the extent that the behaviour of such beneficiary would have similar characteristics as the ones commented.

132. The Loss. For this primary subject of loss in credit insurance, it is indispensable to refer at the same time to the insurable interest, element corresponding to the property damage insurance contract.

Given the particularities of this insurance, the matter related to the insured interest has given rise to controversy among the books of authority by virtue of its determination. Whereas one position states that the interest is laid on credit law, others understand that the logical insurable interest would be the rendering of services of economic content that the debtor is in charge of.

The books of authority have expressed that, 'by means of the credit insurance contract, the existence proper of the credit is not covered; what is covered is its fulfilment or payment, that is, the claim of the creditor before the debtor or, correlatively, the rendering of services of the debtor and, in a mediate form, the subject matter of this rendering of services that is an amount of money'.[98]

What cannot be denied concretely is that the interest in this type of insurance contract has a close relationship with a specific credit and thus coinciding the value of the insurable or insured interest with the value of the credit, before the impossibility of the collection by insolvency, such amount shall be the loss determining the insurance contract.

These amounts that are the assured amounts in the contracts of individual modality, when we are dealing with global contracts documented in floating policies which contemplate one or several groups of credits – which are generated in a defined period of time – are substituted by an assured amount that is known as maximum compensation of the period, generally of annual extension, making it clear again that, this depends elementarily on the contractual agreement.

---

98. Antigono Donati, *Trattato del Diritto delle Assucurazioni Private*, 303.

Starting from the initial definitions of this chapter, if a Bank carries out a money loan, its insurable interest shall be on collecting, according to the modality of the reciprocal agreement, the amount of money lent, plus the agreed interests in the stipulated time. This amount shall be, ultimately, the credit of which coverage is guaranteed by the insurance contract, by virtue of the real interest that the insured (in the example, the Bank) has in relation to the loan property (money).

It is logical to spontaneously believe that the value of the insurable interest must coincide with the value of the credit that in practice 'is insured' as it becomes unpaid on account of the occurrence of insolvency, but that does not imply that the maximum limit of coverage that the insurer is willing to pay must coincide, nominally, with the value of such credit.

This is due to the fact that, in certain types of coverage, an economic maximum limit for the possible obligation before the occurrence of a loss is established as a way of avoiding uncertainty about the extension of the compensation to their charge, among other reasons.

Notwithstanding this – and by the special characteristics of this credit insurance – it is usual for the purposes of strengthening the insured interest, and in order to avoid the occurrence of the loss, to make the insured himself participate in part of the assumption of the risk, by means of the inclusion of overdrafts in charge of him. At the same time, and following the worldwide tendency in insurance matters, the regulations expressly exclude from this final loss suffered by the insured the loss of profit or loss of benefit in the following sense: 'the credit insurance contract covers the loss suffered by the insured; now, two elements compose the insured's credit: the first is the price of resale of the sold goods (price of raw materials, work, general expenses), the second is the benefit of the operation … The loss only affects the first element and, in principle, it is not the same situation as the loss of profit'.[99]

133. Determination of the Compensation. Terms. The property damage insurance contract in which credit insurance is included is compensatory, which is the reason why in this species no benefit can be originated in favour of the insured but only a compensation up to the maximum limit of the loss or the damage experienced, so as not to determine the enrichment of such party.

Thus, it can be sustained that, ultimately, the damage precisely suffered shall have to fix the highest limit of the rendering of services the insurer is in charge of, but always with a maximum equivalent to the assured amount. It is called 'highest limit', as the parties may agree to fix another inferior and even a sort of participation of the insured in the assumption of part of the risk, by means of fixing franchises or overdrafts in charge of him.

As it can be observed – and it has been previously observed in the first volume of this topic – the precise determination of the damage is a significant element of the compensation owed by the insurer, where the proportion of some values – as the insurable interest, the assured amount, and the losses – shall be at stake.

In the specific case of credit, the final appraisal of the compensation supposes the existence of a strict procedure, aiming at verifying the state of insolvency of the

99. R. Michel, '*L'assurance de crédits en Droit Compar*', *Essai Théorique* 134 and 135 (Paris, 1930) quoted also by Francisco Tirado Suarez, in the work quoted *supra*, 490 of vol. II.

debtor that determined the loss and besides the exact finding of the reach of the loss, that is, the final loss experienced by the insured-creditor, by virtue of the non-compliance of his debtor.

As it has been established in the previous items, the loss in this case in the credit insurance contract is subject, as every event, to its verification by revealing facts of the insolvency of the debtor. These facts, sometimes listed by the laws regulating the reorganization proceedings to avoid bankruptcy, in no way can be subject to circumstances compulsorily established, both for being facts and consequently entailing a broad range of possibilities, and since they are a matter that should be decided based on what was agreed by the parties.

In all that concerns the proceedings tending to the identification and evaluation of the reach of intensity of the loss, the analysis must be circumscribed to the study of the contributory elements in order to obtain the amount of the ultimate net loss of the insured. This loss shall be fixed in the contract, at least, by means of a mechanism adequate to reach it.

This mechanism should be certainly and conveniently agreed upon because the matter entails in its nature, major complexities to the extent that the state of insolvency and its effects on the credits carry with them situations of diverse nature that may go from deductions corresponding to recoveries – or other lawful causes – to aggregates deriving from the attempted salvage and expenses derived from the formalities carried out for judicial or extrajudicial collection.

The terms contemplated to reject require complementary or documentary information as well as those needed to carry out the liquidation, and the payment to the insured are the ones that also correspond to apply to this type of insurance contract, with the particularities of the case, existing the possibility of agreeing on a shorter term, but not a longer term than the one indicated in section 49, by virtue of what has been set forth in section 158 of the Insurance Act.

Once the payment of the compensation has been made on the insurer's part, he shall be empowered to subrogate all his rights and actions in relation to the unpaid credit.[100]

134. Burdens of the Taker and the Insured. In a previous paragraph, in which it had been considered the subtopic of the parties and the influence on the risk – even when the positions adopted by some theories were expressed regarding who can be insured by this type of contract – the adoption of a conception in relation to the exclusivity of identifying as such only those creditors, holders of the credit, also became evident. Consequently, as it is obvious, the duties and obligations of the taker and the insured shall be considered regarding the different moments of the credit insurance contract.

Depending to a great extent on the kind of insurance agreed upon (individual or global), the taker or policyholder, as well as the insured – either with the two

100. Argentine Insurance Act No. 17.418, s. 80: 'The rights corresponding to the insured against a third party, by virtue of the loss shall be transferred to the insurer, up to the amount of the paid compensation. The insured is responsible for all acts that may prejudice this right of the insurer.'

positions concentrated on one person or different people – must deeply respect the precontractual specifications in relation to misrepresentation and aggravation of the contractual risk.

In this matter of risk aggravation, it must be very clear that the situations agreed upon in origin – by the creditor, taker, or insured – with the debtors of each credit linked to the credit insurance contract shall not be altered in any manner by agreement of the parties, in a way where predominant circumstances were changed in the agreements without the acceptance of the insurer.

During the effectiveness of the credit insurance contract, the indispensable information that must be supplied to the insurer is closely related to the commercial and business behaviour of the debtor or debtors of the credit obligations of the case. To the extent that the taker and the insured, depending on the assumption, know the pertaining facts, although their authenticities could not be categorically asserted, they must act with prevention regarding the situation of the insurer and communicate them with the appropriate reserve.

This communication of news – as this duty could be called – is generally complemented in the contractual text (policies), with other burdens of the kind referring to information, verifications or document evaluations, accounting books, or miscellaneous data of other people of interest to the company, and commercial relationships of the creditor, of the debtors, or of those that, as third parties, have guaranteed in certain way the obligations contained in the credits to which we are making reference.

The conditions agreed upon in each credit insurance contract shall provide the details of the burdens to comply with and their corresponding extension without prejudice for those that, besides being established in the insurance policy (insurance contract), are also established by Act 17.418 as common duties for all assumptions and that – as it happens in the case of notification of loss – are impositions inherent to the temporal state of development of the insurance.

In this instance, in the analysis of the notification of the loss in the credit insurance contract, it can even be sensed that the considerations are different from those assumptions in which, once a concrete event occurred, the loss is almost totally identified as legal concept, indispensable to create the obligation of the insurer or comply with the service agreed upon or compensate the damage (section 1 of Act 17.418).

135. Notification of Loss by the Insured – Salvage. The notification of the loss by the insured is a fact for which elucidation is not simple, as it is always without exaggerating, invested in multiple complexities that start from its formation, since it should not be confused with the events that could generate it, although they were concrete non-compliances.

Even when from the commencement of this chapter, constant concepts have been explained in relation to its better understanding, in some of the last headings, considerations about the risk, the loss, and compensation have been repeated. These concepts now must be joined with the ones generically acquired on this subject, and thus present a solution to the multiple problems that may arise. That is why the specific notification of loss may be considered implied in successive or progressive pieces of information that the insured/creditor notifies to the insurer every time that he complies with the constant possible compliances of the burden of communicating news that, in order to differentiate it, has been mentioned *supra*.

Notwithstanding how complete, responsible, and in good faith the observation of the safety measures related to informative ends may be, the communication of the particular news of the undoubted knowledge of the exteriorization of insolvency of the debtor is inexcusably compulsory.

In this insurance contract, there habitually appear burdens that express, by means of the performance of certain legal rights, certain peculiarities, as those linking it with the credit or credits, which ultimately are their motivation. These distinctive characteristics are markedly noted in the manoeuvres and procedures that may and have to be done towards the recovery of the insolvent debtor or of its guarantors, amounts that constitute final reductions in loss costs of the insurer.

These legal duties could be summarized as a sort of broad collaboration of the insured with the insurer that starts from the moment the contract is agreed upon, and which major operative scenario shall be the Courts of Justice (besides complying with other established impositions as the ones required by the burden of salvage so crucial in this occasion).

In the topic under analysis, this burden of salvage shall not have the same conditions as the one seen (legislated by sections 72 et seq., of Act 17.418) since, in order to form the enforceability of the compliance with the duty stated therein, it is indispensable that the future and aleatory event would have taken place, and the loss legally in course of attention, at the least.

It is just before the occurrence of the loss when the insured must start preventing the major damages that could derive in the insolvency of the debtor, communicating with his insurer with the purposes of finding the convenient means to diminish the loss via any possible means (which were indicated *supra* as the ones which may increase the recovered sums and those which may reduce the loss to experience, directly through declaring the credit a bad debt). More simply, it could be said that both the duty of salvage and the other legal duties, natural to the collaboration between the insured and the insurer, must be assumed with a preventive nature, in order to obtain the greatest positive outcome.

In order to avoid an inconvenient enthusiasm regarding what has been strictly agreed between the parties to the insurance contract, these collaboration duties – and even the own duties of salvage – must circumscribe to those established mainly in response to the provision of section 36 of Act 17.418.

However, it must be taken into account the duty of collaboration of the insured regarding his defence and representation by the person appointed by the insurer (with the purpose of preventing the unfulfilment of the credit, as consequence of the insolvency of the debtor).

This representation, which limits will arise from, once more, the contractual terms and conditions, in principle, will be considered comprehensive in relation to any other specific proceedings involving the debtor in a possible insolvency.

The previous procedures to which reference was made *supra* had as object to reduce the impact of the loss. Now the comment will elaborate on the subrogation of the insurer and the credit assignment contract, similar to the former in some consequences.

By agreement established in the credit insurance contract, the creditor/insured (the person the insurer agreed to compensate) is usually engaged to assign the latter, the credit following the different provisions established by the Civil Code and – if it were the case – those provided for in the insurance contract.

In relation to the provision of section 80 of Insurance Contract Act 17.418, it is important to point out that, even when the effects of the legal subrogation and the assignment are the same – as they legitimize the insurer that satisfied the originary debt in order to compensate the debtor by the unpaid credit to the effects of recovering the amount – both institutes call for different behaviours.

In fact, whereas in the contract of assignment of credits is required compliance with several previous requirements provided for in the Civil and Commercial Code, in the legal subrogation of section 80 the legitimation is acquired by the law itself, by mere payment of the obligation.

Moreover, there is a significant difference between both institutes. Such difference is centred in the limit established by Regulation 17.418, regarding the extension of the subrogation that admits it only up to the amount of the sum of compensation paid. It should be noted, as a verifying note of what has just been said in the matter of who is the party to the contract denominated insured, that if the insured was the debtor – as it has been wrongly sustained – the right to subrogate of the insurer (according to the terms of section 80) would be impossible and thus, the assignment of credit would also be impossible.

Instead, in credit assignment and more so, in the case of litigious rights, it would be enough that the price was serious and certain, and thus the assignee could have paid an inferior price for the assignment contract to the assignor and then claim the assigned debtor the collection of the credit in its totality.

Before this specific situation that appears in credit insurance, the collateral guarantees the creditor insured has and that, later, before the payment of the compensation agreed in the insurance contract, he could assign to the insurer, acquire a great significance for insurance companies. In fact, according to the provisions of section 1614 of the Argentine Civil and Commercial Code, the assignment of credit does not only include the principal but all collateral guarantees.

The same comment can be made on the subrogation mentioned in section 80 of the Insurance Act, as such regulation does not only operate before the debtor but also before the co-debtors, sureties, and other guarantors of the principal obligation.

136. Prohibition of Section 24 of Act 20.091. Act 20.091 is the one regulating in our country Insurance Companies and at the same time, everything related to the control that the National State must exert over such entities, by means of the SIN.

Without entering into further details about such Act – since it is not one of the main topics of Part III of this monograph – it can be pointed out that, within the powers granted by the Superintendence of Insurance, there is the power of authorizing types of insurance and technical and contractual elements of insurance – as it can be noted from what is set forth in Article V sections 23 et seq.

Due to its extreme regulatory nature, as it occurs in many occasions, Act 20.081 has used to the extreme those powers of control when establishing in its section 24, last part, very questionable prohibitions from which we shall deal with the one related to the topic under consideration, credit operations.

The regulation with confused language in matters so precise as those restricting business freedom and the freedom of contract states: 'Prohibited Plans. It shall be prohibited ... 2) the coverage of risks coming from operations of pure financial credit.'

The technical management of the SIN, keeping the obscurantism that has always applied to interpret legal texts, carried out an explanation of the sense of the law alien to any other sphere but the banking sphere, aimed at the undeserving possibility, from the point of view of such management, that 'Insurance companies dealing with credit insurance could become the main guarantors of payments of amounts of money by non-compliance with contractual obligations in our financial market, circumstance not only risky for the stability of the companies and the rights of the insured of other types of insurance but also, alien to the role of insurance by operation of law.' Further, the regulation stated that, given the significance of the meaning of the legal regulation, it could be clearly appreciated the technical impossibility of its instrumentation by means of an insurance contract.[101]

As it can be appreciated from a quick and superficial reading of such regulation – and of what has been set for by the technical management of the Official Comptroller – it seems that, in the Argentine Republic, credit insurance would not be permitted since we are dealing with an operation of pure financial credit. Nevertheless, as conclusion of what we have been analysing throughout this chapter, credit insurance in the strict sense, that is, as insurance protecting the cases of insolvency, is not in breach of the law.

Even when it is true that the first confusion arises out of the utilization of not very accurate terms regarding the definition of this type of insurance as 'of credit', when it would be much more appropriate to denominate it as 'of property loss due to insolvency' or 'of insolvency', it is not less true that, in order to carry out a serious analysis in relation to its compatibility with the legal system, one must necessarily pass onto the study of the contents of the contract and verify if their conditions do not violate the prohibition mentioned *supra*. More so, first it would correspond to analyse the constitutionality of such regulation.

Following what has been determined by the technical management of the SIN, what is not permitted is that insurance companies intending to operate in this business turn themselves into joint and several co-debtors of the debtor, or that they finish occupying in financial business the place of financial institutions, denaturalizing insurance activity, whose purpose is unique. In consequence, it is plausible that the SIN, following its task of controlling the insurance activity, protects that, in this type of insurance contract, the regulation established in Act 20.091 is not violated, with significant deformations regarding the nature and essence of insurance.

Thus, it must be concluded that credit insurance is viable within our legal system as long as it is carried out according to the principles of insurance, by virtue of which, continuing with this line of thought, it can be affirmed with no hesitation that this type of insurance contracts does not carry per se any violation to Act 20.091.

It is worth pointing out what has been said in relation to the risk covered by this insurance, in the sense that it consists of the property loss experienced by the insurer as a consequence of his debtor's non-compliance with one or several obligations in

101. Superintendence of Insurance of the Nation, Case file 29.055 – 12 Mar. 1993, 97–105.

the presence of a state of insolvency. As it may be observed, it is an uncertain and future event, existing as typical random event, as in any insurance contract.

In this line, it is necessary to clearly point out that, whereas credit insurance does not cover the property loss arising from the mere non-compliance by the simple will of the debtor but, on the contrary, the one originated in a state of financial insolvency – judicially declared or not according to the case – it cannot be held that the insurance company, by means of this type of insurance, is carrying out financial operations.

137. Credit Insurance for Exports. Brief Outline of the Experience in Our Country. The credit insurance for exports may be defined as a type of insurance by means of which an insurance company covenants, by means of the payment of a premium, to partially or totally pay a credit generated from an export operation, in favour of the export's creditor in the case the credit is not paid by the importer, as long as the causes provided for in the contract take place.

More so, this insurance may be considered, in fact, a technical instrument of assistance, of support and a boosting instrument not only for the indispensable activity of exportation for a country but also for the domestic commerce and industry.

From these brief concepts, it can be clearly inferred that we are not dealing with a true contract but with a legal artifice which will attempt to satisfy the needs of cooperation at a State level, in order to favour the exchange that contributes to the political economy and the development of certain areas. Thus, with the capabilities of the institute, it shall be simple and feasible to coincide with the criterion expressed about the impossibility of equalling this institute to a contract.

The commerce of this insurance has been extremely restricted by virtue of the economic reasons arising from the losses that the business created, recurring to the State in order to guarantee those risks that were called extraordinary. These risks were those that did not have a direct relationship with the commercial operation of exports, but responded to external circumstances as it could be matters of politics, natural catastrophes, military conflicts, and other problems not related to the business itself.

Thus, the private insurers limited their performance to taking out insurance that would protect the ordinary risks such as insolvency (failure to pay an obligation related to exportation).

In our country, by means of the repealed Acts 17.267 and 18.189, and currently the one in full force and effect, Act 20.299 of 24 April 1973, credit insurance for exports is regulated as a special system of operations for Argentine export trade or the related activities favouring it, constituted by the National State.

The coverage that is granted by law covers the political, catastrophic risks and any other risks which, by application of the current regulations of the insurance market, are not covered by insurance companies constituted in the Argentine Republic.

The reglementary decree of Act 20.299 in its first section compulsorily lists those risks that the National State assumes under the system of this type of insurance, in an extremely exaggerated way and, later, in its second section, indicates which are the risks that may, possibly, be covered by this insurance.

At the same time, both the Act and its reglementary decree establish that the National Treasury shall be the one affording the needs derived from the credit insurance for exports before the occurrence of losses. In order to do that, a fund must be constituted with the financial obligations arising from the insurance taken out by the State.

As it may be observed, the legal ordering establishes a system that attempts to turn this contract into an encouragement of exportation, placing the National State as guarantor of the payment of obligations unfulfilled by the importer. At the same time and although in some operations, a private insurance company may take part, either on the National State's part or in operations in which it appears per se, tax exemption for such legal businesses is established in the analysed regulations. Even though it could be controversial from the point of view of inequality towards other taxpayers, it is the result of a policy destined to favour the operations linked to foreign trade.

Ultimately, this system created by the law attempts, on the one hand, to create better tax conditions for those guaranteeing these types of operations and, on the other hand, to grant exporters more protection and certainty regarding the effective collection of credit; all that with the purpose of encouraging foreign trade.

§2. The Surety Bond Contract

138. Origin and Precedents. The use of insurance policies the purpose of which was to guarantee compliance with obligations of the debtor started with the so-called fidelity insurance of employees in Great Britain during the first half of the nineteenth century.[102] Such fidelity insurance of employees could be considered, both in its structure and its performance, as similar insurance to the surety bond; when deepening into the subject, it is noticed that they are different types of insurance.

When considering in the first part of this chapter credit insurance in its broad sense, the different types of insurance that in such way were gathered by a simple and pragmatic circumstance as the legal name were considered. Among them, as indicated, is the fidelity insurance of employees of great commercial importance since its appearance in the Anglo-Saxon world – and also in other parts – by means of its different types, as the one covering the ultimate net losses of the insured employer on account of theft, fraud, misappropriation, forgery, etc., or acts of misappropriation (with the purpose of making money or liable of breach of trust) or those protecting similar conditions, but for individuals that work under the order of the damaged insured, not being employees or belonging to his payroll personnel.

This fidelity insurance that nowadays is practised separately from the surety bond (and though in many countries the controlling body of the insurance activity – on

102. María Pilar Barres Benlloch, *Legal System of the Surety Bond* (*Régimen Jurídico del Seguro de Caución*) 35 (Madrid: Aranzadi Press) in the quotation about Jean Bastin, in *La défaillance de paiement et sa protection, l'assurance crédit LGDJ, Droit des affaires* 51–57 (Paris: LGDJ Press, 1991). This last author deems it preferable to locate the origins of the institution of the denominated guarantee insurance in Italy and not in Great Britain. Nevertheless, Bastin seems to refer more to credit insurance in general and not so much to the specific modality of surety bonds.

account of this same principle – puts them together) differs from the surety bond fundamentally in the operational mechanics and in the nexus existing among the linked individuals.

Already in those times of the nineteenth century, the importance of the existence of an insurance granting a personal guarantee on the debtor proper was clear. It was sustained that an insurance of these characteristics would favour the security to the good ends of business and the reduction in the price of expenses in the management of commonly used guarantees.[103] Nevertheless, not all the legal systems admitted this contractual modality. In the first half of the twentieth century, in France, both the books of authority and the legislation consistently rejected this feature.

This criterion is received and accepted by the so-called Renaudin Arbitration from the State Council dated 6 October 1952, when the resolution resolved a controversy between bank institutions and insurance companies on their jurisdiction in matters of guarantees of obligations.

The aforementioned resolution denied categorically the possibility of guaranteeing obligations by means of a surety bond. This motivated the lack of use of the feature in question until France's insertion in the Communitarian Law.

After this and despite what happened in France, the guarantee insurance, among which there is the surety bond, started to develop progressively and consistently until our day.

139. Notion and Legal Concept of the Surety Bond. As credit insurance in the strict sense has been conceived by most of the books of authority as insolvency insurance, the surety bond has been nominated as suretyship insurance by some Latin American voices such as the Colombian H. Galindo Cubides,[104] emphasizing that it grants protection against non-compliance.

The difference between insolvency and non-compliance is the orientation marked by the books of authority that appears as significant in Argentina and that truly draws a distinction between these two credit insurance contracts and surety bonds since the risks that are the subject matter of each one of them derive from separate legal and factual sources.

The surety bond has been conceived[105] as the one carried out to guarantee that the damages the creditor could cause for a non-compliance with a non-direct money obligation are compensated.

To the effects of better understanding the reach of this explanation, it is important to determine what must be understood by non-compliance in Argentine law since it is a word that may give rise to many constructions, from the point of view of not only the creditor or the debtor but also third parties. For fulfilment of obligations it

103. C. Ancey, *Les risques du crédit*, 2nd ed., 175 et seq (Paris, 1932).

104. This author is quoted by Francisco Tirado Suarez in n. 10 corresponding to s. 68 of the book *Comments to the Spanish Commercial Code* (*Comentario al Código de Comercio Español*), vol. II, 421, where reference is also made to the influence on the Anglo-Saxon practice and the American author J.H. Magee and his book *General Insurance*, 8th ed.

105. M. Broseta Pont, *Handbook of Commercial Law* (*Manual de Derecho Mercantil*) 573 (Madrid: Tecnos Press, 2002/2003 and 2008).

is understood the payment of something to the other.[106] In this line, arrears in the payment of the obligation that equals delay is one of the relevant assumptions in order to entitle the creditor to use the remedies that, pursuant to the practice imposed by the law of any origin, are of the nature of those provided for in section 505 of the Argentine Civil Code.

Yet as clear as the responsibility for non-compliance is in the debtor, the existence in the law of some causes of exemption must be taken into account, such as the fortuitous event or act of God and force majeure, which are very controversial subjects regarding their quantitative and qualitative features.

To these two traditional reasons has been added a third right of exemption called 'state of need'. From the point of view of the creditor, non-compliance shall be verified when, at the moment of expiration of the obligation assumed by the debtor, the latter does not meet his obligation totally, regardless of the circumstances or causes that had caused such unfulfilment.

As a consequence of the ambiguity that has just been described, the parties must be very careful and strict at the moment of entering into the insurance contract, meticulously defining what must be understood by non-compliance, in order to interpret that the occurrence of the risk agreed upon has taken place at a definite moment.

From these comments, a very clear conclusion can be derived that is linked to the limitation by the agreement of the parties of the risk in each contractual species. This takes us to note that the legal name of each type of insurance contract does not lead indispensably to the establishment of its subject matter, that is, the specific risk covered, but the generic risk (as fire, theft of movable property, glass, civil liability, etc.). The subject matter of each insurance contract within the denominated species must be limited by cause, space, and temporal parameters.

Given the professionalism and technical knowledge the insurer counts on at the moment of specifically limiting the risk agreed upon, the definition of the concept of non-compliance shall be strict and clear as the burden of an incorrect description in the policy (contract) may depend on it.

Jurisprudence is right when making the insurer responsible for the consequences of a deficient description of the assumed risk in the contract, not only by the technical knowledge already mentioned but also because such party usually draws up the contractual conditions.

Consequently, before a doubt in the construction of non-compliance, the judge should be inclined for the interpretation most beneficial to the insured, which, in principle, would imply a demanding position towards the insurer, thus broadening the original meaning permitting to consider the indifference of the non-compliance as cause of the loss.

In this line, it has been understood that in surety bond insurance, the loss takes place with the sole unfulfilment of the contract by the proponent (debtor of the

106. According to Civil Law, as synthetically pointed out by H. Lafaille, *Obligations I*, vol. VI, 12, n. 36 (Buenos Aires: Ediar Editores S.A. Press, 1947).

related obligation) regardless of the measure of such non-compliance or the culpability or innocence of such debtor, except for the case of excluded risks.[107]

140. Nature and Characteristics. From another point of view – and taking into account the conception that has been commented at the beginning of this second part of the chapter with the note mentioning the ill-fated Professor Broseta Pont – it is appropriate to sustain that in the surety bond insurance, a contract by which ultimately the protection against non-compliance with an obligation is agreed, its legal nature could be no other but a true guarantee.

The distinctive feature of the surety bond regarding other contracts of the same nature is that its grounds are on the insurance techniques, and thus its construction shall be carried out primarily within the parameters that such technique establishes and that are recognized by insurance law.[108]

There is plenty of jurisprudence in Argentina that has decided on a different way regarding the legal nature of the surety bond insurance because it has been resolved in the vertices of doctrinarian positions at both extremes, that is, from sustaining the thesis of being an insurance contract to the opposite of supporting its essence as a guarantor contract. In the footnote several judicial judgments are quoted.[109]

In fact, the possibility that by means of a surety bond the economic risk of a debtor in arrears is erased does not imply that this contract legally becomes a guarantor agreement. There are other contractual possibilities or tools in order to eliminate the economic risk of arrears without classifying them as bail solely on those grounds.

In this line, the insurer must use all his ordinary methods – as technical tools establishing the frequency and intensity – as it is habitually carried out in any insurance contract attempted to be analysed, all of which does not happen in a guarantor contract and there would be no grounds for it to happen.

---

107. National Chamber of Commerce of the Federal Capital City of Argentina, Room C, 8 Sep. 1997, El Derecho Press, 131–321.

108. The surety bond is characterized by the involvement of three subjects and the necessary connection of two contracts. The subjects are: the taker, the proponent, the insured, and the insurer; the first one (a business person devoted to works, provision, or rendering of services) and the second one are connected by a contract from which derives the obligation of the taker and the capacity as creditor of the insured (in relations to the works, provision, or rendering of services). Thus, in this type of insurance, the insurable interest is the business person's compliance with a non-monetary economic service that he must carry out in the future. As guarantee of such service, he insures the creditor so that, in case of failing to carry out the works or perform the provision or rendering of services, he receives a compensation on the insurer's part. National Federal Court of Claims of the Capital City, Room IV, 19 Nov. 1993, Journal *El Derecho*, vol. 160, 610.

109. National Court in Commercial Matters of the Federal Capital, Room B, 24 May 1976, Journal *El Derecho*, vol. 68, 248; National Court in Commercial Matters of the Capital City, Room C, 22 Apr. 1977, Journal *El Derecho*, vol. 76, 607; Supreme Court, 30 Jun. 1992, *National State* (*Ministry of Economy of the Nation, Secretariat of Maritime Interests*) *v. Prudencia Cía. Arg. de Seguros Generales, S.A.* National Court in Civil and Commercial Matters, Room III, 14 Jul. 1998; *Argentine Railway Company* [*Empresa de Ferrocarriles Argentinos*] *v. Agencia Abracsas Turismo S.R.L. and/or National Court in Civil and Commercial Matters*, Room III, 14 Jul. 1998; National Court in Commercial Matters, Room B, 11 Mar. 1997, *Alba Cía. Arg. de Seguros. S.A. v. Delos Electrónica S.A. on ordinary proceedings*.

From this point of view, the Honourable Justices of the Court of Appeals in Commercial Matters accepted that the surety bond is truly an insurance contract when sustaining that 'if the amount of the policy in a surety bond contract taken out in guarantee of the performance of a contract, practically coincides with the advance payment granted by the proponent to the insurance taker, amount that turns out to be the "assured amount"; this leads to the conclusion that in this concrete case, the modality of the proportional rule was adopted, according to which, the insurer shall compensate the insured, up to the maximum damage'.[110] Under such circumstances, the beneficiary is not empowered to claim any payment whatsoever as penalty, unless such thing has been expressly agreed.

As additional corroborating argument of not being the surety bond contract, a secondary obligation to another, but an independent legal contract, it can be sustained that, precisely due to its autonomy, the possible nullity of the related obligation does not bring about the nullity of the insurance contract and its effects, among which would be included those affecting the reimbursement of the premium. Nevertheless, it has not been easy to reach a systematic framing of the surety bond contract since even though the books of authority are unanimous regarding the fact that the surety bond contract is within the group of property damage insurance contract; there has not been such conformity in relation to whether it is damage to things or property.

Within the conception of being an insurance contract, the majority of the books of authority have understood that it is within the contracts denominated property damage insurance contracts, which has also been decided by some laws as, for instance, the Spanish Insurance Act.

This framework brings about some practical consequences since being a part of damage insurance, it is necessarily a compensatory one, although, within it, it could be considered a different type to the strictly conceived as damage property insurance.

Some authors have considered the surety bond insurance an insurance over legal risks (in contraposition to natural and economic risks) because, on the basis of the risk covered, the surety bond covers damages caused as consequence of the non-observance of the obligations derived from specific legal relations, arising out of a credit right.[111]

In fact, in the surety bond insurance, although there is no occurrence of an event alien to the will of one of the parties, it turns out to be that the non-compliance – attributable to the taker and which may trigger the loss – is not from the insured/beneficiary of the obligation of the insurer.

Not anymore as a specific type of insurance contract as it has just been analysed, but due to the singularity of its contractual form, the surety bond adopts the modality of contract for account of a third party.

---

110. *CNCom*, Room A, Decree 30-998, *Rigoleau S.A. v. Solvencia S.A. General Insurance*, judgment 98.592.

111. M. Olivencia, *Surety Bond, Credit, Civil Liability and Reinsurance in Comments on the Insurance Contract Act* (*Seguros de caución, crédito, responsabilidad civil y reaseguro, en Comentarios a la ley de contrato de seguro*) 872 (Madrid: Aranzadi Press, 1982). It also can be seen in the previously quoted work of Francisco J. Tirado Suarez, 424 and 425.

Within the possibilities that permit the modality of contract to which reference is being made, it is feasible to think that the two possibilities are possible, that is, the alternatives of contract for account of a third party and contract for account of whom it may correspond.

Regarding the obligation of the insurance contract which could only be instrumented by means of a credit instrument – as would be a bill of exchange – the contract could be entered into for account of whom it may correspond, that is, without expressly appointing a third-party insured, a circumstance that would allow the insurer to be the taker himself, as it has been seen.

All this is despite the extinguishment of the obligation provided for in section 862 of the Civil Code because, as we know, this extinguishment by confusion does not take place in documents of the aforementioned type when there are other negotiable instruments.

141. Use of the Surety Bond Insurance Contract in Our Country – Most Usual Types:

(a) *Guarantee of Offer.* This specific type of insurance contract counts on the regulatory recognition of the SIN, which has regulated it by means of Resolution 19.064 of 13 February 1987 and Resolution 20.464 of 2 October 1989.

Within this type, there are guarantees granted regarding work contracts that are awarded by means of conquest or bidding process where it is requested by law or the caller of the bid to submit a specific guarantee in order to ensure that if the offeror is awarded the bid, he will accept to perform the works.

The performance of this type of surety bond insurance consists of the insurer obliging himself before the caller of the bid to compensate him in case the offeror/taker of the insurance contract was awarded the bid and – as it has been explained in the previous paragraph – did not comply with the commitment to sign the contract to carry out the work.[112]

From this idea, it arises that, although in the case of this type of surety bond insurance, the formalization of the contract, subject matter of the conquest, or bidding process is covered when the works are awarded, compliance with other obligations related to the contractual relationship is not covered, as would be the works contract or the reimbursement of financial advance payments in order to acquire materials or necessary elements. That is why the caller of the bid, besides demanding the submission of a guarantee to ensure the certainty and seriousness of the offer, must also demand the awarded person the constitution of a guarantee specifically ensuring the compliance with the performance of the contract. These guarantees that are being referred to are compulsory in public works bids at any level, national, provincial, or municipal.

In the case under analysis, the extinguishment of the surety bond insurance contract is produced at the moment in which the work is awarded and the taker is not

112. Javier Camacho de los Ríos, *The Surety Bond* (*El seguro de caución*) – *Critical Analysis* (Madrid: Editorial Mapfre S.A. Press, 1994).

the awardee. It is clear that the provision of section 23 of Act 17.418 shall be considered.[113] If the taker turns out to be the awardee of the bid and the contract for works is formalized – constituting the final guarantor contract demanded by the bidder – the surety bond insurance contract of the offer terminates because the risk (that is, the subject matter of it) has come to an end.

(b) *Guarantee of Performance of Contracts.* Although a brief outline of this type of surety body insurance will be carried out below, it would be advisable to point out from the beginning that the SIN, by means of Resolution 19.064 of 13 February 1987, has acknowledged this type within the surety bonds insurance contracts.

Within this category, there are those surety bonds that are constituted with the purpose of guaranteeing compliance with contractual obligations. By means of this insurance, the insurer covers the insured, up to the assured capital or assured amount, with a compensation in case of non-compliance on the part of the taker of the insurance, with some or all the obligations assumed in a given contract.[114,115]

---

113. National Court of Appeals in Commercial Matters. Room A. Journal *El Derecho* 109, 435.

114. The guarantee granted by means of the surety bond covers verified non-compliances, the losses caused by the non-observance of contractual clauses, every expense carried out by the consignor, and all prejudice caused by the contractor, up to the maximum limit established in the policy. National Federal Court of Claims, Room IV, 19 Nov. 1993, ED, 160–610.

115. The purpose of the surety bond is to guarantee in favour of a third party, the beneficiary, the consequences from the possible non-compliance of the taker, related to the beneficiary by a contract previous to the surety bond contract and to which it is subsidiary. SC, 30 Jun. 1992, *National State (Ministry of Economy. Sec. of Maritime Interests) v. Prudencia Cía. Arg. de Seguros Generales, S.A.*

If there was a main relationship in the surety bond (beneficiary-taker-insurer) with accessory and subsidiary relations in which the co-insurance companies were involved, they did not alter the sole and total obligation assumed by the former in guaranteeing the compliance with the obligations of the taker before the beneficiary. SC, 30 Jun. 1992, *National State (Ministry of Economy. Sec. of Maritime Interests) v. Prudencia Cía. Arg. de Seguros Generales, S.A.*

It is a surety bond insurance contract, the insurance contract entered into with the purpose of guaranteeing the insured, up to the maximum stipulated amount, the payment in cash that he must collect from the proponent he is taking out the insurance with having as aim the immediate payment on the insurance company's part before the mere non-compliance of the debtor. NCinComMat., Room A, 26 Nov. 1981, ED, 97–588.

The surety bond replaces the guarantee demanded by the owner of the works in order to ensure the compliance with the contract; this real guaranty, that the insurance replaces works as a true penalty clause that the insured and the taker establish in advance, as conventional compensation appraisal. NCinComMat., Room C, 8 Sep. 8 1987, ED, 131–321.

In the surety bond, the arrears of the insurer shall have effects only regarding the possible damages that the non-compliance may cause (s. 50, CL) but not those that he may have concerning updating and interests. In fact, as the insurer was constituted into a joint and several guarantor, he shall be responsible for the sentences imposed to the taker and, if the non-compliance of this one caused the loss, since this was evidenced, he shall be liable as principal debtor by the devaluation and interests. NCCom., Room E, 23 Oct. 23 1990, ED, 142–79. In the surety bond insurance contract, the insured finds in the insurer a new responsible party that adds his responsibility to the originary obligor that is supposed to be solvent and to faithfully comply with his obligations since we are dealing with an insurance company, that is to say that it belongs to the guarantee contracts which purpose is the elimination of the risk of arrears. National Court of Appeals in Commercial Matters, Room E, 23 Oct. 1990, Journal *El Derecho*, vol. 142, 479.

The subject matter of this insurance is to cover the economic prejudices suffered by the creditor insured as consequence of the non-compliance of his debtor, taker of the insurance.[116]

As a consequence of this, it is understood that the surety bond covers the payment of what should be afforded by the debtor as guarantee of compliance, given that it is not the case of the insurer plainly and directly becoming the joint and several co-debtor of the original debtor.

In this line, the Spanish Insurance Contracts Act in section 115 establishes that the guarantee granted by the insurer covers in the first place the penalties imposed to the contractor by virtue of the performance of the contract, in the second place the compensation of the damages that the awardee may cause to the Administration on the grounds of performance of the contract, and in the third place the confiscation that may be resolved in the cases of termination of a contract, pursuant to what is established in the same section.

Even when this has been the coverage at the beginning of this type of contract, it cannot be sustained nowadays that, being the obligation assumed by the insurer an obligation to deliver, each time more often the insurer should assume the compliance with the unfulfilled obligation by the own debtor/taker.

Thus, there are many judicial cases that have taken an extreme position regarding this type of insurance contract, considering the surety bond insurer a joint and several co-debtor.

In fact, we can quote the following: 'In the surety bond, the contract entered into assumes the same economic functions of guarantee than a debtor grants a creditor in order to ensure him the compliance with a future monetary obligation.' 'In the surety bond, the insurer constitutes himself as principal payer of any damage caused by the non-compliance with his obligations on the works contractor's part.'

As it can be concluded from the reading of these judgments, the position established by both rooms can be justified in cases as the ones mentioned, that is, when the insurer clearly assumes in the contract the same obligation as the taker regarding the creditor insured, but it is not admissible when it arises from the contract that an amount established by the parties as compensation for the prejudices that the non-compliance of the debtor may cause to the creditor is being covered.

Ultimately, the generalization arising out of these judgments may be dangerous if each case is not analysed in particular since what is assumed in a specific surety bond contract may substantially differ from what is assumed in another.[117]

---

116. *See ibid.*

117. The surety bond is an insurance contract (Act 17.804) under the terms of s. 1 of Act 17.418 and not a guarantor contract. To ensure the characteristic of guarantor contract would imply so much as granting such characteristic to any guarantee granted by third parties in favour of the creditor (vote of Mr Alterini, Esq.). NCCom., Room B, 24 May 1976, ED, 68–48. The controversial nature of the surety bond (Decree (7607/62)) was not an obstacle for our positive law to admit it as a true insurance contract as from the mentioned decree. This fact has not ceased, nevertheless, to have an impact on certain characteristics of the system related to this insurance. NCCom., Room C, 22 Apr. 1977, ED, 76–607. The regulations and principles inherent in insurance contracts are applicable to the surety bond insurance contract, since it does not contradict the essence of the legal relationship, which consists of the entering into of a guarantee contract. *National State (Ministry of Economy. Sec. of Maritime Interests) v. Prudencia Cía. Arg. de Seguros Generales, S.A.*

Many of the mistakes that have happened in these types of judicial judgments derived from situations that, fortunately, have stopped influencing negatively the insurance in our country.

The concrete reference is, first, the ending of the burden deriving from the State monopoly of the reinsurance and the preeminence that, by the power of economy, the NRI assumed during many years; second, the burden suffered as a consequence of the inflation devastating Argentina for more than forty years. Its presence and effects have been so devastating that our mentality (although now we are ashamed to remember it) was frequently managed with legal parameters distorted by that vice that was permanently damaging us. The famous indexation that, although to many may appear to be a soap opera product of feverish hallucinations, got to be inherent to our daily life and even to manage part of our attitudes and activities. In judicial matters, obsession did not play a lesser role because, in some occasions, it deteriorated the concepts, altering the comprehension of existing realities, besides the nowadays forgotten inflation.

§3. Guarantee of Maintenance or Quality

142. This category of surety bond insurance is related to the works supply or rendering of services in which the consignor requires from the provider of the service, the subject matter of the obligation, the assurance on the quality or good functioning for a specified term of the works or the services that are the subject matter of the request. By means of this insurance, the insurer covers the possible prejudices that the insured may suffer as a consequence of such lack of quality or malfunctioning, or by equal circumstances affecting a service.

By virtue of the great subjectivity that is implied in terms such as 'quality' and 'defective service', the clear and precise determination of all these concepts, both in the insurance contract and in the related supply, turns out to be very important in order to operate with this type of insurance.

In this sense, it corresponds that in the guaranteed contract, certain parameters of quality, service, and maintenance are fixed in order to analyse in the corresponding case whether the non-compliance on the part of the taker has been verified, or whether they are mere disconformities of the parties.

The legal business of surety bonds appears as a real contract of guarantee, under the form and modalities of the insurance contract. OS, 30 Jun. 1992, *National State (Ministry of Economy. Sec. of Maritime Interests) v. Prudencia Cía. Arg. de Seguros Generales, S.A.*

Even when the surety bond contract maintains its nature of insurance, it acts as a substitute of the guarantee demanded by Act 13.064 and by the conditions of the bidding process, which the contractor consented to and by virtue of which the surety bond was taken out. Thus, since in none of these bodies of laws is it demanded as requirement of viability for the performance of the guarantee on the part of the consignor, the agreement of the contractor – and his guarantor – in the of liquidation of damages, it can be concluded that the consignor entity may provide per se the appraisal of the damages. National Court of Claims, Room IV, 19 Nov. 1993, Journal *El Derecho*, vol. 160, 610.

§4. Guarantee of Customs Obligations

143. Due to the existence of great import and export activity, Customs authorities have to deal with a great number of obligations due to the payment of customs taxes and duties, as well as in order to oversee compliance with the different operational activities of exports and imports that may bring about the payment of considerable amounts of money.

In view of these circumstances, it is habitual that Customs requests certain guarantees as a means of preventing non-compliance with such obligations, and thus avoiding the consequences of unpaid contributions. Among the possibilities to cover such guarantees, there is this type of surety bond contract.

In relation to the matter under analysis, there have been many cases where problems related to non-compliance of the taker of the insurance, which is, in turn, a debtor of Customs, have taken place due to taxes derived from import-export operations.

These problems have their origins in a wrong position held by the Customs National Administration when assuming that the guarantee of the surety bond is not limited by the terms of the insurance contract. On the contrary, their belief is that the coverage extends to the amount corresponding to the obligation of the taker/debtor.

To be true, this would not bring about any problem if such extension was so agreed in the insurance contract, but it occurs that, in most of the policies submitted as guarantee, a maximum amount of the coverage of the insurer is established, which is accepted by Customs itself (through the lack of an express objection to the limit provided and accepted by a silent administrative conformity). If Customs expects that in surety bond insurance contracts this quantitative extension is covered, it should demand so at the moment of receiving the guarantee and not when the contract is finished on account of the occurrence of the risk.

In this line, it must be taken into account that when Customs receives the insurance policy (contract) as guarantee to fulfil the requirement of guarantee, it expresses its manifestation of consent, as provided for in the Civil Code, sections 913 et seq. Even, ultimately, would be applicable – due to its proximity – what is established in section 12 of Act 17.418, which empowers the insured to challenge – within thirty days of receiving a policy – any clause that differs from the ones of the insurance application.

In the case under comment (many times caused by Customs, with an attitude that takes us to futile legal proceedings), it is obvious that the intention – that has been made public by some of the regulations or provisions of the institution – is to apply such broader extension effect, comparing it to the one contemplated by section 12 of Act 17.418.[118]

In order to conclude this item, it is highlighted that the State's Attorney General's Office with Jurisdiction in Appeals, arising from this type of controversy, has favourably ruled on the limits established in the insurance contract, and thus the

118. This wrong position of the Customs National Administration can be consulted in the administrative case files of such entity, Nos 601.510/96, 606.654/96 and 602.304/94.

guarantee assumed by the insurer is no other than the one established in use of the right of autonomy of the will of the parties (section 1197 of the Civil Code).[119]

144. Analysis of Non-compliance in Surety Bond Insurance Contracts. Insurer's Powers. In our country, this special insurance contract has been constantly criticized from the same official sphere that adopted it when having to insure the obligations assumed by its suppliers, generally by means of conquest or bidding processes as it has been already considered.

This degradation of the legal business caused by the lack of openness to the new forms and institutions, which the law incorporates on a daily basis as a consequence of the simple observation and adaptation of the reality to human actions that are naturally acceptable, meant, like in many other occasions, to adjust original features to old parameters, using these principles as a Procrustean bed, chopping off every convenient advance preventing without cause its full usage with unnecessarily limitative pretexts or arguments regarding their function, instead of permitting the creative collaboration of the human being.

This has been so much so that it can be read in judicial judgments that the surety bond has been buried under the influence of the guarantor contract, whose similarity is recognized, but without reaching the extreme to take out all individuality or cause unrest with the phantom of reprehensible conduct.

The non-compliance, basis of the surety bond insurance contract, must derive from the responsibility of the debtor of the related obligation and not from a circumstance that is alien to the will of the subject in question.

Any obligation may be unfulfilled and not necessarily as a fault of a debtor. It could be due to an exemption applied to the arrears of payment – as has been seen in the assumption of fortuitous case of force majeure – except that those had been assumed by the obligor.

This non-compliance – at least the one that is the responsibility of the debtor – will bring about the need for an analytical reconsideration on the part of the insurer, in order to recognize from such situation the legal basis of the right of the debtor to be compensated. This takes us to the duty of notifying the occurrence of the loss and the material event from the insured to the insurer.

Although the insurer has the exact knowledge of the term agreed for compliance with the related obligation – as he was already entitled to demand compliance of the contractual terms of the case – it is the duty of the insured, the creditor of such obligation, to inform about the non-compliance and thus the occurrence of the loss, pursuant to the provisions of section 46 of Act 17.418 that is also, although in essence, repeated in the insurance policies (contracts).

---

119. *See* the following statement from the case, State's Attorney General Office, Room E, Case file 8753-A, *Siglo XXI Compañía Argentina de Seguros v. Customs National Administration on Appeal*, 14 Oct. 1997:

> That, considering the assured amounts in surety bonds ... it is appropriate to conclude that the complainant is supported by law when assuming that the additional right provided for in s. 18 of Decree 1554/86 was not guaranteed, as it arises from the intent of the involved parties translated into the aforementioned documents ... The complainant must undoubtedly respond up to the maximum amounts provided for in the policies.

In this same line, it must be taken into account how uncheckable it is, under any assumption, to establish with precision and certainty that the taker of the insurance/debtor of the obligation subject matter of the insurance has not timely complied with notice of the loss, and whether such non-compliance is not his responsibility. In other words, to establish whether the loss has occurred or not in order to limit its extension and, within the term provided for, pay the compensation as agreed upon.

This takes us to remembering that the surety bond does not take in its structure the condition of immediate performance, as would be the case of execution proceedings. There are terms the parties must respect.

It corresponds that the notification of non-compliance or loss that the insured carries out is notified to the non-compliant with the related contract to which the aforementioned notification refers. It must be remembered that in this contract, the part which non-compliance's consequences were attempted to be protected is precisely the person who in the surety bond contract is denominated taker or policyholder. Thus, it is of extreme interest to establish with this informative notification whether the taker, accused of non-compliance with the annexed contract, validates or not such claim of the insured who, obviously, is his co-taker.

This so-called notification of non-compliance must be formulated in the briefest possible term for the insurer to issue a decision about the possible loss. Thus – and as it is an obligation alien to the relation between insurer and insured reciprocally – it is important that it is contemplated without using evasiveness in the insurance contract.

As it has been explained in this part, the loss in this class of insurance contract is of a legal order and not merely material, as the event giving rise to it can be characterized in other types of property insurance: the assessment of the notification, the manifestations of the debtor about it, and the considerations of the legal evaluation of the non-compliance's compatibility with the contract, subject matter of the referred obligation shall establish the debit and amount on the insurer's part and the insured's credit against him.

145. The Taker of the Surety Bond and His Responsibility. The insurance's taker assumes responsibility before the insurer that has paid a loss. Once the event has occurred and the loss has been accepted, the latter must proceed to compensate the beneficiary of the indemnity, that is, the owner of the insurable interest or, in other words, the insured, pursuant to the terms and conditions of the insurance contract, as well as the very specific conditions regarding this modality of contract, contained in Act 17.418.

Once the loss has been paid, there are different means enabling the insurer to claim the compensation that he has paid against the person that turned out to be responsible for the occurrence of the loss.

One of those means would be the subrogation provided for in section 80 of Act 17.418, which establishes, with an inappropriate terminology, that the rights corresponding to the insured against a third party by virtue of the loss are transferred to the insurer up to the amount of corresponding compensation.

Nevertheless, for this legal subrogation derived from the non-compliance with the insurance contract by the insurer, section 80 provides as a condition – which ordinarily is not important as it does not usually bring about impediment for the claim – that the owner of the rights, the purpose of the subrogation, is not the taker of the contract.

Retracing our steps, it must be pointed out that this regulation contains the expression 'against a third party', and the taker or policyholder of insurance is not a third party, that is, a party alien to the contract. On the contrary, it is one of its parties.

Within the context of Act 17.418, the elimination that implicitly derives from what is set forth in section 80 is in agreement with the one corresponding to section 70 regarding the causing of the loss. The causing of the loss on the part of the taker, as the one coming from the insured, releases the insurer to use the exact legal words.

In this order of ideas, it would be impossible – due to its lack of sensibility – that the insurer was enabled to execute the taker of the contract by subrogating to the rights of the insured. Nevertheless, an adequate interpretation of the precepts, as well as of the other parts of the law in full force and effect, since they lawfully permit the drastic dispensing of the consequences of section 70 – otherwise there would not exist this type of insurance contract – would also permit the subrogation, although the responsible party of the loss is the taker, as it is truly the debtor of the related obligation.

In order to subrogate to the rights of the insured, the insurer must evidence the payment of the loss and that the taker of the insured, as debtor, did not meet the obligation that had been guaranteed and that such conduct originated the loss.

Deepening into what refers to the responsibility that the taker may have in the loss in the surety bond contract, it turns out easily understandable the appreciation regarding losses incurred during the duration of its effectiveness and, in consequence, how indispensable it is to punish this attributive factor of negligence or malice in the non-compliance of the obligation of the debtor. Since the same existence of the contract is not punishable, as it has been indicated *supra*, what is punishable is the causing of the loss or the event that causes the loss because, otherwise, its occurrence would be created or helped, circumstances neither wished for nor accepted by law.

Thus it has been sustained, before the regulations that expressly confer a special action to the insurer in order to be reimbursed by the taker of the surety bond contract that this corresponds with a solution that comes from another sphere. The latter refers to the action of the guarantor against the debtor.[120]

Another means that makes the action of recovery of what has been paid to the insurer possible is the inclusion of such power in the insurance contract. In fact, it is common to see contracts habitually entered into with this type of clause, without prejudice of the legal permission of section 80 of Act 17.418.

---

120. It is practically possible to combine this explanation with Joaquín Garrigues, as can be seen in his book *Land Transport Contract* (*Contrato de Seguro Terrestre*), quoted frequently *supra*.

It is clear that, in order to justify such inclusion in the policy, before the characteristic that its own copy is issued by the insurer, it must be included in the agreement of wills of the parties, a thing that is achieved – as it happens with the rest of the contracts – by means of its inclusion in the request or application for the insurance subscribed by the proponent.

Even when we have acknowledged the existence of this type of clause, it is not less true that there are no cases in practice in which the claims for recovery are invoked, as the already commented regulation of the Insurance Act turns out to be more favourable. Also, as means enabling the action of recovery against the non-compliant taker, there is the possibility of requesting the insured/beneficiary of the insurance, at the moment of collecting the compensation established in the contract and signing the corresponding receipt, to proceed to assign the rights he is entitled to against the debtor/taker.

146. The Burdens of the Insured and the Relationship with the Taker. Pursuant to what has been expressed when making reference in this chapter to the burdens of the insured regarding credit insurance, non-compliance with an obligation on the insured's part may bring about the release of the insurer in relation to his contractual obligation and, therefore, the loss of the benefit of the insured.

In the specific case of the surety bond contract, even when what has been generically manifested in such part is applicable, it is worth mentioning a distinction among the consequences coming from the non-compliance with a duty of the insured or the taker.

In effect, it is apparent that if there is non-compliance with an established burden on the insured, he will lose the right that the contract grants him, as long as such penalty was provided for in the same contract, according to the governing principle of sections 36 et seq., of Act 17.418.

The case of non-compliance with a burden of the taker is different, as it would be a non-valid solution for the law to admit that non-compliance with a burden on the part of the person who has unfulfilled a principal obligation guaranteed by the surety bond contract may prejudice the creditor insured releasing the insurer.

As a logical consequence of this, the books of authority have resolved in a great number of opportunities that non-compliance with a burden of the taker can never prejudice the insured at the time of being compensated before the non-compliance of the former:

> If the collection of the indemnity was subrogated to the prior verification of the insured of the noncompliance of the taker, the purpose of the surety bond insurance contract would be compromised as its reason to be, the immediate execution of the guarantee, would be prevented.
>
> Honourable Justices of the Court of Appeals in Commercial Matters of the Federal Capital, Room A, 26 November 1981, Journal El Derecho, vol. 97, 588.

More so, it cannot be admitted that the insurance company demands the demonstration of the non-compliance of the creditor/insured before the notification of the loss as condition of the payment of the indemnity, but only of those elements that logically and reasonably may serve to have the non-compliance as evidenced.

In such sense, it is acceptable that prior notice is required to the taker as it is a means of knowing his conduct, and if the taker rejects the notice, therefore, denying the non-compliance, he is being charged with:

> The obligations and burdens of the surety bond insurance contract are in the hands of the owner or proponent, the debtor under the surety bond, and not in the hands of the insured-creditor. From there it is concluded that, neither the misrepresentation nor the lack of payment of the premium have an incidence on the coverage or that the provisions related to the release of responsibility, on account of lack of payment of the supplements of the gross premium be valid before the insured, because they do not suspend its coverage.
>
> The insurance is kept in full force and effect, until the debtor has been released from his responsibility. In consequence, he must pay the gross premiums corresponding to the periods in which his responsibility has been extended in itself.
>
> Honourable Justices of the Court of Appeals in Commercial Matters of the Federal Capital, Room C, 22 April 1977, Journal El Derecho.
>
> By virtue of the nature of the surety bond insurance, the obligations and burdens of the contract are also in the hands of the taker, that is, the debtor under the surety bond and not only the insured. Consequently, the insurer will not be able to claim that a noncompliance has taken place on account of the burden imposed by section 46, paragraph 2 of LS if the taker has not carried out any request whatsoever to the taker who is always the noncompliant and, thus, who is in better conditions than anyone to give the explanations of the case.
>
> NCCom., Room B, 23 October 1990, ED, 142–479.
>
> In the surety bond, the insurer shall not be able to know what has happened if he does not require the ratification of the existence of the loss, that is, the noncompliance and that, could be only irrefutably achieved by requesting the taker the necessary information which shall depend on the circumstances of the case and that, pursuant to the characteristics of the loss, shall be considered admissible or not by the intervening Judge.
>
> NCCom., Room B, 23 October 1990, ED, 142–42.

Now the agility on the part of the insurer to make enquiries and request information to the taker will be of utmost significance in order to issue, within the contractually agreed term, his decision on the right of the insured (if it is effectively the occurrence of a loss produced according to the risk description formulated in the surety bond contract).

In summary, it shall be accepted as condition of the payment of the obligation assumed in the insurance contract, those burdens that had been imposed on the insured by its specific situation, within the guaranteed legal business. This implies that there should be an extreme analysis of each case in order to determine the burdens imposed on the insured, and thus the possibility that the insured may provide the information and comply with the behaviour established by the insurance contract.

One of the most common burdens is to notify the loss within ten days as from the awareness of the non-compliance. This burden that has its correlate in insurance law itself – which demands a shorter three-day term – has a reason to be, which justifies its inclusion in the contract and, thus, its acceptance, since its purpose is to permit the insurer the knowledge within useful time of the occurrence of the loss and thus prepare temporally its actions in order to recover from the taker what must be paid, as a consequence of the non-compliance.

It must always be taken into account that early information of non-compliance will allow the insurer to take certain measures in order to protect from the potential probability of the declaration of insolvency of the taker of the surety bond contract and, besides, to notify the possible guarantors of the taker if the insurance company required him some additional guarantee at the moment of entering into the surety bond contract.

147. The Contract of Fidelity Insurance. At the end of this chapter (that has been devoted to credit insurance and surety bond insurance contracts), some paragraphs shall be devoted to introducing the study of the different types of fidelity that, for some important books of authority, constitute an autonomous type that must not be annexed to any of the preceding species.

This contract has as purpose to insure the risk of damages or losses of an economic type that usually derive from the dishonesty of some individuals that take advantage of some circumstances present in the in-house labour relationship or external professional assistance.

This type of insurance contract has not been contemplated by Act 17.418 or by its immediate precedents, either. Thus, both the generic risk and the concrete risks that are the subject matter of the contracts of employment must be reported in the group of clauses of external insurance practice within which, in some occasions, it is noticed very old deficient translations that do not coincide with the spirit of the terminology that should be used or is used in other places in a more convenient way.[121]

For this same reason, for continuing to use conditions of policy coming from other languages and different customs, there are policies referring to the need that the unfaithful employee takes advantage of his conduct, without finally considering the language characteristic.

In the sense mentioned in the previous paragraph, this type of coverage of infidelity is profusely commercialized in bank coverage, precisely covering the fidelity of their employees or the individuals providing professional assistance to them, specifically related to activities that could be more permissive than others in this matter.

The risks more often contemplated as purpose of the contracts of insurance of this kind – and always due to the losses of final or definite order that may experience the insured – are related to those coming from fraud, misappropriation of funds, embezzlement, forgery, as well as any fraudulent act of the aforementioned individuals.

121. A very old policy in use among us, evidently of a British origin, contained a clause that in Spanish stated that infidelity of employees covered 'the mysterious disappearance of certain property'.

In the insurance contracts, assured values must be established without any doubt, as well as the individuals who must have them under custody or who must take part in operating with them, coverage times, opening of treasures, external and internal security measures, and – dealing with bank institutions – the double control burden and periodic audits.

As a distinctive note in fidelity insurance – in comparison with the surety bond – it is worth pointing out that the taking out is not by means of the same modality of for account of a third party or for account of whom it may correspond, but it is a habitual contract in which the taker turns out to be, ordinarily, the same insured/ owner of the insurable interest.

As it will be soon noticed from the analysis of this contract, the moral risk or moral hazard arising out of the quality of the individuals collaborating with the insured is very important, whose honesty shall be decisive regarding the probabilities of maintaining the insured's property intact.

In this line, it is clear that the insurer must, when being proposed the list of individuals of prospective cover, that is, the employees of the insured, professionals or related individuals, he shall reject those whose background does not meet certain established standards.

What has been said regarding net loss to compensate and the subrogation of the insurer and other means of recovery is also applicable to this contract:

(a) Importance of the infidelity as generator of damages. In the last years, there started quite an important amount of losses, caused by infidelities of people tightly linked to the damaged companies. Such was the concern that a very well-known international recruiting company carried out a market survey on the affected market performed on about a thousand companies of different industries or businesses. The amazement was huge when, at the moment of finishing the study in 1996, some worrying reports came to light since, from the total of frauds under analysis, 51% had an internal cause and, from those, only 5% were from management positions whereas the remaining 46% were domestic frauds carried out by employees.
(b) Exclusions from coverage. Although each insurance market and each insurer has established and is establishing specific guidelines to exclude certain risks, it is feasible to locate them within the following types: exclusion for family relationships, some actions of employees are not covered if they have a certain degree of consanguinity with the insured. In the cases of companies, this happens with the family relationship established with directors or managers; exclusions of relationships determined by type of shareholders of the insured company, in proportion established, so as not to fall over those shareholders with very low percentages; exclusions for recklessness of employees, as these do not imply infidelities. In any case, there is express exclusion.
(c) Term of coverage. Different from other contracts and as a prominent characteristic of this insurance contract, the coverage requires a special precision referred to the discovery of events contemplated as generators of the fact that shall constitute the losses. It is very common that the acts carried out by the unfaithful employees are not immediately recognized until after they were committed

because, among the manoeuvres of infidelity, there is also very closely contemplated the one tending to their concealment. This takes us to another characteristic that is almost a prerogative of this insurance contract. The reference is to the term required for the notification of loss on the insured's part. The complexity of the cases takes us habitually to extend the term to a year after the expiration of the contractual term to comply with the requirement of notification to the insurer.

Chapter 5. Liability Insurance

148. Importance of Civil Liability Insurance. In this matter, we face a subject to which liability is attributed for the prejudicial consequences that the acts or omissions of an individual may have over another individual, both because of non-compliance with the generic duty of not harming another or by non-compliance with an obligation arising from a contractual or legal relation. The third-party victim of the damage shall be the creditor of a compensatory obligation, and the person responsible for the damage shall be the debtor of such obligation. In any of the assumptions is possible a plurality of individuals.

It is worth pointing out that this is not the only solution to redress the damage suffered that our law contemplates because, on some occasions, the prejudiced party may be constituted by operation of law as creditor of a social security welfare service, different and independent from what has caused the civil responsibility – as could be a retirement by disability, compulsory or optional life insurance, or compensation for a labour accident on one's way to or from work.

In some cases, where the law establishes the social security welfare benefit, it is prohibited to claim it against the person who could have caused the prejudice, except that it was evidenced his acting with malice. In our legislative system, we have, for instance, the system of Labour Risks Act, provided by Act 24.557, which was passed in September 1995 and that profoundly changed the previous system.

In every assumption, the damaged party is the creditor to a welfare or compensatory social service benefit, but it has been provided for a system in which the debtor of such benefit is the State, the corresponding social security body, or the private or public entity established by law to afford such redress, as, for instance, Labour Risk Assessing Entities.

In other words, a system of redress is generated either by a way of social security benefits or insurance by which is granted the direct right of the victim to a social security benefit where obligor becomes a subject recognized as a person before the law, different from the party responsible for the damage.

Instead, in civil liability, the possible debtor shall always be the individual responsible for the damage, that is, the person who is the author or to whom was assigned by some factor of attribution provided for by law the prejudicial consequences suffered by the damaged party.[122]

The civil liability insurance contract precisely covers that the property of the responsible insured is held harmless. In other words, the insured – when he was responsible for a damage covered by the civil liability insurance contract – does not prejudice his property due to its duty to respond for the damage.

122. If there were to be applied, in the specific case, different systems of remedy of welfare, independently from the redress obligation, derived from civil responsibility, the problem still current of accumulation or juxtaposition or layering of the respective benefits would be generated. That is to say, the problem of whether the first remedy has to be discounted from the civil responsibility compensation or not.

Taking into account these prejudicial consequences, not only for the victim but also for the responsible party – since it could appear a debt on his property – it is noticed the significance of the use of a system as the one encouraged by the civil liability insurance contract.[123]

Studying the history of civil responsibility of the last decades, it can be noticed with absolute certainty that the priority of the analysis in question has been moved in order to favour the victim of the damage who has thus achieved a total significance in the objectives of law, turning this into a clear social purpose. It has become less important to reflect on who the responsible party is, and the matters related to questions of the damaged subject and of the damage to be compensated have gained importance. In other words, the study of the charge of responsibility to the obligor, by virtue of different factors of attribution legally established, has lost significance and, however, the grounds of active legitimation of the claimant as well as the elements of composition of the fair indemnity to be granted to the individual who suffered the damage have gained prominence.

In this dimension of the analysis of the development of civil responsibility and the civil liability insurance contract, a link has existed that may be perfectly defined as a reciprocal interdependence,[124] although in the facts that have more frequently and more intensely taken place in the last two decades of the twentieth century, it could be spoken of more as reciprocal interference: not so reciprocal between civil liability insurance and civil responsibility,[125] but between civil responsibility and civil liability insurance.[126]

The effects in the legislation of the evolution of the analysis of responsibility already have been widely considered, a change that has been translated mainly into a progressive but constant broadening of the grounds of attribution of liability. The guideline of evolution of legislations in this sense has been that, before the existence of a damage suffered by an individual, it must be established who must remedy it.[127]

If, however, attention was drawn, not to the debtor but to the other extreme of the legal relationship of civil responsibility, that is, the claiming creditor – or the victim that suffered the damage – legislative and jurisprudential processes of constant broadening have also developed about who is a legitimate party to claim compensation.

---

123. This could have been the concept that, in part, inspired Vivante in his exceptional view about land insurance. Vivante, *Il Contratto di assicurazione*, vol. I (Milan: Hoepli Press).
124. Joaquín Garrigues, *Land Insurance Contract* (*Contrato de Seguro Terrestre*), 358 et seq.
125. In this simultaneous way, that we do not share, has been conceived the thought when the expression was used in the *Insurance Contract Act* (*Ley de Contrato de Seguro*), vol. XXIV, 515 (Madrid: Journal of Private Law Press, 1985).
126. *See* in this sense the exposition of Mrs Nasri in the World Congress of Insurance of AIDA that took place in 1988 in Rabat, Morocco.
127. A work of Hans Möller, published in Assicurazioni in 1961, 386 et seq., about the aspiration of society to security and its influence, both in civil liability law as in insurance demonstrates, that an irradiation of the insurance of responsibility has been produced by the broadening of responsible parties. This notable conception, explained with coherence and certainty by the author, has been taken as important precedent by Professor Garrigues, in Ch. XII of his previously quoted work.

At the same time, the categories of damage were extended, arriving at a much more detailed analysis of the damages suffered by the victims.[128] Different factors have contributed to this, some decisive, notorious, and others vague, on occasions hesitant. In this sense must be remembered the substantial progress of ideas as from the change occurred in the legal books of authority when admitting the alleged culpability, via jurisprudence[129] mainly with praetorian decisions and later with legal reforms or conventions and international treaties, especially in Argentine law with the inclusion of these last treaties in the National Constitution text when it was reformed in 1994.

It must be taken into account that, among the factors to which reference is made in the previous paragraph, also appears as opposed curious fact the primitive non-admission of any other grounds but culpability of the responsible person; more recently, there has been a profusion of regulations that oblige the insurability of responsibilities derived from other sources different from culpability.

To that, we must add the need of an intensive utilization of the productive property that takes us both to the demand of its immediate redress, when they are damaged, and to the obligation of compensating with indemnities the impossibility of their usage, even temporary, as a consequence of a harmful event.

It must be remembered that in recent times an attempt has been started to change the denomination of the law of obligations – which traditionally corresponded to this part of the law that deals with liability – by another name with the aim of introducing a greater range of included cases, before the need to always find a solvent debtor. That is why a new 'damages law' has appeared focused on the prejudicial consequences of the victim, but substantially establishing amounts and appropriate mechanisms to establish extension and redress.

Influence must not be lessened on factors that determine the multiplication of the potential damages third parties may cause and, thus, generators of civil liabilities. Among them, there can be found examples as the multiplication of the means of generation of richness, the need to constantly adjust the conditions of competition and scientific advances that rapidly are used in a practical form for the development of a greater production of goods and services.

Thus, civil liability insurance has become an important instrument of transfer of the assumption of responsibility and compensation of such harmful consequences, undesired by the technological evolution, by the increment of the velocity of exchange, by the globalization of commercial traffic, and by the expansion of consumption of goods and services. That is to say that civil liability insurance achieves a dispersion of the prejudicial consequences – although involuntarily – that comes from the growing use of goods and activities that are hazardous for third parties.

---

128. Azpeitía, Lozada & Moldes, *Damage to Persons* (*El daño a las personas*) (Buenos Aires: Abaco Press of Rodolfo Depalma, 1998). Although on frequent occasions positions different to the ones that can be completely accepted are considered, arriving – for the criterion of several authors – to inconveniently summarize the books of authorities or jurisprudence adverse to the criterion expressed in general in the cited work, an expressive and transcendental creation can be found about damage in all its respects.
129. In the last part of the nineteenth century – and during almost the whole twentieth century – the jurisprudence of the courts of practically all countries have been filing, at least in their application, regulations establishing, even indirectly, the culpability in the act as sole cause of responsibility.

Before the presence of activities and goods of risk, it is in the first place important to take into account the need to formulate policies of prevention of its harmful consequences. Yet independently from the preventing actions, when they do not exist or they are not enough, or they fail in the specific case, it is necessary to take into account the personal and economic prejudice that represents the damage suffered by the victim, for himself, for the responsible person obliged to compensate it, and for society in general.

With civil liability insurance is avoided the use of individual, commercial, and productive and even institutional or governmental goods, since the development of the activities considered necessary in the day-to-day life may have negative consequences that imply a loss-making result in the individual or collective economies. This is what has synthetically occurred in the world, which turned the civil liability insurance contract as legislated towards the decade of the 1960s in the Argentine Act of 17.418, in civil liability insurance, of a nature practically alien to the contractual nature, thus decisively inclined towards a solution similar to one of a social type or of obligatory protection requested by the State.

Thus, in considering civil liability insurance law, it must be clarified as obligatory guideline in the Argentine sphere that Act 17.418 clearly determined that the insured, as owner of the insurable interest and beneficiary of the coverage, is the responsible taker of the damage or other nominated damages in the corresponding policies, by virtue of specific circumstances. The damage by the event generating the civil liability of the debtor shall only be a preferred creditor of the insurer for that risk. The possible damaged parties of the prejudicial events shall be indirectly benefited by the application of the civil liability insurance contract, and certain jurisprudence has pointed out that the civil liability insurance contract safeguards the indemnity of a credit and not the indemnity of a loss.[130]

This position evidently tends to produce a categorical change in the purpose of civil liability insurance, aiming at the benefit of the creditor of the obligation, that is, the party prejudiced by the damage, and not the debtor of the aforementioned obligation, that is, the insured civilly responsible person. In other words, the risk would be different; clearly, this principle turns out to be different from the one established by section 109 of Act 17.418, since in this one, the protection is for the person responsible of the damage, that is, the owner of the property that is the subject matter of the insurable interest that could be affected.[131] Therefore, it is an insurance contract that protects the indemnity of the property of the insured. This is the reason why it is a contract of compensation and not because, as a consequence of such safeguarding, it accomplishes the satisfaction of the damage that the third party may experience.

This has been the legal doctrine followed by the Supreme Court of the Province of Buenos Aires with categorical resolutions in relation to the fact that civil liability

130. Cf., Appeals in Civil and Commercial Matters, of Bahía Blanca, Room 1, *Di Marco, Carlos v. La Perseverancia del Sur SA. on damages*, Case file 90.060, 23 Nov. 1993; Rev. of Prov. Jurispr., year 5, No. 9, 822.

131. Section 109 of Act 17.418 expressly establishes that the purpose is to hold the insured harmless for whatever this one owes to a third party on account of civil liability provided for in the contract as a consequence of an event occurred during the agreed term.

insurance does not constitute a stipulation in favour of a damaged third party since it is entered into in the interest of the insured.[132]

Thus the direct action of the victim against the insurer that our legislation in full force and effect does not provide for is deemed convenient, as will be seen in another part of this chapter. Only the guaranteed subpoena of the latter in the action filed by the claimant against the insured is accepted.

In reality, the insurer pays the third party the compensation owed by the insured for the purposes of fulfilling the only obligation he has, which is to hold his property harmless, to the extent that the relationship with such insured determines it.

149. Types of Civil Liability Insurance. As it is unnecessary to give many details in facing this subject, it is convenient to start by speaking about the noticeable proliferation of insurance of this species that have appeared during the last half of the last century. With the intention of finding a simple system, we are going to choose an idea, legally interesting, which is not a longstanding one,[133] against those that arise out of conceptions about the nature of the responsibilities covered or the nature of the damages caused to others as are: the contractual and extra-contractual, the material, and the corporeal, respectively.

The reference is the division of such type of insurance into the one of responsibility – in relation to an object or a precise and limited purpose from the beginning – and the one whose purpose is undetermined at the beginning, as it cannot be supposed at that time, to whom or to which property a damage can be caused and, of course, what would be the amount of such possible damages. This separation is clearly presented in the example of the coverage of the lessee or bailee for the loss of things that are the subject matter of the leasing or the loan for use and that should be returned, and of the owner of the user of a motor vehicle by injuries to third parties or by damage to third party's things, in the case of the second group.

From there arise all the differences among insurances with concrete assured amounts, insurances with assured amounts determined to a maximum, within which there is certain imprecision as to the amount by which the insured shall be held harmless and also with the insurance by unlimited assured amount. In the first ones, since the value of the insurable interest shall depend on the sale value of the property which shall determine the liability, the principle of the proportional rule shall be inexcusably applied. In the second ones, in which it is not feasible to adequately use the principle of compensation, since there is no concrete property to which the insurable interest may refer, it is only possible to determine the damage once the prejudice to the third party is established by a joint agreement among all the related parties or by sentences and proceedings or claims.

In the first, damages shall always be caused to things that have a very specific price of sale, whereas in the second assumption, as the property is the one affected, even being negative, it may be more damaged as liability increases.

---

132. SCJBA, Act 1st of Appeals in Civil and Commercial Matters of La Plata, Room II, *Rivera, Ricardo E. and other v. Pujol, Eduardo and other on damages*, Case file 214.266, 27 Apr. 1993; Prov. Jurispr. Rev., year 5, No. 8, 713.

133. *See* an approximation in Y. Lambert-Faivre, *Droit des Assurances*, 9th ed. (Paris: Dalloz), Part 2, Ch. 4, especially the first article, protected responsibility, item A.

150. The Risk – Its Description. As in any other type of civil liability insurance, the risk to cover (as purpose) must be and it is required to be described by the parties, without the possibility of extensive or analogical interpretations. Arguments are constantly heard in relation to this type of contract that, directly or indirectly, intending to be emotive, usually introduce considerations that would be useful for a modification of the regulation, but inadequate for the construction of the one in full force and effect, since these arguments are alien and contradictory to the legal text.

In line with the previous paragraph, we understand that the generic risk, the civil liability risk, shall be the unmistakable and patent class of the subject matter of this insurance, in the same way that, for their respective cases, fire, theft, agriculture, or animals are for our legislation. Yet from the assured amount as maximum coverage of the insured, passing through its duration and reaching the event or events civil liability could derive from, these specifications cannot be in any way established by law, but solely through the contract, except, of course, that the assumption of a non-contractual different kind of insurance or a regulation of public order responding to the corresponding interests was considered, pursuant to section 21 of the Civil Code.

In relation to the comparison that derives from the principle established in the previous paragraph, it is basic to stress that the expression 'civil liability', in some way, is more restricted regarding the possibility of participation of different situations or different types of notions or designs within the same group. The denomination responds to a manifestation of a legal type, accurate regarding its intelligence of involving one way of occurrence, a thing that does not happen in other types of insurance mentioned such as fire or robbery, which can be referred to insurable interests of different species, as well as animals or agriculture may be subject of different events.[134]

What has been mentioned *supra* does not deny the possibility of a specific construction of an insurance contract covering the liability of an insured, when there appear doubts coming from a faulty circumscription of the individualities of the risk and, as consequence, uncertainty about whether an occurred event is or is not covered, it just means that there must always be remembered that there are logical general guidelines as it may happen with any other contract and specific guidelines, typical of insurance contracts.

To conclude with this matter of the description arising out of the contract, it is not appropriate to extend the risk covered, and such risk must not be analogically interpreted, always respecting the agreed coverage of the risk:[135]

(1) *Risk Causal Limitation.* In the civil liability insurance contract, the insured will be held harmless by the risk specifically established in the contract when

134. Cf. Y. Lambert-Faivre, *Droit des Assurances*, 630 et seq.

135. *See* Supreme Court of Justice of the Province of Buenos Aires, Agreement 28.723, *Aranda, Mario v. Valli, Héctor R*; 18-III-80, *Journal Outline of Jurisprudence of the SCJBA* 294 (Province of Buenos Aires: Lawyers Bar Association, 1980).

the occurrence of the event provided for, from which the damaging consequences to third parties will derive, takes place; consequence that, due to the factor of attribution established in the contract shall fall over him.

From this, it is deduced that the care in the correct description, especially of the causal conditions, turns out to be of absolute significance for the related parties. In this order of ideas, it is worth pointing out the need to contemplate certain specific circumstances as the insured interest and his owner, taking care in this sense, of the specification of the type of liability that shall be covered by the insurance contract. Also, the activity or thing from which the civil liability covered would be derived and who shall be considered third party, in order to establish the extension of the insurance coverage regarding this last subjective element of the damage that may be caused.

(2) *Civil Liability of the Individuals Involved by the Risk Covered.* In this item reference is made to those individuals who may be responsible for the event that prejudiced a third party. This is the insured to be held harmless by civil liability, which may be attributed to him pursuant to the specification of the insurance contract.

In the first place, the person insured is the person who was the taker of the contract to protect his own civil liability, as holder of the insurable interest coming from his capacity as owner, according to the provisions of the contract. Yet there are also situations in which, apart from being the taker, another subject could be insured since that person could be the holder of an insurable interest, different from the owner's and that, at the same time is feasible of being protected. For instance, this would happen in relation to the driver of a motor vehicle that materially was involved in an accident; although he was not the taker of the insurance, he shall equally be considered as insured, as it is established in the contracts (policies) in force in our country.

(3) *Exclusions of Coverage. Different Assumptions to Consider.* In order for this type of description of risk to turn out operative, they shall be described with absolute clarity by the clauses used in the coverage exclusion and indispensably, above all, in contracts the purpose of which is a multiplicity of risks, or more simply, what we call today multi-risk contracts.

As a consequence of what has been sustained about the civil liability risk, the jurisprudence has interpreted that the limitations or exclusions to the coverage are opposable to the third-party claimant. Thus, it has been decided that when section 118 of Act 17.418 uses the expression 'within the insurance', it is not exclusively limiting a monetary extreme but also equally involving different exclusions of liability to be provided for in the contract.[136]

136. Supreme Court of the Province of Misiones, 13/04/98, *Acosta, Felicia v. Casola, Rubén*, Journal *La Ley* of 28 Dec. 1999; National Court in Commercial Matters, Room B. 1981, Journal *El Derecho* 97.401.

Confirming and more so broadening this conclusion, other judicial judgments have provided that all the clauses – even those restricting the guarantee of indemnity – are opposable to the damaged third party without distinguishing the nature that these could have,[137] as they have, as basis, the principle of restrictive appreciation of all implied extension of the coverage.

However, in the risk of civil liability, if by the circumstances provided for in the insurance contract or by law, the damaging event was not included as generating cause of the liability, the redress of the damages produced on the part of the insurer of such risk of civil responsibility could not be claimed.[138]

Among the conditions of coverage contractually provided for, there are some that require certain permissions to carry out a specific activity controlled by the State, as, for instance, the driving of land motor vehicles. This requires the civil liability insurance contract of the driver of the vehicle, in keeping with the general conditions of the policy common to our business in the line motor vehicles. Such demand constitutes a rigorous condition of coverage, which omission implies inexistence of such coverage and not an expiration clause.

In such assumption, if damage was caused by the motor vehicle when it is being driven by a person that fails to hold driver's licence, we are before the assumption of a risk without coverage, alien to the contract or – as it has been inappropriately called – an assumption of non-insurance.

(4) *Type of Liability to Cover.* In such sense – and as it has been reminded at the beginning of this chapter – according to the Argentine legal system, civil liability may be contractual or extra-contractual. It can be agreed that both are covered or one could be covered and the other could be excluded. In some assumptions in which it is agreed to cover the civil liability of the insured that could derive from a specific activity exercised by him, in case of doubt, it must be considered the relation of cause of such activity with the damaging fact, except that the exclusion of one of the two types of responsibility had been expressly excluded.

Usually, when covering the extra-contractual liability also covered is the liability generated by any of the factors of possible attribution. Nevertheless, it would be legitimate to restrict these attribution factors by the simple reason that this is a limitation of risk of the causal type. Anyway, civil liability arising from torts cannot be covered because they cannot be subject matter of the contract the risk related to the malice generating the event.

This determination can be later on restricted by the formulation of precise exclusions, with a greater precision regarding the type of liability covered as risk, leaving outside of the coverage, specific civil liabilities.

The establishment of types of civil liabilities to be covered according to the types established in our legal system determines the quality of the risk agreed upon, as

137. Court in Civil and Commercial Matters of Lomas de Zamora, Room 1st, Case file 36.679, 29 Dec. 1992; Provincial Jurisprudence Journal, year 4, No. 1, 71–75.

138. Supreme Court of Justice of the Province of Buenos Aires 29/8/89. Provincial Jurisprudence Journal, vol. 1, No. 4, 404.

the damaging causes by which there is liability in relation to the contractual or extra-contractual responsibility are different.

In this respect, it is worth remembering that, in the extra-contractual liability, a person is liable for the immediate consequences, for the mediate consequences – to the extent that they were foreseen or could have been foreseen by using the attention of the case and knowledge of things – and for the casual consequences – when they should have turned out according to the aims of the doer of the fact, in such a way that this last one supposes certain intentionality, due to the fact that the unlawful act so conceived would be an intentional fact and, therefore, an exclusion from the coverage of the insurance, on account of the existence of malice (sections 903, 904 and 905 of the Argentine Civil Code).

However, the contractual liability only includes those immediate and necessary consequences (section 520 of the Civil Code), and it just will include the mediate consequences when the unfulfilment of the obligation was with malice (section 521 of the Civil Code), assumption also excluded from civil liability insurance on account of the malice, as it arises out of section 114 of Act 17.418.

It must be always taken into account that these circumstances shall proceed, when the risk would not have been otherwise determined between the parties because, if a generic reference is made to the risk covered, it is obvious that the description has been left to what is established in the specific regulations, by the, at least, dispositive quality that the regulations have, to replace the will of the parties.

However, the coverage of contractual or extra-contractual liability also has consequences in the determination of the risk since the application of the statute of limitations to one system and the other is different. When a statute of limitations of ten years is provided for the actions derived from the contractual liability and of two years for the ones derived from extra-contractual liability, the dimension of the risk assumed is also diverse in one and another assumption.

(5) *The Description of Risk by the Covered Civil Liability.* The question around this is whether the civil liability of the insured is only covered under specific circumstances or, on the contrary, if it is totally covered.

That is to say, reference has been made to the specific liability related to a precise thing or things or determined or undetermined individuals or to the broad liability, that it is not restricted to certain thing or individualized persons.

In the first case, the insurance contract must point out which type of liability is covered, either in relation to the activity of the insured or by establishing the thing that, as it is of the property of the insured or for being under its guard, may generate him responsibility.

It is also worth pointing out that when covering the specific civil liability, this can be limited by means of a combination of activity and thing covered, as, for instance, in the case of the one derived from the transporter duty, by which is protected both the one derived from the business transport activity and the one derived from the things by means of which the transport is carried out or even the responsibility towards third parties, which can be derived from the transported things.

(6) *Individuals Whose Damages Shall be Subject Matter of Compensation.* Individuals considered third parties. Taking into account that the risk covered is tightly linked to the possible damage caused by a third party and that it may generate the responsibility of the insured, it corresponds to clarify who are considered third parties.

One first approximation would permit us to say that a third party is that person that is not insured. This concept, even when correct is insufficient and, above all, inexact as not all those that are not insured bear the quality of third parties in order to be holders of the right to claim to the insurer. In this sense, it cannot be considered as example that person that driving the motor vehicle turns out to be injured and attempts to attribute such objective responsibility to the owner or guardian of the motor vehicle.

Yes, it can be mentioned that, due to the provisions of the insurance contract are not considered to hold that capacity, by virtue of certain bond or proximity with the insured or nexus with the generator of the liability.

Among these it is worth mentioning the relatives up to certain degree of consanguinity or affinity, the spouse, the concubine of the insured or the managers of the insured company, or the manager unforeseen as third party, independently from the activity that he was performing at the moment of the event invoked, in order to attribute responsibility to the insured.

Contrary to what has been previously stated and for the same reasons about freedom of contract, some individuals that in principle would not be naturally considered third parties could be so, by means of expressions provided for in the contract (policy), as it would turn out to be the failure to consider third party the employee, as long as the event took place in opportunity of work or with work purposes, or the person transported by an ambulance as patient.

151. Loss in the Civil Liability Insurance Contract.[139] For the best understanding of the problem, we must start with the analysis of the loss in the civil liability insurance contract.

The same as in other insurance contracts, in civil liability insurance contracts, the loss shall be as well the occurrence of the risk provided for in the contract. In order to start with this very difficult subject, it is indispensable that it is clear that we are talking about covering the generic risk of civil liability and the guarantee to the insured to hold him harmless, by virtue of the responsibility that has been provided for in the contract, as consequence of a determined fact which equally took place during a specified agreed term.

In this line marked by section 109 of Act 17.418 and that has been transcribed *supra*, it is natural that if there was no obligation to hold the insured harmless, there would not be a loss to compensate or, in other words, it would not have taken place the risk whose effects were desired to avoid.

---

139. Section 50 of the French Act of 1930, later on identified in the *Code des Assurances* under s. L 124-1, and one of the direct precedents of the Argentine Act No. 17.418, established '*Dans les assurances de responsabilité, l'assureur n'est tenu que si, à la suite de fait dommageable, prévu au contrat, une réclamation amiable ou judiciaire est fait à l'assuré par le tiers lésé*'.

The immediate question that brings about the aforementioned conclusion is: Why being the risk subject matter of this contract, cannot the indemnity of the insured and not of the damaged third party (however, alien to the contract) be considered where there is no change in regulations?

Thus, in the same way that without claim from the legitimate party, there is no damage for the insured (responsible party), it shall suffice the claim of the third party for the immediate consequence, the proceedings necessary to determine if there has been a loss, which essentially will imply the guarantee of indemnity of the insured.

About the subject under analysis many discussions have been held, for more than seventy years (to judge by note 18 that still is at the end of page 370 of the book of Joaquín Garrigues, *Land Insurance Contract*).

What matters is how the authors summarize this matter. We must remember that the opposite situations sustained went from the criterion of our law that has just been stated to the diametrically opposed of making coincide in civil liability insurance law, the triggering fact or omission with the loss.[140]

Our opinion is that, beyond personal thoughts about the convenience that it could bring about for the damaged parties to establish legally, but with absolute clarity, that we are dealing with social insurance contract with a purpose defined by law or a third-party insurance contract or, even better, an insurance contract for account of whom it may correspond and thus, aimed at benefiting the damaged third party – as it is conceived today in Act 17.418 – must not be judged by any other thing but the reality of the regulations and not the personal wishes of anybody.

In order to change something so substantial, the regulation requires its transformation and not a praetorian interpretation, although that seems to be the apparent desire.

It should be noted that if that was the real intention of the legislator, the plain and simple modification of the current precept should not be a complex thing to do by the National Congress.

The unavoidable legitimate conclusion is that, as long as the damaged third party does not claim, there will not be loss.

On the contrary, thanks to an alleged additional guarantee of the insurer, although mistakenly, it could be considered that, without liability, there could be loss if the third party wrongly claimed compensation since the insurer must defend the insured from this attack to the integrity of his property.

From all this, it could be logical to conclude – as synthetic expression – that the civil liability insurance contract in Act 17.418 is an insurance contract against claims of civil liability.

It is possible, from the contractual law point of view, to grant insurance in relation to other imaginable risks, as long as the loss is coherent with other schemes.

140. As authors and works considering loss in a coincidental way with the third-party claim, i.e., the position that has been sustained in the text and as that may be derived from Act 17.418, that can be quoted: Joaquín Garrigues, *Land Insurance Contract*, 370; M. Picard & A. Besson, *Les assurances terrestres en droit francais*, vol. 1, 4th ed., 357 et seq (Paris: LGDJ, 1975); Jacob Nicolás, *Les Assurances*, 2nd ed., 265 (Paris: Dalloz Press, 1979). Most of the Books of Authority have issued their opinion against this idea in our courts.

Nevertheless, still left to be resolved is the commercial problem of coverages for this assumption and, fundamentally, the inconveniencies that could arise from the authorizations coming from Act 20.091 or from other ruling of the kind.

152. The Concept of Triggering Fact and Its Report to the Insurer. The characteristic of this type of insurance, in comparison to other many insurances of the kind of property damage is the ordinary circumstance of differentiating ideas included in the terms 'loss' and 'triggering fact' of the responsibility or damaging fact or, as some legislation states it in a simple manner, accident.

It must be remembered that when Act 17.418 considers the loss in section 46 in a generic form, imposing the duty of notification to the insurer within three days of knowing it, it also includes the physical fact of occurrence of the risk affecting the insurable interest in the matter of property damage insurance.

It is clear that the duty under analysis must obviously be related to the report of the consequences caused by the fact, which omission on the part of the insured cannot be invoked by the insurer as punishable non-compliance if he has taken part in some way in the related events, which implied his knowledge and his acting in consequence.

To express it from another perspective, what we have intended to point out is that when occurring the loss in insurance contracts, the future and uncertain event covered takes place; yet, in property damage insurance, because of the appearance of the exclusive insurable element denominated insurable interest, the occurrence of the loss discounts that there has been a damaging event precisely affecting that insurable interest.

What has just been pointed out takes us to the certainty that, in property damage insurance, the burden of reporting the loss must be absolutely complete, informing both situations: the occurrence of an event that possibly constitutes a loss – from the legal standpoint – and the estimated extension of the material damages that, later, shall be circumscribed and evaluated in order to be compensated.

Going further into the species of property damage insurance, anyone will coincide that all the information to be reported to the insurer must, at the same time, be registered in the civil liability insurance contract, one of the contracts included in such species.

This last affirmation is tightly linked to the burden of section 115 of Act 17.418, as it is repeated in the text of the regulation that has just been mentioned and it is reinforced by means of section 117, identical to the one provided by the last paragraph of the mentioned section 46, always of Act 17.418.

153. Obligations of the Insurer. It is important to focus on the burdens that the insured has, and they must always be studied together with the analysis of the fundamental obligation of the insured of complying with the agreed service, as well as with the other supplementary obligations that, in each case, could exist.

In the civil liability insurance contract, this connection is deeper due to the so special details deriving from this species and from specific subjects as, for instance, the loss already considered.

Thus, in the consideration of the obligations of the insurer, it shall be attempted to strengthen the link without altering the substance of one or the other:

(a) To pay to the claiming third party the corresponding compensation. In the first place, there appears very clearly the fundamental obligation assumed of holding the insured harmless by means of meeting the corresponding indemnity that may be established by a jurisdictional final sentence or by a valid transactional agreement.

The valid time to comply with the obligations would be the one provided for in the law or the aforementioned final judicial decision.

When the obligation of the insurer comes from a transactional agreement, it must be established the term of payment therein, being it indispensable the establishment of adequate terms to timely comply with the purposes pursued in order to hold the insured harmless as well as preventing him from being attacked or threatened for having considered that the term established for the payment turns out to be in violation of the duty of good faith.

This would lead to a feeling of a special despair added to the uncertainty felt after experiencing a loss, which is per se dramatic no matter what type of property insurance contract we are dealing with, more so when dealing with a civil liability insurance contract.

Insisting on this specifically, a longer opportunity of payment must be agreed in the civil liability contract for the insured to pay the third party, as this would grant the insured the certain and clear possibility of affording the additional damages, as consequence of the enforcement of the judgment.

This obligation of the insurer combines with the significant burden of the insured of notifying the loss that has been provided for, generically, in section 46 – and elliptically – in the last part of section 115 of the same Act 17.418[141] for the civil responsibility insurance contract.

Although, in our view, the aforementioned burdens are different for the insured, they bear certain correspondence between each other. On the one hand, there is the duty of communicating to the insurer the fact which could generate his civil liability; on the other hand, there is the burden of notifying the insurer the filing of the demand on the damaged complainant's part.

The reader is required to be specifically acute from now on, as here there will be concentrated the most significant decisions, which many conclusions of a permanent nature shall derive from.

As can be noticed, due to the idiosyncrasy of this type of insurance contract, a fundamental burden is added to the insured.

It is noticeable that the same reasons given when studying the burden to notify the loss in section 46 are present in the occurrence of the fact or omission that triggers the possible civil liability of the insured.

141. It is transcribed s. 115 completely as its texts bear similarity with s. 46 and also establish as different, the burdens of notification of the loss, the burden of notification of the event from which liability may arise and the burden of giving notice to the insurer of the judicial claim of a third party. The regulation states: 'The insured shall notify the event – from which his possible liability arises – in the term of three days as from occurred, if it is known to him or if he should have known about it; or from the claim of the third party, if it was not of his knowledge before. He shall give immediate notification to the insurer when the third party enforces his right judicially.'

It is thus worth remembering that, as the claim of the damaged party constitutes the loss of the insurance contract, it may occur that the notification of the judicial complaint to the insurer occurs at the same time than the notification of the triggering fact of the possible liability or even an additional independent burden, as it has been rightly stated.

The information of the insurer of the occurrence of a fact (or omission) – from which the liability of the insurer could arise – in the other property insurance contracts is concreted together with the notification of the loss, as it has been stated, within the term agreed upon in section 46.

In other words, the event of the loss and the event of the fact originating the possible civil liability of the insured never occur at the same time or jointly; on the contrary, the latter always is previous to the claim of the damaged party.

For such reason, it is indispensable that the insurer is notified of the circumstance mentioned, so that he can carry out all the convenient acts in order to safeguard himself and the insured from the inaccuracies and inconveniencies that a third party may oppose when claiming the civil liability of the insured.

(b) Payment of the costs and extrajudicial expenses. It can be estimated as supplementary obligation of the insurer, the one referred to the payment of certain expenses and judicial and extrajudicial costs, accrued by several reasons, which may arise from the claim of the damaged third party.

This obligation arises diffusely from sections 110 and 111 of Act 17.418 and has not been a product of a risk covered by a provision set forth by a legislator, but it is an economic compensation to the insured, alien to the risk itself but contemplated in Act 17.418 (as it will be seen shortly).

Section 110 has not intended to establish – nor could it have been able to with any coherence sustaining its position regarding risk – that the legal management of the insured was by risk covered. It only limits itself to demanding the insurer (as other provisions of the same kind have) to anticipate funds to spend in relation to instructions that could be provided for the salvage, tending to avoid or diminish the risk and, of course, to reimburse those that could have been met by the insured and that are contemplated in section IV of Chapter II of Title I, specifically sections 72 and 73.

This anticipation of funds – which could even consist of the complete payment of the expenses caused by the instructions of the insurer in the specific details of this type of salvage, pursuant to the nuances of section 111 of Act 17.418 – is an obligation of such party since it conceptually deals with expenses originated from the loss or arising thereof.

A binding burden of the insured is to grant the insurer the management of the proceedings. Originally, as a consequence of the way the insurers used to commercialize this insurance contract, this was established in the corresponding policy conditions.

It turned out that, as the insurer had a great interest in lessening the amount of the compensation that jurisdictionally would be granted to the damaged party and, for that purpose, counting on the legal defence of the insured was of great importance, the insured did not care about this point – at least in most of the cases – where the fundamental guarantee of the insurer seemed to be large enough to cover the assured amount of the compensation.

As a consequence of this duty of the insured and the corruption of the relevant existing customs, there started to crop up from the profusely spread cases of this type of insurance – and from motor vehicle insurance – related legal proceedings, abuses and questioning, even regarding the legitimacy of the clause which granted the legal management to the insurer.

It must not be forgotten that, in our country, only a few years after Act 17.418, in civil liability insurance contracts deriving from the use of motor vehicles (which was practically the only application at the time), the practice of two bodies of the State was installed.

One was the Postal Savings National Office (*Caja Nacional de Ahorro Postal*), and the other the NRI (*Instituto Nacional de Reaseguros*). Towards the first years of the decade of 1970, the former – which had inconveniently entered, on account of political reasons, the insurance business – started to commercialize the civil liability insurance contract of motor vehicles, establishing a coverage without limit to the benefit of the insured.

All that, thanks to the NRI support who, as official reinsurer monopoly – also for political reasons – granted the reinsurance coverage to the rest of the market.

This fact undoubtedly meant an enormous benefit to the insured. The insured surpassed many inflationary years thanks to the State which, in certain way, carried on its shoulders the expenses for the damages caused by traffic accidents. All this created a general habit which distorted the relation which always must exist among risk-premium-service of the insurer.

Despite the different systems of the law which have maintained the duty of the insured to grant the management of the legal proceedings, stress started to be put on the fact that we are dealing with an obligation of the insurer in the benefit of the insured, obligation that cannot be unfulfilled by the former and that also generates others.

Lastly, it corresponds to making a brief reflection on the right that could correspond to the insured of assuming – in the civil proceedings – a co-participation for the legal management of the proceedings and, in criminal proceedings, the true enforcement of his defence.

In criminal proceedings which may be brought about, as consequence of the triggering fact of civil responsibility of the insured, proceedings which may lead to the personal conviction of the insured, the right to totally assume his defence with the legal representation he may decide is indisputable. The waiving of this right in advance is inadmissible, and it may affect the principle of personal freedom[142] even if it is a monetary penalty since there is the possibility of becoming a penalty involving personal restraint.

142. In criminal proceedings, it is not possible to discuss even theoretically the undeniable right to appoint a lawyer the accused is entitled to, as it is a right tightly linked to being subject to a fair trial before judges appointed previously to the event of the proceedings.

As in the civil liability insurance contract, the case of underinsurance is impossible, the situation could be complex regarding the payment of the legal fees, on account of the defence of the insured, which shall be covered by the insurer and the insured.

It may occur that, as the assured amount establishes the maximum amount that the insurer may satisfy for the covered risk, the amount that the insured shall pay by the damage caused to third parties will be superior to the former.

In such assumptions, section 111 of Act 17.418 contemplates a proportion for which it is applied the relation between the values arising from the two concepts that have just been mentioned: 'If the insured must support part of the damage, the insurer shall reimburse the expenses and judicial costs in the same proportion.'

This will not be the case if the civil proceedings claim for damages has been caused by an expressly unjustified decision of the insurer.

(c) Acceptance of the acknowledgement of the facts by the insured. As section 116 of Act 17.418 imposes as specific burden to the civil liability contract the prohibition to the insured without consent from the insurer to acknowledge his liability or concrete a transaction related to the claim, it also reconciles it with the obligation of the insurer to accept the acknowledgement that the insured may make of the facts occurred, although they could serve as guideline for inferring the liability of the aforementioned insured.

The specific burden that prohibits the acknowledgement of his liability implies placing the insured in front of the obstacle for drawing conclusions of legal nature, which would cause an elemental corollary of the acknowledgement of his debt and thus would be the triggering fact of the fundamental obligation of the insurer.

It cannot be considered of this species, the acknowledgement of the facts occurred and less so when, as it states section 116 of Act 17.418 in its last part, it is an act performed during jurisdictional interrogation.[143]

154. Other Obligations of the Insurer in the Civil Liability Insurance Contract. As a clarification starting this paragraph, it is worth taking into account that, although it is not strictly a concrete obligation of the insurer, the demands related to the guaranteed subpoena and the direct action against the insurer call for the same treatment.

In order to consider these aspects, it is indispensable to take into account that, from the point of view of Argentine law, the civil liability insurance contract is not a contract in favour of third parties, and its object is the risk of holding the insured harmless.

Before this conception and, as long as the contractual effects are not extended to third parties – to begin with – it is clear that the protection that the insurer granted by the contract can only be expected by the insured who receives the benefit of the insurance.

143. The word 'jurisdictional' instead of 'judicial' is important here, as the right of telling the truth of the insured cannot be omitted, whoever the judge is.

In this synthetic outline of the constitution of this contract, it must be considered that, notwithstanding what has just been stated, the protection of the damaged third party has been present in the long and constant evolution of law, which has found along the way, systems enabling such coverage in all contracts.

The damaged third party by civil liability has found redress against the insurer of his debtor, that is, has been able to file claims in the same way that an action is conceded to every creditor when the debtor fails to pay an obligation via the subrogation of the action against the debtor of his debtor.

They have always been also granted other ways of redress by means of revocation or the Pauline action, that, as we know, has as purpose the revocation of all the fraudulent acts of the debtor which would prejudice his creditor, even when indirectly going through the most complex action of enrichment without cause.

As it can be easily noticed, this position suffered the onslaught of a world that was attempting to change the recipient of the insurance guarantee, above all because most of the insurance taken out was directed to civil liability generated by motor vehicles traffic accidents which were experiencing a great increase and also because of the acceptance of this type of insurance as compulsory, by means of the new interstate European agreement (within which, the green card may have been one of the most motivated and with greatest effects agreements).

The compliance with the obligation of the insurer to pay the sentence – by which compensation in favour of a damaged third party is awarded – is related to the participation of the insurer in the judicial process, by which the third party files an action against the insured he attributes civil liability to. In our legal system, such participation is accomplished by means of the so-called guaranteed subpoena to which we shall refer *infra.*

155. Guaranteed Subpoena. The guaranteed subpoena as a proceeding of hybrid nature of protection of the damaged third parties rights requires considerations of significance, similar to the ones that have been dedicated to the insurer's obligations as its performance shall make great demands on the latter.

Regarding its legal nature, it is possible to state that in our books of authority much has been said and written, especially about whether the guaranteed subpoena constitutes or not a direct action of the damaged third party against the insurer.

It neither adds to our case to introduce ourselves in the details of the matter nor to extend in considerations sustained in favour of each one of the positions assumed by the authors.

It suffices, to the effects of informing about the subject, to express that the predominant position – as it has been sustained by most of the Courts – has been that the guaranteed subpoena is not a direct action.

Before Act 17.418 was passed, it was resolved by plenary judgment of the Court of Appeals in Civil Matters of the Federal City that the victim of a traffic accident did not have a direct action against the insurer of the agent of the damage.[144]

At the same time, after the passing of the law, it was resolved that its section 118 did not have the reach to confer such direct action to the damaged third party against

144. National Court of Appeals in Civil Matters, full court, 16 Dec. 1954, *Landa B. v. Viejo, Sixto and other*. Journal *La Ley*, vol. 77, 11; Journal of Argentine Jurisprudence, vol. 1955-I-291.

the insurer but by granting a privilege concerning the credit of the former, subtracting him from the risk of insolvency of his debtor and granting him even the opportunity to enforce the sentence against the insurer.[145]

Thus, the guaranteed subpoena is provided for in an assumption of coactive intervention, being a typical institute, differentiated from the direct action.

It is believed that this construction is correct as, in keeping with the system provided by law, the insured is indispensable; legal proceedings must be carried out against him where the insurer must attend. It is a special action which cannot avoid involving the insured, which must be sentenced so that the judgment is enforced against the insurer.

To sustain that an action is a direct action but conditioned to certain requirements different from the ones governing it equals to plainly and simply misappropriating the name of an action and granting it different attributes, without any justification.

That is why it is noticed that the true reason to categorize the action of guaranteed subpoena of the insurer as direct action is no other but intending to extend the qualities from true direct actions to this false direct action.

156. Requirements and Effects of the Guaranteed Subpoena. Concerning the legitimacy and opportunity, it is worth mentioning that both the damaged party and the insured may promote the guaranteed subpoena of the insurer until case is brought to trial.[146]

A specific effect of the guaranteed subpoena is limiting in time the demurrers related to the corresponding insurance, which the insurer may file against the claimant of the compensation, since as he has been subpoenaed as guarantor, no demurrer arising after the loss can be filed against such damaged party.

That is to say that demurrers can be filed arising from such contract, as long as those had appeared before the loss.

Besides – and may this contribute as clarification – demurrers that were filed by the aforementioned insurer, by virtue of reasons related to the alleged responsibility of the insured or the active legitimation to act, shall be opposable without temporal limitations in relation to the insurance contract.

Regarding the concept of loss, as it has been stated many times in the preceding paragraphs, in the civil liability insurance contract, this is not a term equivalent to the originating fact.

Nevertheless, the books of authority in general have established the identification of the loss with the generating fact for many years now in this matter.[147] In this sense, it is considered that such jurisprudence must be modified except that, of course, Act 17.418 was modified via the Congress of the Nation.

157. Damaged Party's Privilege of Credit. In the same section 118 of Act 17.418 it is established a special right that is called privilege of the damaged party on the assured amount and its collaterals.

---

145. National Court of Appeals in Civil Matters, Room D, 2 Apr. 1970, *Unión Comerciantes v. Martínez, Oscar and other*, Journal of Commercial Law and Obligations, year 3, Nos 13–18, 789.
146. Act 17.418, s. 118, paras 1, 3.
147. *See* case Room III of 29 Apr. 1983, published in Journal *El Derecho*, vol. 105, 369.

It is clear that the right truly granted by the regulation under comment is not a privilege as, in order to enjoy that legal preference, it is essential the condition of being the creditor to someone.

In other words, the law does not grant any privileges to whom is not creditor by virtue of what arises from section 3877 of the Argentine Civil Code when providing the supplementary characteristics of privileges in relation to credits on which they depend.

Thus, the privilege is inherent to the credit, and it could not be a matter of an independent legal act without involving, at the same time, the credit that works as principal obligation.[148]

Without specifically entering in an argumentation about the negative position sustaining the wrong denomination of the privilege used in section 118 of Act 17.418 – since it is a subject clearly exceeding the purpose of this monograph – it can be firmly established that the Argentine Civil Code, with more than a hundred years of effectiveness implemented a resistant system which still provides a good assembly which makes it impossible to interpret its repeal through an isolated section of an Act like Act 17.418, which does not have any relation with the insurance matter in question that, precisely, has no other beneficiary than the insured.

However, not being the civil liability insurance contract a contract in benefit of a third party (damaged party), but in the benefit of the insured (who must be held harmless), it must be taken into account that, not even in the most favourable hypothesis, a collateral right or privilege could have been granted to the right of credit of such damaged party if we notice that the credit that he himself has against the mentioned responsible party, does not hold any kind of privilege whatsoever.

In fact, it would seem that, contrary to reality, when the prejudiced party is more protected by the presence of the insurer, a privilege that he would not have enjoyed when the insurer did not exist would appear, but due to the inexistence of such insurer or thanks to the corresponding demurrers, he would have found himself less economically protected.

The idea of protection stemming from section 18 of Act 17.418 is not understood and less so the idea of those sustaining positions forced to justify wrong, illogic positions in order to defend a wrong text – as it implies the granting of an impossible privilege.

Nevertheless, section 118 exists with undoubted certainty of language; thus, criticism can and must be only carried out in order to correct the legislative future, the methodological, scientific, or logic errors that may have been incurred, but in no way to force an interpretation that seems to affirm as absurd as it would be the inexistence or ineffectiveness of the express text of a regulation.

In our opinion, such position solely equals to an intellectual disorganization – not exempted from emotional connotations – that, with senselessness, ambitioned a praetorian achievement to calm own interests or passions, fact that was timely criticized in other paragraphs.

In this line, although it would seem alien to the concept of privilege, the legal provision of section 118 quoted *supra*, grants a right to the damaged party which consists of an undoubted preference to collect within the assured amount, the

148. *See* ss 523 et seq., of Civil Code (Principal and Collateral Obligations).

amount of the compensation to be agreed upon or agreed solely in proceedings in which the insurer would have been subpoenaed in guarantee and would have thus been exposed to the possibility of broadly and without restrictions defend himself.

158. About Some Subspecies of Civil Liability Insurance. Although it is a certainty that the world advances technologically by leaps and bounds in comparison to what used to happen forty or fifty years ago, it turns out that, despite the process of globalization that has been developing since the last decade of the twentieth century has not yet come to an end, it is very complex to foresee the legal system design that could sensibly order the rights of individuals that might be affected by those changes.

This, without disregarding the rights of those who are a prominent part of the management of such globalization, producing goods according to new schemes and the influence which, above all, modern methods have on the habits of the great mass of population, with the great impact of the publicity introduced, although undesirably, in the very same intimacy of our homes.

In what has been said, there is still something to be manifested explicitly, but that must be understood: civil liability and the insurance related to it necessarily shall adopt some specific parameters, as there have been established through the last years, for example, in the matter of motor vehicles and products, subjects in which liability without culpability has been consolidated and also responsibility for manufacturing defects and professional liability for malpractice.

From these three variables commented as an example, without thinking at all in a complete list of the different existing types which, ultimately, are originated from multitudinous consumption and production patterns, it is perceived as on a starring role, the one related to the use of motor vehicles, one of the greatest significant civil liabilities due to the vastness of assumptions involving both, quality and quantity.

The civil responsibility coming from maritime or aircraft transport of a considerable magnitude has been left behind with less significance granted to it, as the commercial managers of such businesses have acted with shrewdness when defending their interests, obtaining limitations to such compensations both, in what is related to amounts and, specially, in all related to liability.

In the matter of motor vehicles, the events involving third parties have seen themselves incremented in frequency and intensity in keeping with the greater amount of existing vehicles in use and more intense mechanical rendering of services.

This decisive intensification of the cases which formed a new species (motor vehicle civil liability) has progressively been influencing the gender civil liability.

With time, concepts, ideas, books of authorities and even solutions dealing with civil liability derived from the use of motor vehicles started to be erroneously applied to generic civil liability cases from other genesis, as it has happened many times with professional liability, product liability, etc.

In other words, curiously enough, assuming an incomprehensible position, it is attempted to apply solutions for other subspecies of civil liability insurance to the insurance for damages derived from motor vehicle circulation, as, for instance, the 'claim made' clause, very convenient in those cases of 'long tail' losses.

Another demonstration of modern types of civil liability insurance contracts that have achieved great significance in modern business, commercial and industrial environments would be the civil liability insurance contracts for directors and managers that is known through the universal denomination of Directors and Officers Liability and specifically by means of the abbreviation of this expression in English D & O.

In this civil liability insurance subspecies, there has been in Spain not so long ago a resounding judgment (as it was the case connected with a very powerful financial entity) which was resolved in a peculiar way, a new case in relation to the 'claim made' clause.[149]

In a different direction from what we have been analysing, the civil liability insurance contract for motor vehicles has generated, by means of the repeated application of one of its components – the legal management by lawyers when appearing the claim of third parties – a convenient coverage that is the 'legal defence insurance'.

159. The Compulsory Insurance of School Liability. The Argentine Civil Code provided for in its section 1117 the 'reflex' liability of the headpersons of schools and master artisans for damages caused by their students or apprentices of more than ten years of age.

The same regulation established the exemption from this responsibility if it was proved that they could not have prevented the damage with the authority that their position conferred to them and their due care.

Such responsibility could be both, for damages suffered by other students and by third parties, as long as they were caused by students or apprentices of more than 10 years of age (Argument, section 921, Civil Code).

Notwithstanding this, due to the application of other regulations of the Code, there could exist liability of the school or their owners, as a consequence of damages suffered by the students, as long as this factor of attribution of responsibility could be proved on the basis of general rules; either by culpability of the headperson or a teacher in charge of the students or by responsibility for risk or vice of things or property under the custody of the school or by non-compliance with the duty of general guarantee, in case of being the relationship between the school and the students considered a contractual one.

In this regulatory context, school liability insurance used to be taken out in order to cover damages that could cause the students of more than 10 years of age. Notwithstanding this, the Province of Buenos Aires used to take out insurances for personal accidents with the students of the province schools as beneficiaries, with a relatively low assured amount.

By Act 24.830,[150] the applicable system of responsibility was modified, reforming the originary section 1117 and establishing compulsory school liability insurance.

149. *See* the journal *Risk Management and Insurance* (*Gerencia de Riesgos y Seguros*) *of Fundación Mapfre Estudios* Year XVII, 70 (Mapfre S.A. Press), 39 et seq., in which there is an appropriate analysis of the case in question, from the always attracting authorship of Eduardo Pavelek Zamora.

150. Act 24.830 was passed on 11 Jun. 1997, enacted on 3 Jul. 1997 and published in the OB (Official Bulletin) on 7 Jul. 1997.

Regarding this new regulatory system, the responsibility of headmasters and teachers is suppressed in the specific way seen in the previous paragraphs, notwithstanding the liability that could derive from the application of general regulations and which could impose the same duty to the owners of the establishment, be them private or state establishments.

Such liability does not refer solely to the damages caused by students or apprentices of more than 10 years of age but also to the damages suffered by students regardless of their age, only excluding those assumptions of tertiary and university education establishments.

The liability shall be always applied to students that were under the educational authority control.

It has been established with the reform that the only cause of exclusion of liability shall be a fortuitous case, limiting the possibilities of release from responsibility.

The new section 1117 imposes to the owners of public and private schools the taking out of civil liability insurance; thus, it has been established a new compulsory insurance in this matter.

Chapter 6. Motor Vehicle Insurance

160. Insurance Contract Act 17.418. In the scheme proposed by the editor of this monograph for this Part, it is possible to deal with the insurance covering motor vehicles from two points of view: (1) the corresponding to damages typical of this subject matter of insurable interest; (2) the corresponding to the responsibility for damages caused to third parties, their persons or things.

As we shall later refer (in Part IV) to the damage typical of motor vehicles, now we will elaborate on the responsibility for damages to third parties, their persons or things.

In Argentine law, especially, in the Insurance Contract Act 17.418, there is an important characteristic of civil liability insurance, responsibility that, from an extra-contractual point of view, corresponds to the owner, user and driver of the vehicle, responsible for the accident causing damages to third parties or their property.

There is no detailed and general legislation specifying a protective insurance for third parties and their property.

That is, to our understanding, due to the reality that such insurance would never participate in the nature of a contract and would not correspond to nominate it, precisely, in an Act that, as Act 17.418 legislates on insurance contracts.

The insurance protecting third parties and their property for damages as consequence of motor vehicle accidents – as those existing in other countries – has not yet deserved any Act in our Congress.

When it was *supra* dealt with civil liability insurance, some considerations applicable to this space were made that we shall not quote again but that are completely applicable.

As a conclusion of this subject we can summarize that, as the technique of insurance may be used without the need of a connection to the legal institute of contracts, a compulsory insurance protecting third parties specifically for damages as a consequence of motor vehicle accidents could be perfectly legislated. Yet and obviously, this should be done taking care of other related circumstances, as well as establishing that, in order to afford the compensations a tax, rate, or contribution be established, zealously collected and not less carefully invested and reserved to honour the purpose of authentically redressing the damages caused.

161. Other Appreciations about Liability for Damages by Circulation of Motor Vehicles.

Since towards 1925 Finland started to legislate, on the basis of the theory of risk, matters related to motor vehicle circulation,[151] the regulation about insurance corresponding to this type of responsibility started to pose special characteristics that, the same as the language utilized in order to refer to it by the experts, started to cause distrust about the denomination of civil liability insurance, which openly but, without deeper technical or legislative certainty continued, in full force and effect.

---

151. This Act was followed by others of the same tenor as, for instance, those of Norway (1926), Denmark (1927), Sweden and Austria (1929), Benelux (1955), France (1958), and Italy (1969) to name a few.

From practically those moments, the reality of this insurance, beyond the words used, started to outline the preliminary draft of a different protection to the one that had been in use until then.

This idea of change that started at the same time of the extensive variants of attribution, which gradually started to appear in the issue of liability, mainly pointed out to the protection of personal victims or their property, becoming these, the habitual risk that usually was covered, safeguarding the insured from yet a different risk, compensating the damaged party.

This has been disguised with the formulation used by section 73 of the Spanish Act of 1980, with the provision that states: 'covering the risk of the appearance of the obligation, in charge of the insured, to compensate a third party'.[152]

In such way, the civil liability insurance contract started its evolution of formation with a different element to the one it had had in the previous contractual custom, changing towards a social insurance or a compulsory insurance in keeping with the political will of the legislator.

This transformation that took place for social reasons, in response to the change occurred in the determining causes of civil responsibility, should have produced some evolution in the denominations of the different affected institutes and not maintained relentlessly the old names. This is what happened with the most significant of them all, the civil liability itself as in most cases, the 'civilly liable responsible person' has not been or, to be exact, is not, a responsible person with the connotation of culpability that the term used to have. The attribution of liability does not imply equivalence with culpability.

It is not clear what the reasons are to continue talking about an insurance contract of civil liability when it is easy to realize that what is being concealed is: first, a non-contractual insurance and second, an insurance that may as well be qualified as 'against damages' and, for both reasons, it is worth attempting to achieve an appropriate theory of the assumptions involved.

In Argentina, for more than forty years, we have turned our back on the civilized world to which our ancestors decided to belong to. From the middle forties of the twentieth-century Argentina has experienced an involution in many respects.

We are specifically referring to its extraordinary legislative quality that has been emblematic since the Congress of the Nation started in the second half of the nineteenth century.

Due to many and varied reasons (that do not correspond to deal with now), there was a weakening of the institutions – with errors and ambiguities – which made the government idle away and avoid facing situations that the rest of the countries – which have held direct relationships with us before the World War II of 1939–1945 – started to resolve as it should have been done here, in order to overcome precisely the backward state that those regrettable years meant for all humanity.

Thus, we were alien to modifications of laws as the ones mentioned before, to the extent that, in this specific and very technical area of insurance, in the preliminary

152. It is so specifically determined the protection of the liability insurance contract in Spain in relation to the damaged third party that when with shrewdness, reference was made to the obligation of the insured to compensate, simply with this expression it was intended to avoid its consideration as insurance for account of a third party.

draft of year 1959, it was designed a compulsory insurance for motor vehicle civil liability which was never passed or accepted at a legislative level.[153]

This strangeness to the new regulations that were dealt with all around the world, apart from bringing about an omission when it comes to setting out changes by means of Acts – as it was needed – was mixed with the judges' tendency to use extensive constructions of the laws to accommodate them to their wishes or way of thinking or, even, to the new currents of thought, concluding all this in the transformation of these judges in imitations of ancient praetors.

This circumstance – which got to be quite common – was one of the starting points for the re-elaboration and justification of the theory of arbitrariness of the Supreme Court of Justice of the Nation.[154]

What we have just stated about the criticism to books of authority and jurisprudence on civil liability insurance and on the lack of adequate legal provisions in damage matters caused by motor vehicle accidents is no impediment to sustain the social convenience of compulsory insurance for damages caused by motor vehicles as the one we have established and even of granting more protection in this line.

In other words: the civil liability insurance contract as previously construed as well as the other general clauses of ordinary use in our market are admissible, but it is not a type governing other subtypes.

Damages arising from accidents caused by the circulation of motor vehicles require a special Act of compulsory insurance with guidelines about amount, obligation, and other specifications of nature, extension and reach, different from the current ones.

Finally, the coexistence of the civil liability insurance and the aforementioned compulsory insurance would be possible since not only an overinsurance could not take place but also the priority of application of the former over the latter could be perfectly established via the compulsory Insurance Act.

162. Compulsory Insurance for Damages on Account of the Circulation of Motor Vehicles. The SIN issued Resolution 38.708 Annex I by means of which the conditions for the compulsory insurance set forth by section 67 of the Act called National Traffic and Transport Regulations (*Reglamento Nacional de Tránsito y Transporte*) are established, permitting the taking out of civil liability insurance by possible damages caused to third parties with motor vehicles.

For that purpose, it has been taken into account, on the one hand, 'the purpose of the protection of the victims of traffic accidents and, on the other hand, the cost of

153. It is not explained how it was not noticed the significance that this design of compulsory insurance had. This general appreciation mistake has been more than inconceivable if we notice the efforts that, a bit afterwards were made both, from the books of authority and the jurisprudence to get off the legal scheme of Act 17.418, with hard and laborious argumentations.

154. The arbitrariness doctrine, though historically dated in 1909 – and yet before – by authors like Linares, truly in their disqualifying function of certain judicial sentences reached its peak almost immediately after the military coup of September 1955, when it was intended the redress of certain excesses committed before the aforementioned year. An interesting study regarding this can be seen in the exceptional book of Carrio Genaro, *The Extraordinary Remedy by Arbitrary Sentence* (*El recurso extraordinario por sentencia arbitraria*) (Buenos Aires: Abeledo-Perrot Press, 1967).

the coverage so that it is possible to allow the community the easy access to this contract',[155] establishing for those purposes, minimum amounts of compulsory taking out for the following risks:

(a) Death or total and permanent disability.
(b) Partial and permanent disability in the proportion corresponding to the amount of total disability, according to the percentage of disability undergone by the victim of an accident.
(c) Hospital expenses, establishing a low limit.
(d) Funeral expenses establishing another low limit.
(e) Limit for an event equal to the double of the one foreseen for death or total and permanent disability cases.

Hospital and funeral expenses shall be paid by the insurance company within three days of being claimed and of being irrefutably evidenced – whenever the value of the services is reasonable. The insurance company shall not be able to file any demurrers supporting the lack of responsibility of the insured. Nevertheless, the payments performed by the insurance company on such concepts shall be considered as carried out by a third party subrogating to the rights of the creditor, and they will not bring about any assumption of responsibility.

155. Such grounds arise from the whereas clauses of the mentioned Resolution 21999 of the SIN.

Chapter 7. Legal Aid Insurance

163. As it is the general case, also in Argentina, the insurance covering this topic refers to the legal defence in controversies against third parties originating judicial proceedings where the interests of the insured are or may be the purposes of holding the insured harmless from the judicial costs arising thereof.

It has been only recently that this coverage has appeared as independent from others. Traditionally, it only appeared in relation to civil liability and specifically motor vehicle civil liability.

There is no regulation whatsoever in Act 17.418 (insurance contract) referring to this type of insurance; therefore, as in the other cases, it is feasible to establish in the policies dispositive clauses to this respect, provided that they do not alter unchangeable generic regulations.

Chapter 8. Aviation and Space Insurance: Marine Insurance

164. Insurance Contracts Act 17.418 does not deal either with risks arising from the marine or the aviation activity. Much less with what could be related to both spaces.

The Act has left it to special acts regulating maritime and aircraft law (Act 20.094 January 1973 called Navigation Act and incorporated into the Commercial Code; and Act 17.825 17 May 1967 and its modifications constituting the Aircraft Code).

These specific Acts contain enough provisions related to the maritime and aviation spheres – which are their main topics – in order to sufficiently cover the matters related to the utilization of vessels and aircraft, the commercial business they are applied to, the liabilities arising from those specific uses and the insurance used to cover the individuals participating in those activities.

The specialities of one and the other prevent us from developing in these succinct pages, explanations regarding these insurances as, in order to do so, special treatment should be given to subjects specifically related to each of them so that, later on, the analysis of their risks and available coverages could be carried out.

Chapter 9. Theft and Embezzlement Insurance

165. These types of insurance, in general, are neither very much spread nor massively commercialized in the Argentine Republic. There are some home insurance coverages (household policies) and some policies covering bank activity risks (especially in the assumption of fraud), but there are no general regulations about this type of insurance, except for those applicable to all coverages arising from the Insurance Contract Act.

Chapter 10. Agricultural Insurance: Hail Insurance – Livestock Insurance

166. Coverage for Damages to Agriculture.

Even though in Argentina the agricultural-stockbreeding activity has been essentially developed since the very beginning of its local and foreign trade, the insurance protecting the values needed for its production has not had a significant development. It has kept modest levels, spreading and increasing in specific zones where dangers derived from climate factors may cause considerable damages due to the volume of the crops to be harvested.

This insurance is, in fact, an insurance contract covering risks of agricultural exploitation of the type agreed between the parties, within the limits established in keeping with the rules that we have been mentioning. Section 90 of Act 17.418 exemplifies it, with the risk to be covered, although here, it is necessary to point out that the most frequent coverages are hail, fire, and, frost and then strong winds, excessive rains, wet soil (inconsistency of soil, only due to rains, which makes grain harvesting impossible).

As conditions of coverage to underline, the most habitual would be the following:

(a) for hail, a franchise is generally established in 6% of the assured amount corresponding to the affected surface;
(b) for fire, the assured amount may amount to up to 50% of the amount corresponding to hail and up to 100 kg per hectare, with the same franchise as hail;
(c) for re-sowing: the amount of a similar franchise and the limitation to only one event.

Fundamentally, it is important to consider that these three risks are basically and jointly commercialized.

For other risks less covered with policies, the following can be considered: for strong winds, franchises of 15% in the case of sunflowers and 6% in others.

For frosts, a deductible franchise of 20% of the assured amount.

For excessive rains causing chlorosis and decline of profitability, it is applied a compulsory overdraft of 30% of the assured amount corresponding to the affected plot.

In the assumptions of strong winds, frost, excessive rain, and wet soil, preexisting conditions waiting periods are established, which are calculated from the twelfth hour of the day the insurer accepted the proposal, as provided for in the policy.

The provisions of clauses of the policy establish with detail, pursuant to the insurance applications in each case, the preexisting conditions waiting periods according to the type of crop to cover and the Zone 1 or 2 it belongs to in accordance with its corresponding climate extension, as well as the maximum assured amount and the minimum premium for each contract.

167. Animal Insurance Contract. None of the regulations of Act 17.418 regarding agriculture or animal's insurance contracts is of an imperative nature.

Thus, in both insurance contract species, the agreements of the parties are fundamental to establish all the conditions in their respect.

The insurance covering risks about animals is obviously referred only to accidents or life of the animals mentioned in the contract and, in a similar way, to the obligation assumed by the insurer in life insurance. The insurer must meet the value of the assured amount for these risks, including also veterinarian assistance for the treatment of the ill or hurt animal. It is really a burden of the insured to actively take care of providing the assistance of an adequate professional.

In any case, as this animal coverage depends on the extension agreed upon in the contract, in relation to the type of animals and the quantity and environment covered, the contractual conditions may vary as well.

Chapter 11. Catastrophe Insurance

168. In general, catastrophic risks are a reason of express exclusion in the different coverages which is closely related to the reinsurance conditions that may be obtained.

This is no obstacle for their inclusion, as there is no legal impediment for such a thing.

Chapter 12. Credit and Caution Insurance

169. For methodology preferences – without questioning the index established in this publication – the analysis of the credit and surety bond insurance has been carried out in Chapter 4. Please refer to the corresponding section.

Chapter 13. Technical Insurance

170. Technical insurance does not have a specific legal regulation, and it is widely spread in the business world. In general, it coincides with the definition of Large Risks which, in spite of not being expressly considered in the Insurance Contract Act, have been specifically regulated by its own reglementary rules.

Thus, it is permitted that the insurance contracts entered into between professionals have a system of differential authorization, regarding their terms and conditions.

Part IV. Motor Vehicle Insurance

171. Material damage insurance in relation to this type of insurance is the most widely known. The coverage shall be in response to causes expressly stated in the insurance contract.

The coverage may be for total or partial damages, in relation to each one of the following causes.

Given the cost of some of the risks, the usually protected with full coverage are fire, theft, larceny which contemplates the 80% destruction of the value of the vehicle. In this type of coverage, it does not matter whether the damages are own damages or damages against third parties or property.

It does not matter in these coverages the driver's liability while driving or if the driver was stopped.

To these own risks, it must be necessarily added a third party liability coverage due to the reasons expressed in the chapter of civil liability.

It is important to emphasize that, in general, for economic reasons, the coverage of damages usually is taken out without taking into account partial damages or with franchises or overdrafts in charge of the insured.

For many years now, in the insurance contract against damage of the vehicle it is included a civil liability coverage which, as previously stated, contemplates the payment of compensations for damages to an individual or third parties' property which must be afforded by the insured.

172. Reference. On account of methodology reasons, since for Argentine law civil liability insurance on account of the driving of motor vehicles is a species of the civil liability insurance contract, it was analysed in Chapter 5, Part 3 of this monograph. Therefore, we kindly request the reader to refer to that chapter for further reference.

It has also been analysed the insurance for own damages to the vehicle, subject matter of the insurable interest.

It is worth remembering – point that has been previously made in Chapter 5 – that the civil liability insurance contract deriving from motor vehicle driving pursuant to Act 17.418 which, in turn, legislates the conditions for the drawing up of policies, makes of this legal feature an insurance contract and no other thing.

Therefore, and as a consequence of being a contract, it has been also systematically sustained that it is impossible to treat this legal feature as part of a social protection system or simply as welfare insurance, where the agreements of the parties could be rendered ineffective due to irrelevant administrative or legal decisions.

It is acknowledged the development in the world of civil liability in regard to motor vehicle driving and the benefits that the establishment of insurance may bring about for the victims, especially taking the statistics of this type of accident into account.

This circumstance of number, extension, and severity of the damage has, unfortunately, increased in our country over few years. It would be quite urgent that the Congress of the Nation dealt with a formal and material Act in relation to the subject so that, after debating and hearing experts' opinions, an Act appreciating all the aspects of the problem could be drawn up and passed. In relation to the insurance covering the motor vehicle driving and the material and personal damages arising from these activities – subject we are dealing with here – all social realities should be contemplated in order to protect them by means of adequate methods, with appropriate contributions from the community and the national provincial and municipal states.

In order to end these clarifications, it is sustained that the civil liability insurance contract derived from the motor vehicle driving could be maintained as it is, that is, as an insurance contract, but releasing it from the conditionings that, at present, authoritarian guidelines have imposed upon it.

Part V. Insurance of the Person

173. Comments on the Division Carried Out by Act 17.418 Between Property Damage Insurance and Insurance of the Person. Insurance of the Person. The Argentine Insurance Contracts Act has established in Chapter III of Title I, the specific category of insurance of the person, as opposed to property damage insurance.

Just as a reminder for the reader, property damage insurance is in Chapter II under the same title. Finally, there is a subdivision of Chapter III in three sections (I, II and III) which are respectively called life insurance, personal accidents insurance, and group insurance.

Argentine Act 17.418 adopted a similar scheme to the French Act of 1930. This regulation in France established a general part for insurance denominated of non-maritime damages and, under Title III, it provided for regulations referred to insurance of the person subdivided, in turn, into general dispositions, life insurance (*assurances sur la vie*), and in popular insurance.

Before deepening into the analysis of Chapter III of Act 17.418, we would like to express our negative opinion on the contents and apparent categorization of insurance under such denomination; apparent because the regulations specifying this part of the Act, at no moment form a clear pattern responding to such nomenclature.

In our opinion, those who drew up the Act, its bill and preliminary draft introduced the name of a type of insurance in a bipartite way, fact in fashion during those years, answering to the French books of authority of the time with lawful basis on the Act of July 1930.

For the Argentine books of authority, there has not been such a justification in order to introduce such a characteristic in our legislation; thus a reform is needed.

For the French theory unanimously – not for the one influencing mainly the Argentine Act 17.418 – it was indispensable to separate very clearly the principle of compensation – reason of existence of property damage insurance – from the rendering of services – reason of existence of the insurance of the person – that considered such services as independent from the damage which could be caused by the occurrence of the risk covered.

As A. Besson sustains, this insurance has been characterized, above all, by not having as purpose to redress a damage; the insurer must pay the amounts assured in the contract, regardless of the existence or significance of the damage to be redressed.

The insurable interest as starting point of any property insurance contract – in order to avoid the utilization of the insurance legal business as generator of benefits – is not a condition for the insurance of the person, as there are no reasons of public order.[156]

In this same sense, it is important to point out that for the French books of authority – which unanimously rejected the idea of obligation or the need of having to evidence the insurable interest in the insurance of the person, as it is not a compensatory insurance – it was required an express provision similar to the one contained in 131-1 of the Code of Insurance, establishing that, in matters of life insurance and accidents suffered by individuals, the assured amounts shall be established in the contract.[157]

As it has been mentioned before, in insurance law in Argentina, the category 'insurance of the person' was introduced by means of a concrete expression of the law, although reasons like in French law did not exist. The division referred to does not respond either to any parameters identifying a specific class of insurance beyond the one that Uría pointed out very simply about realities, which shall be timely developed.

It is evident that the name 'insurance of the person' provided by Act 17.418 is captivating, and it would be even more so if a general theory of such insurance species could be concreted. Nevertheless, it is worth remembering that – as the Spanish professor used to say – in a way, the insurance of the person has as purpose the coverage of the risks related to the human being. Yet, it is important to notice – as Garrigues did notice – that such a general theory is impossible to elaborate.

The impossibility of such elaboration, used to say Mr Joaquín Garrigues, is because life insurance constitutes the dominant matter of the whole problem of insurance of the person. It obeys to different principles than other insurance of the same kind. Garrigues mentioned the fact that life insurance is a pure amount insurance,[158] alien to the concept of damage, whereas the others, such as accident and illness, are a mixed form.

Yet, as attractive as this denomination and, above all, the harmonic possibility of dividing insurance into property and personal insurance may be, we must not rush into wrong conclusions as, for instance, that a person can be the subject matter of any type of insurance.

The subject matter of the insurance contract is, as we have seen, the risk.[159] Garrigues in a note makes a reflection about this matter, insisting once more in the inexistence of an insurable interest in the insurance of the person. He concludes – in

156. *See* M. Piccard & A. Besson, *Les assurances terrestres en droit francais*, 690.
157. The purposes article states that the insurance of the person, different from damages insurance is not a compensatory insurance and that, in case of a loss, the insurer must deliver amounts established in the policy. *See* comments of M. Piccard & A. Besson, *Les assurances terrestres en droit francais*, 690, n. 439.
158. Joaquín Garrigues, *Land Insurance Contract*, 481 and 482, n. 1.
159. Emilio H. in Bulló, *Insurance Law and Other Related Business* (El *derecho de seguros y de otros negocios vinculados*), vol. 1, 170 et seq. *See* para. 33 in Ch. III about risk as subject matter of the insurance contract.

complete opposition to his previously held position – that the subject matter of the insurance is the risk it is covering, and thus, it is neither the risk that may have taken place nor the person.[160]

With what has been explained, it can be appreciated the legal loopholes brought about by the denomination of insurance of the person and, therefore, in keeping with the reality of this so-called insurance of the person in our legal system (which is that it is mainly represented by life insurance and legislated by Act 17.418)[161] it would have been preferable to choose the denomination life and non-life insurance to refer to them.

From a different point of view, it is important to notice that, for certain books of authority – and this shall be contemplated later on – within life insurance, a division must be made between insurance which risk is related to death and insurance referring to bodily injuries (i.e., something different from death) as death, technically, does not 'damage' life (the case of accidents or illness) but it extinguishes it. Although, and yet, from another point of view, it damages life in a superlative degree.

---

160. *See* Garrigues, *Land Insurance Contract* (*Contrato de Seguro Terrestre*), 484 (at the end). *See* opposing position of Garrigues mentioned in the text, 114.
161. Something similar happens in other modern laws as in Spanish laws and in the aforementioned French Insurance Code.

Chapter 1. Workmen's Compensation and Occupational Disease

174. The system of Work Risks in Argentina is regulated by Act 24.557, effective since 1 July 1996, and it constitutes, in fact, a subsystem of the Social Security Services with universal characteristics (it includes the total of workers, even the non-registered ones) and automatic characteristics (the right to receive the social services starts as from the notification of the events causing the damages derived from work).

Act 24.557 was amended by Act 26.733, enacted in October 2012, and several executive orders which updated the amount of the services or else extended the list of diseases and reviewed the provisions on safety, security, and health.

It is not ruled out that a new amendment will take place which shall be discussed in the National Congress in December 2016.

This system is developed by implementing a balance resulting from compensations and benefits from each one of the sectors (workers and employers) with the purpose of improving the prevention and redress of work risks.

The regulation expressly establishes the obligatoriety of this insurance for all those employers who had not opted for self-insurance.

The fundamental managing agencies of the system of work risks are the so-called Labour Risk Assessing Entities (*Aseguradoras de Riesgos del Trabajo*) (ART); private entities under the legal form of corporations that must be authorized to work as such by the SIN.

The ARTs in the event of labour contingencies (labour accidents or illnesses related to the profession) have the specific and sole purpose of granting monetary benefits or services in kind.

The services in kind include not only medical and pharmaceutical assistance but also the granting of prosthesis, surgical aids, rehabilitation, professional retraining, and funeral services.

Regarding monetary services, they shall vary according to the disabilities. Their determination shall be in charge of Medical Committees dependant on the Superintendence of Retirement and Pension Funds (*Superintendencia de Fondos de Jubilaciones y Pensiones*), depending on whether they are temporary, permanent, or definitive, partial or total disabilities or when the death of the damaged party has taken place. All of them are calculated pursuant to the formulas and maximum amounts set forth by the provisions of the Act.

By means of Act 24.557 it was created as State entity comptroller of the system, the Superintendence of Labour Risks (*Superintendencia de Riesgos del Trabajo*), autarchic entity within the Ministry of Labour of the Nation.

Chapter 2. Bodily Injuries

175. This chapter deals with what is known in Argentina as 'Personal Accidents Insurance', whose classification as Insurance of the Person has been criticized. It was denominated like this by the Insurance Contracts Act, when dealing with it within Chapter III (Insurance of the Person) in its second article.

Many regulations in connection with life insurance are applicable, and the risk protected is related to the health and life of the insured.

In general, its provisions are dispositive, except for the topic related to risk aggravation contained in section 132 of the Act which may be changed only in the insured's favour.

The coverages provide for the payment of a defined amount upon the death of the insured or in the case of disability (which parameters are established in a table of disabilities drawn up to such effect) appointing beneficiaries.

The assured amounts may be freely established.

Chapter 3. Private Health Insurance

176. Private Health Insurance has not spread in Argentina to a great extent. The Insurance Contracts Act does not deal with it either.

Nevertheless, there are existing approved plans, and some entities have started to develop this type of insurance.

A system of prepaid medicine entities has been developed instead. By means of the payment of an established amount of money, a medical service is provided, in some cases, by the same institution or entity devoted to the direct rendering of medical service and, in others, by entities which are intermediaries between the entities providing the service and the patients.

It has been widely discussed in the country whether these hybrid entities carry out insurance operations or not.

Up to the moment, the controlling authority has considered that they do not carry out such activity, reason why it has implicitly excluded them from its system.

Chapter 4. Life Insurance

§1. Individual Life Insurance

177. Concept. In the previous paragraphs, it has been evidenced that life insurance is the most significant category within insurance contracts of the category insurance of the person.

All its variables could be individualized and, at the same time, this species could be defined as the contract by which the insurer, as consideration for the payment of the established premium covenants to pay the beneficiary or taker, the amount established in case of death or survival of the insured at a specified time.

Life insurance was long resisted in the civilized world because life was used as a game or bet, reason that, paradoxically, as time went by, determined its impulse – since gambling has always been an interesting entertainment with profit possibilities.

The development of life insurance was progressively favoured by governmental measures that rescued the value of the system and also by the scientific findings of the indispensable exact techniques of statistics, which brought about the precisions of the tables of mortality.

The higher French Courts also had an important influence supporting the legal business with the theory of 'stipulations on behalf of third parties', granting the beneficiaries a right of their own and not derived from somebody else's right.

This posture was of great influence and served as support to the institute as the right of said beneficiary, which emerged from the stipulation on behalf of a third party, was considered as arising from him and not from the stipulator.

Ultimately, the spirit of provision and saving of the population was boosted, favouring the development of insurance (by means of the reduction of tax rates), a trade alien to unfavourable consequences, as it was the case of real estate loans emerging from excess funds.

178. Causes That Boosted Life Insurance. In other words, it is considered that, on account of the extraordinary boost of the life insurance activity, some significant causes from different orders took place at the same time.

We notice: (a) a moral cause; the natural provision and sense of saving, existent in all the social classes of the population; (b) an economic cause, the gathering of capitals for investment, preferably allocated to interest-bearing loans for construction; and (c) a social cause, permitting the support of individuals (primarily relatives) upon the death of the principal.

The State encouraged due to these important causes the increase of life insurance by means of a better tax treatment and protective legislation towards the insured.

In life insurance, there is no such thing as compensation which is an essential consequence in property damage insurance.

The characteristic of this type of insurance is that its purpose is not the redress or compensation of a loss, as the insurer must pay an amount established in the contract regardless of the need of the effective occurrence of a loss or the appraisal of its economic value.

However, due to the characteristic of this insurance of amount or capital, an event of overinsurance, underinsurance, or multiple insurance (which is the legal taking out of several insurances, covering the same risk or the right of the beneficiary to collect more than one insurance) could never take place.

The criticism to the denomination of insurance of the person and the distinction of categories between property insurance and life insurance does not mean, from any point of view, that we must elaborate from simulated, unreal or groundless concepts or that there are different genders.

We cannot forget that there are extremist theories sustaining that a business which did not find its basis on the purpose of compensating could not be considered insurance, but it would have a different nature which would be the purchase of a capital (paid by the insurer) as consideration for the payment of the premiums or also a fungible deposit.

The concepts are not fake, simulated, groundless, or unreal. They do not exist in different genders, either.

The essential element, the subject matter of the contract is the risk and that same and sole purpose makes both, property insurance and life insurance species of the common gender insurance.

The classification of insurance contracts, almost universally accepted as from its utilization by the European Community, poses the fundamental division of life and non-life or property or things insurance contracts – more for a controlling reason and the greater protection of the insured than for an inner need of insurance law.

For the Argentine legal conception is a classification based on the existence or not of an insurable interest, element that, for us, only exists in property insurance contracts but not in life insurance or insurance contracts that Act 17.419 calls 'of the person'.

For the Anglo-Saxon books of authority which consider that, for any kind of insurance, it is necessary the existence of an insurable interest as condition of validity of the business being agreed upon, it could be possible to conceive an insurance of a non-compensatory nature since the insurable interest is not conceptually a synonym of indemnity.

More so, according to the same books of authority, although there could be non-compensatory insurance, there could not exist insurance without an insurable interest.

This position is not applicable to our law, as for Act 17.418, the insurable interest is a consequence of the compensation principle of the insurance contract – denominated of property or things – and that indispensable element (for that type of insurance) is not indispensable at all for the so-called insurance of the person and, specifically, for some life insurance contracts.

179. Independent Legal Institute. It is worth remembering that, although life insurance from the point of view of economy may be considered as a way of provision or saving in relation to insured and beneficiaries, as any other more specific business, it has its place in law, independent from any economic or technical aspect which may serve as purpose in each specific case.

With this, what is intended is to express the importance of granting technical aspects to any business without leaving aside its legal aspect which characterizes it and governs it. These are conclusions reachable from a technical point of view, not from the global analysis of any business which may have the false or wrong assumption of taking its parts as a whole.

The insurance contract is a contract different from any other, although it may have similarities with other legal features or may be composed of different realities.

In this perspective, it is important to take into account that, for some, the life insurance contract includes more than one business, and several legal operations coexist, maintaining their independence.

Life insurance has, at least, two different aspects that are technically contemplated. One is the insurance aspect; there is a risk on the life of an insured. The other is the financial aspect: the risk[162] is displaced from the person of the insured to the protection and trustworthiness of a financial collocation that, as any other, turns into a financial risk.

We stress the fact that the risk does not include the damage since, from the insurance point of view, the risk is the future and possible fact causing an aleatory event, alien to the idea of damage.

180. Technical Complexity. The institute of life insurance, as many others, is not simple at all but, on the contrary, is the complex result of the harmonic gathering of many institutes.

If we dissect their elements, leaving no connection among them, we could achieve an endless number of strange deductions or results that would arise from a profound analysis of the whole, since methodically it is not true that a part of the non-physical science of Law had to be a partial expression, equivalent to the whole.

If this criterion was followed, we could conclude that the same flair needed by the anatomopathologist to penetrate into the details of the physical knowledge of the body under study is the same used in life insurance with other kinds of economic and commercial operations.

With the same criterion, we could think of businesses or matters arising out of a purchase of capital, where the insurer pays a price represented by the amount of the premiums or a fungible deposit of the type of savings account or an aleatory loan, with the obligation of returning the premiums paid, with interest and the corresponding capitalization.

In this last case, there is the danger that the aforementioned premiums are paid for a term longer or shorter than the necessary term for their return.[163]

We stress the fact that this procedure is not effective in this situation because, although it is apt for the analysis of physical facts, it is not apt for moral, legal, or religious facts (which enquiring and cognitive methods are others).

To deal with a law institute – as if it was part of physics, medicine, or another organic science – is to violently confuse matters and to create a great spiritual disorder for both, those who have the interest of knowing and those who wish to improve their knowledge.

---

162. Yvonne Lambert-Faivre, *Droit des Assurances*, 718.
163. Joaquín Garrigues, *Land Insurance Contract*, 489 and n. 8.

Life insurance thought under the concept of risk of duration of a human life is decisively an aleatory contract because, although the event is not uncertain (as the death of the insured shall fatally occur at some point), it is uncertain the moment of its occurrence.

In the words of the great Spanish professor Joaquín Garriges, the uncertainty is not '*an*' (if) but '*quando*' (when).

The legal feature that we have to contemplate is life insurance, although it may be composed of many elements inducing us to believe in the possibility of separating them.

Let us remember again that the parts of a whole are not necessarily complete parts by themselves.

An inherent part of a legal act may have its own individuality, but it is also possible that this individuality disappears when we consider the whole.

Life insurance is death insurance as the risk, which occurrence enforces the obligation of the insurer, is the death of the insured.

As counterpart of this type of insurance and when the risk whose occurrence making enforceable the obligation of the insurer is the survival of the insured after a specified date, the loss determining the obligation of the rendering of services is, clearly, more uncertain.

Between both situations, life and death insurance, that is, in all the assumptions where the risk is related to or connected with a matter of duration of human life, there are other possible assumptions that have given rise to combinations of the other two, including a double subject matter.

In this respect, it is worth remembering that this has been called mixed insurance because the commitment assumed by the insurer is multiple or, at least, double, as: (a) on the one hand, he must pay the capital agreed to the insured if he reaches the age provided for; and (b) on the other hand, he must pay the beneficiary if the insured dies before that term.

We have to agree once again with Garrigues who has sustained – as well as others as Besson and Picard – that the expression of double insurance or insurance of double purpose is deceiving since it makes believe in the existence of a sole insurance with specific characteristics when, in fact, there are two layering insurances: one for the case of death and another for the case of survival or simply, of life.

It constitutes, for Garrigues, a sole contract with contemporary and alternative coverage of two opposed risks, from which one is 'incertus an' and the other is 'incertus quando'.[164]

181. Classes of Life Insurance. It is well known that the mathematics supporting the actuarial science is the technical support of life insurance. Due to these technical bases, it is perfectly understood the wide range of possibilities available to satisfy the different needs or interests of those requesting a policy.[165]

---

164. *Ibid.*, 490, n. 9 and especially the bibliography contemplated therein of Piccard and Besson, Hémard, Donati, and Gasperoni.

165. *See* G. Lamelot & J. Leriche, *Assurance Vie*, 3rd ed. (Paris: Belfond Press, 1994).

Precisely on account of this range of possibilities and the development of this type of insurance – which will continue to develop as time goes by – life insurance contemplated in Argentine Act 17.418 have been elementarily existent during the first fifty years of the twentieth century.

Nevertheless, it is necessary to attempt a list in this monograph of the different classes of life insurance mostly used in our sphere. It is also necessary to remind of the fact of the great inflation prevention during around fifty years, the indispensable saving in order to concrete this type of business and provisions. It has only been in the last fifteen years or so that the life insurance business started to establish again in Argentina, although in recent times history seems to be repeating itself:[166]

(a) *On Account of the Risk.* In the first place and taking into account the type of risk that will be the subject matter of the contract, we could divide this insurance into: death insurance or life insurance paid upon the death of the insured and life insurance proper or survival insurance.

In both cases, the random event determining the advantage of one of the parties shall depend on an uncertain event,[167] the death of the insured or the survival of the insured.

The future random event, that is, the risk, according to the view, shall be the death or survival of the insured to a defined date or moment.

We have already sustained that it is not a third type of life insurance but just an insurance contemplating the two risks mentioned as causes of the losses and, therefore, two independent insurances that shall play successive roles.

More so, we can think of a sole contract where two guarantees or two alternative coverages – certainly contemporary – are granted by the alternative risks of survival and death.[168]

(b) *On Account of the Contract and Obligation of the Insurer.* In the second place and taking into account the duration of the contract and the obligation of the insurer, these insurances may be divided into: permanent or temporary life insurance.

In permanent life insurance, the insurer covenants to pay the agreed amount at the moment of the death of the insured, regardless of the moment of its occurrence, after the contract was agreed.

166. We are making reference to the time elapsed as from half of 2007 onwards, although – as it always occurs with inflation – the development is every time quicker and more traumatic.
167. *See* s. 2051 of the Argentine Civil Code.
168. *See* Picard & Besson, *Le Contrat D'assurance*, T.I, 720; Lambert-Faivre, *Droit des Assurances*, 397. This author underlines that this combination of risks is the most practical one, as the insured is under the impression or sensation of always winning. Yet, it is a more expensive option because it must be paid the counterpart of two different and contradictory risks, from which only one will actually take place.

In temporary life insurance, the payment of the amount established in the contract shall only be carried out if the death of the insured takes place within a determined period, that is, within the term provided for or, in other words, if death occurs before a determined date, that is, within the period of coverage agreed upon.

(c) *On Account of the Moment and Kind of Payment of the Loss.* In the third place, for that insurance that we have denominated as life insurance proper, that is, that in which the risk subject matter of the insurance is the life of the insured at a specific moment, it could be divided into: insurance that will pay a deferred fixed annuity, insurance that will pay a life annuity (*rente viagere*), or insurance that will pay a temporary annuity.

It is also possible to speak of insurances that will pay a variable capital, most of the times increasingly and in arithmetic and geometric progressions.

This means the insurer will have the obligation – if the random event of the survival of the insured after a defined date takes place – to pay periodic life annuities or for an agreed-upon term.

(d) *On Account of the Moment of Payment of the Premium.* In the fourth place, the classification may be referred to the time of payment of the premium.

The insurance of death, denominated of permanent life, was originally designed through the payment of a sole and advanced premium. Later on, payments in instalments were implemented thus appearing: insurance with payments of temporary premiums and with payments of life annuity premiums.

In the insurance of payments of temporary premiums, the periodic payments of the premiums are made for a determined number of periods (e.g., twenty-five years), and after this time, the taker stops making the payments, being insured for the rest of his life and, in case of death, the insurer has to pay the obligation assumed.

Another thing: permanent life insurance, with the payment of a sole premium is certainly a product very difficult to commercialize in the market as the premium would be very high. Only under very special circumstances and only some special people could afford it. However, we know the dubious use that many takers of this kind of insurance have made, by deficiencies of the imposition of taxes.

182. Modern Types of Life Insurance. Universal life insurance. Unit life insurance. Taking into account the possibility of mixing the different forms of life insurance, it is necessary to analyse some of these combinations, especially those modern ones inspired in practical reasons.

In the commercialization of products, the insurers have found many times the emerging difficulty of comparing insurance from its actual profitability point of view with other types of financial investments as investments to a specified term, investments in bonds or shares, negotiable obligations or investment funds.

They have also encountered the lack of transparency of commercialization, production costs and inflexibility imposed by the payment of premiums.

Thus, in the American and British markets, these new modalities have acquired certain characteristics that have permitted them and permit them to compete successfully with the typical bank investments.

These characteristics make life insurance to be identified: (a) with the possibility that the client or taker could have a direct intervention in the type of collocation of the premiums; (b) with a greater transparency in regard to the items composing each premium and expenses; and (c) with the flexibility acquired by the payment of premiums, both regarding their amount and their opportunities.

With all this new perspective – that does not restrict to the items mentioned *supra* finally, and on a completely technical criterion, the modern operations with permanent life insurance may be gathered as insurance of flexible type (universal life) and insurance related to internal or external investment funds (unit link and total link).[169]

This policy of commercializing temporary insurance in Argentina, where life insurance had practically disappeared due to the inflation suffered since 1950, had a reception from a different source.

The scarce insurers that had commercialized group insurance – with some kind of premium which may imply mathematical reserves – before a jurisprudence of wrong content started to promote temporary group insurance with which no other prospects of possible insurance had quite an acceptable placement in environments of modest but steady income.

Years later, when inflation seemed to have disappeared from the country (until recently), life insurance made a strong return because the final operations of pension funds could finally be concreted.

After the first euphoric moments of this new modality, the insurers noticed that they could only truly compete with other segments of the saving market by offering a product that continued to be safe, improving notoriously its financial characteristics.

Following a technical criterion, the other varieties are the unit-linked insurance plans (of variable capital).

According to the most commonly used expressions, this modern insurance is nominated in units of account, insurance in shareholding or insurance related to investment funds, and it is, ultimately, universal life insurance with some advantageous innovations for the investor.

The high inflation of the past and the interest of the stock market forced the creation of new methods of investment that could be of the appeal of a greater number of individuals, fact that was not accomplished in the Argentine weak market either.

In fact, it was not an exclusive or excluding way of commercializing life insurance, but certainly a new modality started to be developed from the 1980s. In that

169. José Elías Gallegos Díaz de Villegas, *Classical Modern Modalities of Permanent Life Insurance* (*Modalidades clásicas modernas del seguro de vida entera*) (Madrid: Mapfre Press, 1997). This Spanish actuary establishes the following division: Flexible type of insurance (universal life insurance); insurance related to internal or external investment funds also known as unit link insurance (unit link and total link insurance).

decade, the information technology (IT) development made a multiple impact on the financial world, permitting an unforeseen speed for the management of an incredible amount of data.

These two circumstances that were inconceivable before opened the doors to walk unknown paths which broadened and broadened more each time.

Thanks to technology, access to a greater public was possible, spreading systems and financial means in order to look for and find the growth of individual savings, weakening the division that used to exist between insurance and banking businesses.

It must be remembered that both activities due to habits, customs, and ancient fears, after having been closely linked by the merchants (who acted as brokers, bankers, and insurers) that conceived commerce as something strategically unique – eight centuries ahead of the current bancassurance – split in two, each of them with exclusive purposes. Thus, a bank did not operate insurance, and an insurer was not allowed to carry out business deals.

This unique purpose in both activities (that besides exclusive is excluding), during several decades for security reasons and consumer protection of one and the other diluted in the need and thirst for obtaining the acceptance and penetration of new financial products with deeper financial characteristics, which can be distinguished with some difficulty by its origin or speciality, either a financial banking business or an insurance business.

It has been so varied, multiple and even heterogeneous the conjunction of one and the other activities that, only after some years of having started, the witty name of '*bancassurance*' as indication of inclusion appeared.

Simply as an anecdote, this denomination was brought about by the French and spread towards 1989. Then it formed similar terms coming from Germany as *allfinanz* and its translation into French of *assurfinance* that in Spanish means offering commercially at the same time insurance and financial products that are somehow supplementary.

This joint work is easily noticed in life insurance due to the type of products that it involves and almost with preference, the preeminence of banks which, as from the decade from 1981 to 1990, penetrated the insurance business since some companies belonged to bank groups or simply by means of the product distribution by banks with which agreements were entered into.

What is undoubted is the growth of the retirement funds – privately administered – as an immediate consequence of the world crisis of the social security and welfare systems since banks started to look into it as novelty business which brought forward, in the field we were commenting on, a new boost in bank institutional development, which added activities related to life insurance.

In our country, a more important presence of capitals related to banks, in the insurance business has been noticed, either because financial institutions shareholding groups have taken positions in the capital of insurance entities or by the appearance of new dominant groups of insurance companies that, at the same time, acquired majorities in the capital of banks.

At the same time, some insurers have taken portfolios that depended on banks for their commercialization when disappearing or entering in liquidation proceedings insurers, traditionally linked to such banks.

183. Modalities of Life Insurance by Subscription: Individual Insurance and Group Insurance. Apart from the different forms that life insurance may take, it is possible to establish a division in relation to the manner of subscription by the number of people linked together:

(1) Individual subscription. In relation to the individually subscribed contracts, as they are a common gender, they have legal and contractual provisions applicable to others and, in general, everything that has been considered in previous paragraphs may be applied to this type of subscription, without prejudice of also being applied to group insurance. Nevertheless, some specific aspects will be detailed later on. Within this group there is permanent life insurance for more than one holder.
(2) Group life insurance. Our Argentine Act 17.418 has failed to systematically provide elements that may clarify the real characteristic of this contract.

Only Article III of Chapter III may be said to include some concepts in sections 153–156.

Such concepts can only weakly allow for the inference of an organic theory about this type of contract, and even then, the aforementioned four sections bring about some confusing theories.

In the universal doctrine a quite specific idea has been formed by means of certain practices of the insurance community around the world and, above all, by some regulations later on provided for in some countries.

There are some constant characteristics in this modality of subscription of life insurance which can be perfectly applied in Argentina because of the principle of freedom of contract (except that they violate morality, goods customs, and laws of public order or laws of superior rank):

(1) The name of group insurance is not a clear notion. Ivonne Lambert-Faivre, with her habitual grace when writing describes it as 'flou', that is, vague, out of focus, a blurred image.[170]

In doctrine, with time and thanks to the help provided by posterior laws of better design, by means of the juxtaposition of different opinions, an important element could be extracted: the need of a link among the individuals forming the group, link that must be of the same nature, regarding the individuals forming the group and the person gathering them.

(2) The link in question generally is a contract or an institution. In the first assumption, it could be labour contracts, loan contracts, etc.; in the second, the relationship could be to belong to the same association (club, trade union, Non-governmental Organization (NGO), etc.).

170. Y. Lambert-Faivre, *Droit des Assurances*, 9th ed. (Paris: Dalloz Press, 1995).

The link must also be alien to the will of forming a group or the purpose of forming the group, if not, a group could be easily constituted by means of the adverse selection of the risk, with risks aggravated on purpose or, as it is said in the specific language, substandard risks.

This balance was noticed by means of experiences carried out with time, and it was also noticed that there was no need to establish a minimum number for each group.

It must be clear that this type of life insurance is unique regarding risk selection and distribution.

(3) Life group insurance is carried out by one person that agrees with the insurer a precontract or a regulatory contract as, even when there is a contract between insurer and subscriber binding all individuals composing the group, the truth is that, without the express will of these individuals established in the aforementioned agreements, there would not be a definitive contract.[171]

Therefore, the subscriber does not exactly play the same role than the taker in other modalities of life insurance as it has other capacities and further, he does not act for account of third parties as this insurance is not of that nature. Further, neither the subscriber covenants on behalf of the insurer nor does he on his own name.

The subscriber is in fact a coordinator of the group that does not assume any obligation before the members of the group.

Logically, some obligations can be assumed outside insurance law and the duties of this contract, as, for instance, to collect the premium to pay the insurer by automatic means as discounting it from wages or including the premium in periodic instalments paid in a contract of savings and loan or any other that could be agreed upon as, for instance, a contract by the administrator of a closed group of a savings plan with defined purposes.

(4) The premium to pay is of an amount in relation to the average age of the members of the group and it is calculated on the basis of a percentage of the salaries of each individual or on any other common parameter (e.g., amount of the loan).
(5) Even when group insurance adjusts well to the more diverse wishes of life protection in society, it is specifically important to help credit operations and labour.
(6) Group insurance is temporary and annually renewable, generally by implied continuation. Nevertheless, some group life insurance has been based on a level premium; this insurance is often called permanent group insurance.
(7) As component of the group, subject matter of the precontract with the subscriber it will suffice his conformity to be insured. Whoever entered the group thereinafter will have to comply with the conditions that were established in such precontract.

---

171. M. Picard & A. Besson, *Les Assurances Terrestres*, 456, n. 3.

(8) If membership to the group stops, the insurance ends. The same happens when a certain age is reached.
(9) Instrumentally, the contract is drawn up in one copy that remains in power of its subscriber and constitutes the policy. Each member of the group adhering to the system is handed in a certificate of coverage in which the essential elements are evidenced.
(10) The beneficiary may be, pursuant to the risk covered, either the own insured or a third party, including in the last concept, the taker, under the circumstances of section 120 Act 17.418 that, to our judgment, is connected with the second part of section 156.

This second part – which provides for the possibility that the beneficiary may be the taker – is, to our understanding, a repetition of what is set forth in section 120. That is the only understandable meaning of the expression 'lawful economic interest', that is, an insurable interest that does not exist in life insurance and only exists for damage insurance.

In summary, group life insurance is habitually presented in two groups: (1) workers of the same company; and (2) debtors of a same creditor by a defined type of credit. Notwithstanding this, any element can get groups together, except the wish to insure, taking this line of insurance very far.

184. Personal Elements of Life Insurance. Either as a need or as a mere possibility due to operational reasons, life insurance may cause effects on different individuals from those that have taken it out.

It is interesting to resume some concepts about death insurance. The agreement could never be carried out with the taker or policyholder as, being the insured, he would disappear when occurring the loss, that is, when his own death is taking place. It is then evident that, in this type of insurance, the beneficiary shall always be a person different form the insured.

It is also apparent that the taker and the insured could be different individuals, as long as, the insurance, as any other type of contract, may be agreed upon in the benefit of a third party without this third party taking part of its creation.[172]

Remembering that in insurance law, the taker or policyholder is the person that enters into the contract with the insurer and is obliged to pay the premium and that the insured, in life insurance is the person constituting the risk, we, therefore, have the traditional trilogy marked by authors[173] completed with the beneficiary. This last

172. This position has been ratified by the jurisprudence (*see* judgment registered in Journal El Derecho, vol. 17, 742, Room F, Court of Appeals in Civil Matters of the Federal Capital City 12 Apr. 1966).
173. It is not a matter of senseless denomination. It is absolutely indispensable in order to differentiate correctly the roles of each one of the parties. As our Act 17.418 has made wrong use of the denomination 'insured', so have the judicial judgments on the related subjects, calling, for instance, taker, the insured. *See* judgment quoted in preceding n. 200.

person is not a party to the contract but is the contractual recipient of the payment that could be carried out by the insurer in the event of occurrence of the loss, that is if the risk is verified.[174]

185. The Insured. According to what has been stated it is possible to take out life insurance on the taker's life or on a third party's life. These are the cases established by section 128 of Act 17.418. Thus, the Argentine Act determines that the subject of life insurance, the insurer, may be any person with the characteristics that the same section 128 establishes – and which has found support in the same ethics and protection guidelines for any possible dangerous acts as the French Act of 1930 when considering that this was a contract in the benefit of a third party.

In the beginning, life insurance in the benefit of a third party, when the risk was the death of the insured, deserved criticism and strong objections as it was considered that this business could result harmful since the beneficiary, in spite of being the taker or the policyholder, could cause such death in order to collect the amount agreed.

Vivante in his *Comment to the Italian Commercial Code*, when referring to section 449, page 381, gives his personal impression against the objections, a very advanced thought for the time, his contemporary authors and even authors who came after him. In his translation to Spanish, Garrigues,[175] puts emphasis in the following: 'The requirement of interest upon the life of a third party, apart from the difficulties of evidencing when such interest really exists and if it is lawful (e.g., interest on the life of a mistress, more *uxoris*), does not prevent the abuse it intends to stop. For these purposes, modern laws have substituted such interest for the requirement of consent of the third party (or his legal representative) on whose life the contract is constituted.'

It is understandable that these objections had not been passed onto the survival insurance as the risk of the life of a third party could not deserve them. Such circumstance is not related to a danger on the life of this type of insured. This comes from the senseless comparison sometimes mistakenly made between the term 'risk' and something harmful.

186. Mistakes of Act 17.418. A closer look on section 128 of Argentine Act 17.418 places us in front of an error in the way the regulation is formulated as different concepts and guidelines are mixed containing precepts gathered without any need referring to the insured and the taker.

In fact, when going through the cases that section 128 Act 17.418 present, it is clear that nobody is prevented from being the insured, in the second paragraph, on the contrary and after this general provision, the possibility is denied to those that, in specific cases do not adopt a specifically expressed conduct.

Lastly, in the third part, the same provision prohibits this condition of insured to specific persons. In detail:

---

174. Cf. M. Picard & A. Besson, *Les Assurances Terrestres*, vol. I, 4th ed., 732 (Paris: LGDJ Press, 1975).

175. Joaquín Garrigues, *Land Insurance Contract*, 502, n. 7, point D, and n. 26.

First Mistake

The limitation does not have an objective base, but it is presented on overtly subjective guidelines. The situation provided for by this regulation is related to the fact that a person under the age of 18 can solely enter into a contract to insure his own life if the beneficiaries are specifically his relatives.

Our opinion is that the problem is not in the quality of the insured but on his quality of being an underage (under the age of 21). This one, notwithstanding his minority incapacity could take out life insurance being, at the same time, the insured, under the conditions of relationship established at the end of the text of that second part of section 128.

This means that the generic principle of freedom of the first paragraph is limited by a situation alien to the capacity to be an insured. It derives from a general incapacity arising from his minority from which he is released only when the beneficiary complies with the conditions established as well in this second part of section 128 of Act 17.418.

Second Mistake

There is an absolute prohibition that would render the contract void.

The limitation expressed in section 128 states that the incapacity of young adults is to take out life insurance on their own life but not death insurance, as provided for in the third paragraph. There is no reason for Act 17.418 not to establish at least the differences that traditionally have existed for both types of insurance.

In our law, there is no provision which clearly differentiates life insurance for survival from life insurance upon the death of the insured, as, for instance, there is in the Spanish Act 50/1980, section 83.

Therefore, this apparent indifference of Argentine law could bring about inconvenient constructions. Nevertheless, the sense of the criterion is clear and uniform.

Not even within the bitterest opponents to the possibility of appointing a third-party insured, there is a reason to prevent this assumption in the cases of survival insurance.

The loss and consequently the benefit of the collection of the assured amount shall occur as a consequence of the survival of the insured to a defined date and, therefore, there would not be a cause for the beneficiary to prevent such survival.

In the opposite side of this generic principle of acceptance provided for in section 128, there is the absolute prohibition to become the insured. In this case, it is only in the case of death insurance and for individuals under the age of 14 and of a category of persons, the legally deprived of civilian rights (interdict), that our laws do not contemplate.

In any assumption of death insurance constituted on a third party, that is, when the insured is a different person from the taker, it is always required the consent in writing from said insured and, if the insured was disabled or incapable, his legal representative's. The contract thus is prohibited for the two assumptions of prohibition mentioned *supra*.

Our Act 17.418, following the immediate precedents, introduced the category of legally deprived of civilian rights as a category next to minors below the age of puberty (under 14). It was not taken into account by the authors of this Act that there is not such a term in our civil legislation to generically and legally refer to some types of incapable.

Nevertheless, to bring some sense to this definition, they must be considered as those declared incapable by an authority with jurisdiction, different situation from the minors below puberty that are incapable without the need of any declaration.

Coming to a close, we will deal with the absence of written consent in the aforementioned situation. In the first place, there is the omission of the consent of the insured of age and capable. Such omission of consent would not bring about any negative effect as there is no penalty established either directly or indirectly. It would not be a void act or an act prohibited by law (section 18 Argentine Civil Code).

The jurisprudence has not dealt with the subject,[176] and the foreign books of authority do not appear to have analysed it in depth, presumably because they deal with different laws from the ones we are dealing with.[177]

The comments of the authors of the Spanish Commercial Code[178] – who are authorized authorities – sustain that the consent provided in written by the insured is an assumption iuris et de iure (assumption that does not admit evidence to the contrary) of the existence of an interest. An assumption that may be presented by some other means as it points out the second part of section 83 of the aforementioned Spanish Act.

As there is no penalty for this conduct, it cannot be inferred that law has implicitly intended to establish a penalty to the validity or existence of the contract. However, the problem would be the determination of the subject enabled to attempt the nullity of the insurance contract before the omission of consent since the nullity by operation of law is not possible (or the nullity by another person but the insured, as he should demonstrate his interest in the nullity action).

Although not expressly stated, the lack of consent may be rectified after the contract between the insurer and the taker as the consent may be implicit, despite the expression 'written consent' apparently decisive of section 128.

As case of implied consent, we can refer to the assumption that, although no conformity written form is signed in relation to it, the insured third party will carry out the medical examination that the insurer may require.

The reason is that the fears existing at the beginning in relation to the life of the insured third parties today no longer exist. Vivante affirms so and, however, it would be very unfair to prevent the appointed beneficiary from receiving the assured amount with no concrete grounds of damage from the insured.

In the second place, the omission of consent may be referred to the case of the legal representative of an incapable or disabled. The solution must be the same as there are no reasons to adopt another one (provided always that the prohibitions of section 128 did not apply).

---

176. *See* preliminary draft Halperín, s. 146 Part XVII of the article initiating the work and bill treatment in committees of 1961, s. 128 and item XXXII of the initial exposition.
177. The French law directly punishes the omission of conformity of the insured with the nullity of the contract and the Spanish (s. 83), in spite of not establishing explicitly the sanction, allows for other constructions, mixing consent, and interest of the existence of insurance.
178. Fernando Sánchez Calero and Francisco Javier Tirado Suarez, commentators, *Comments on the Commercial Code and Special Commercial Legislation* (*Comentarios al Código de Comercio y Legislación Mercantil Especial*), vol. XXIV (Madrid: Journal of Private Law, 1989), 120 (Insurance Contracts Act, vol. 3, s. 80 at the end).

187. The Beneficiary: Insurance for the Benefit of a Third Party. In the case of death insurance (death insurance established upon the risk of death of the insured, regardless of its permanent or temporary life insurance denomination), the beneficiary that shall collect the assured amount must necessarily be a person different from the insured.

Section 143 of Act 17.418 apparently limits the possibility of appointing a third party as beneficiary in the case of death insurance as the text refers specifically to 'the case of death' and further, by the way it is drawn up, it seems to refer to the appointment of that third party as if it was an exceptional power.

In our opinion, what has been wished to transmit is that the right of the third-party beneficiary is not transmissible by inheritance since the right is acquired with the event of the death of the insured. If the appointed beneficiary had not been alive, he would not have transmitted a right that in life he was not entitled to. However, section 143 also sets forth that the beneficiary must be specified at the moment of the loss (occurrence of the death risk), taking into account for that the concrete information that the taker provided or, if it were the case, the basis of the substituting decision of law (cases section 145 of Act 17.418).

In no way could it be an excluding requirement of law the restriction of the appointment of a third party as beneficiary solely in the case of life insurance paid upon the death of the insured. First, because there is no reason for such restriction and, second, because the possibility of a third party as beneficiary, considering third party as any person alien to the contract, seems to be inherent to the letter of section 128.

This second part denies the capacity to the underage young adults of taking out life insurance (becoming takers) if third parties are appointed as beneficiaries in the language used by law.

However, the expression 'it can be agreed' – with which section 143 starts – cannot be understood as a possibility granted by law in order to reach an agreement that would change this fact, as it would be unnecessary due to its redundancy.

The law admits the agreement of parties without requiring the special authorization of dispositive regulations (section 1197 of the Civil Code), reserving the concept of unchangeability for the cases provided for in Regulation 21 of the same Civil Code.

Thus, the regulation must be simply interpreted as establishing the requirement of the survival at the moment of the death of the insured, precisely the aspect that stops being significant at the beginning of section 143 for onerous third-party beneficiaries when it states that their acquisition of rights could take place, previously.

However, to empathize this point, it must be considered section 148 that, although unnecessarily, expressly admits the extension.

Moment of Acquisition of the right. This subject is much more interesting.

For a long time, different theories have been elaborated about the legal situation of a beneficiary different from the taker in life insurance paid upon the death of the insured (death insurance).

Thus, hypotheses of every kind have been sustained, from that it is the same case as a business management to that it is a case of an obligation with alternative creditors – with all the possible nuances in between expressed by French and German ancient books of authority.

After some hesitation which divided French and German books of authority,[179] towards the end of the nineteenth century, the cassation court of France provided the theory of the stipulation on behalf of third parties, granting the beneficiary of death insurance a right of his own, separating him from any matter arising out of hereditary rights[180] and decisively encouraging the insurance in favour of a third party.

This position sustaining that the beneficiary acquires an originary right that derives directly from the insurance contract and not from the insurance taker, thus implying an autonomous situation. He is no one's successor or assignee.

The right is constituted over him when occurring the risk provided for and a novation is unthinkable.

The power of appointing a beneficiary and its extensions in Act 17.418 is different from what occurred in property damage insurance where the institutes were clear.

In life insurance the lack of precisions brings about disorganization in the regulations, conceptual dispersion and an inappropriate terminology.

This is the case with the concept of beneficiary. This point should at least have been dealt with in a provision, as section 84 of Act 50 of 1980 of Spain where it is stated: 'appointment of the beneficiary, manner and substitution'.

It is important to start by pointing out which individuals are authorized to appoint the beneficiary before this silence of the Act.

It is a contract in the benefit of a third party which is not a party to the contract, and the power of establishing or admitting this third party is on the hands of the taker or policyholder who is in charge of paying the premium.

This assertion which logically follows the contract in the benefit of a third party in our opinion, accepted by most of the books of authority has, nevertheless, not been strictly followed by some of the laws granting such right to the insured, as it happens in the Colombian Commercial Code (section 1146) and the Mexican Insurance Act (section 163).[181]

It must be certainly noted that the taker must be understood as the person obliged to the payment of the premium, as if the taker dealing with the insurer was not in charge of such payment, he would not be genuinely the taker in the explained sense, as it happens in group insurance with the coordinator.

This power is a truly personal right, extreme and broad except otherwise agreed, revocable to the will of the taker. This agreement to the contrary may be expressed or understood. The latter takes place when other conditions of the contract make the irrevocability natural in the context as it happens, for instance, when the appointment of the beneficiary comes from a binding agreement between him and the taker or in group insurance where the taker delegates to the insured such power.

Consequences of the originary right of the beneficiary:

179. J. Baleydier & H. Capitant '*L'Assurance sur la vie au profit d'un tiers et la jurisprudence*', *Livre du Centenaire du Code Civil*, T.I, 516 et seq (Paris: 1904).

180. M. Picard & A. Besson, *Les Assurances Terrestres*, Vol. I, 708 et seq.

181. Francisco Javier Tirado Suarez, *Insurance Law Contract* (*Ley de Contrato de Seguro*) vol. III, 139.

(a) The capital or the agreed annuities never form part of the taker or policyholder's assets. His creditors do not have the power of challenging the contract and attacking the appointment of the beneficiary. This situation is presented both, from the individual and group perspective. In other words, once the loss has happened and the capacity of beneficiary has been accepted, the rights to collect the assured amount correspond to such beneficiary or his creditors.

In relation to the amount of premiums paid, only the creditors could expect a Pauline action or a simulation action or an action of revocation of reorganization proceedings.

It is worth noticing that section 147 of Act 17.418 is not very well drawn up as it refers to the insured. At least, it should have said taker. This mistake is evident as the insured, person on which the risk is constituted, is not obliged to pay the amount of any of the premiums.

The mistake of the section is much more evident when we notice the confuse ending when referring to the salvage by the bankrupt or individual in reorganization proceedings or the right on the insured capital, as if the event provided for had taken place.

The insured could never as such, exercise redemption rights or collection of capital. If, besides being an insured, an individual had the capacity as taker or policyholder, his salvage right would come from that capacity.

Finally, for the insured to collect capital as beneficiary once occurred the event, it would be precise that we were dealing with an individual that, besides the insured in a survival insurance turned out to be the beneficiary or, failing that, the taker.

In life insurance paid upon the death of the insured, the insured could never be the beneficiary since, as the insured is the person on which the risk of death is constituted, his death would cause the impossibility of holding the contract.

Therefore, it is not necessary an express agreement as Act 17.418 has established regulations that will account for the lack of appointment of the beneficiary with which it must be clear that Argentine law, as many others, could not be calling correctly beneficiary, the insured, as it is an individual that plays a different role in life insurance.

It is a serious mistake to consider that the right to appoint a beneficiary corresponds to another individual but the taker or policyholder and more so, if it is taken into account that the other person is the insured.

Insured, in life insurance, is the denomination that is given to the individual on which the risk is constituted. It has no link with the rights emerging from the insurance contract. In this line, section 128 is clear when stating its role.

(b) If we take a look at the legitimate heirs of the taker, the situation is similar because they do not have any right to expect damages derived from the assured amount. The legitimate heir is the individual that has the right to a legitimate portion of the decedent's estate. He has no right on the insurance amount as this is different from the estate and it is not a part of it.

Nevertheless, the legitimate heir could have the right to a hotchpotch or abatement of the insured amount until the concurrence of the amounts of premiums paid by the taker since it is attempted to safeguard – as much as possible – the legitime ('forced share'), a position that is not currently followed by legislations similar to ours. Those legislations usually establish guidelines of protection for the cases in which the sums paid for the premiums are too high in relation to the purchasing power of the taker or in extreme situations where insurance is taken out to sole premium, which could be a concealed donation.

(c) In marriage law, there is no right of the surviving spouse to claim the assured amount as part of his/her marital property. In summary, the surviving spouse of the taker appointing a third party as beneficiary of the insurance would not have the right to ask for half of the amount or amounts of the insurance by invoking his/her marital rights of the marital society dissolved by the death of the spouse.[182]

Having established that the capital or annuities do not form part of the estate, the following situation could take place if section 144 did not provide for the exaggerated disbursement of the amount of the premiums.

In the case of a marital society, before the lack of a precise regulation, the payments of the premiums of an insurance contract – in the assumption of the death in the benefit of a third party – are an impediment in order to expect a benefit to the beneficiary's expense, except that the premiums paid were exaggerated or disproportionate according to the decedents estate and the marital society. A greater impediment would be if it could be shown that the premiums were paid with own funds.

188. Manner of Appointment of the Beneficiary – Lack of Appointment – Appointment Revocation. Argentine Act 17.418 has provided for the written form of appointment, but it establishes emphatically that it does not require specific formalities,[183] despite any requirement that the policy may introduce.[184]

This principle of section 146 is final.

It is so final that if it was required a form under penalty of nullity for the document being used, the fact of applying such punishment in relation to the institute requiring the formality would not bring about the same penalty over the appointment of the beneficiary of the life insurance contract. For instance, the assumption of appointment of a beneficiary contained in a will that had irregularities in the testamentary form required by law and was not valid for testamentary purposes.

182. Y. Lambert-Faivre, *Droit des Assurances*, 808.

183. 'A formality is the establishment of forms by law which must be observed in the carrying out of legal acts' R. Salvat, *Romero del Prado, general part Civil Law*, vol. II, 242, n. 1646 (Buenos Aires: Tea Press, 1954).

184. 'It is valid the modification of the appointment of a beneficiary of life insurance by the obliteration or erasure of the name and ID of the originary beneficiary and the posterior registration of a new one. Section 146 of Act 17418 is very clear about the appointment being made in written without any established formality (in the case, neither a challenge nor the invocation of forgery of the document were carried out).' National Court of Appeals in Civil Matters Federal Capital, Room B. 29 Apr. 1980. Journal El Derecho, vol. 88, 716.

The validity of that appointment of beneficiary is independent from the document as testament. The appointment of a beneficiary of life insurance by means of a will does not change the nature of the act of appointment of beneficiary, which shall always be considered a living act (*inter vivos* act).

However, a written declaration naming the beneficiary shall suffice as section 146 provides. Such declaration must undoubtedly carry the signature of the issuer following the principle of private instruments. It is provided for the imperative regulation of not admitting special forms in the policy; for that reason, it could not be established the requirement of a public instrument.

The consent of the insurer is not compulsory in our law and his participation is not even necessary before the moment of the loss.

What is only needed, pursuant to section 146 is the knowledge of the insurer about this appointment, even when the appointment was made after the loss:

(a) *Notification to the Insurer.* The use of a grammatical and logical expression after the 'informality' provided for in section 146 demonstrates that the notification to the insurer is necessary to cause effects, but that it is not necessary for it to take place before the occurrence of the loss because the posterior notice suffices.

Our Act followed the precedent of section 63 of the French Act and section 167 of the preliminary draft Halperín, which in turn, was based on the Swedish Act (section 103).[185]

The fact that the notification grants the beneficiary the possibility of exercising his rights does not contradict with the lack of necessity of notifying the insured of the appointment.

Consequently, there is no consent to consult the insurer about the person of the beneficiary.

In summary: the stipulation on behalf of third parties in life insurance is truly a very special institute and only relates indirectly to a similar institute of Civil Law. Here, the appointment of the beneficiary only depends on the taker's will.

It is not a receptive declaration neither in relation to the beneficiary nor in relation to the insurer, and it has no effect before the occurrence of the loss, except that the taker would have waived the power of changing beneficiaries or that it was an onerous beneficiary.

The notification to the insurer does not need the insurer's approval for the appointment to be effective; it only implies notification to the ends of its passive legitimation. This is a fact of significance for all the interested parties and fundamentally for the insurer who shall pay.[186]

---

185. Francisco Javier Suarez, *Insurance Contract Law* (*Ley de Contrato de Seguro*), vol. III, 146, n. 43. The Suarez translation of s. 103 of the Swedish Act of 1927 states: 'In order to have effects, the institute of the beneficiary or its revocation must be notified in written to the insurer or at least be mentioned or quoted by him in the insurance policy.'

186. J. Garrigues, *Treaty of Commercial Law* (*Tratado de Derecho Mercantil*), vol. II, *Securities* (*Títulos-Valores*) (Madrid Press, 1955), 2. The commercial traffic nowadays as well as life and habitual businesses, even those related to the most simple circumstances require certainty, security, and celerity that make easy the recognition of right and easier even to exercise them. *See also*

This matter of passive legitimation is fundamental in the economics of life insurance as the regulation about it must overcome all confusion and delay in the payment of the loss; situations that may be brought about when it is not reached by other means a legal construction of the facts, documents or situations.

To begin with, the most important fact for the insurance case – as for all other obligations in our law – is to be certain that both the debtor and the creditor, that is, the insurer and the beneficiary, without prejudice of any other who may claim so, are entitled to rights.

Therefore, it is always important to be aware of the regulations in full force and effect related to the aspects of compliance with the obligation as means to make certain the act of payment.

As the appointment of the beneficiary is an act carried out by a private document, there could naturally be problems derived from its authenticity and the opportunity of such appointment when it is controversial.

Nevertheless, as it happens with many other institutes of different branches of law, this institute, inherent to life insurance, deviates from the strict regulations that have governed as from who knows when towards others more similar.

The regulation in section 146 providing for the 'informality' of such act cannot and should not be considered different from any experience occurred in the legal sphere throughout the years, as a laboratory experiment.

Its contents are very important even when their authors could not see such fact, as there is no purposes article manifesting it.

Maybe from this omission derives the fact of not having been prepared precisely and exhaustively the significance of the regulations preceding this one.

(b) *Effectiveness of the Appointment.* The current French Act containing this principle in section L 132-25 clearly provides for the fact that the good faith insurer paying the insured capital, according to his knowledge about the identity of the beneficiary is released.

This is the construction that undoubtedly works for section 146 of our Act 17.418 regarding the provision of notification to the insurer. Otherwise, the institute of the beneficiary and the easiness provided by the inexistence of any formality would not have much effect since it was always needed the certainty of the date and the acknowledgement of the private document. In other words, the easiness that was intended for life insurance not preventing with formalities, the will of the taker owner of the business, would be distorted when complying with the payment of the insurance and, the legal imposition of doing so within fifteen days of section 49 second part of Act 17.418 would be impossible.

Beyond the natural and ostensible differences in the matter of notification to the insurer of the appointment or revocation of the beneficiary, something similar to what happens in the notification to the debtor of the assignment of credits takes place.

Georges Ripert, *Legal Aspects of Modern Capitalism* (*Aspectos Jurídicos del Capitalismo Moderno*) 129 and 130 (Buenos Aires: Bosch Press, 1950).

Nevertheless, the notification to the insurer of the appointment of a third-party beneficiary grants the act effectiveness, and thus, it grants the drawnup document the value of expression of the will of the grantor at a defined time which, at the least, may be established as the moment when the insurer was notified.

Finally, the notification to the insurer implies to make the capacity of the appointed beneficiary known, until another appointment is carried out, circumstance that, pursuant to section 904 of the Civil Commercial Code, would determine the acknowledgement of the best right of the different claimers, in case of controversy.

(c) *Revocation.* This takes us to the right of revocation of the appointment of the beneficiary established in the last two lines of section 143.[187]

The revocation is the declaration of the will of a taker, by means of which the appointment of the beneficiary ends.

The revocation may be carried out by simply indicating this fact or by means of a manifestation in the terms required by law (in written) appointing another person.

The revocation of the beneficiary may imply granting the benefit to another beneficiary at the same time; thus, the revocation would only be partial.

The fact that no act of manifestation of the will is required does not mean that the beneficiary does not need to be notified of the appointment in order to agree in his capacity as creditor or reject the benefit and that, fundamentally, the insurer be notified in the same way as provided for in section 146.

If, after the beneficiary is appointed, the taker is declared incapable, the revocability may be only declared by a judge with jurisdiction on incapacity proceedings, once the declaration of incapacity was resolved with the force and effects of a final judgment. It must be clear that this revocation cannot be accompanied by a new express appointment and that the decision of the revocation must have grounds on the only interest of the taker that now has become incapable as, without such interest, the truly personal right of taker could not be attributed.

As Picard and Besson[188] clearly state in section 132-9 of the French Act, this right is denied to legal representatives.

In our opinion, one thing is that the Court, interpreting the convenience of the one declared incapable and acting on his behalf, could revoke the appointment, and another thing is that the legal representatives could have the attribution of such truly personal right.

If the appointment of the beneficiary is revoked and the taker lacks legitimate heirs and the benefit corresponds to the State, there is no possibility of substituting

187. At the end, s. 143 states: 'Except for the case when the appointment is for a valuable consideration, the taker can freely revoke it even when the contract has been entered into.'

188. Cf. *Le Contrat D'assurance*, vol. I, 4th ed., 795 et seq (Paris: LGDJ Press, 1975). The article referred to textually states '... *le droit de révoquer cette stipulation n'appartient qu'au stipulant et ne peut, en conséquence, être exercé de son vivant par ses créanciers ni par ses répresentants légaux*'.

the will of the taker in the case of supervening incapacity either as, when substituting his will there must be at least signs that such appointment was what the incapable would have desired when capable.

When the appointment of the beneficiary is onerous (for a valuable consideration), there is no freedom of revocation of such appointment.

Section 143 clearly states so and also establishes that when the appointment is onerous, it could be provided that the acquisition of the own right of the beneficiary is established before the loss.

As there is no specific definition regarding the term 'onerous' in the Act, it must be understood as the appointment of a beneficiary which costs money or is otherwise paid or, if preferred, an appointment for a valuable consideration which must be complied with by the appointee as beneficiary.

Within this category it must be considered every appointment of a beneficiary caused by the compliance with an agreement with such beneficiary, that is, an agreement where the subject matter of the agreement was the appointment of this person as beneficiary. There is also no freedom of revocation of the beneficiary when the taker-policyholder would have waived such right.

The second part of the subject of this part refers to the situation of life insurance when there is no appointment of a beneficiary. This situation that rarely presents in individual insurance frequently happens in group insurance.

The lack of appointment of a beneficiary can derive from an omission of the capable person to carry out the appointment or from a situation that renders him incapable or the appointment ineffective or void. The Act establishes only one solution to the problem, whatever the reason. Act 17.418 in its fourth part establishes that then, it will be understood that the heirs were appointed.

(d) *Harmony of Section 145.* In our opinion, section 145 is one of the few regulations that has achieved harmony in life insurance and has resolved different situations in a clear and simple way. In this section, there are provisions related to the plurality of beneficiaries with omission of the parts, with the attribution of the capacity as children when generically appointed and with the attribution of heirs.

The appointment of heirs as substitute beneficiaries established by law does not imply that it is necessary that they accept the inheritance as such. The reference in section 145 is only what it is, a reference in order to enable a legal appointment. The heir thus, by virtue of the legal precept, is a beneficiary of life insurance. He must only have the will to inherit, but that is no impediment as he can be beneficiary without collecting his inheritance.

With relation to which children must be considered, the same section 145 provides that it would be those conceived and surviving at the time of the loss.

In our opinion, to be considered a person to be included as beneficiary, the conditions of the Argentine Civil Commercial Code must be complied with, regarding the existence of the persons.

The ineffectiveness in appointing heirs as beneficiaries shall come from grounds of disinheritance (by law or incapacity to inherit).

The Act does not resolve the situation of ineffectiveness regarding appointments. In our opinion, it shall correspond that the part of the ineffective beneficiary is accrued in the benefit of the others, pursuant to hereditary portions (expression textually used by the law for a situation very similar to the one under comment).[189]

Another aspect that deserves specific consideration is the assumption of simultaneous death of the insured and the beneficiary.

It must be always perfectly clear that if the beneficiary does not die before the insured, as he has not reached the possibility to assume such right,[190] there would not be any right added to his property. Thus, the assumption of simultaneous death arises from the books of authority determined by section 85 of the Argentine Civil and Commercial Code.[191]

In case of vacant succession on account of the inexistence of legitimate heirs, it should be construed whether the State must intervene to collect such estate of life insurance without beneficiary expressly appointed, subsidiarily appointed by law or not.

The question is if the State has the right arising out of the last paragraph of section 145 of Act 17.418.

Such extension of the right would not correspond as the State would be attributed with a right to benefit extensively without cause or reason whatsoever, though sporadically. Nevertheless, if the situation arose, as there cannot exist property without owner, it should be granted such right of beneficiary to the State.

The right of taker-policyholder of appointing a beneficiary is not subject to any restriction except the provision in such sense.

It is a right that is completely accepted in this business and, therefore, is a matter of negotiation, in our view.

This negotiation takes place up to the moment in which the beneficiary becomes such that is at the moment of the death of the insured, as provided for in section 143, as from there he holds a right of his own.

The characteristics of the beneficiary, established in the same section to validate the contract carried out by a young adult, are required at the moment of the loss, that is, the death of the insured.

Besides that case originated by the natural event of death of the insured, the right of the beneficiary could also be triggered in some other way. Those would be the waiver by the taker of the contract to change the beneficiary and the appointment of an onerous beneficiary.

---

189. Cf. s. 145, third paragraph end where it is stated: 'If a quota share is not established, the benefit shall be distributed pursuant to hereditary portions.'
190. This position is based on the truly personal right of the beneficiary and although it is a full right as from his appointment, except revocation if corresponded, it cannot be exercised but as from the occurrence of the loss (death or survival of the insured). The insurance contract is not a conditional contract and the beneficiary is not a conditional creditor.
191. Section 109 of the Argentine Civil Code states: 'If two or more people died in a common disaster or under any other circumstances, so that it cannot be known which one died first, it shall be presumed that they died at the same time, without enabling the transmission of any right between them.'

The death of the insured is no cause for the acquisition of any right by the beneficiary. The death of the insured is, on the one hand, a covered risk and, on the other hand, the moment of acquisition of an originary (not derived) right.

The right to appoint a beneficiary corresponds to the *dominus negotii*, that is, the taker or policyholder, as Professor Morandi correctly states in page 329 of the aforementioned work.

The taker or policyholder of an insurance contract is the stipulator that is obliged to pay the price (the premium) and thus is the owner of the business.

It is that so that in Article 1, Chapter III of Act 17.418, section 145 expressly considers it in the third and fourth item with direct and concrete mention to the taker.

Garrigues, referring to the matter in question, states that: 'The inaccuracy consists of confusing the insured with the beneficiary of the insurance in life insurance.'[192]

The Spanish law, different from ours, expressly contemplates the issue and, apart from the position assumed in section 7, section 84 refers to such right of the taker.[193]

In French law, the situation is similar since, as Picard and Besson pointed out, the persons of the insured, beneficiary and taker are legally different, although they can be identical or different from the human point of view.[194]

The problem of lack of concrete reference to the way of appointing a beneficiary as necessary guideline for revocation has not been sufficiently analysed in our country or in foreign laws with similar features since it has been resolved by the laws in an indirect way.[195]

189. The Taker or Policyholder – His Position. Still remains to be carried out an analysis on this topic to establish its role in the life insurance contract in the benefit of a third party and the moment at which the rights could be extinguished.

In the previous paragraphs, it has been developed the underlying subject to all kind of life insurance, both life insurance proper and survival insurance.

This underlying subject has to do with the nature of the legal business being carried out and, mainly, with the assimilation that has already been performed in the preceding pages to the feature of contract on behalf of a third party and the position that, in the contract, the taker and the alien beneficiary have.

In contracts on behalf of third parties two different cases can be seen. An advantage in favour of a third party, alien to the creation of the contract, or that an obligation is promised to a third party, also alien to the creation of the contract.

In other words, in the first assumption, a part covenants to perform a service in favour or to the benefit of a third person, alien to the agreement.

---

192. J. Garrigues, *Land Insurance Contract* (*Contrato de seguro terrestre*), 69. *See also* Jordi Carbonell Puig, *Life Insurance Contracts* (*Los contratos de seguros de vida*) 173 et seq (Barcelona: Bosch Press, 1994).
193. Cf. Tirado Suarez, *Insurance Law Contract* (*Ley de Contrato de Seguro*), vol. III, 133 et seq., and n. 39.
194. Cf. M. Picard & A. Besson, *Le Contrat D'assurance*, vol. I, 462 et seq., and 732.
195. For instance, the Spanish Act in s. 87, of a markedly reglementary nature, when providing for a concrete reference to the way used to appoint the beneficiary as necessary for the revocation, notably diminishes the problem.

In the second assumption, a person promises the creditor that a third party – who this person does not represent – shall perform the services established in the agreement.

The second case is left aside for the purposes of our study of life insurance.[196]

The first assumption is the appropriate as the service will be rendered by one of the parties, the debtor, who has engaged to provide it to an alien third party, according to the agreement entered into with the other party.

The latter does not have preeminence regarding the beneficiary as he neither guarantees the compliance with the obligation of the debtor nor makes a promise in favour of a third party or in the interest of a third party.

Our preference is the denomination of stipulation on behalf of a third party, despite that all the ones accepted by the books of authority have a similar sense in general (although they are different theories on the legal nature of the institute):[197]

(a) Before the insurer, the taker or policyholder has, in the first place, the right to pay the premium at the times agreed upon.

This fact grants action to the taker so that the insurer, counterpart to the contract, receives the owed amount and provides the corresponding receipt.

Nevertheless, such right of the taker is not followed by a corresponding act as this does not bring about to the insurer, any action to claim payment.

It is thus curiously established to the benefit of the taker, the same right that the law always grants debtors of services and, nevertheless, it does not grant the creditor of such service, the insurer, any action to secure the payment.

In our opinion, in life insurance, the payment of the premium more than an obligation to the taker is a burden, and also, if such action was granted, there would be a conflict with those regulations establishing the rescission of the contract caused by the lack of payment of the premium.

This duty arises from Act 17.418. On the one hand, section 27 textually states in its first line the duty to which we are referring when stating: 'The taker is the obliged to the payment of the premium.' This regulation is generic for all types of insurance.

On the other hand, the delay in payment or the lack of payment, according to the terminology of the Act, in the agreed term, implies the rescission of the contract pursuant to section 134.[198]

This section carries a terminological mistake when mentioning the insured as empowered to rescind without limitations the contract and, at the same time, a conceptual error when granting such power after the first period.[199]

196. *See* ss 1161, 1162, 504 and 1936 of the Argentine Civil Code.

197. Héctor Lafaille, *Civil Law* (*Derecho Civil*), vol. VIII, Contracts I (Buenos Aires: Ediar S.A. Press, 1953), 362 et seq., and his thesis *Life Insurance on Behalf of Third Parties* (*Seguros de vida a nombre de terceros*) (La Semana Médica Press, 1907), especially Chs V, VI and VII.

198. Section 134 states 'The insured shall rescind the contract without limitation after the first period of insurance. The contract shall be considered rescinded if the premium is not paid within the agreed upon term.'

199. *See* in previous note the text of the first part of s. 134.

It is not the insured who could rescind. It is the taker, the policyholder as he is the *dominus negotii*.[200] If the insured was at the same time the taker or policyholder, it is evident that this person, of course, would have that right. In gathering both capacities in the same person, it is added the taker to the insured, only capacity enabling him to do so.

However, the contract shall exist after the agreement of wills, regardless of whether the premium of the first period has been paid or not.

The debt on account of the premium exists as from the moment of the agreement yet, as it is not enforceable but from the moment of delivery of the policy (section 30), it implies for life insurance, the possibility of terminating the agreement if the debtor is in arrears.

(b) Also before the insurer and before the beneficiary, the taker has the right to appoint the beneficiary, right that is complemented by the power of revocation of the appointment and expressly reappointment of another beneficiary.

These powers of the taker cease when he had waived them and when there is an onerous beneficiary.

It is a stipulation on behalf of third parties with some autonomy of the right of the third-party beneficiary regarding the insurance; that is, the third party has an originary and not derived right in the insurance contract.[201] The third party acquires a right of his own at the time in which the event occurs (section 143).

(c) The taker has the right to choose, according to section 138, in the case of 'conversion to paid insurance of a lower amount or shorter term' or 'rescission with payment of a defined amount'. It is also entitled to the loan right provided for in section 141.

It must be clarified that these assumptions are for the cases of contracts where the rights of the beneficiary have not been constituted on his person, that is, that the taker has not waived the right of revocation of the beneficiary or that it was an onerous beneficiary.

190. Other References and Characteristics of Permanent Life Insurance. Different from property damage insurance (where the aleatory characteristic is on the occurrence or not of the risk and, consequently, the insurer shall only have to pay the insurance if the event takes place), permanent life insurance is an insurance that, unavoidably, shall have to be paid by the insurer by means of the payment of the assured amount upon the death of the insured (individual on which the risk is constituted).

200. *See* Francisco Javier Tirado Suarez, *Insurance Law Contract* (*Ley de Contrato de Seguro*), vol. III, 145.

201. J. Garrigues, *Land Insurance Contract* (*Contrato de Seguro Terrestre*), 492 et seq. (especially notes 12 and 15).

This is completely true except for the cases where the Act releases the insurer from the payment, fact that does not happen very often (for instance, cases in sections 136 and 137).

It is not necessary to state that, despite the simplicity of the reasoning about the unavoidable payment, life insurance is not a source of financial loss for the insurer, but it represents a very important business due to the benefits it provides.

These benefits arise from the system that is followed by millions of individuals, which determines that the payment of the premium by the taker does not turn out to be an economic burden impossible to afford.

It is to say that the payment that, in principle, will have to assist all the insured cases is neither an absolute loss for the insurer nor a disproportionate increase of the price which as counterpart must pay the taker, in spite of the fact that the occurrence of the loss is one hundred percent certain.

The price of the insurance, as we have sustained,[202] is conditioned by certain factors from which, the most significant are the frequency and intensity of the risk, factors that in the life insurance line are located in the tables of mortality.

These tables provide us with, in defined groups by similar ages, the probabilities of the amounts of deaths each year, that is the amounts of losses that will happen during each period and, consequently, indicate the insurer which shall be in each fiscal years his payment commitments to the beneficiaries of the events of loss.

With these parameters, considering for a moment that these premiums of these life insurances are paid in cash at the beginning of the relationship, it is indispensable for the insurer to invest these funds in property so that they can give profitability that will translate into additional income to the premiums received to build up a premium fund to pay each loss.

It is important that it is very clear that the insurer knows the homogenous amount of its obligations and that, at a certain point in the future, he will have to afford the payments, so by being updated – thanks to the tables of mortality of the moment when he will have to carry out each payment – he can plan in a lucid manner, the time when to finish each investment in order to dispose of the necessary money to timely cancel his obligations in favour of the beneficiaries.

191. Reality of the Business. Up to now, we have been talking about the hypothesis of payment of the premiums in permanent life insurance in cash.

Nevertheless, this is not so in the actual facts of business as, if this was real, only a few individuals would have the real capacity to insure themselves, and the amount of a premium of a considerable value would scare away most of the interested population.

In life insurance, the risk is more intense as the insured grows older; therefore, the amount of the premium must necessarily increase.

In other words, the price of life insurance shall be more expensive for the older the insured, as the occurrence of the loss, death, shall be directly influenced by the passing of time.

---

202. *See* Emilio H. Bulló, *Insurance Law and Other Related Business.*

This natural increase of the premium would prevent the payment of an instalment as the risk in course would increase very substantially the premium that, coming from a low value at young ages, would reach a very high value at older ages.

This would conspire against business as the cost, at the same time, would increase to amounts impossible to pay by most of the interested parties, above all because the greater cost would be during their years of lower income.

Over the course of time, the possibility of a very clever procedure was invented in order to give a solution to the problem and reach a wider marker. The solution was to obtain the possibility of payments in instalments during the duration of the insurance.

Instalments of an always identical value and, fundamentally, of an amount adequate to the general sectors of the population.

Following this procedure, it can be noticed that the difficulty arises from the issues that will come from arranging the higher amounts of premiums that, during the first times, shall be paid and the lower amounts of premiums that, during the last times, shall be equally paid.

In the beginning, the value of the level premium, in fact, will compensate a risk of lower importance and, in the end, the opposite will just happen.

Ultimately, the equivalent value of the obligation to pay the loss on the insurer's part would be established in instalments that, if maintained equal, would pay different considerations in each period.

The real invention was to find a value for the premiums periodically paid but always identical without affecting the equation premium = insurer rendering of service = risk.

This has been called level premium that instead of being calculated independently for each year is established regarding all the periods of the insurance, making reserves and investing adequately the amounts collected in excess of risk covered during the first years.

The insurance business requires a mathematical calculation of great accuracy, on the one hand, and a more than careful administration on the other because, knowing that, at a certain moment in the future all and each of the existent insurance in the portfolio will have to be paid, the reserves generated by each case mathematically when reaching the age limit shall equal the value of the insurance or the value of the insured capital.

As reality establishes by means of tables of mortality that there will be more losses in intermediate ages than at the limit age, what is important is to determine how these insurances will be paid at each age, that is, from where the money will come from to satisfy those assured amounts.

The answer is simple. In each loss occurred at intermediate ages that go from the commencement of the insurance to the payment of each loss, that is, when yet the reserves have not equalled the assured amount, the assured amount to pay by the insurer shall be constituted by the mathematical reserves that the insurance in question may have plus the amount that is left to complete this assured amount; amount that each insurer will obtain from the accrual of all the premiums of risk, similar to what happens in damage insurance.

Simply, the level premiums of life insurances separately are, on the one hand, the risk that shall be run during the paid period and, on the other hand, the amount to reserve in order to create the capitals that, unavoidably, will have to be paid.

Yet: what are the mathematical reserves? They are the funds that the insurer keeps, without disposing of them in order to partially afford the payments that he will have to perform as the losses take place and the disbursements that, for other reasons, he will have to perform in certain occasions (this will be seen in the cases of rescission and nullity).

These mathematical reserves are called like that because they are sums that are saved or kept for a specific purpose, without spending them. They are established by a purely mathematical calculation whose sources are: (a) the amounts in excess that, regarding the real risk, the level premiums represented during the course of the first years of insurance; (b) the financial proceeds from investments where those amounts in excess were allocated.

In the technical insurance environment, it is possible to establish a difference between the part of the premium that belongs to the risk that will certainly be run during the period in question – and that is called in actuarial terminology risk premium – and the part of the premium that, exceeding that risk premium will serve to collaborate in the creation of the mathematical reserves and that is called savings premium although it is not comparable with the banking operation.

In this type of insurance contract what is significant is the coverage of the risk, as this is the fundamental aspect for the taker, who wishes to be insured in relation to the risk of death.

The insurance contract, thus, is fundamental in the business that the parties agree to.

Nevertheless, from the economic point of view, the invention of the level premiums as marketing method generates as rightly sustained by Gallegos Díaz an outstanding element as it is saving, which allows for the creation of reserves.

It is true, though, that in insurance, saving is of less quality than in specific financial products; fact that requires, commercially, to be counteracted in order to prevent its logic competition but which, however, allows for the functioning of other institutes as reduction, advances, and loans.

The quantum of the level premium paid each time depends on the interest rate element since the higher the calculation rate, the lower the flow of needed money and, on the contrary, the lower the calculation rate, the higher the amount to pay by the taker.

Likewise, the interest rate considered to be the profitability obtained by investments shall directly influence the mathematical reserve regarding the amount of the instalments to pay or the assured amount.

Thus, the interest determination is of vital importance since, in case that the other variables are constant, the relation between interest rate and premiums shall be inverse.

It must always be taken into account that this is an operation of financial balance between the service and the consideration. An insurer offering a considerable technical interest could be seriously jumping – with the purpose of gaining businesses – into a more than sure insolvency.

Thus, the insurer must be prudent when estimating the rates that he shall obtain from his investments as it may not differ from what he will have to pay according to his calculations and that will finally be represented in the value of the premium paid by his insured.

Without entering in mathematical calculations, taking into consideration the long terms in this type of insurance, as well as the interest capitalization, it may be stated, for instance, that a rate of technical interest of 6% for twenty-five years is considerable.

192. Risk Aggravation and Other Modifications of the Risk. There are certain duties of the taker, some inherent to this type of insurance and others, generic for all insurance:

(a) *The Precontractual Duty To Avoid Misrepresentation of the Status of the Risk.* The principle of section 5 of Act 17.418 is absolutely applicable to the variants that, regarding misrepresentations effects, some other provisions of the Act provide for.

This principle fundamentally governs the subject as misrepresentation or false declaration of the risk, even carried out in good faith, render the contract void.

The effect of nullity is tempered with the assumptions of readjustment of the contract as provided for in sections 6 and 7 of Act 17.418 since in life insurance there are technical and commercial circumstances and others of the trade which originate a very special economic relation between insurer and taker.

Due to the possibility of the existence of a different taker than the insured, in life insurance in the benefit of third parties, the notification and the conducts assumed by one and the other influence, without prejudice of the acts 'not in good faith' or 'in bad faith' (*see* section 129 of Act 17.418).[203]

(b) *The Contractual Duty of Not Aggravating the Status of the Risk.*[204] The institute of risk aggravation incorporated in Article X of Chapter I is totally applicable to life insurance.

This generic situation, the same as the institute of misrepresentation, due to the technical and commercial circumstances and circumstances of the trade specifically of life insurance, is partially modified by some specific regulations which temper the severity of the possibility of terminating the contract or stress such severity.

The provision which considers the conducts and the notification of taker and insured when it is a life insurance in the benefit of a third party is a case of strengthening of such severity (section 129 of Act 17.418).

---

203. *See* Emilio H. Bulló, *Insurance Law and Other Related Business*, vol. I, 107 et seq., n. 211, para. 17, and specifically 111 and 112 regarding malice and good and bad faith as well as 'not in good faith'.

204. *See also* Emilio H. Bulló, *Insurance Law and Other Related Business*, vol. I, 198 et seq., para. 38, about aggravation of risk.

In connection with the first case, tempering the possibility of rescission of the contract, the following can be mentioned:

(1) Non-aggravation of the risk for reasons not specifically established in the contract. The law establishes as specific requirement for a circumstance of risk to be invoked as grounds of risk aggravation to be notified and, therefore, to be so established in the contract as such.

In this sense, section 132 of Act 17.418 is assertive. In our opinion, this must be prudently construed since, as it is a covered risk, it is not possible to carry out constructions regarding its extension either by excess or defect as the subject is not regulated by law but established by the parties.

(2) The case of inaccuracy in the indication of the age of the insured. Even when the age of the insured is significant due to the nature of the risk covered to the effects of establishing the guidelines of the contract (premium, salvage value, etc.), it is true as well that the inaccuracy in the indication of the age could not affect the will of the insurer as it could be readjusted.

This principle contained in section 131 of Act 17.418 is similar to the provisions in sections 6 and 7 for the case of misrepresentation without malice and in good faith.

The reason for this possibility acting towards the survival of the contract is that, technically and economically, the life insurance contract generates between taker and insured, a complex set of operations mixing saving, insurance and even banking concepts demanding the appropriate care in order to safeguard the rights of the taker who carries out payments in the present containing part of what, in the future, will be needed to carry out the consideration.

So as not to confuse the subject, we shall limit to repeat that the payments for the premiums of the taker contain a part which shall be consumed in the consideration of the risk of each period and another part that shall be consumed in posterior periods.

This last portion is what is called 'savings premium' (without it being a saving in strict legal language) and combines to form the so-called mathematical reserve.

Consequently, the system established by Act 17.418 in section 131 is the following: The inaccurate indication of the age of the insured allows the insurer to claim for the rescission of the contract only when the real age of the insured exceeds the limits that such insurer had fixed in the practice in his business in order to assume the risk.

The insurer establishes beforehand and with a general criterion the technical and commercial guidelines that he deems adequate to create the 'mutuality' with the insured[205] as this is his obligation to permit its control.[206]

---

205. *See* E. Bulló, *Insurance Law and Other Related Businesses* (*El Derecho de Seguros y de otro negocios vinculados*), vol. I, 62 et seq., para. 8 about intensity and frequency of the risk.
206. *See* Act 20.091.

On these bases, the insurers establish their plans and conditions to which their obligations will adjust and, therefore, in life insurance, they must establish the maximum limits of age under which they are willing to cover the risk. Thus, If the real age of the insurer was superior to the one taken into account as maximum age or limit, the possibility of termination would be logic. It would not be logic if it was the case of a real age superior to the indicated by the insured but inferior to the limit.

In fact, the insurer, when fixing his technical cases with an age limit, is establishing an exclusion to the risk for the cases where the insured exceeded that limit.

The other two solutions provided for in section 131 are the ones of the cases where the contract cannot be terminated.

The first solution in the second part of the section is the reduction of insured capital in the assumption of an older age. The second solution, in the third part of the section, is the reimbursement of the already paid premiums by the taker and the mathematical reserves in excess and the reduction of the premiums to be paid when it was the opposite situation, that is, with a real age inferior to the one taken into account for the contract.

A necessary clarification. We have been using the subject of age as an assumption of aggravation of risk. This is our opinion as the age of the insured, essential base to know the true status of the risk, is one of the possible assumptions of aggravation with sufficient grounds to claim for the rescission of the contract.

(3) The change of profession or activity by the insured is a special assumption that must follow the general principle of aggravation of risk of section 37 beyond the regulatory appearance that the text of section 133 may induce as, ultimately, it does not alter the principle as nor does section 132.

If we stop in the first part of this section, we notice that this appearance leads us to thinking that the words used actually say more than what they truly say.

A circumstance or a series of circumstances would be decisive to ratify as fair the contract's termination of an insurer regarding an insurance when: (a) the case constitutes an aggravation, a situation that increases the frequency or intensity of the risk existing at the moment of the agreement of wills; (b) the case of existence at such moment, to the expert's judgment, of an augmented risk would have determined the impossibility or inexistence of the contract or that the conditions of such contract would have been modified.[207]

Therefore, if the matter is the activity or profession of the insured, the aggravation shall consist of an increase in the intensity or frequency that, to the expert's judgment, constituted the aggravation of risk which, if having existed at the moment of the agreement of wills would have prevented the contract or modified its conditions.

Related to the change of activity, having kept the need of the experts' judgment and the reference almost concrete to the manner of handling business of the insurer are suitable.

207. *See* s. 37 of Act 17.418.

193. The Premium – Special Situations. At the risk of being repetitive, we consider it important to stress certain situations that may occur in life insurance as well as certain rights of the individuals involved:

(a) *The Payment of the Premium.* In the first place, in life insurance, there appears the right of the onerous beneficiary to pay the premium as provided for in section 134 second part.

In life insurance, the right (and duty) of the payment of the premiums belongs to the taker or policyholder in keeping with section 27 – which applies to all kind of insurance.

This onerous beneficiary, to our belief, has the same right of the taker to demand obligations from the insurer receiving the payment of the premium and the insurer, again, is not granted with any prerogative to protect his right to collect.

On the contrary, let us remember that the lack of payment of the premium must be interpreted as rescission of the life insurance contract pursuant to section 134.

This lack of action to claim payment of the premium on the insurer could not be strongly held by law as it would have turned out to be an inconvenient situation, and although it uses a language, attempting to make the situation objective, it establishes a compensation as by operation of law.

Section 27 establishes so when both, property damage insurance and life insurance, use the expressions 'owed compensation' and 'owed service'.

That is to say that, even when the Act does not require the action compelling to the payment of the premium, it does not expect, however, that the insurer is obliged to pay the service without being compensated by his unpaid credits.

This power of the onerous beneficiary in life insurance is exclusive and excluding as it cannot be assumed by any other person. Concretely we are referring to any other third party, as could erroneously be interpreted from section 28 of Act 17.418.

This section is not compatible with section 134, and they are even contradictory as the power to pay is granted to the third-party beneficiary, and there is no change of influence on the insured in life insurance.

In fact, the harmony between the two precepts could only be achieved if we take into consideration that in life insurance the applicable regulation is section 134 of Act 17.418, regulating the sole right of the onerous beneficiary.

Thus, section 28 shall remain as a right of the insured, that is, the owner of the insurable interest (individual running the risk) in life insurance.

Before the great possibility of the taker of rescinding the contract, inclusively by simply not paying the premium in the agreed-upon terms, it does not seem compatible the right that many times law grants to a third party of paying an obligation on behalf of somebody else (applied to the reason of existence of life insurance and its institutes), since paying does not only bring about the release of the debtor but the maintenance of the bond in the benefit of a third party; bond which, the party that compromised to the payment of such consideration, the premium, would seem not to wish to continue following his attitude of non-compliance.

Instead, the onerous beneficiary has been introduced in the contract in a special manner by the taker and insurer, acquiring his right originally and without the possibility of being revoked.[208]

It must be noticed the special situation that in life insurance paid upon the death of the insured in the benefit of a third party acquires the person of the taker and the bond that he establishes with his actions. It must also be noticed that Act 17.418 mistakenly again calls the insured the person who can rescind the contract if not paying the premium.

Neither the insured is obliged to pay the premium (*see* section 27) nor has he any right by the fact of being insured to pay it. The only person authorized by exception is the onerous beneficiary (*see* section 134).

Yet, section 27, when dealing generically with the premium (Chapter I) expressly states that the payment is the obligation (besides being an obligation is a burden) of the taker or policyholder, and in this, the Spanish books of authority completely coincide with the principle of our law.[209]

The payment of an agreed premium when it is a level premium (as it happens in most of the cases) contains two portions of a different value and purpose, at least, temporarily.

It has been pointed out that a part of the premium, the risk premium, has the purpose of meeting the technical value that the risk assumed by the insurer has during the ongoing period (year, month, etc.).

The other part of the payments carried out in each of those periods of time has as purpose: meeting an equal value for the benefit both, of the takers and of the insurer.

Regarding the former, because of the relief concreted in the increase of the amounts that should be paid for the risk premium, as the age of the insured advance. Regarding the latter, for keeping the price constant, which allows him to make insurance accessible to the market.

Despite the reciprocal benefit of the invention of the level premium that took life insurance through the path of commercial success due to the massive answer that was obtained, it is logic to notice that the future benefit of the taker obliged theoretically to pay premiums each time higher is coordinated with a present drawback. On the one hand, in each one of the first periods to be paid there would be a considerable remaining amount regarding the risk premium that would have strictly corresponded. On the other hand, the insurer receiving that plus would, at the same time, gain an interest when investing that extra money.

Although legally it is not a saving, economically such premium in advance is a saving, as it must be kept to be used ahead, following its purpose.

In such manner, the concept of saving, although not strictly corresponding – as it must be legally separated from the person paying the premium – has always remained linked and has always generated in business conscience, a sense of responsibility. This has been not only for such application but also for its correct

208. *See* Act 17.418, s. 143, part 2.

209. J. Garrigues, *Insurance Land Contract* (*Contrato de Seguro Terrestre*), 106 states 'The person obliged to pay the premium is the taker or policyholder of the insurance that may be or not, simultaneously, the insured. In life insurance, the beneficiary is not authorized to pay.' In a note it is added that this is another difference that justifies the separate exposition of the obligations in the two kinds of contract.

determination, generation and individualization items that are subject matter of very concrete protective regulations of public order in all controlling legislations.

(b) *The Contractual Change.* In the second place, there is the right of the taker to demand a specific change in the contractual relationship. Such is the case of the right of loan of section 141, or the right of salvage or conversion of insurance to a paid one of different amount or term provided for in section 138.

These changes are related to the mathematical reserve and, in consequence, to the characteristics of the premium in life insurance.

As in every insurance, the specific risk run for a specific period of time is technically compensated with the payment of the pure premium or net premium in the English jargon of the trade, which added to others, compose the commercial premium that is the one paid ultimately by the taker.

In permanent life insurance, the risk of occurrence of the event originating the loss, that is, the death of the insured turns out to be each year or period that goes by, an aggravated risk in relation to the periods already passed. The insured shall be during each ongoing period of more age and, in death insurance, the passing of time determines a higher frequency and intensity in the occurrence of the risk.

This increase in the possibility of occurrence of the risk should be logically contemplated in the increase of the premium to compensate the greater risk and, thus, the natural premium as Garrigues[210] calls it (which should be variable, augmenting its amount together with the insured's age).

This reality that Garrigues quotes could not be translated into the insurance business due to the great increase in the amount to be met by the risk premium in the older years (years during which, the strength and energy of work lessen and the production as well, and with that, the possibilities of income).

It could not be convenient either, to state it commercially and thus, form a psychological point of view that would be permanently stressing the unavoidable end of human beings, their death, which evidently would not be a positive factor for the marketing of a product or service.

This inconvenience of very severe consequences for the development of the business was overcome thanks to the possibility of establishing the level premium, always constant during the years that must be paid and for a value which allows for its payment without the aforementioned efforts.

Yet, it must be clear that the amount to pay periodically for the level premium shall be in the first cycles of the insurance, higher than the corresponding to the pure, net or natural premium and later – as age advances and thus, the habitual consequences of its effects – inferior to the risk premium which would really correspond to meet due to the frequency to be faced.

This higher amount paid for the premium during some periods, plus the interests capitalized which can be accrued, shall help to constitute a reserve for the years where it will lessen.[211]

210. J. Garrigues, *Land Insurance Contract* (*Contrato de Seguro Terrestre*), Chs XVI–VII, 519 et seq.
211. Y. Lambert-Faivre, *Droit des Assurances* Ch. 2, Title II.

In fact, in a figurative sense, if we were to divide permanent life insurance, we would notice that it is constituted by complex economic businesses. On the one hand, there is a temporary insurance with basis on the risk and, on the other hand, a complex financial business of saving; a system to save money and invest it, with capitalization in order to make a profit of such investment.

When coming across a permanent life insurance, as insurer, a capital that shall be payable at some moment in the future, statistically calculated pursuant to the tables of mortality as applicable must be provided.

(c) *Amount of the Capital To Create*. The amount of this capital to be created shall be in inverse proportion to the time that is left to reach the end provided for. During the year zero of the insurance, that is, the first year of effectiveness of the insurance, the risk capital on the insurer's part shall be of the same amount as the value of the assured amount. As periods go by which would imply, within a normal situation, the payment of the level premiums, technically, the risk capital will decrease in the same amount that the mathematical reserve increases.

During the time the loss does not take place, the capital that shall be provided at the end of the contract with the payment of the assured amount will be gathered. If the loss did not occur at a moment previous to the termination of the contract, the shortage from the mathematical reserve shall be paid in as it has been explained with the risk premiums of the other insurance calculated appropriately to suffice – as it happens in all lines of insurance.

This division that with an economic sense has been posed cannot be reflexively translated into the legal scope because, within it, some concepts belonging to other disciplines may be represented but in no way introduced as an absolute value.

If economically and technically there is more than one business or operation, they should not be necessarily accepted from the legal point of view. In fact, it is quite obliged to anticipate if their inclusion is acceptable or possible.

The so-called risk premium or natural premium 'represents' the cost of the obligation assumed by the insurer that is the payment of the assured amount when the random event takes place.

In order to carry out that complement and keep the insurance contract alive through time, that difference in excess that will exist from the higher premiums received during the first periods and their interests should be zealously taken care of by the insurer, recipient of such payments in excess – which in advance, from the economic point of view, carried out the taker. These payments in excess must be reserved by the insurer for the protection of the taker of life insurance, obviously in guarantee of the beneficiary and decisively in guaranteeing the system.

According to mathematical teachings, the pure premium is the value that the insurer must receive so that, complying with his plans or provisions both, in investments and profitability and opportunities of loss occurrence, the expected economic value of the operation turns out to be zero.[212]

212. *See* Gallegos Díaz de Villegas, *Classic and Modern Modalities of Permanent Life Insurance* (*Modalidades Clásicas y Modernas del seguro de vida entera*), Chs III and IV.

These amounts are called mathematical reserves and they are called like that because they are amounts that the insurer cannot dispose of (as they are technically destined to the payment of future obligations of the taker in order to keep the balance among risk, premium, and obligation of the insurer).

Although when considering in the third volume of this monograph, the commercial side of the business and its corresponding control, we will analyse in depth certain technical aspects, among them, the need for the creation of reserves or provisions for the payment of losses of ongoing risks, unpaid, unknown or unreported losses, it is important to comment on one of this types of technical reserves, the mathematical reserves which purpose it to cover future payments that the taker must carry out.

(d) *Brief Reference to Technical Aspects.* Continuing with what was being said, a premium of equal amount to be paid annually is determined, containing two different components: one referred to the part of the risk that temporarily exists and that may present each period (called pure premium, net premium, etc.). This part of the premium has the same role as the technical or pure premium established in property insurance: to technically compensate the risk which shall be run during the period that is being faced and it is related to the frequency and intensity – statistically found – for the risk in concrete.

In life insurance, this frequency is found in tables of mortality of a statistic value imponderable for the amount of cases in observation and the unbelievable possible findings. The other component is called savings premium or reserve premium – although as previously stated, this idea is not related to the business of such name as, legally, it does not share its nature.

The denomination of mathematical reserves is because, on the one hand, a protection over this money is established with a specific purpose and, on the other hand, the reserve is distinguished in the technical-economic aspect from the other reserves or provisions related to property insurance by virtue of precisely being calculated in a mathematical[213] way by actuarial science.

Very briefly recalling what has been mentioned in Part I of this monograph about the calculation of probabilities regarding the frequency of the risk and, above all, about the loss deviation, ultimately, the insurer, by guaranteeing with his property the accuracy of his estimates, carries out the function of homogenizing risks and amounts of distribution, saving or reserving premiums or parts of premiums of the amounts entered during each period, necessary to afford payments which will have to be done.

In the closing of each fiscal year, the insurer, regardless of its legal form, must draw up his general balance sheet. In such balance, all the income and the justifications for that income shall be registered. At the same time, all expenses, its justifications and the expenses that will influence the near future and are already totally or partially known will have to be indicated.

213. M. Picard & A. Besson, *Les Assurances Terrestres*, vol. I, 491, 768 et seq.

As in insurance business, the losses to be paid could have been originated from contracts during that same fiscal year or during different years; it is important to take into account that, in the balance sheets, these obligations must be registered somehow, either by indicating the amounts to pay with accuracy or reserving the amounts entered by premiums, technically adequate amounts. Consequently, even when the definitive income of these premiums is established, it is established a balancing entry of provision for the assurance of fulfilment of obligations.

As the first of the methods would be impossible, the solution to the problem is the reserve or safeguarding of such premiums by means of effective and defined investments, according to the provisions established by the comptroller laws and the subsequent results of the insurer.

This subtopic of the premium in permanent life insurance that, by its own force, requires permanent attention and care must be analysed more extensively to allow for its better understanding despite our lack of mathematical formation.

Resuming the matter and going on with the subject premium, we must take into consideration that the pure premium is only for the purposes of considering the counter value or necessary price of the insurance to respond to the technical aspect, separated from any other expense.

It is clear that the cost of business for the insurer is not purely the risk since, besides that, it must be taken into account that there are always other expenses or costs coming from commerce or from the administration of accumulated funds or from the use of banking services and management.

It is due to the existence of these annexed and necessary costs that the insurer needs that these costs do not have influence on him. On the contrary, the business would not be profitable and he would be taken to bankruptcy. The way to avoid such influence is transferring to the taker or policyholder such costs by means of additional surcharges to the pure or net premium. The amount of the pure premium plus the additional surcharges is called commercial premium or rate premium.

In the words of José Elías Gallegos Díaz de Villegas on account of the principle of actuarial equivalence, in the origin of the operation of life insurance, there is equality between the future obligation of the insurer and the taker or policyholder.

Yet, as time goes by and if the loss does not take place, the value of the assured amount is incremented in accordance with the decrease of remaining time until the random moment in which the assured amount must be paid, whereas the current value of the owed or outstanding premiums decreases when diminishing the value of the profit.[214]

The author in question – who we have followed very closely on account of his clarity – finishes his explanation of the principle by drawing the conclusion that, at a concrete moment along the duration of the insurance, the future obligations on the insurer (the obligations for the services that he will have to pay) must be higher than the taker's (the obligations of the premiums that he will have to pay). If it was the other way around, the taker would be more inclined to rescind the contract than to continue it.

214. *See* Gallegos Díaz de Villegas, *Classic and Modern Modalities of Permanent Life Insurance* (*Modalidades Clásicas y Modernas del seguro de vida entera*), Ch. 5.

In other words, the insurance that originally has a zero value, over the course of time changes its position, granting a positive value in the benefit of the taker which equals the difference of the obligations to comply with in the future that the parties hold against each other, insurer and taker. This value preceded by the plus sign in the benefit of the taker of policyholder is the mathematical reserve.

194. Right over Mathematical Reserves. The topic analysed takes us directly to an interesting legal problem regarding the ownership of these mathematical reserves since, from the strict economic point of view, during some periods at least, the taker delivers the insurer a value, superior to the technically necessary to cover the risk.

The insurer receives during certain time, payments that exceed the technical price of the risk funds that, if not applied to their original purpose, could be understood as suppression of the cause of payment.

New theories have considered that the amounts corresponding to the mathematical reserve belong to the taker and, thus, there are laws granting them to the taker either in the case of a not favourable termination of the insurance or when the taker rescinds the contract deciding not to pay the premiums.

We do not agree with this position. Beyond some rights acknowledged to the taker, he is not the owner of the mathematical reserves.

It is worth remembering that this opinion (that the taker has a right of credit regarding the insurer) was quite accepted in general in the past as it was established by some very respectable books of authority and modern laws that started to rule at the beginning of the twentieth century, with certain regulations related to privileges or preferences of the takers.[215]

It must be remembered that it seems that the actuarial artifice of the level premium benefited the marketing of the insurance paid upon the death of the insured, allowing for the payments to be always equal but lower to the payments that should be made in the course of some periods. Also this appearance benefited the public because this means extended this type of contract almost unlimitedly.

Benefits thus, have been reciprocal – for the insurer and the taker – and it is of good faith to maintain this equivalent of services at all levels during contractual life.

We must take into account that the mechanism of laws or contract provisions, in order to protect the existence of the insurance before the easiness of rescission – which, however is protected – must be operative; otherwise, agreements would not have incentive to be held throughout the years when the reasons and motives for the taker to have taken out the insurance could become concealed behind the payments to be performed.

In our opinion, this equivalence is achieved when the taker is protected for the payments that he technically carried out in excess – although they were aiming at his benefit – to enable somehow that the differences in less, that the premiums to pay are applied to his benefit and not to an unjustified enrichment of the insurer or as an out of proportion penalty for rescission.

It is not convenient for new institutions as it happens today in the commercial world and, thus, in commercial law to be labelled with the old categories of civil law.

215. M. Picard & A. Besson, *Les Assurances Terrestres*, vol. I, 769.

The nature of mathematical reserves and their effects, typical of insurance – as, for instance, are the reduction or the loan – must not respond inexcusably to traditional legal features that have been invented for absolutely different situations to the ones that are being commented.

Ultimately, because of legal and political security reasons, it is imposed that all payments carried out by the taker to the insurer as premiums in life insurance comply with the purpose that they had, that is, that they are considered definitive payment for existing and legally valid debts.

Such payments are understood, from their payment on, as the species that helped to cancel the duty of the payer-taker, and they are property of the insurer as it would be any other property acquired with the money received in lieu of payment.

Thus, we do not share the opinions of the books of authority sustaining that mathematical reserves are property of the insurer but of the taker or the books of authority that understand that the right of the taker on reserves is a right of credit with preference or privilege.

Yet, it must be clear that this protection must be considered from the opposite side. When establishing a salvage value or a guarantee value in the benefit of the taker, it should be established, at the same time, a non-abusive logic penalty for the rescission of the contract and its prejudicial consequences (the damages caused by the adverse selection of risks, the loss of profit derived from the anticipated withdrawal of the investment which the insurer may have already carried out and, consequently, calculated in order to project his business).[216]

The books of authority and positions sustaining the taker's ownership of mathematical reserves, to our belief, have used an argument which is typical of public law insurance: the regulations protecting the control of the State over insurers and that insensibly turned into a milestone the support of inexistent rights for the taker as there would be no reason to expect them.

From a long time ago – especially taking into account the different parts of the operation which finally constitutes life insurance and the interest in public savings that the State has – once the technical-mathematical bases sustaining the great development of all the products that can be commercialized were perfected, a series of protective regulations on the takers started to be issued so as to avoid the failure of bad administrations of the insured portfolio of such a great business for all involved parties.

As the calculation of the premiums must respond to three principles (equity, sufficiency, and freedom of competition), it is necessary that the management of the insurer is controlled in order to avoid that a reckless or simply non-technical behaviour could destroy the general trust in the system.

Thus, some parameters of protection are inspired not in the protection of the insured specifically or in their rights as such, but in the protection of the mutuality proper and in the protection of the system.[217]

---

216. Jean Bigot, *Traité de Droit des Assurances*, vol. I, 313 (Paris: LGDJ Press, 1996), *Réglementation de la Provision mathématique*.

217. Gallegos Díaz de Villegas, *Classic and Modern Modalities of Life Insurance* (*Modalidades clásicas y modernas del seguro de vida*).

Act 17.418 has established – as so many others in other countries of the world – a change in the original relationship that does not imply a novation for change of purpose of the legal act that constitutes insurance, even in the assumptions in which it is not a contract.

In the following paragraph 195 entitled 'The Contractual Changes', some special situations that may take place in life insurance shall be analysed.

Starting by reduction, Tirado Suárez[218] explains it when he states that 'it is the transformation of the insurance policy into an insurance of the same modality released from the payment of the premiums, which capital shall correspond to the mathematical reserve constituted pursuant to the table of guaranteed values included in the special attached conditions'.

This conceptual definition attempts to translate into legal language and knowledge, the technical-actuarial assessment of the idea of reduction which we could ordinarily define as the freezing of the existing operation, that is, the insurance taken out under the same existing conditions but for a lower capital as no future premiums will be paid.

In other words, as no premiums will be paid in the future, there will be a breakage of the relation premium and service of the insurer.

195. The Contractual Changes: Reduction, Salvage, and Loan. In this part some effects typical of permanent life insurance as a consequence of the existence of mathematical reserves shall be analysed.

Although the fact that the taker with the payment of the level premiums implies payments in excess in relation to the risk run by the insurer during the first years of insurance and that this may have awoken arguments in favour of certain rights of the taker on the reserves created and their interests, what is true is that, at least, this took the taker to be alert about the allocation and utilization of the money.

In insurance life occurs the same thing that happens in any other insurance (that we know as property insurance). In such insurance, the value of the risk premium is increased, apart from the amount represented by the payments made by the takers, it is included the amount of the interest which such money received by the insurer shall produce.

This is put in very simple words, as it is not being considered the commercial costs or the specific expenses on the insurer that are logically translated into the commercial premium so as not to increase the pure or risk or technical premium.

The risk premium is the consideration that the mutuality of insured pays according to the frequency and intensity of the risk insured in order to technically maintain a fair price which compensates in each established period, the cost of that risk. All that on the statistical basis that may be found.

In everyday life, the taker of the insurance is not interested in the details or cost of the risk or technical premium. He is only interested in the commercial premium that he will have to pay and based on that, he will make the decision and he will take as important parameter, its price.

218. Javier Tirado Suarez Francisco, *Insurance Contract Law* (*Ley de Contrato de Seguro*), vol. III, 352 et seq.

The taker has no interest in the frequency or intensity of the risk or the statistics to be applied. He is not interested either in the profitability of the money paid to the insurer.

The same should happen with permanent life insurance, but as they are investments in the long run performed in a very well-known scope by everybody and the allocation of the level premiums (the portion called savings premiums) is known, the commercial contest of the offering portion of the market has established the stage for this business contest around the financial business and also the profitability that will arise in relation to the investment of reserves and finally, in relation to each individual case.

We have been through the development of the commercial behaviour in the last years and the appearance of the so-called universal life and united linked as response to the unfavourable competition from financial and banking institutions.

Even when it could have been a less aggressive contest, it is possible to imagine a similar situation during the times before 1970 and, above all, as from the Second World War 1939–1945, situations that have improved the insurance product in the benefit of the insured.

It can be noticed then, that mathematical reserves that each year increase, determine the factor of commercial competition among insurers. Also and throughout time, some behaviours developed, finally forming steady and constant conducts which definitely helped towards the better collocation of the product.[219]

These mathematical reserves have been extending their effects by means of the appearance of new institutes that, in all cases, have improved the investment conditions by means of other features.

Our law – as well as many other foreign laws and most of the books of authority – allocates the application of mathematical reserves to other purposes than the originally provided for.

Three are those possible purposes: (a) reduction; (b) salvage; and (c) loan.

As starting point in order to start the analysis of the three possibilities, it is necessary to stress that they are only admissible in cases in which some measurable mathematical reserve has been done (this does not happen in every life insurance contract).

In this line, not all insurances start generating mathematical reserves as from the moment in which the contract or the payment of the premium starts but at a posterior moment, generally after the payment of the second or third year or, in other words, as from the third year of effectiveness of the contract.

Thus, the excess of the level premium over the risk premium corresponding to those first years is allocated to the amortization of part of the acquisition expenses of the insurer, expenses that to a certain extent, generally, the controlling legislations authorize to activate.

219. In the beginnings of life insurance, the obligation of the payment to the insurer when occurring the loss was linked to the punctual payment of the premiums, as any interruption meant the lack of any right to the assured amount.

It is also important to point out that in our law there is no legal provision obliging the creation of mathematical reserves in all life insurance assumptions as, by nature, some of this type of insurance will not be compatible with obligatorily establishing such kind of reserves.

This is the case of survival and endowment insurance and temporary insurance paid upon the death of the insured.

In survival insurance where the risk covered is that the insured stays alive after certain period, the adverse selection of the risk would derive from the will of the taker who may decide to rescind his contract when finding out that he has a condition that could kill him before the occurrence of the loss (survival) and thus, it would not be convenient for him to continue paying the insurance premiums.

In temporary insurance paid upon the death of the insured, as the premium that is paid is the risk premium, no reserves of this type of contract are created:

(a) *Insurance Reduction.* With this denomination we are making reference to the possibility of converting insurance that was taken out, in insurance for a lesser amount, without continuing to pay any premium.

The reduction of the assured amount must be carried out for the same amount that would be obtained for an insurance of the same nature, as it may correspond, according to the age of the insured at that time, paying one sole premium equivalent to the guaranteed value of the policy.

This conversion or modification is absolutely opposed to the salvage as, the salvage includes a rescission first and the reduction essentially implies the maintenance of the relationship under certain different guidelines – as the fact of being a contract released from the payment of new premiums.

The conversion is, legally, a unilateral declaration of the taker. Apart from being unilateral is receptive as it becomes effective by simple reception from the insurer of the manifestation of will, without any act required on his part.

In the contract, this right of reduction of the insured capital must be established as well as the guaranteed salvage values.

The reduction of the assured value may derive from a specific claim of the taker or else from a legal solution upon the occurrence of certain circumstances.

Section 138 of Act 17.418 establishes the right to carry out the claim.

Again the Argentine Act uses a wrong denomination when establishing as condition, that the insured must be up-to-date with the payment of the premiums.

Once more, the insured is not the debtor of the premiums and he does not constitute a person allowed to pay them.

The insured in life insurance is the person on which the risk is established. A taker may be the same insured but, his right to pay the premium comes from his condition of taker and not for simultaneously being the insured.

Legally, this solution of reduction of capital insured or the salvage solution are established in sections 139, 7 and 6.

In general terms, the Act first respects the will of the taker to decide about which solution he prefers and, before his real or assumed silence, allows for a solution which opts for the survival of the relationship.

(b) *Insurance Salvage.* It is the possibility of the taker of releasing from the insurance contract, receiving part of the mathematical reserves accrued by the insurer that are known as salvage guaranteed value.

The right of salvage implies the rescission of the existing insurance contract, and it is an express voluntary act of the taker or a legal solution before the absence of his decision.

Section 138 establishes this right in subsection b) and the legal option is determined by sections 9 and 140.

The guaranteed amounts of salvage are those that the insurer covenants to pay to the taker, according to the technical plans that he has drawn up and that are always lower to the mathematical reserves as, in all cases, it is assumed some compensation in relation to the insurer for the damage that the rescission of the contract may cause him, the expenses incurred and the expected benefit.

It can be noticed that, so that the salvage is possible in life insurance, it is an indispensable requirement to comply with the technical assumption that the mathematical reserve has been created and further that, with the salvage, the risk of appearing a reverse selection or as it is called in the insurance jargon 'anti-selection'[220] could not be concreted.

In other words, the salvage could neither have a role in temporary insurance that does not generate a measurable savings premium with which the mathematical reserve starts to be formed nor in survival insurance.

In the latter, as death is not the covered risk as the risk is survival, it can be assumed that the taker will rescind it since, as the health of the insured is deficient, he will probably not reach the necessary age for the insurance to be paid.

Certainly, the salvage arises from the assumption that there is no compulsory obligation from the taker to pay the premium in all the periods, as he can deviate from that via a very easy rescission of the contract (since he ends the contract by his own will).

It also corresponds to the salvage or the value of the salvage when the loss occurs during the term that the insurer has in order to challenge the contract on grounds of being null and void, as a consequence of misrepresentation of the risk (section 9) and also as a consequence of the release of the insurer by any other cause, after having elapsed three years as from the moment of entering into the contract (section 140).

Such release must be broadly understood as the term of three years is the term of incontestability established by section 135 as the maximum within which the insurer may make use of the exclusion of risk by suicide, crucial assumption of causing of loss in the matter of life insurance.

If the insurer is compelled to pay the agreed amount once the three years of effectiveness of the contract have elapsed, despite the suicide of the insured, the release grounds of the insurer, by force, must be contemplated in the same way.

---

220. This word does not appear in the Spanish language but its use is possible dividing it into its two parts: 'anti' and 'selection'.

(c) *Insurance Loan.* It is the possibility to obtain from the insurer, certain amount of money with or without a purpose pursuant to the contract technical plans and in relation to the bases that should be indicated in the policy.

These technical plans must be adjusted to the reserve that may correspond.

This loan – and it can be agreed so in the contract – will be granted in order to pay the unpaid premiums and, obviously, as long as we are dealing with mathematical reserves.

The legal nature of this institute – which is called loan or advanced payment – is unquestionable. These names that, to our criterion, are antagonist respond to different concepts.

Advanced payment gives the idea of a prepayment of something and, if an advance is carried out – in the economic language – it means that something was previously owed to the moment it had been established.

On the contrary, when we speak of a loan, it indicates that the person who receives it (in this case, the taker) becomes the borrower with the obligation of returning the borrowed amount.

Yet, as in this operation the money is not returned, it is not possible to speak of a loan and, as there is always a charge of interest on the amount received, it is not possible to speak of advance payment since it does not correspond to meet interest for money of one's own property.

Our law, as many others and part of the books of authority, categorizes the business that is being considered expressly as loan on grounds of section 141.

The latter were found not only in the two parts that provide for the regulation but also in the two Titles preceding them.

This brings about confusion about the legal nature of the institute. This is a significant problem as, if it was effectively a loan, it would be unavoidable the obligation to return it, without prejudice of having to pay interest, as in any other commercial operation.

The problem appears on account of using for situations that come from new commercial operations, words that have specifically defined effects and consequences of others.

The most simple solution would be to grant the words 'advance' or 'loan' an expanded meaning for this matter or to use other different words which could denote a meaning, alien to the traditional legal criterion and more in keeping with the commercial act that they are attempting to protect, obtaining from those provisions, the protections sought for.

Thus, for instance, in the Act, it should be provided for that the taker may receive money coming from the mathematical reserves, if certain situations take place.

This right to receive money which comes from mathematical reserves created by the insurer – whether it is called advance payment or loan – in some occasions, according to the legislations or contracts is established by means of a pledge. This pledge on the policy instrumenting the insurance contract is done by means of the delivery of the policy to the insurer as evidence of the debt and the pledge owed.

In Argentina this is not so, unless there was a specific regulation authorizing it.

It is not possible the scenario of a pledge on a loan provided for in section 141 since the insurer has no possibility of demanding the return of the amount lent, apart from the possible compensation that has been already mentioned.

Furthermore, although a pledge was possible in our system, it would require a specific contract since, as the policy is not a credit instrument or, more specifically a negotiable instrument (commercial paper), there is no endorsement as guarantor in order to instrument a pledge.[221]

Contractually, it could be instrumented the right to the 'loan' or to receive a defined amount from the reserves. It should operate automatically to pay the unpaid premiums at their due date, pursuant to section 141.

However, the taker can, at any time, return the sum of the amount withdrawn (the 'loan') and the corresponding interests, which would bring the contract back to its original terms.

This solution is not established by law, but it is a simple derivation of the reinstatement established for reduction in section 142.

196. The Risk Covered in Life Insurance. Extension. In an analysis of the risks and purposes of each type of insurance it is important to remember, following the books of authority that in life insurance or survival insurance, the risk always has the uncertainty derived from the duration of life of human beings.

It is almost unnecessary to point out that, in life insurance paid upon the death of the insured, the natural aggravation of the risk is inherent since, as time goes by, the probability of passing away of the insured increases.

In life insurance the specific risk is of vital importance, as death is a generic situation that is necessary to separate since, it can come as a consequence of normal or abnormal risks that should, in principle, be excluded in order to maintain the homogenization of the insured risks.

The risk, apart from being the subject matter of insurance is a polysemous concept and requires precision.[222]

It is clear that the description of the risk must be carried out according to the technical needs the insurer realizes of, if it does not require defined specifications. The uncertainty derived from the declaration could only be attributed to the latter and not to the taker or the insured, except, of course, in case of misrepresentation or in case of malice or bad faith.

The homogenization of the risks assumed by the insurer is as important in life insurance as it is in property insurance, but it is a burden of the insurer to establish them clearly. If not he is undeterminably obliging himself in the case of death of the insured to respond, whatever its reason, except exclusions or limitations expressly indicated.

The acquired immune deficiency syndrome (AIDS) condition had quite a huge impact on recent years as it was an illness previously unknown and that did not have precedents of any nature.

---

221. *See* Part I of this monograph, Ch. II, para. 28.

222. E. Bullo, *Insurance Law and Other Related Businesses* (*El Derecho de Seguros y de otro negocios vinculados*) vol. I, para. 33.

In the time that followed immediately after the appearance of the first cases of death as a consequence of the disease, it started to be filed the demurrer derived from the ignorance of such disease to the date of the taking out of the insurance.

It was adduced that the risk came from an inexistent cause until then and that it was a risk unknown and that it could not have been taken into account from the results of the existing tables of mortality.

In 1988, in the Canary Islands, Spain, a Symposium carried out by the Council of the Presidency of the International Association of Insurance Law (AIDA), one of the Spanish representatives, Mr Julio Castelo, posed a question on the possibility of the insurers of releasing from paying as losses, the cases insured which died of AIDS precisely due to the aforementioned reasons. Above all, because of the total previous ignorance at the moment of the contract of the insurer who could have done nothing as the disease was inexistent regarding its prior knowledge at the moment of the contract and even before during the precontractual stage.[223]

The attendance engaged in a very interesting discussion. It is important to notice that in October 1988, the cases of the illness just started to be spread and known.

Finally, at those first times, a conclusion was drawn that it could be opposed to the exception of demurrer derived from the theory of unpredictability, exception that given the factual existent circumstances was the logic solution to follow.[224]

197. Coverage Exclusion in Life Insurance. In life insurance, the coverage exclusion of certain risks and the release of the insurer – the consequence of coverage exclusion – must be established in a defined and clear way so as not to confuse which is the true description of risk or introduce in the insurance harmful confusions.

Regarding causing of the loss, Act 17.418 has established similar provisions to those of property insurance.

We do not share the denomination of causing of the loss that the Act uses in relation to property insurance in Article III because it is not correct since, as it has been previously stated, the loss for insurance law is the occurrence of a risk specifically covered and which, consequently, sets off the guarantee promised by the insurer.[225]

This causing of the event covered that determines the release of the insurer by coverage exclusion is specifically established regarding three situations: (1) insured's suicide; (2) deliberately caused death of the insured by wrongful act of the taker; and (3) death of the insured during the course of a criminal act or by lawful application of the death penalty.

223. This precedent has been quoted in an article with reference to the random nature of the insurance contract. *See* 'Reflections over some matters related to the general theory of insurance' [*Reflexiones sobre algunas de las cuestiones vinculadas a la teoría general del contrato de seguros*], Journal *Derecho y Empresa* (DYE) of the Austral University, Company Sciences School, year 1997, 7 and 8, 33 et seq.

224. This solution – that was first discussed in length – was suggested by who was leading the Argentine Delegation: Mr Juan Carlos F. Morandi, Esq., supporting his argument mainly on the civil legislation of our country as well as others.

225. In the denomination that the Act provides and that we have observed in other papers and from the teaching profession, it is criticizable the use of the word 'loss' in a generic way as if it is something more limited to damage property insurance as it has connotations of prejudice or damage.

Some legislations as well as some books of authority called this causing of the loss – as our law calls it – intentional damage, which excludes the risk as intentional fault is a synonym of produce, originate, cause.

French law is maybe one of the legal systems that has encouraged their books of authority to study this subject further.

In general, coinciding with many of these authors, the fundamental reason of risk exclusion as a consequence of intentional damage from the insured, the beneficiary or the taker stems from the fact that accepting them in the guarantee of the insurer would be to take into account false grounds that would alter the so-called random guarantee that allows for the application of the mathematical laws of statistics.[226]

It must not be forgotten that the risk must be treated as a random event, alien to the acts or the will of the parties.

Although, in fact, the expression intentional fault in fact, as suggested by the same foreign books of authority, must be considered 'damage or intentional' as the contrary case would bring about doubts on the origin of the coverage of the risks caused in civil matters with malicious intent of the driver.[227]

The causing of the loss or intentional fault – as the French Law calls it – is to violently cause the occurrence of the risk, subject matter of the contract which, unavoidably, brings about the intention of achieving the payment of the compensation by the insurer in order to benefit:

(a) *Suicide*. With reference to life insurance paid upon the death of the insured, three cases have been mentioned of our Act 17.418 where it has been seen the coverage exclusion or release of the insurer and that are, coincidently, the same provisions established by other legislations.

The first assumption in which the risk is excluded and that is established in the Act as release of the insurer from paying the assured amount is the case of suicide of the insured act that means, materially, bringing one's life to an end and, at the least, it is linked to a voluntary act of the suicidal subject.

This is the definition required by section 135 of our Act to achieve the grounds of risk coverage exclusion.

Until the end of the nineteenth century, the laws and codes did not accept the death by suicide for morality and public order reasons and only as from the 1930s in the twentieth century certain grounds of responsibility started to be granted to the insurer, limited to the amount of the mathematical reserve.[228]

Today, this acknowledgement is consistent, and it finds support in technical reasons.

In Spain, where the Act of 1980 has brought about a new force in the books of authority, its section 93 uses an expression quite similar to the one the Argentine

226. *See* T. Motteau D' Elbruel, '*Assurance Francaise*' Nos 705 and 706, February/March 1995, 51 and 54, '*La faute intentionelle en l'exclusion légale de l'art.*' 113-1.
227. The construction of this aspect has evidently more a legal support than a support of a political legislative nature as nowadays, coverage exclusion related to crimes coming from a malicious intent could not be harmonized with certain existing rights of the damaged third parties.
228. Javier Tirado Suarez Francisco, *Insurance Contract Law* (*Ley de Contrato de Seguro*), vol. III, 315 et seq.

Act uses and its precedents of 1959 and 1960: suicide is defined as 'the death caused consciously and voluntarily by the own insured'.

In France, section L 132-7 of the Insurance Code with the modifications of Act 3 January 1981 provides us with an identical terminology to the Spanish one.[229]

This conception about the intentionality of suicide that – as common denominator – has been accepted and included in the most modern and distinguished legislations of Latin Law (e.g., the three mentioned examples) obviously derives from the concept of suicide as voluntary act.

The will, as we know, is the power of the soul with which one desires, wishes, or has the intention or liberty to choose or reject things.

Coinciding with this criterion on the need of suicidal intentionality to cause risk exclusion (release of the insurer) the example of the death of the actress Marilyn Monroe which occurred as a consequence of the ingestion of sleeping pills is given.

The French author Lambert-Faivre rightly expresses that the fact of having taken a fatal dose of such kind of products does not prove on its own the will to commit suicide as the ingestion could have been the product of a mistake and thus, the death would be accidental.[230]

Something similar, though the opposite case, could be said regarding death in certain traffic accidents.

From the point of view of certain doctors, judges, and insurers, many of these accidents are not such but suicides for those driving the motor vehicles.

Both examples aimed at showing that in order to prove suicide, it is required the demonstration of the attempt to commit suicide as, from the starting point, the good faith of the insured is presumed and consequently, the inexistence of suicide until otherwise certainly evidenced. However, it is essential a risk exclusion which, as any other exclusion, must be evidenced by the insurer.

Confirming what has been stated, the denomination of voluntary suicide has nothing to do with the external behaviour of the insured since, as it is a suicide, such action always implies to kill oneself (Latin pronoun sui).

It has to do with the interior attitude since, if the insured was in a state of perturbation or mental illness, it would not be a voluntary act but a fortuitous case pursuant to some books of authority.[231]

It is not our opinion that the suicide exclusion as grounds of coverage is unlawful as it is a limitation of responsibility, and section 135 is one of the unchangeable regulations[232] (that can be only changed in the benefit of the insured).

In Part I of this monograph, it is mentioned the dispositive effect of the regulations of Act 17.418 regarding the concrete risk they refer to, as the parties have plenty of powers to limit the risk.[233]

---

229. The text of the section states that the insurance paid upon the death of the insured has no effect if the insured delivers himself voluntarily and consciously to death within the course of the first two years of the contract. *Textes du Code des Assurances*, 13th ed. (Paris: L'Argus, 1995).
230. Y. Lambert-Faivre, *Droit des Assurances*, 291 et seq.
231. Halperín-Morandi, *Insurance* (*Seguros*), vol. II, 874 (Depalma Press, 1983).
232. *See* the book mentioned in the previous note in the same page 874.
233. *See* vol. I of the treaty quoted several times, lastly in preceding n. 211, 172 et seq., para. 34. Especially, *see* 172, n. 4.

Suicide as coverage exclusion is possible to be agreed upon in full, that is, as a conscious or unconscious suicide, but the agreement about it must be totally clear to avoid the possibility of any other construction.

In this way, the mere fact of taking one's life could be construed at the least, as demonstrative of certain mental perturbation that numbs or blurs the correct evaluation of the situations and the reasoning, causing a mental state of incapacity to understand the act.

Thus – and though it was shared that killing oneself always invokes a non-totally rational or voluntary act – it should be accepted as coverage exclusion non-pathological suicide.

It should not be interpreted by the expressions voluntary and conscious that the suicide was being considered even before existing the insurance, as it would be conditioned by such will.

If a person takes out insurance on his own life or on the life of a third party, taking into account the possible death of the insured (because of a more than likely suicide), such insurance would be null and void due to malicious misrepresentation and we would not be dealing with coverage exclusion.

A last matter to take into consideration would be the omission instead of the action of the insured. (The insurer that intentionally prevents some act that had as purpose to improve his illness and, as consequence, dies.)

Two cases in the jurisprudence have brought about this situation.

It is only important to point out that both cases have been resolved in connection with their characteristics; the general books of authority's conclusion being to accept that suicide, in certain assumptions as the ones referred to, may not respond to a concept of own material doing or a violent act on oneself.[234]

234. As stated in the following court opinion: Federal Court, Comodoro Rivadavia, Argentina, 5 Jun. 1989, ED, 134 –295:

> The recurrent negative of the patient to receiving a blood transfusion recommended by the professionals in charge of him is a slow suicide carried out by a non-violent means and not by his own hand; it is an omission from the suicide victim who does not admit treatment and in such a way, lets himself die. It is a person that for religious reasons attempts to take his life by omission.

In Honourable National Court of Appeals in Civil Matters of the Federal Capital City, Room H, 21 Feb. 1991. Journal *El Derecho*, 144–122, the Court states:

> Not arising out of the case that the conduct of the patient constitutes any type of suicide it must be respected the will of such person and the solution shall be imposed by the nature of the rights at stake that shall determine that the patient is the only and irreplaceable arbiter of the situation. The principle exposed must not yield although there could be a threat to life. This is so because it is him who will face the risks, the sufferings, the immobility, the possibility of a survival full of deficiencies and limitations and a surgical intervention that, sometimes, only offers the probability of a temporary extension of life, especially in this case that the amputation of a leg is not for healing purposes or to stop the disease that originated this condition in the patient.

(b) *Deliberate Causing of the Death of the Insured.* The second of the cases of coverage exclusion legislated by the Argentine Act 17.418 is the one established in section 136 regarding the deliberately caused death by a wrongful act of the taker.

It is our opinion that the deliberate death of the insured by the acts of the taker of the insurance, apart from the moral and ethics criticism that such behaviour deserves, technically has the same grounds as suicide.

The matter is to describe the behaviours that caused the occurrence of death (not coming from a random event proper but dependent on the will of one of the parties).

This regulation of the Argentine law has some specific characteristics that indicate that only the deliberate unlawful action from the taker of the insurance contract that causes the death of the third party has the release effect.

This expression prevents the consideration of coverage exclusion for the death of the insured third party by an action whose author is not the taker or the possibility that he could cause the event without having committed a wrongful act. For instance, that the author of the death of the insured is a third party or even the beneficiary or that death occurs as the consequence of an act which some circumstance does not permit to classify as unlawful.

It is not considered as unlawful the death of the insured by homicide by recklessness caused by the taker as it would be death as a result of a car accident. It is an assumption of coverage exclusion but it lacks intent (which requires the legal status of deliberate action).[235]

The attempted homicide as it is not a case provided by law is not a fact that causes coverage exclusion by legal provision. Nevertheless, it would be judicially possible to present it as specific grounds of exclusion by means of an express agreement in the policy.

(c) *Death of the Insured during the Course of a Criminal Act or by Lawful Application of the Death Penalty.* This regulation is provided for in section 137 of Act 17.418 of Argentina. It has, as in the other two cases that have just been analysed, the same grounds.

On the one hand, the insurer releases himself if the occurrence of death is a consequence of his participation in a criminal act, that is, if the insured passes away during a criminal act. On the other hand, if he dies as a consequence of a judicial sentence of death.

The first of the assumptions has been construed by the jurisprudence as referring to an act with a defined purpose, with previous plans or combined actions towards the commitment of a crime but not all activity – many times with no consultation, unpremeditated, circumstantial, and accidental – which may cause a crime.

There is no reference in the books of authorities to the second case since death penalty was only applied during brief periods in the country, and none have

235. Cf. Y. Lambert-Faivre, *Droit des Assurances*, 295 and 408.

occurred after the passing of Act 17.418, except for some isolated occasions and by application of military or criminal emergency laws.

In a judgment many years ago, although the Court provided for an adequate legal frame for a case where there were mentioned plans of an attempt to commit a crime in which the insured lost his life, a mistake was made because, instead of plainly and simply applying section 137 – establishing the release of the insurer – the Court resolved the matter by declaring the insurance null and void.[236]

198. Loss of the Right of the Beneficiary. This penalty provided for in section 136 punishing the beneficiary that deliberately caused the death of the insured by committing an unlawful act is, with no doubt, a different consequence from the release of the insurer established for an identical situation on the taker's part, already seen and that is provided for in the same section of Act 17.418.

Our Act is, in this respect, similar to section L 132-24 of the French Insurance Code, pursuant to the modifications introduced by the Act of 3 January 1981.

When section 136 establishes the loss of the right of the beneficiary of the insurance in the case of death of the insured when such beneficiary deliberately causes the loss with a wrongful act, it establishes a direct penalty to the beneficiary for morality and not technical reasons – as the insurer is not released at all and remains contractually obliged to the payment of the assured amount.

The direct penalty of the doer is evidently the right choice since it must follow morality and public order.

Nevertheless, the solution of the mentioned section is incomplete and even contradictory with the principle followed of causing of the loss since, if this causing or intentional fault, breaks the characteristic of random event that the insurance in other cases has, that is enough reason to consider the inexistence of such random nature when the intentional damage or the causing of the loss comes from the person who is directly interested in achieving the occurrence of such event.

Thus, it is not shared at all the legal solution to the problem which has grounds on the wrong legislative policy of considering the protection of the assignees of the taker and obliging the insurer to pay the assured amount, pursuant to what we have been mentioning, by the application of section 145 last paragraph.

Technically, the intentional participation of a beneficiary in the death of an insured responds to an interested human reason that should exclude it from being a loss and, before its occurrence, the insurer should be released from the payment of the insurance by the same reason of the other assumption: coverage exclusion, in our opinion, much more fair.

The same reason is imposed by the French Insurance Code since, when it was reformed by the Act of 3 January 1981, it was introduced the fact of linking the death of the insured to the beneficiary's acts. Before, the insurance did not have effects regarding the beneficiary; in fact, it did not produce any effects whatsoever.

This exclusion in our law in no way would be a source of benefits to the insurer since, as he would be released if the logical term of three years elapsed, he should reimburse the heirs of his taker the value of salvage (section 140).

236. *See* E.D. V.5, 421.

If the three years had not elapsed, the amounts collected by the insurer from the premiums still would not have achieved the creation of measurable mathematical reserves, and there would not be any salvage value at all.

The taker, before the death of the insurer, pursuant to the provision of section 145, must pay the assured amount, as the appointment of the beneficiary must be interpreted as ineffective.

Needless to say that section 140 would not be applied, as the insurer owes the agreed service.

Logically, if there was more than one appointed beneficiary, the assured amount would go to the others.

If among the co-beneficiaries, the portion that would have corresponded to that other beneficiary punished by law pursuant to section 137 is divided or not shall be a factual question to be resolved according to the case and the terms of appointment agreed upon.

199. Misrepresentation in Life Insurance and Its Consequences. Previously in this same work, the institute of misrepresentation has been seen in a general way and, specifically in relation to property insurance, although some concrete references have been made to life insurance.

Section 6 devotes to the problem related to this type of life insurance.

The consequence of the misrepresentation without malice when it is claimed during the corresponding term grants the right to the insurer to choose between the nullity of the contract with reimbursement of the premium received less the expenses that would have been caused (solution in keeping with civil law in the generic matter of judicial acts) and the readjustment of the contract to the true status of the risk.

This last choice would take place as long as the insured agrees to it.

Nevertheless, for life insurance, the solution of section 6 is different as, in the second part, the provision states the possibility of imposing the insurer the readjustment under the compliance of some other provisions: (a) that the nullity of the contract was prejudicial for the insured; (b) that the contract was readjustable to the judgment of experts (with the same extension that the one commented in the case of misrepresentation); and (c) that the contract with the readjustment could have been entered into according to the commercial practice (use and custom) of the insurer (specifically).

In any case, misrepresentation of life insurance, except when it is classified as malicious or in bad faith (as those facts imply the release of the insurer), would bring about the salvage; therefore, there would not be a benefit without cause for the insurer.

It must be also contemplated in detail the concept of incontestability.

The limitation of three years imposed by section 130 in order to admit the invocation of misrepresentation on the insurer's part does not act but like other similar existing regulations of the insurance contract, a moderate criterion of not malicious or bad faith misrepresentation in order to prevent a long period in which there would be uncertainty about the possible right to the assured amount in the contract of life insurance.

Our Act has been criticized by some authors by the apparent restriction of the limitation solely in relation to misrepresentation.[237]

The criticism of the great author quoted in the preceding note is a bit rushed into as in section 5, misrepresentation is contemplated in a similar way to false declaration.[238]

200. Participation of the Benefits. As it is reminded by some authors, the long-term management of life insurance and, more precisely, of the mathematical reserves that such insurance generate determines important resources that have been identified and are identified in the products offered by insurers.

This financial activity is important in order to promote such insurance, as the benefits of such managements are publicized in order to encourage the taking out of insurance by investors.

Thus, it is possible to very clearly distinguish the income coming from the technical aspect of the business and the income that comes directly from the financial management carried out by the insurer.

More than about income, it is necessary to speak about the technical and financial benefits since what is interesting for investors is this, precisely, and not merely the income. The management of business must inexorably tend not only to a commercial productivity but also necessarily to profitability.

The technical benefits are those originated by a lower number of losses than the assumed by means of the correct application of the table of mortality or a more adequate selection of risks assumed or finally by a more effective administration regarding acquisition and management costs.

The financial benefits are those whose origin are the interests received by investments as well as, in principle, the surplus value of such investments when they take place.

When the insurer establishes a technical plan of life insurance, it sets out a level premium to be paid periodically on a mathematical basis which, although conservative, is always hypothetical.

As time goes by, the correspondence between the estimated and used parameters can be established with both scopes in mind, the technical and the financial.

If the result of the comparison is an improved result regarding the accomplished financial benefit, that is, the compensation to the taker for the financial business of

---

237. J. Garrigues, *Land Insurance Contract* (*Contrato de Seguro Terrestre*), 511, n. 36. In the 1982 edition under the copyright of the same author there is a mistake, in our opinion, a typographic mistake which indicates s. 30 of Argentine Act when, in fact, it is s. 130 of such Act 17.418.

238. In the Spanish denomination of the institute to which we are referring (*reticencia*) habitually the misrepresentation (*reticencia*) and the false declaration are concepts taken as similar and with identical effects. Section 5 of the Insurance Act, following the preceding text of the Commercial Code (s. 498) when considering the subject in general, states: 'Every false declaration or misrepresentation of circumstances known by the insured, even in good faith.' Even though, truly, both terms indicate different concepts, it cannot be ignored that the legal similarity that the Act grants the nullity grounds legislated under s. 5 (misrepresentation of known circumstances and false declarations of known circumstances) have, grammatically, semantics in common: 'to suggest, permitting to reveal or give to the understanding'. In the judgment *Suc. Risso Patrón v. Círculo Cerrado and Plus Ultra*, Judge Mr Juan Carlos Morandi, Esq. briefly referred to the similarities between both terms.

insurance has not been sufficiently rewarded, it does not seem prudent that the insurer gains profit excessively, receiving an exaggerated benefit since, commercially, he should have lost.

This has been precisely what has happened, beyond any theory about the sensibility of accessing a participation of the benefits.

However, not only benefits were agreed regarding a fiscal year closed during the existence of the insurance but also currently participations are agreed on benefits exceeding certain limits, participations in proportion to the assured capitals, on the premiums paid by the taker or on the mathematical reserves of the contracts.

The reserves are, in general, the ones that are usually the basis of the distribution of benefits.

There is no regulation that obliges to pay insurance contracts with a participation in benefits, but the policies issued by the insurers usually agree so.

201. Devaluation of Money. One of the greatest problems in life insurance comes from the monetary devaluation and the effects of inflation.

In our country, inflation has taken place with great force and throughout a long period of time, possibly as it has not been witnessed in other parts of the world. This has taken the national and provincial judges to enforce extreme judicial regulations that, with the years, mitigated the effects of the loss of value of the currency, without the possibility of avoiding the damage that the applied remedy (indexation) produced.

The problem of the inflation causing this devaluation has been so important that it generated both, in the country and outside our country, a strong devotion to its study and attempts of solution.

The effects were so great that some people suffering its effects were disoriented to the point of getting confused when attempting to find solutions to the problem.

In life insurance, there were not many experiences because, due to the effects of these evils, during a long time, there was no possibility to save money which meant a total separation from the taking out of permanent and survival life insurance.

A monetary devaluation of incredible measures destroyed life insurance to the extreme that the insurers with the biggest portfolios decided to pardon the payment of premiums, as they took too much work to collect, and the quantum of the instalments did not justify the administrative management or the simple collection tasks since the paper where they were instrumented was higher than the instalment to be paid.

It is clear that the damage was felt at all levels, even the moral level, since all the country went through a global crisis for more than thirty years which distorted the economy in a way that only those that have lived it could completely understand.

The indexes of inflation of those years from June 1953 to June 1983 were of more than 1,407,000%.[239] This amount also was darkened by the ones that provided the cost of living increases and other similar during many years.

239. Carlos Lago, 'Inflation and Life Insurance in Argentina' ('*La inflación y el seguro de vida en la Argentina*'), Argentine Insurance Journal, Company and Responsibility, 3–4, 101 et seq.

In summary: several times, the national currency has seen its value transformed, reaching the amount mentioned by adding thirteen zeros in order to permit comparison and exchange with other hard currencies.

This lack of experience about monetary devaluation in matters of life insurance could not be covered by the experience before the same kind of phenomena in foreign countries – via books of authority, laws or jurisprudence – as ours was of outrageous proportions and the damage caused to life and survival insurance businesses was complete. All capability of saving of individuals and companies was lost.

Furthermore, the jurisprudence in Commercial Matters of the Capital City – which then enjoyed great prestige in the whole territory – logically for those times, maintained the need of existence of arrears in the insurer as necessary factor for the revaluation of the currency of payment of the insurance to proceed[240] and this, for a long time made it impossible to expect that the Courts could issue judgments on the matter by revaluating life insurance, despite the many cases of property insurance.

Between December 1982 and April 1983, two of the rooms in which the Court of Appeals of the Nation in Commercial Matters was divided into for organizational purposes of the Capital City had the opportunity to sentence in the matter of revaluation of the amount to pay by the insurers.

The importance of these matters both due to the significance of the subject and due to the fact that it was sentenced for the first time the monetary revaluation without arrears of the obliged to pay[241] and more so, the significance of one the sentences of these cases issued later on by the same Court (consequence of accepting the Supreme Court of Justice of the Nation an extraordinary remedy by arbitrariness) requires a further analysis, specifically of the latter.

It is important to emphasize that due to the time elapsed in judicial proceedings – which practically permitted to eradicate inflation as from 1991 – the sentences of justice were just interesting for the books of authority, without having influence on the present (as the inflationary period was finished) until recently.

Both judgments are jointly analysed as they were contemporaneous and from the same insurer, and they had primary different decisions before very similar situations:

(a) The judgments were on 29 December 1982, case file *Pacheco de Alvear José A.*, and 20 April 1983, case file *Mitelman Simón*, rooms D and E, respectively, Honourable Court of Appeals in Commercial Matters of the Federal Capital City.

(b) They were about permanent life insurance cases with limited premiums payments although one of the judges of Pacheco de Alvear classified one of them as survival insurance or endowment as they were called.

240. *Mussa de Gómez de De La Vega María H. v. La Defensa S.A.*, E.D. V.81, 273.

241. Alberto Bianchi, 'The Notorious Diversion of Economic Reality as a Consequence of Arbitrariness in Sentences' ('*El apartamiento notorio de la realidad económica como causa de arbitrariedad de las sentencias*'), Journal El Derecho, vol. 116, 772, n. 16. It is completely advisable to review the comments of this article, in which the first case by the Supreme Court is precisely commented on.

(c) Whereas in Room D in the first of the judgments, the revaluation of the assured amount was accepted,[242] with a very peculiar way of selecting the grounds for that, Room E, the second judgment disallowed a case of very similar nature.

(d) Later on, in this last case, Room A of the Court of Appeals, as a consequence of a Supreme Court of Justice decision on a remedy for arbitrariness had to issue again the final sentence. Even when accepting revaluation at the beginning in life insurance without being the insurer in arrears (against what was set forth in the plenary session *Mussa de Gómez v. La Defensa*), it was a partial acceptance. Above all, it was an acceptance where only the circumstances existent in this type of operations were taken into account; if not, the sentence would have been extremely unjust and contrary to law.[243]

(e) In Room A also took place a sentence of significance via the vote of the judge speaker, without using the high-sounding manner of his colleague in Room D (*see* note 124) or entering in clichés for the time or concepts vacant of meaning, despite the enthusiasm of being the leader of this judicial start point.[244]

(f) There were some significant matters that were crucial as, for instance, the brief but shrewd analysis of the characteristic of the premium paid by the taker which differs from the same concept in property insurance – practically the only ones existing in the market by the reason already expressed, at that time (lack of savings due to inflation).

A part of the premiums paid by the taker must be reserved, and, the other part, the risk premium, is the portion that is applied to be consumed in each period to cover the provided risk as in property insurance.

In such a way, insurance can never be revaluated by the devaluation of the currency suffered in the previous periods for amounts that were consumed during those periods by covering the risk.

It must not be forgotten that the mathematical reserve is a provision that arises from the fact of the intelligent invention of the level premium but that the impact on the benefit that the insurer must obtain can only be attributed to the amounts effectively subject matter of the reserve in his power and not to the amount that, periodically has been used as consideration for the risk effectively run in each occasion.

(g) It was also very crucial the analysis of the first vote regarding the limitations of investments in order to obtain benefits that the insurer is allowed to do pursuant to Act 20.041 and the regulations of the SIN. They do not admit to surpass the limits of investment allowed for the protection of profitability and also for security reasons.

The simplistic criterion of revaluation according to concrete indexes (as the consumer or wholesaler indexes) would be truly unjust as they are different guidelines.

---

242. *See* judgments in Journal El Derecho, vol. 112, 615 et seq.
243. The judgment in Room A in the case *Mitelman*, new sentence indicated in the text, must be fully read as example of the situation in question. Journal El Derecho, vol. 116–203 et seq.
244. It is advised to read carefully the arguments of the first vote.

(h) From almost the same point of view, another vote mentioned the way of payment of life insurance in relation to time. The payment in instalments permitted by the level premiums meant during inflationary periods that the value of the instalments was not always the same and the assured amount was devaluated with time.

Let us suppose that the established premium of the taker of life insurance was twenty annual instalments of a defined amount of ARS 100 each. If, during the course of twenty years of the payment of other instalments there was an inflation that represented ten times the monetary devaluation per year elapsed, it is obvious that the taker did not comply with the original obligation, as the necessary money to pay 20 times ARS 100 had, at each of those moments, less purchasing power.

In consequence, to accept a devaluation of 10 times the value of the assured amount would be excessively in favour of one of the parties, as it is not taken into account the consideration, the premium that also was similarly devaluated.[245]

This reasoning completely ruined the reasoning of one of the members of Room D which, at a moment, had caused, mistakenly, a blind and general interest.

As further information, the provincial courts do not have jurisprudence (or jurisprudence of importance) about the revaluation of the currency in life insurance. This derives from the fact that the jurisdiction where suits had to be filed was the Courts of the Federal City as they are trials against insurers which usually have their real domicile in the City of Buenos Aires.

202. The Act of Pledging the Policy of Life Insurance. Frequently in our life we hear about possible business (as pledge or assignment) of the policies instrumenting life insurance.

These references are caused mistakenly from situations that take place in other countries.

It is necessary to clarify that these financial operations are not similar to the ones of appointment of the beneficiary, a right that can only be exercised by the taker of the insurance contract, except when a beneficiary for a valuable consideration has been already appointed (fact from which there is no return except with his express consent or acceptance).

In fact, in life insurance, the assignment and the pledge of the policy or the assignment or pledge of the right of the appointed beneficiary is not possible in keeping with our regulations since, the right as beneficiary, as it has been already pointed out, is acquired originally when occurring the event, that is, the death or survival of the insured.

Before that and except the beneficiary was onerous, the appointment can be freely revoked.

The right of the beneficiary can be assigned once the loss has taken place, that is, when the beneficiary starts being a creditor of the insurer for the assured amount. This is because it is a right composing his assets. Yet, the beneficiary could not

245. *See* judgment after *Mitelman* case, issued by the same National Court in Commercial Matters, Room B. NC.Com., 22 Feb. 1989 (ED. 134– 486).

assign in advance the right that he would have at the moment of occurrence of the event since, until then, he would not be the owner thereof.

The onerous beneficiary, effectively, can assign since his appointment cannot be revoked without his consent. In this assumption, it is also admitted to establish a moment before the production of the event for the acquisition of his right (section 143).

Nevertheless, it is worth mentioning that a random credit may be the object of an assignment pursuant to section 1446 of the Civil Code, reason why opinions could appear contrary to this, if it is not duly construed that the right of the beneficiary is not a random right since, before the loss, he has never had any right to the benefit. The loss, to his regard, is not a random event or condition.

His right arises autonomously from the occurrence of the loss since, if this did not happen, it could never be sustained that there was a right but that it ceased.

This assignment that can be carried out by the beneficiary, as by any other creditor, must comply with all the requirements that the Argentine Civil Code establishes.

A different thing is the right that could have the taker-policyholder as *dominus negotii* of assigning or pledging the rights arising out of the insurance contract regarding its insurer.

When the matter of the transfer of rights of the insured in property insurance was analysed, it was clear the link that this transfer had with the insurable interest, unavoidable principle in the general theory of damage property insurance.

On account of the same right sustained in that chapter which stated that in life insurance, there is no insurable interest, it would appear that in life insurance contracts, the taker, who has as part of his property the right to appoint and change without restrictions the beneficiary, obtain loans on the assured amount, require the salvage or forgiveness thereof, etc. would also have the right to pledge and assign such right.

This assignment and pledge are possible since the rights of the taker – as long as they are in the market – are negotiable, with the restrictions arising out of the assignment of credits.

It has been previously sustained that the policy of insurance is not a negotiable instrument but that we could place it within the concept of instrument of passive legitimation.

However, the instrumentation of the life insurance contract must be contained in an exclusively nominative policy. It is so set forth by section 13 of Act 17.418 in its last part.

With what has just been established, it must be clear that this transmission of the rights of the taker could never be carried out under the form and with the effects of a policy endorsement.[246]

246. In the best of cases, if the application of s. 1456 of the Civil Code was fully respected, an endorsement could only have the effects of assignment.

§2. Group Life Insurance

203. This way of subscribing life insurance has been developed in item 189, E). In order to avoid repetition, for further information, please refer there.

Chapter 5. Pension Funds

204. In Argentine law, pension funds do not constitute insurance. There are two systems of retirement or pensions: the State system which, despite the errors of the past, is still in existence by a system called 'pay as you go' (*de reparto*) or the private system under the system of capitalization which has recently appeared, precisely because of the bad experiences with the old public system.

The control of the private activity is under a specific Superintendence with broad powers which go beyond the scope of insurance.

Part VI. Insurance Intermediaries

Chapter 1. Law of Establishment and Supervision

205. In Argentine law, the Insurance Contracts Act that we have been analysing and that constitutes the only organic existent regulation in the matter of the relationship arising out of the insurance contract between the parties does not contemplate any provision regulating the concrete manner of managing the intermediaries or 'insurance brokers or agents'.

Three sections of such Act, 53, 54 and 55 set forth some provisions on the scarce powers of those auxiliaries authorized by insurers for the operations in which they take part as representatives or proxies of the insurers proper. They are similar to those arising from the mandate contract with some extensions to allow for certain modifications of the contract and zone. Their relationship is circumscribed to the insurers as, traditionally, that was decided by the books of authority and the jurisprudence.

The commission – except otherwise expressly agreed in the contract – used to arise from the gross premium that was paid for the taking out and that obviously included it.

It is clear that the taker of the contracts was the only one empowered to approve the participation of one or another intermediary.

Towards February 1981, it was enforced Act 22.400 whose subject matter was insurance brokers, with a partial regulation of their activity, modalities of performance, imposed rights and duties as well as the obligatoriety to be registered in a register.

It divided the brokers into individuals of two kinds: insurance direct advisors, whose purpose was to concrete insurance contracts by assisting insured and insurers and insurance organization advisors who, besides the aforementioned task, had to train, manage and advise the former (insurance direct advisors) that formed part of an organization. These organizations are possible to be constituted using any of the company types admitted by our law.

Act 22.400 prevents from being intermediaries those who are not enrolled in the especial register created by such Act and administered by the SIN in charge of imposing penalties.

Regarding payable commissions, the regulation determines that the insurance advisors will agree on them, pursuant to the agreement with the insurer, except otherwise exceptionally established by the authority of application.

The mentioned amount shall arise from the price of the insurance that the taker shall carry out, subject that arises from the Act since it determines that the right to collect by the auxiliaries in question emerges at the moment of the payment of the premium.

Part VII. Reinsurance, Co-insurance: Pooling

206. Reinsurance: Generalities. To start with, reference shall be made to the end of Chapter 2 where some characteristics of this chapter have been advanced. The reinsurance contract is also regulated in four sections (159–162 inclusive) Title II, Act 17.418.

Its denomination denotes with certainty that we are dealing with one activity subject to another preceding it and, in order to avoid confusions between them, Act 17.418 contains the appropriate precept in section 159 (of undeniable reality) that states: 'The insurer can, in turn, insure the risks assumed, but he is the only one obliged regarding the taker of the insurance.'

Our country has had important precedents in relation to insurance and its commercialization as the first company started to operate in 1796.

Regarding reinsurance, there is a lack of interest. Its business was during many years carried out by foreign companies from their institutional headquarters, except for some representative offices that, during many years they have had in our country.

With an interventionist criterion, the Argentine State has many times intruded on the two mentioned business, without taking into account that the private activity has shown always the ability to perform with excellence without the need of guardianships or interventions.

Towards the middle of the 1940s after the general elections of 1946, the elected government – of a clear statistic tendency – started the same as with other activities to introduce itself into the reinsurance market (as an advance of what its administration would tend to do with insurance business as well).

After a few dabbles, it constituted itself in the monopolist reinsurance with the creation of the NRI of very negative effects during the years it lasted.

Finally (and abruptly due to its final operational crisis), reinsurance, even when being controlled by the SIN has become a commercial activity that, as insurance is free, as long as some requirements are complied with.

207. Outline about Types and Classes of Reinsurance. In the first place we could divide them into treaty or general reinsurance and simple or specific reinsurance. From the good faith characteristic point of view – which is the most important in this type of operations – it will be clear that, except for some assumptions, the treaty or general reinsurance is the most frequently used.

In the second place, and from another perspective, we can notice the existence of quota share or proportional reinsurance; reinsurance of surplus or surplus treaties or reinsurance of risk surplus; reinsurance of loss surplus or damage or reinsurance of compensation surplus; reinsurance of surplus or reinsurance of annual loss surplus or loss surplus proper; or reinsurance of loss percentage or stop loss reinsurance.

Reinsurance contracts, even when having many common characteristics with the insurance contracts, must be construed with certain differences. Not only because they are intrinsically different but also because they link professional parties that oblige them to use a clear terminology of the commercial speciality, and they are not susceptible to a protective appreciation.

It is absolutely important that it is noted that the taker or the insured of the insurance contracts that are subject matter of reinsurance does not have, in principle, influence between them in any sense.

208. Co-insurance and Pooling. Please refer to Part II, Chapter 6, where this matter has been developed.

209. Prevention. In the Argentine Republic, the prevention of risks has been left to the insurers themselves, counting for that on some private support, with no support from the State.

This situation has been caused by the useless existence of the NRI, body that, while existing, did not take any measures in relation to subjects as precaution or care.

There is the case of one insurance company that for about fifteen years has been collaborating in the sector in all that is related to motor vehicle circulation.

It is a corporation that has gathered around ten of the most significant insurers and contributed with a substantial improvement to motor vehicle circulation, inside the national territory, as well as contributing in the field of care assistance to victims of accidents.

The company quality can be appreciated in the way they carry out their company activities and in their management towards the preservation of the environment.

Its origin – in relation to the cohesion of its members – came from the work that highlighted at the time prior to the constitution of the corporation this item is making reference to, the insurance company Mapfre, through its homonymous branch in Argentina, the main shareholder of the organization, which denomination is Cesvi, identical to the one existing in Spain which carries out developments in many countries, especially in the American Continent.

Selected Bibliography

Current Sources. In Argentina, with the legislative transformations that took place with the drawing up of Acts 17.419 of insurance contracts and 20.091 of control of insurers, it turned out to be clear that the bibliography that had existed and had been praised until those decades of 1960 and 1970 was only left for historical studies or for those scholars who did research.

That is the reason why authors of the importance of Raymundo Fernández with his commented Commercial Law Code and Carlos J. Zavala Rodríguez with his work of similar title are mentioned in this sense (although absolutely praising the doctrinal eloquence of their texts).

In modern times, after the first half of the twentieth century, as general bibliography in insurance matters, the following is listed:

Bulló, Emilio Horacio. *Insurance Law and Other Related Businesses* ('*El derecho de seguros y de otros negocios vinculados*'). Vols I and II. Edited by Rodolfo De Palma. Buenos Aires: Ábaco Press, 1999 (Vol. I) and 2001 (Vol. II). (A third volume is in press at present.)

Halperín, Isaac. *Insurance*. Vols I and II. With commentary by Juan Carlos Félix Morandi. Buenos Aires: Desalma Press, 1983.

Selected Bibliography

Index

The numbers here refer to paragraph number.

Index

www.ingramcontent.com/pod-product-compliance
Lightning Source LLC
Chambersburg PA
CBHW071425230926
51846CB00001B/125
* 9 7 8 9 4 0 3 5 3 5 5 7 9 *